A COMMENTARY

ON

THE COLOSSIANS

A COMMENTARY

ON THE

GREEK TEXT OF THE EPISTLE OF PAUL

TO

THE COLOSSIANS

JOHN EADIE, D.D., LL.D.

EDITED BY THE REV. W. YOUNG, M.A., GLASGOW

Wipf & Stock
PUBLISHERS
Eugene, Oregon

Wipf and Stock Publishers
199 W 8th Ave, Suite 3
Eugene, OR 97401

A Commentary on the Greek Text of the Epistle of Paul to the Colossians
By Eadie, John
ISBN: 1-57910-163-1
Publication date 10/2/1998

PREFACE

THIS volume has been composed on the same principles as those which guided me in my previous Commentary on the Epistle to the Ephesians. My aim has again been to trace and illustrate the thoughts of the inspired writer; to arrive at a knowledge of the truths which he has communicated, by an analysis of the words which he has employed. I have used every means in my power to ascertain the mind of the Spirit; and my eye being single, if I have not enjoyed fulness of light, my hope is that some at least of its beams have been diffused over my pages. As the purity of exegesis depends on the soundness of grammatical investigation, I have spared no pains in the prior process, so that I might arrive at a satisfactory result. One may, indeed, compile a series of grammatical annotations without intruding far into the province of exegesis, but it is impossible to write an exegetical commentary without basing it on a thorough grammatical inquiry. The foundation must be of sufficient depth and breadth to support the structure. Nay, after the expositor has discovered what meaning the word or clause may bear by itself, and as the Grammar or Lexicon may warrant, he has then to determine how far the connection and development of ideas may modify the possible signification, and finally determine the actual or genuine sense.[1] For the only true sense is that which the author intended his words should bear.

[1] In making these remarks, I refer to, but certainly find no fault with, the following two treatises, *A Critical and Grammatical Commentary on St. Paul's Epistle to the Galatians*, *A Critical and Grammatical Commentary on St. Paul's*

Now there is ample wealth of grammatical assistance. Apart from formal grammatical treatises and dictionaries, one might almost compile a Grammar and Lexicon from such works as Schweighäuser on Herodotus, Stallbaum on Plato, Poppo on Thucydides, Kühner on Xenophon, and other productions of similar scholarship. Still, when all this labour has been gone through, the higher art of the exegete must be brought into requisition. The dry bones must not only be knitted, but they must live. Successful exposition demands, on the part of its writer, such a psychological oneness with the author expounded, as that his spirit is felt, his modes of conception mastered, and his style of presenting consecutive thought penetrated and realized. And there is need, too, of that Divine illumination which the "Interpreter, one among a thousand," so rejoices to confer on him who works in the spirit of the prayer, "Open Thou mine eyes, that I may behold wondrous things out of Thy law." May I venture to hope that, to some extent, I have come up to my own theory?

What others have written before me on the epistle I have carefully studied. Neither ancient nor modern commentators in any language have been neglected. But I have not been so lavish, as on my last appearance, in the citation of names,

Epistle to the Ephesians, by C. J. Ellicott, M.A., Rector of Pilton, Rutland, and late Fellow of St. John's College, Cambridge. London, 1854–55. Mr. Ellicott is an excellent Greek scholar, but in many of his corrections of myself, and on points of Greek Grammar too, I cannot acquiesce, though in a few I admit his modifications. I hope he is aware, at the same time, that in Scotland every Greek scholar is and must be self-taught, since at our northern Universities we get little Latin and less Greek, and enjoy no leisurely Fellowships. Yet with all the necessary apparatus of German scholarship in our hands, why should we really be behind England, save in the privilege of early and minute tuition? Indeed, English scholarship, in two of its latest efforts in this direction, does but give an English dress to continental erudition. Jelf has not absorbed the individuality of Kühner in his improved translation. Liddell and Scott have modestly avowed the sources out of which, to a great extent, their very useful Lexicon has been wrought out. However, we wait hopefully for the New Testament of Tregelles, and for the Lexicon believed to be in preparation by the Master of Balliol. Mr. Ellicott has unconsciously misnamed our last work, in a point of view against which we protested in our preface, and somewhat extraordinarily and in opposition to what Prof. John Brown himself has said, he hastily ascribes his Exposition of Galatians to a collegiate authorship.

except in cases of momentous difficulty, or where some peculiar interpretation has been adduced. Names, I well know, are not authorities; and such a complete enumeration of them as I attempted has, I find, been sometimes misunderstood in its principle, and sometimes misrepresented in its purpose.

If my labours shall contribute to a clearer understanding of this portion of the New Testament, I shall be amply rewarded. I believe that the writings of the apostle, whatever their immediate occasion and primary purpose, were intended to be of permanent and universal utility; and that the purity and prosperity of the church of Christ are intimately bound up with an accurate knowledge of, and a solid faith in, the Pauline theology. I dare not, therefore, in the spirit of modern rationalism, say in one breath what the apostle means, and then say, in another breath, that such an acknowledged meaning, though fitted for the meridian of the first century, is not equally fitted for that of the nineteenth; but must be modified and softened down, according to each one's predilections and views. The privilege of individual deduction from inspired statement is not questioned—the attempt to glean and gather general principles from counsels and descriptions of a temporary and special phasis is not disallowed; but this procedure is totally different from that ingenious rationalism which contrives to explain away those distinctive truths which an honest interpretation of the apostle's language admits that he actually loved and taught.

I have still to bespeak indulgence, on account of the continuous and absorbing duties of a numerous city charge; and for a careful revisal of the sheets, and the compilation of the useful index which accompanies this volume, I am indebted to my esteemed friend the Rev. John Russell, Buchlyvie, Stirlingshire.

13 Lansdowne Crescent, Glasgow,
October 1855.

THE LITERATURE OF THE EPISTLE

—o—

I.—COLOSSE, LAODICEA, AND HIERAPOLIS

COLOSSE was a city of the greater Phrygia, or that province which, under Constantius, was called Phrygia Pacatiana, and was situated on the river Lycus, about five furlongs above the point where it joins the Maeander. The spelling of the name has been disputed. The common appellation, **Κολοσσαί**, has, in the inscription of the epistle, the support of Codices D, E, F, G, the Vulgate, and several of the Fathers, among whom are the Greek Chrysostom and Theophylact, and the Latin Tertullian and Ambrosiaster. Some ancient coins exhibit the same spelling,[1] and it occurs also in Herodotus,[2] Xenophon,[3] Strabo,[4] Diodorus Siculus,[5] and Pliny.[6] It appears to be the correct and original form of the word. On the other hand, **Κολασσαί** has the high authority of A, B, C, of the Syriac and Coptic Versions, and not a few of the Fathers and classical writers.[7] Lachmann and Tischendorf adopt it. This form, therefore, was also a current one. It seems to have been in common use among the people, and was probably the spelling employed by the apostle himself. Among the subscriptions to the Acts of the Council of Chalcedon, held in A.D. 451, occurs that of the metropolitan of Laodicea, who, speaking of the bishops under him, mentions—**'Επιφανίου πόλεως Κολασσῶν.**

[1] Eckhel, *Doctr. Numis.* iii. p. 147, who cites the terms Κολοσσηνοί and δῆμος Κολοσσηνῶν.

[2] vii. 30. [3] *Anabasis*, p. 6, ed. Hutchinson, Glasgow, 1817.

[4] *Geographia*, vol. ii. p. 580, ed. Kramer, Berlin, 1847.

[5] *Histor.* xiv. 80, 8. [6] *Hist. Nat.* v. 32.

[7] It stands as a various reading in Xenophon and Herodotus. and also in Polyaenus, viii. 16.

The city was of some note in its early days. Herodotus calls it *μεγάλη πόλις*; and Xenophon bestows upon it the epithet *εὐδαίμων*. Strabo, however, while he classes Apameia and Laodicea among the greatest cities of Phrygia, ranks Colosse only among the *πολίσματα*, as if its ancient greatness had already been eclipsed by the prosperity of the neighbouring towns. Ptolemy takes no notice of it. Laodicea and Hierapolis, mentioned in the second chapter of the epistle, were but a few miles from it, and all three in the year 60 A.D. suffered terribly from an earthquake.[1] Indeed, as Strabo observes, the whole district or valley of the Maeander was volcanic, and liable to earthquakes—*εὔσειστος*.

In the middle ages, Colosse was known by the name of Chonae, as is stated by Theophylact[2] in the commencement of his commentary, and by the Byzantine Nicetas,[3] who, after his birth-place, surnamed himself Choniates. A village named Chonas still remains, and the ruins of the ancient city have been discovered and identified by the modern travellers Hamilton and Arundell. The lofty range of Mount Cadmus rises abruptly behind the village, presenting that remarkable phenomenon [4] which seems to have given its second name to the town, and was connected with one of its singular superstitions. The legend is, that, during a period of sudden and resistless inundation, Michael, descending from heaven, opened a chasm, into which the waters at once disappeared, and the fact is, that a church was built in honour of the archangel, in which he received Divine honours. This subsequent idolatry affords a curious illustration of the tendency which, under the clause "worshipping of angels," the apostle formally notices and rebukes in the 18th verse of the second chapter of his epistle.

The other towns mentioned in the epistle are Laodicea and Hierapolis. The former had often attached to it the appellation—*ἡ ἐπὶ Λύκῳ*, or *ἡ πρὸς τῷ Λύκῳ*—that is, "Laodicea on the Lycus," to distinguish it from other towns of similar name,

[1] The statement of Orosius on this subject must not be taken as correct in all points. Orosius, *Hist.* vii. 7. Winer, *sub voce.* Tacitus, *Annal.* xiv. 27. Wieséler, *Chronol.* 455.

[2] Πόλις Φρυγίας αἱ Κολοσσαὶ αἱ νῦν λεγόμεναι Χῶναι.

[3] Χώνας . . . πάλαι τὰς Κολασσάς. *Chron.* p. 230, Bonn.

[4] Herodotus, *loc. cit.*

one in the same region, another forming the port of Aleppo, and a third close to Mount Lebanon. Its original name was Diospolis, and it received its later designation from Laodice, the wife of Antiochus II., by whom it was patronized and considerably enlarged. As the metropolis of the Greater Phrygia, it was a city of some size, splendour, and trade, covering several hills with its buildings, having a rich and active population within it, and a fertile country round about it, watered by the Lycus, and two other and smaller streams.[1] But the scourge of the place was the frequency and severity of the earthquakes. On being devastated by the earthquake referred to, it soon rose to its former grandeur—*propriis opibus revaluit*;[2] but after many a convulsion and overthrow, the place was at length abandoned. Its ruins attest its ancient grandeur. Remains of two theatres may yet be seen, with many of their marble seats; temples may be traced by their foundations; but of the architecture and ornaments of churches almost no trace can be found. "Vast silent walls," about the purpose of which there is considerable doubt, are striking objects amidst the desolation. The Turks now call it Eski-hissa, or old castle, a translation of the common Greek term applied to old sites, Paleo-castro.[3]

East of Colosse, and to the north of Laodicea and visible from its theatre, lay Hierapolis. It was famous for its mineral springs, which produced beautiful stalactites, and all forms of encrustations, and for the mephitic vapours which filled a cavern on the hill-side.[4] These peculiarities may have originated its sacred name. It has been visited and described by several travellers, such as Smith, Pococke, Chander, Arundell, Leake, and Fellows. The remains of three Christian churches are visible, and the theatre and gymnasium are prominent among the ruins. Fellows has the following entry in his *Journal*,[5] pp. 283, 284:—"Up the valley towards the south-east stands Mount Cadmus, and I heard that at its foot, about twelve miles from Laodicea, there were considerable ruins, probably of the ancient city of Colossæ. Descending

[1] Strabo speaks of ἡ τῆς χώρας ἀρετή, and adds also τῶν πολιτῶν τινες εὐτυχήσαντες, xii. 8, 16. Rev. iii. 17.

[2] Tacitus, *Annal.* xiv. 27.

[3] Kitto's *Cyclop. sub voce.*

[4] Called the Plutoneum. Strabo, lib. xiii. Pliny, *Hist. Nat.* v. 29.

[5] *Journal written during an Excursion to Asia Minor*, London, 1839.

rapidly into the flat and swampy valley of the Lycus, we crossed in a diagonal line to the city of Hierapolis, six or seven miles from Laodicea. My attention had been attracted at twenty miles' distance by the singular appearance of its hill, upon which there appeared to be perfectly white streams poured down its sides; and this peculiarity may have been the attraction which first led to the city being built there. The waters, which rise in copious streams from several deep springs among the ruins, and are also to be found in small rivulets for twenty miles around, are tepid, and to appearance perfectly pure. This pure and warm water is no sooner exposed to the air than it rapidly deposits a pearly white substance upon the channel through which it flows, and on every blade of grass in its course; and thus, after filling its bed, it flows over, leaving a substance which I can only compare to the brain-coral, a kind of crust or feeble crystallization; again it is flooded by a fresh stream, and again is formed another perfectly white coat. The streams of water, thus leaving a deposit by which they are choked up, and over which they again flow, have raised the whole surface of the ground fifteen or twenty feet, forming masses of this shelly stone in ridges, which impede the paths, as well as conceal and render it difficult to trace out the foundations of buildings. The deposit has the appearance of a salt, but it is tasteless, and to the touch is like the shell of a cuttle-fish. These streams have flowed on for ages, and the hills are coated over with their deposit of a filmy semi-transparent appearance, looking like half-melted snow suddenly frozen." From this whiteness of the southern and western declivities of the rocky terrace on which the city stands, a whiteness consisting probably of a deposit of carbonate of lime, it is now called Pambuk-Kaleh, or Cotton Castle.

The inhabitants of Phrygia boasted of a high antiquity, and the Egyptians confessed their own posteriority. Herodotus tells at length the absurd story of the experiment of King Psammetichus, by which was discovered the priority of the Phrygian language.[1] It is certain that they were inclined to wild superstitions. Their religious worship was a species of delirious fanaticism. The self-mutilated Corybantes were the

[1] ii. 2.

priests of Cybele, who under the sacred paroxysm cut and gashed themselves, as they reeled, whirled, and danced in frantic glee to the braying of horns and clashing of cymbals, while the forests and mountains echoed the wild clamour of their orgies. The national propensity of the Phrygians was towards the dark and mystical, and they were specially attracted to any mania or extravagance that claimed a near knowledge of, or a maddening fellowship with, the spirit-world. Ravings and convulsions were the sure tokens to them of inspiration. Deficiency of intellectual culture left them the more the creatures of whim and impulse, so that the errors mentioned by the apostle in his letter to the Colossians, and characterized as "intruding into those things he hath not seen, will-worship, and neglecting of the body," were peculiarly fitted to such a temperament, and calculated to exert a strong fascination upon it. The knowledge of this correspondence between the errors propounded and the eccentric propensities of the people, must have deepened the fears and anxieties of the apostle, and led to that stern and thorough exposure which characterizes the second chapter of the epistle. We know that at a subsequent period similar delusions prevailed in the province. The reveries of Montanus originated there about the middle of the second century, and spread rapidly and extensively. The leading features of Montanism were a claim to ecstatic inspiration, the gift of prophecy, the adoption of a transcendental code of morality, and the exercise of an austere discipline. Its votaries were often named Kataphrygians, from the region of their popularity. The heresiarch himself was born on the confines of Phrygia, and his first disciples, as might be expected, were natives of that country, nay, two of its towns were fondly supposed to be the New Jerusalem predicted in the Apocalypse.

II—THE CHURCH IN COLOSSE

But who originated the Christian community at Colosse? Was it the apostle himself, or some other missionary? The question has not yet been answered beyond dispute. The early Greek commentator Theodoret held that the apostle planted the church, though he indicates that even in his day there was a diversity of opinion on the subject. In later times, Dr. Lardner has formally stated sixteen arguments in defence of his belief, that the author of the epistle was the founder of the church. Dr. Wiggers, in the *Studien und Kritiken* for 1838, has espoused the theory of Lardner, and it had been previously advocated by the reviewer of Junker's Commentary, in the ninth volume of Rohr's *Kritischer Prediger-Bibliothek.* In express opposition to these views, Dr. Davidson has written at length with great candour and precision.[1]

The arguments for and against the Pauline origin of the church are of two kinds—inferential and critical.

1. It is stated in the Acts of the Apostles, xvi. 6, that Paul and his companion "had gone throughout Phrygia," and then, xviii. 23, that "he went over all the country of Galatia and Phrygia in order, strengthening all the disciples." There arises a strong presumption from these accounts, that during this first or second visit the apostle must surely have reached Colosse. This is Theodoret's argument—that as Colosse was in Phrygia, and Laodicea the capital of the province was in its vicinity, it could scarcely happen that the apostle should not visit both places. Dr. Lardner endorses this judgment, and says, "This argument alone appears to me to be conclusive." Now, it is beyond doubt that the apostle made extensive journeys in the province of Phrygia, but it is nowhere stated that he was either in Colosse, or even near it. In the first instance referred to, the route was from Antioch to Syria, Cilicia, Derbe, Lystra, Phrygia, Galatia, Mysia, Troas, and thence over to Europe. The record of the tour is vague. True, indeed, Colosse lay on the great road from Iconium to Ephesus, but the apostle did not visit Ephesus till after his return from Europe, and then he sailed to it directly from the port of Cenchrea, and after a brief visit took shipping again for Cæsarea. The term Phrygia, as has been remarked by Conybeare and Howson (i. 291)—"was merely a geographical expression, denoting a debatable country of doubtful extent." The journey performed in reaching Mysia, for the purpose of going into Bithynia, and then through Mysia down to the

[1] *Introduction,* vol. ii. p. 396, etc.

coast at Troas, would seem to indicate that the apostle's route lay greatly to the north of the city of Colosse.

With regard to the apostle's second journey, the language is also indeterminate. Only it was a journey of visitation, and if there was no previous sojourn in Colosse, and no existing church in it, then the apostle was under no inducement to turn his steps towards it. He came from Antioch into Phrygia and Galatia, and thence down to Ephesus. If he had taken the great road to the Ægean, through the valley of the Maeander, he must have come near Colosse; but the probability is, that he passed again farther to the north—for he passed, in fact, through "the upper coasts," or table land.

The apostle was for more than three years at Ephesus, and we may be assured that evangelizing influence would be diffused through the surrounding country. Qualified preachers would visit the various districts, proclaim the gospel, and gather together small communities. Probably by one of such disciples might the truth be carried a hundred miles eastward to Colosse, during the period "when all they which dwelt in Asia heard the word of the Lord, both Jews and Greeks." There is nothing in the brief allusions in the Acts of the Apostles to warrant the supposition that Paul himself had preached in Colosse. His apostolic journeys never approached it. We know not his proximate reasons for not visiting it, nor can we tell from what or how many motives, apart from direct revelation, his route, in any case, was originally chalked out, and afterwards modified or departed from altogether. The course we may venture to propose for him might, for anything we can know, have presented insuperable difficulties, even though we should be able to defend it by a reference to geography and itineraries, based on the researches and discoveries of modern travel. And we are sure that if, when in Phrygia, the apostle did not visit Laodicea—its capital, it was because there was more pressing work for him elsewhere, while a higher power and wisdom were guiding him in all the points of his busy and sublime career.

The second class of arguments in favour of the notion that Paul himself founded the church in Colosse, is drawn from a critical estimate of the general spirit and occasional sentiments of the epistle itself.

Dr. Lardner adduces the apostle's earnest belief, that the Colossians rightly knew the truth (i. 6), as evidence that probably himself had taught them. But the inference is strained, and the context disallows it; for the proper translation is—"which bringeth forth fruit, as it does also in you, from the day ye heard it, and knew the grace of God in truth, just as ye learned it from Epaphras." The proof based upon *καί*, in the phrase *καθὼς καὶ ἐμάθετε ἀπὸ 'Επαφρᾶ*, is not valid, for the best MSS. exclude *καί*, though Wiggers contends that the theory we espouse and are now defending may have led to its exclusion. See our commentary on the place.

Nor is there tangible evidence in the declaration made in i. 8, where the apostle tells how Epaphras had declared to him and his companions their love in the spirit. Even taking Dr. Lardner's interpretation of the phrase as meaning their affection for the apostle himself, how can it prove a prior and personal acquaintance? For surely Christian love does not depend on personal interview or recognition, else it would be impossible for any one to love the whole "household of faith." Nor can the presence of Epaphras at Rome, his intimacy with the apostle, and the accounts which he brought of the spiritual condition of the Colossian believers, be any presumption that they were the apostle's own converts; for who that has seen the workings of his large heart would limit Paul's interest to those churches gathered by his own preaching?

The apostle, indeed, says to the Colossian church,—"If ye continue in the faith grounded and settled, and be not moved away from the hope of the gospel, which ye have heard, and which was preached to every creature which is under heaven; whereof I Paul am made a minister: who now rejoice in my sufferings for you, and fill up that which is behind of the afflictions of Christ in my flesh for his body's sake, which is the church; whereof I am made a minister, according to the dispensation of God which is given to me for you, to fulfil the word of God." But no part of this language will warrant the inference which some would put upon it. He does not say that he had ever preached to the Colossians, he only says that he was suffering for them. And those sufferings arose purely from his being the apostle of the Gentiles, as indeed he indicates in a subsequent clause. There he intimates to them that the persecutions which harassed him arose from his special relation to the Gentile churches. In no other sense than in this general one, could he be suffering for the Colossians, for personally they were in no way instrumental in causing his incarceration and appeal. The charges against him involved nothing said or done at Colosse, the church there was not implicated in the least degree. But for their evangelical liberty and that of all the churches of heathendom the apostle was bound in fetters.

No stress can be laid on the use of the word ἄπειμι in ii. 5, though Lardner, and Wiggers after him, appeal to it, as implying that the apostle had once been present in Colosse. His language simply is,—"For though I be absent in the flesh, yet am I with you in the spirit, joying and beholding your order, and the steadfastness of your faith in Christ." The apostle, however, does not say I am *now* absent, as if he referred by such a contrast to a previous period. The contrast is of another nature. It is such an absence as brings out the idea of presence in spirit—"I am away from you, and yet I am with you—personally at a great distance, but still in spirit in the very midst of you."

It is also said, iii. 16,—"Let the word of Christ dwell in you richly in all wisdom; teaching and admonishing one another in psalms, and hymns, and spiritual songs, singing with grace in your hearts to the Lord." It puzzles us to understand how Dr. Lardner could extract from this admonition any proof "that the Colossians were endued with spiritual gifts." The descriptive counsel refers not to any extraordinary endowment, nor yet to the composition of sacred melodies; but merely to the chanting of them. That "grace" which was in their hearts is the gift of God to all believers.

Again, if, as we have seen, the record of the affection which the Colossian believers bore to the apostle be no evidence of personal intimacy, neither can any "full proof" of it be discovered in the brief note—"all my state shall Tychicus declare unto you." If, as the apostle of the Gentiles, Paul encountered such persecutions, would not they for whom he so nobly suffered be deeply interested in him, and would not he respond to such natural anxiety, and inform them, through

Tychicus, of many things with which he did not choose to cumber an epistle?

The salutations sent by him to Colosse are neither in number nor familiarity any additional argument, and certainly do not bear out Lardner's affirmation, that "Paul was well acquainted with the state of the churches in Colosse and Laodicea." For might not the names of the six men who send their Christian greetings be well known to the Colossians? The apostle might know that Nymphas had a church in his house without his ever being in it himself; and being 'such an one as Paul the aged," he surely needed not the formality of a personal introduction to Archippus, in order to take the liberty of sending him the brief and emphatic charge—"Take heed to the ministry which thou hast received in the Lord, that thou fulfil it." On the other hand, how many, various, tender, and special are his salutations sent to the church in Rome, where he had never been!

Dr. Lardner argues, again, for a personal intimacy from Col. iv. 3, 4, a passage which contains the apostle's earnest request for the prayers of the Colossian believers, and that they would remember his bonds; but Dr. Lardner also supplies the answer himself, when he admits that "such demands may be made of strangers." Nor can his theory be sustained by his appeal to the Epistle to Philemon. Philemon was a convert of the apostle's own, but Dr. Lardner candidly allows that his conversion, though "it might as well have been done at home," yet "might have been done at some other place." It is certainly a very slender ground of argument which Wiggers adopts, when he appeals to the conjunction of Timothy's name with the apostle's in the inscription of the epistle. For surely as a special companion of the apostle, and engaged so often in missionary work and travel, Timothy must have been well known at Colosse; and, as Dr. Davidson well remarks, "among the various disciples of the apostle who were at Colosse, it is not improbable that Timothy had a part in instructing the church." Indeed, some regard him as probably its founder.

But, lastly, a principal ground of dispute is the passage occurring in Col. ii. 1, 2,—"For I would that ye knew what great conflict I have for you, and for them at Laodicea, and for as many as have not seen my face in the flesh; that their hearts might be comforted, being knit together in love, and unto all riches of the full assurance of understanding, to the acknowledgment of the mystery of God, and of the Father, and of Christ." Theodoret based his theory upon one interpretation of the words. "Some," says he, "are of the opinion, that when the divine apostle wrote this epistle, he had not seen the Colossians. And they attempt to support their arguments by those words. . . . But they should reflect, that the meaning of the words is this—I have not only a concern for you, but I have likewise great concern for those who have not seen me.[1] And if he is not understood in this sense, he expresses no concern for those who had seen him and been taught by him." That is to say, Theodoret supposes two classes of persons to be referred to—the Colossians and Laodiceans who had seen the apostle's face, and another indiscriminate class who had never enjoyed his personal ministry. The words may of themselves bear such an interpretation. But it is objectionable on various grounds. The adjective ὅσοι may refer back to the persons mentioned, and may thus introduce a common characteristic—for you and them in Laodicea, and indeed not only you, but all in the same category, who have never seen my face in the flesh. The clause—"and for as many as have not seen my face in the flesh," has no harmonious connection, if it stand so disjoined from the previous clause as to point out in sharp contrast other believing communities. With this exegesis one might infer from the language of the following verses, that all who had not seen the apostle's face in the flesh were beset with the same dangers as the church in Colosse. For the virtual prayer is, that they might be fortified against that false philosophy which was raising its head in Phrygia, by the full-assured understanding of that gospel in which are deposited "all the treasures of wisdom and knowledge." But surely among the many churches who had not seen Paul, there must have been many to whom the prayer in its specialty was not and could not be adapted, and for whom this "conflict" was not necessary. That "conflict" was excited by the danger which menaced Colosse; but all the churches unvisited by the apostle could not be in similar jeopardy, so as to create

[1] Ὅτι οὐ μόνον ὑμῶν ἀλλὰ καὶ τῶν μηδέπω τεθεαμένων με πολλὴν ἔχω φροντίδα.

a similar solicitude and prayer. It is true that the care of all the churches came upon him daily, and all of them shared in his intense and prayerful anxiety. Yet it was his pride (if the expression may be pardoned) to originate Christian societies. He thus speaks—"Not boasting of things without our measure, that is, of other men's labours;"[1] "Yea," says he again, "so have I strived to preach the gospel, not where Christ was named, lest I should build upon another man's foundation."[2] This distinction, so boldly drawn by the apostle, brought the churches founded by himself into a very special relationship with him. Is it at all likely, then, that if he had founded the churches of Colosse and Laodicea, and had occasion to tell them what a conflict he had for them, he would modify and weaken the statement, by adding, that his feeling for them was quite the same with that he entertained for churches with which he had never had any personal connection? Would not the sentiment just quoted from the epistles to Rome and Corinth be somewhat at variance with that supposed to be so expressed to Colosse? Would it have been a source of peculiar comfort to the churches of Colosse and Laodicea, if Paul had founded them, to tell them, that notwithstanding his personal intimacy with them and their imminent danger, they were not a whit nearer his heart than the remotest Christian community of which he had but the slightest intelligence? The apostle possessed too much of our common nature thus to dissipate his friendships in vagueness, and he had too much knowledge of human nature to attempt to create a response to his own anxieties by so expressing himself. No, he had not visited these churches; but special circumstances gave him a tender interest in them. His peculiar interest in the churches planted by himself might be matter of notoriety in the district, and they of Colosse and Laodicea might be disposed to feel that they had not such a claim on the apostle as the churches of Galatia in their vicinity. But the crisis which had occurred roused the apostle to a sense of their danger; that danger gave them a warm place in his bosom, and to assure them of this, he declares his anxiety that they knew what a conflict he had for them, and for all around them, indeed, as many as had

[1] 2 Cor. x. 15. [2] Rom. xv. 20.

not seen his face in the flesh. The reference in ὅσοι is plainly to their own neighbourhood, particularly including Hierapolis, which is afterwards mentioned, and which might be menaced by the same form of error. They had not enjoyed his teaching, and they had the more need of his prayers. If he had seen them in the flesh he might have warned them; or, as in the case of Ephesus, uttered his presentiment of danger, and endeavoured to fortify them against it. The translation of Wiggers, "also for them, to wit in Colosse and Laodicea, who have not seen my face in the flesh," is too restrictive, and takes for granted that Paul had been in both those places, but had not been brought into personal contact with all the members of the churches. We give the words a wider significance. We doubt not that several members of those churches may have seen the apostle during his long stay at Ephesus. The apostle, however, does not contrast them with others who had not enjoyed the same precious opportunity. He speaks not to individuals but to communities, and classes with them others around them similarly circumstanced. In the following verse, he mentions all the parties in the third person, as if they all stood in the same category.

It is also to be specially observed that the apostle, though he combats error, never refers to his own personal teaching, or hints at what himself had delivered on these subjects of controversy at Colosse. Though the introduction of the gospel seems to be referred to, the apostle in no sense or shape connects it with himself. Very different is his style in the other epistles when he recalls the scenes and circumstances in which the churches had been planted or watered by his personal ministrations.

The probability is that the church in Colosse was founded by Epaphras, of whom the apostle says, "who is for you a faithful minister of Christ;" and of whom he also testifies: "Epaphras, who is one of you, a servant of Christ, saluteth you, always labouring fervently for you in prayers, that ye may stand perfect and complete in all the will of God. For I bear him record, that he hath a great zeal for you, and them that are in Laodicea, and them in Hierapolis."

In conclusion, the view which we have advocated is generally that of the writers of Introduction, with the exception of Schott, Börger, and Neudecker; and with the exception of Theodoret, Macknight, Adam Clarke, Barnes, and Koch on Philemon, it is also the view of the great body of commentators upon the epistle, such as Calvin, Suicer, Flatt, Bähr, Huther, De Wette, Junker, Steiger, Olshausen, Böhmer, Meyer, Schrader, Bloomfield, and Baumgarten-Crusius.

III —THE GENUINENESS OF THE EPISTLE

In the early church the genuineness of this epistle was universally acknowledged. No misconception of its contents or prejudice against them, led to any suspicions about its authorship. No inquisitive spirit found anything in it unworthy of the apostle, or unlike his usual modes of thought and style. No heretic seems to have been bold enough to exclude it from his canon, though in the first centuries it must have often confronted some prevalent forms of error and superstition. Eusebius therefore placed it among the Ὁμολογούμενα, or books which were confessed on all sides to be of apostolical origin. Tertullian has quoted this epistle about thirty times, and in such a way as clearly to evince his belief in its Pauline origin. The nineteenth chapter of his fifth book against Marcion, is a summary of its contents, so far as they served his polemical purpose.[1] His great authority throughout is Paul, whom he simply names *apostolus.*

At a prior date, Clement of Alexandria has also many allusions to it. For example, in the sixth book of his *Stromata,* after maintaining that Paul does not condemn all philosophy, he quotes Col. ii. 8, with the preface—ὡσαύτως ἄρα καὶ τοῖς κολασσαεῦσι.[2] In the fourth book of the same Miscellany he quotes that section of this epistle[3] which enjoins the duties of domestic life, and ascribes it to Paul, who was the prime authority to him as to Tertullian. It is found also in the anonymous canon published by Muratori,[4]—a document of the beginning of the third century. The Syrian churches

[1] *Opera,* ed. Oehler, vol. ii. p. 330, etc.
[2] *Opera,* p. 645, ed. Coloniæ, 1688.
[3] Do. p. 499.
[4] *Antiq. Ital. Med. Ævi,* tom. iii. p. 854.

had it in their collection, as is evident from the old Syrian translation. Origen, in the eighth chapter of the fifth book of his reply to Celsus, has a quotation from Col. ii. 18, 19, prefaced by the remark—*παρὰ δὲ τῷ Παύλῳ ἀκριβῶς τὰ Ἰουδαίων παιδευθέντι . . . τοιαῦτ' ἐν τῇ πρὸς Κολοσσαεῖς λέλεκται.*[1]

In Justin's dialogue with Trypho, no less than four times is Col. i. 15, 16 referred to or quoted, the point of the quotation being the term *πρωτότοκος*.[2] The same term is also cited by Theophilus[3] of Antioch, who wrote toward the latter end of the second century, and is found in his three books to Autolycus.

Many distinct and lengthened quotations are found in Irenaeus, who flourished about the same period as Theophilus.[4] Thus, in the third chapter of his first book *Against Heresies*, he says the following things are spoken plainly by Paul—*ὑπὸ τοῦ Παύλου δὲ φανερῶς*, and he cites first Col. iii. 11, and then Col. ii. 9. Or, again, the quotation of Col. i. 21, 22, is introduced with the words—*et propter hoc apostolus in epistola quae est ad Colossenses ait.* Indisputable citations or allusions cannot be brought from the apostolical Fathers. Marcion included the book in his canon, giving it the eighth place in his catalogue. There can be no doubt at all of the unanimous opinion of the primitive church on the subject; in Italy, Africa, Syria, Asia Minor, and Egypt, there was no conflicting testimony.

Through the intervening centuries, and up to a very recent period, the genuineness of the epistle was also acknowledged to be beyond dispute. Indeed, when Bähr wrote his commentary on it in 1832, he says, in his Introduction, "it has been hitherto universally acknowledged, and has been called in question by nobody, not even by De Wette." A few years later, however, Germany began to present an exception. Schrader, in his note on Col. iv. 10, took occasion, from the message sent by the apostle about Mark, to find a difficulty, and out of it to raise a suspicion that the epistle

[1] P. 236, ed. Spencer, Cantab. 1677.
[2] *Opera*, ed. Otto, vol. ii. p. 286, 336, 418, 452.
[3] Lib. ii. p. 100, ed. Coloniae, 1686.
[4] *Adver. Haereses. Opera*, vol. i. p. 41, ed. Stieren, 1853. Do. p. 756.

might not be Paul's, as it wants the individuality found in some other of his epistolary compositions.[1] Mayerhoff, in 1838, made a bold and formal assault, and he has been followed up by Baur and his disciple Schwegler. Mayerhoff's[2] posthumous treatise, edited by his brother, is certainly far from being conclusive. Proceeding on very vague and unsatisfactory principles, it abounds with a somewhat mechanical selection of words and phrases, picks out *ἅπαξ λεγόμενα*, and gives prominence to what are reckoned un-Pauline forms of expression and thought.

But the course of criticism is thoroughly defective. For if the apostle have a special end in view, he must employ special diction. If that end be peculiar, the style must necessarily share in the peculiarity. If in one epistle he explain his system and in another defend it, the expository style may surely be expected to differ from the polemical style. If in one composition he combats one form of error, and one set of adversaries, can you anticipate identical phraseology in another letter in which he assaults a very different shape of heresy, patronized by a wholly diverse band of opponents? Individuality would be lost in proportion to such sameness, and the absence of it would be the surest proof of spuriousness. No sound critic would test the style of Colossians by that of 1st Thessalonians, or throw suspicion on the former because it does not reveal the same aspects of thought and allusion. Nor would he place it side by side with Galatians, and roughly say that both are polemical, and that therefore the same topics of controversy and trains of thought should be found in both. Who would reject 1st Corinthians because the favourite and almost essential term *σωτηρία* is not to be found in it, or throw Philippians out of the canon because words so significant and Pauline as *σώζειν* and *καλεῖν* do not occur in it?

Mayerhoff's first argument is that of lexical difference, and he instances the want of *σώζω* and its derivatives, and of *καλέω* and its derivatives used with reference to the Divine kingdom. But in this epistle the apostle has no occasion to

[1] *Der Apostel Paulus*, vol. iv. p. 176, 1836.

[2] *Der Brief an die Colosser, mit vornehmlicher Berücksichtigung der drei Pastoralbriefe;* kritisch geprüft von Dr. Ernst Theodor Mayerhoff, Berlin, 1838.

employ these terms, for his primary object is not to expound salvation or our calling to it, but to defend the personal and official glory of its great author and finisher—Christ. No wonder that the expressive term *Χριστός* occurs by itself at least twenty times in the epistle. Again, the words *νόμος* and *πίστις* do not occupy a prominent place; and no wonder, for the object of the writer is not, as in Romans and Galatians, to explain the nature and relations of faith and law. "The particle *γάρ*," says Mayerhoff, "occurs only six times; but in Philippians seventeen, and in Romans one hundred and fifty times." But surely, if the adverb be so prominent a feature of the apostle's other writings, he must be a very bungling forger who would not plentifully sprinkle his pages with it. An imitator would not venture a copy with so few instances of the characteristic *γάρ*. The use of such a term would rather lead a forger to multiplication, till its very frequency detected him. We agree with Olshausen, who says, in the first section of the Introduction to his Commentary, "he that can take account of such mere accidents, and that so seriously (*ernstlich*), that he reckons how often *γάρ* occurs in each epistle, decides his own incapacity for judging on similarity and difference of style." In opposition to the scantiness of *γάρ*, Mayerhoff produces the frequency of *ἐν*, which occurs in the first two chapters sixty times; and in the whole Epistle to the Philippians only fifty times. But would an impostor hazard such a profusion of this monosyllable? Besides, a very large number of the instances refer formally or by implication to union with Christ—a darling idea of the apostle, and one which in this epistle he is so naturally led to insert. When the apostle combats a system of proud and false philosophy, need we wonder at the recurrence of *γνῶσις*, or the emphatic form *ἐπίγνωσις*?

And then as to *ἅπαξ λεγόμενα*. Where now should one expect them? Certainly when a writer is busied with some unusual theme. And so it is in Colossians. Out of above thirty distinct *ἅπαξ λεγόμενα* which we have noted in the course of our study of this epistle, no less than eighteen occur in the second chapter, where the novel form of error is discussed and refuted, and the majority of them are characteristic terms. Such are the distinctive words, *πιθανολογία*, *φιλο-*

σοφία, χειρόγραφον, θεότης, σωματικῶς, εἰρηνοποιέω, ἐθελοθρησκεία, νουμηνία, ἀπόχρησις, ἀφειδία, πλησμονή; with other terms associated with them, as *στερέωμα, ἀπέκδυσις, συλαγωγῶν, καταβραβεύω, προσηλώσας, δογματίζω, ἐμβατεύω.* Now, if the apostle be under the necessity of describing a system of error which he has described nowhere else, may we not expect words which occur nowhere else, or must his free spirit limit itself to vocables already employed by him on former occasions? Is the new conception to be deprived of a new expression? Must the apostle, for the purpose of authenticating his writings, bind himself to a meagre and worn-out vocabulary? Shall we refuse to this master of language what we freely yield to every other author? If in a writing of one age we discover some terms which belonged to an earlier one, but had faded into disuse, or some which came into currency only during a later epoch, we justly look upon it with suspicion. But every author has surely liberty to range among the terms of his own period, and to employ the most fitting of them to embody his thoughts. If he never wrote so before, you infer that he never thought so before. If Mayerhoff had set himself to describe the symbols of the Apocalypse, he must have used many phrases not found in this treatise, and therefore with equal propriety, and on the same evidence, might some reviewer argue that the author of such a production could not be the author of this attack on the genuineness of the Epistle to the Colossians and the three pastoral epistles.

Nor is there any greater force in Mayerhoff's objections, based on grammatical differences. Of his charge of tautology we find no proof. When he stumbles on phrases very like the apostle's usual style, he affirms they are not really resemblances at all. He complains of the absence of anakolutha; and when he does meet them, he detects something wrong or un-Pauline in them. Some connective particles are absent in this epistle; but *ἄρα*, one of them referred to by him, is not found in Philippians, nor does *διό*, another of them, occur in Galatians; while *οὐχι*, which occurs fourteen times in 1st Corinthians, is not found in Philippians, nor here, nor in Galatians. On such irregularities no argument can be founded. Thus, the particle *τέ*, which occurs often in

Romans, is found neither in Galatians nor 1st Thessalonians. The conjunction *ἐάν*, occurring twenty times in Romans, is found forty-five times in 1st Corinthians, but is absent from Philippians; and, again, *ἤ* is met with fifty-two times in 1st Corinthians, but only twice in Philippians.[1]

There is nothing peculiar in the forms of construction adduced by Mayerhoff. He next accuses the writer of this epistle of hunting after synonyms, but the examples which he selects are in no case synonymous.[2] Who but Mayerhoff would lay any stress on the various diction in the formula of salutation? If the apostle, in such a prominent place, had been in the habit of using a uniform formula, then the least cunning of impostors would have been sure to copy it with slavish correctness.

Not less futile are Mayerhoff's criticisms on differences of idea or expression to be found in the epistle. He discovers a host of parallel repetitions, which in reality are either not repetitions at all, or repetitions for an avowed object. Col. i. 1, 9, 10, 13, 14, 18, etc.

Another objection, based on a gross misconception, takes up the very different aspect under which the *νόμος* is viewed here, from the representations given of it in the other epistles.

[1] Huther, *Commentar*, p. 423.

[2] We present those which he has given out of the first and third chapters, and we refer to the following exposition for the distinctive meaning of the terms:—I., 6. καρποφορούμενον καὶ αὐξανόμενον—I., 6. ἀκούειν καὶ ἐπιγινώσκειν—I., 7. σύνδουλος et διάκονος—I., 9. προσευχόμενοι καὶ αἰτούμενοι—ἐν πάσῃ σοφίᾳ καὶ συνέσει—I., 10. καρποφοροῦντες καὶ αὐξανόμενοι—I., 11. εἰς πᾶσαν ὑπομονὴν καὶ μακροθυμίαν—I., 18. ἀρχὴ et πρωτότοκος τῶν νεκρῶν—I., 21. ὑμᾶς, ποτὲ ὄντας ἀπηλλοτριωμένους καὶ ἐχθρούς—I., 22. ἁγίους καὶ ἀμώμους καὶ ἀνεγκλήτους—I., 23. τεθεμελιωμένοι καὶ ἑδραῖοι καὶ μὴ μετακινούμενοι—I., 24. παθήματα et θλίψεις—I., 26. ἀπὸ τῶν αἰώνων καὶ ἀπὸ τῶν γενεῶν—I., 28. νουθετοῦντες πάντα ἄνθρωπον καὶ διδάσκοντες πάντα ἄνθρωπον—III., 2. τὰ ἄνω ζητεῖτε, τὰ ἄνω φρονεῖτε—III., 5. πορνεία et ἀκαθαρσία—πάθος et ἐπιθυμία κακή—III., 8. ὀργὴ καὶ θυμός—βλασφημία et αἰσχρολογία—III., 10. ἐνδυσάμενοι τὸν νέον (ἄνθρωπον) καὶ ἀνακαινούμενον—III., 12. ἐκλεκτοὶ τοῦ θεοῦ ἅγιοι καὶ ἠγαπημένοι—σπλάγχνα οἰκτιρμοῦ et χρηστότης—ταπεινοφροσύνη et πραότης—μακροθυμία et ἀνεχόμενοι ἀλλήλων—III., 16. ἐν πάσῃ σοφίᾳ διδάσκοντες καὶ νουθετοῦντες—ψαλμοῖς, ὕμνοις, ᾠδαῖς, etc.—*Mayerhoff*, pp. 35, 36. Huther, in reply, presents the following similarities out of Philippians i.:—V. 3. ἐπὶ πάσῃ τῇ μνείᾳ ὑμῶν— —ἐν πάσῃ δεήσει μου ὑπὲρ ὑμῶν— —τὴν δέησιν ποιούμενος; v. 7. ἐν τῇ ἀπολογίᾳ καὶ βεβαιώσει τοῦ εὐαγγελίου; v. 9. ἐν ἐπιγνώσει καὶ πάσῃ αἰσθήσει; v. 10. εἰλικρινεῖς καὶ ἀπρόσκοποι; v. 11. εἰς δόξαν καὶ ἔπαινον θεοῦ; v. 15. διὰ φθόνον καὶ ἔριν; v. 20. κατὰ τὴν ἀποκαραδοκίαν καὶ ἐλπίδα μου; v. 24. μενῶ καὶ συμπαραμενῶ; v. 25. εἰς τὴν ὑμῶν προκοπὴν καὶ χάραν τῆς πίστεως.—*Huther*, pp. 427, 428.

Now, not to say that νόμος does not occur in this epistle at all, it may be relied, that it is not law as a Divine institute which is here referred to, or the law which is spoken of so often in the Epistle to the Romans. What is spoken of here is the ceremonial law, which was abrogated by being fulfilled in the death of Christ, and not the moral law, which is as immutable as the legislator. What total ignorance of the object of the apostle to say, that because he speaks of "elements of the world," "commandments and doctrines of men," and "traditions of men," he gives these names to the Divine law, and then to infer that such doctrine cannot be Paul's, since he always looks upon the law as Divine, holy, and spiritual! It is surely one thing to speak thus of the law, and quite another thing to reprobate human additions to it.

There is no doubt, as Mayerhoff says, that in Colossians some acts, which are often ascribed to Christ, are ascribed to God; but such a variation not being confined to the epistle is no mark of un-Pauline peculiarity. And lastly, Mayerhoff's objection to its Christology cannot be sustained. For the form which it has assumed has most evidently a reference to such shapes of error as were propounded at Colosse, and the terms which the errorists used may have been selected by the apostle and sanctified by their legitimate application to the Divine Redeemer. Baur[1] and Schwegler[2] also adduce the doctrine of Christ's pre-existence taught in Ephesians and Colossians, as proof that the two epistles were not written by Paul. The objection carries its own refutation.

In fact this whole process of assault is one of capricious subjectivity. One writer decides that the Epistle to the Ephesians is spurious, because it is only a verbose expansion of that to the Colossians; and another, with equal taste and correctness, affirms that the Epistle to the Colossians is spurious, because it is an unskilful abstract of that to the Ephesians; while, according to the judgment of Baur, both epistles must stand or fall together.

To gain his purpose, Mayerhoff has compared throughout the two Epistles of Colossians and Ephesians. But surely the real similarity which they present may be easily accounted for,—that similarity being found chiefly in the concluding

[1] *Der Apostel Paulus*, p. 422. [2] *Nachap. Zeit.* ii. p. 289.

and practical portions. Schneckenburger has pronounced this similarity—a similarity in unimportant things—to be "a mechanical use of materials." But the one epistle is very far from being a copy of the other. There is a distinctness of aim with occasional identity of thought. The great body of each epistle is different, nor do they slavishly agree even in what may be termed commonplaces. There is, indeed, far less similarity than is commonly supposed—all that is special about each of them is wholly different, and even in the paragraphs where there is similarity, there is seldom or never sameness, some new turn being mingled with the thought, or some new edge being given to the admonition. As is noticed in our Commentary, even where the apostle addresses spouses, children, and slaves, and refers to the same duties, there is yet variety in the form and reasons of advice. The one letter is general, the other is special; the one is didactic, the other controversial. The one presents truth in itself, the other developes the truth in conflict with parallel error. And there is no servile imitation, no want of life and freshness.

Mayerhoff's last argument is based on the date of the errors which he imagines to be refuted in this epistle. He holds that the heresy of Cerinthus is aimed at and exposed by the writer, and he infers that as the false doctrine of Cerinthus was not developed till after the apostle's time, therefore the apostle could not be the writer. The truth of his chronological statement it is impossible for him to prove. It would seem that Cerinthus was soon after this in Ephesus, and in antagonism with the Apostle John; so that, even though it could be proved that Cerinthus was the person the writer had in his eye, it would not follow that he could not be the apostle of the Gentiles. Mayerhoff's view of the nature of the false doctrines condemned is not very different from our own, but there is no necessity to identify them thus with Cerinthus, and then to assign his era to post-Pauline times. Olshausen says that Cerinthus may have been by this time in Colosse, though he adds, that he could hardly have that influence which should mark him out as the leader of a formidable party.

Baur and Schwegler subscribe to not a few of Mayerhoff's critical objections based upon the style of the epistle. But

Baur holds it to have had its origin in the Gnosticism of the second century. Mayerhoff admits that Baumgarten has shown that such a hypothesis is untenable against the pastoral epistles, though he himself is bold enough to attack them on other grounds. But the Gnosticism of the second century in its theosophy and angelology presupposes, in fact, the existence of those apostolic documents. The citations from Hippolytus have sadly perplexed those critics of Tübingen—as they show that books of the New Testament are quoted by him fully half a century before those German scholars allowed their existence. (See our Introduction to *Commentary on Ephesians*, p. xlv.)

The attacks on this epistle are therefore of no formidable nature, and the opinion of the church of Christ, in so many countries and for so many centuries, may be acquiesced in without hesitation.

IV—THE FALSE TEACHERS IN COLOSSE

There has been no small amount of erudition and research expended upon the question, as to what party or parties in Colosse held the errors condemned by the apostle. The attempt has often been made to identify these errorists with some formed and well-known sect. But there is not sufficient foundation for such minuteness. All that we know of the false teachers is contained in the few and brief allusions to their heresies. And these allusions are not systematically given as an analysis of their system, but only as occasion required, and for the purposes of confirming the opposite truths. The probability is, that the false teachers had at that period no fully developed system—that they held only a few prominent tenets, such as those which the apostle condemns; and that they were rather the exponents of certain prevailing tendencies, than the originators of a defined and formal heresy. They were thrown up by the current, and they indicated at once its direction and its strength. Many ages in the church have exhibited a similar phenomenon, when the errors which certain men promulgate appear, from their seductive power and immediate success, to be but the expression of those sentiments which had already taken a deep and latent hold of the general mind.

The errors in Colosse rose within the church, and were produced by a combination of influences. Had they grown up without the church, they would have appeared with a hostile front, inviting an instant and a sturdy resistance. If Jew or heathen had announced his creed, none would have listened to it, save as to the challenge of an avowed enemy. It is only when error is nursed in the bosom of the church itself, not like a poisonous weed transplanted from the desert, but like the tares among the wheat, that truth is in the greatest danger. If we reflect for a moment on the mental tendencies of those early times, as seen both in the Phrygian temperament and in the Jewish characteristics; if we remember how strongly the Oriental spirit was leavened with the desire to enter the spirit-world by theosophic speculation, and attain to sanctity by ascetic penance, we need not wonder at the indications of error contained in the epistle to the church in Colosse.

Our inference therefore is, that the theory which holds that those false teachers were Jews without even a profession of Christianity, is utterly untenable. The arguments of Eichhorn,[1] Schultess, and Schoettgen, in vindication of this view, are very unsatisfactory. Nowhere in the epistle are they branded as unbelievers, or spoken of as unconverted antagonists of the gospel. Their error was not in denying, but in dethroning Christ—not in refusing, but in undervaluing his death, and in seeking peace and purity by means of ceremonial distinctions and rigid mortifications. Such a nimbus of external sanctity as Eichhorn ascribes to them would not have dazzled the Colossians, if it had surrounded a Jewish brow; nor would ritual observances have possessed any seductive power, if inculcated by Jewish doctors, as Schoettgen names them. Neither Pharisaic nor Essenic rigorists would have been spoken of by the apostle in the style in which he describes the false teachers at Colosse. Stern denunciations would have been heaped upon them as the rejecters of the Messiah, and disturbers of the church. But the errors promulgated in Colosse were wrapt up with important truths, and were therefore possessed of dangerous attractions. They were not a refutation of the gospel, but a sublimation of it. The Colossian errorists did

[1] *Einleit.* vol iii. p. 288.

not wish to subvert the new religion, but only to perfect it; did not even under the mere mantle of a Christian profession strive to win the church over to Judaism, as Schneckenburger [1] and Feilmoser [2] think; but to introduce into the church certain mystic views, and certain forms of a supereminent pietism, which had grown up with a spiritualized and theosophic system. In other words, they were not traitors, but they were fanatics. They did not counterfeit so as to surrender the citadel, but only strove to alter its discipline and supplant its present armour. In the Apocalyptic epistles, the pseudo-apostles at Ephesus, the synagogue of Satan at Smyrna, the woman Jezebel, the prophetess at Thyatira, and the Nicolaitans or Balaamites in Pergamos, whatever their errors and immoralities, were all within the church, and wore at least the mask of Christianity. Neither could the errorists at Colosse be the mere disciples of Apollos, or of John the Baptist, as extra-ecclesiastical sects. Heinrichs and Michaelis want a historical basis for such an assertion, for we cannot tell how long Apollos taught ere the apostle imparted to him full instruction; and there is no doubt that he would at once communicate his more perfect knowledge to all his brethren. His teaching was but a preparatory step to Christianity. The false teaching at Colosse is not spoken of by the apostle as a rude and undeveloped scheme which stopped short of Christianity; but a system which brought into Christianity elementary practices, vain superstitions, and attempts at an unearthly and sanctimonious life. If it was pleased with the unfinished, it also soared, by means of it, into the transcendental. Apollos was indeed a Jew of Alexandria, and there is little doubt that some elements of Alexandrian or Philonic Judaism were to be found in Colosse, but found in connection with Christian belief, or were combined with such views, feelings, and professions, as had warranted admission into the church.

These errors did not involve of themselves, though they might soon lead to, immoral practices. It was not, as in Corinth, where debauchery prevailed, and impurity had been associated with the pagan worship, where the Lord's Supper

[1] *Beitr. zur Einl.* p. 146.

[2] *Einl.* p. 149. See, on the other hand, the well-known treatise of Rheinwald, *De Pseudo-Doctoribus Coloss.*, Bonn., 1834.

had been profaned, and the idea of a resurrection had been more than called in question. Nor was it as in Thessalonica, where a vital doctrine had been seriously misunderstood, and sundry minor evils had begun to show themselves. In Galatia there had been a bold and open attempt to uphold systematically the authority of the Mosaic law, and enforce its observance on the churches as essential to salvation; but the apostle meets the crisis with a stern and uncompromising opposition. And there was in Rome, too, a proud and self-righteous Jewish spirit, that relied on illustrious Abrahamic descent and conformity to the letter of the law for justification. Therefore the apostle formally proves by a lengthened argument, that to guilty and helpless humanity the only refuge is in the grace of God and the righteousness of Christ.

But the case was somewhat different at Colosse. The teaching was of a more refined nature. It does not seem to have insisted on circumcision as a positive Mosaic rite, but as the means of securing spiritual benefit. It was not dogmatically said, "Except ye be circumcised and keep the whole law of Moses, ye cannot be saved;" but circumcision appears to have been connected with those ascetic austerities by which purity of heart was sought for, symbolized, and expected to be reached. The apostle's argument is, Ye are circumcised already—ye have, through faith in Jesus, all the blessings which that ordinance typifies—ye have been circumcised with the circumcision of Christ. Distinctions in meats and drinks, the observance of holidays, "the show of wisdom in humility, will-worship, and neglecting of the body," were not haughtily imposed as a Pharisaic yoke, but were regarded and cherished as elements of a discipline which hoped to attain religious elevation by a surer and speedier way than that which the gospel presented. The theoretic portion of the error was somewhat similar in origin and purpose. Its object was to secure spiritual protection, by communing with the world of spirits. It aimed to have what the gospel promised, but without the assistance of the Christ which that gospel revealed. It took Christ out of His central Headship, and dethroned Him from His mediatorial eminence. It was a philosophy which longed to uncover the unseen and climb to heaven by homage done to the angelic hierarchy.

That such tendencies should coalesce in one and the same party is not strange, for self-emaciation has been usually connected with reverie and visions.

We may scarcely put the question whether those errors had a heathen or a Jewish source. That they sprang up within the church we have seen already, but some suppose them traceable to a foreign influence. Clement ascribed them to Epicureanism; but indulgence and not self-restraint was its character. It might indeed covet festivals, that it might enjoy a surfeit; but if it made a distinction among meats and drinks, it would be only to abstain from some of them, not for sanctity's sake but for palate's sake, and to prefer others not as lean and scanty fare to the neglect of the body, but as luxuries to revel in under the motto, "Let us eat and drink, for to-morrow we die." Tertullian again vaguely thought that philosophy in general with its theory and ethics was condemned. But the apostle needed to guard the Colossians only against such forms of philosophic falsehood as were taught among them, and most likely to enthral them. See our comment on ii. 8. Grotius has contended that the Pythagorean system is referred to, and Macknight has found it in the maxims, "Touch not, taste and handle not" (that is, as he means), anything the eating of which involves the previous taking away of its life. But Pythagoreanism could only in Colosse have an indirect influence through Plato and his Alexandrian imitators. That the language of Paul has some resemblance to that of Philo is well known, for modes of expression which at length were common among the Hellenistic Jews may have originated in the studies and speculations of Alexandria. Yet any one who carefully reads Gfrörer's Essay on this subject, or the virtual review of it by Jowett,[1] cannot fail to perceive, that with many features of likeness, there are very numerous points of dissimilarity. The spirit of the two writers is in perfect contrast; nay, the same words even have a difference of meaning in their respective productions. Yet with all his mysticism, Philo has much that every intelligent and pious Jew must have believed—forms of

[1] *The Epistles of St. Paul to the Thessalonians, Galatians, and Romans, with Critical Notes and Dissertations.* By Benjamin Jowett, Fellow and Tutor of Balliol College, Oxford, vol. i. p. 363.

thought and faith that Paul did not need to renounce when he became a Christian. But to build much on mere verbal similarity is very unsatisfactory, for Köster has shown, in an ingenious Essay,[1] how much the apostle's diction resembles that of Demosthenes; and Bauer and Raphelius had before him pointed out similar instances from Thucydides and Xenophon.

Heumann, again, pleads for the Stoic and Platonic philosophies as the object of apostolic warning, but with no probability. When we remember the numbers of Jews colonized in those portions of Asia Minor, and how so many of them that passed over into the church were still zealous for the law, and when we see what nomenclature the apostle employs in describing these errors — "circumcision," "handwriting of ordinances," "festivals, new moons and Sabbaths," "a shadow of things to come,"—we are forced to the conclusion, that the false teaching pointed out and reprobated must have had a Jewish source, having grown up among those who had once observed the Levitical ritual, and who carried with them into the church many of those predilections and tendencies which the idealized Mosaism of that age had originated and ripened. The application of the term "philosophy" to these errors, and the accusation of the "worshipping of angels," form no argument against our hypothesis, for the Jewish writers apply the name to their own religious system, and traces of the strange idolatry may be found in later Jewish books.[2]

The tendencies or teachings described by the apostle seem to be allied fully as much to the Essenic as to the Pharisaic school. Formality, ostentation, censoriousness, hypocrisy, and a righteousness satisfied with obeying the mere letter of the law, are not hinted at by the apostle—the demure face on the day of fast, prayer in stentorian voice at the corner of the streets, and the trumpet which heralded almsgiving, are no portion of the picture. Rather does the description harmonize with what we know of the Essenes, and with what they might be if they embraced Christianity. If the Christianized Pharisees were apt to become Judaizers, the Christianized Essenes were as likely to become mystics in doctrine and

[1] *Studien und Kritiken*, 1854.
[2] See our Commentary on ii. 8, 18.

ascetics in practice. Recoiling from the precise formality of Pharisaism, they glided into impalpable speculations. The Pharisee might boast of his sanctity in the outer court, but the Essene strove to pass the vail into the inner chamber and commune with its invisible inhabitant. What the Pharisee laboured to attain by the punctilious minutiæ of a cumbrous ritual, the Essene hoped to reach by severe meditation and self-denying discipline. In short, the Essenes were philosophic Jews, who in trying to get at the spirit of their system, and to reach its hidden nature and esoteric teachings, wandered as far from its real purpose as did the sensual and pompous Pharisee. The Pharisee overlaid the law with traditions, so that it grew into an unshapen mass, and this tendency may be described under the phrases "elements of the world," and "tradition of men." The Essene, on the other hand, was noted for his mystic aspirations, theosophic studies, and self-subduing modes of life, and these characteristics appear to be marked in the clauses, "philosophy and vain deceit," "worshipping of angels," and intruding into the invisible; while both the Pharisaic and Essenic leanings combined may be thus glanced at: "Let no man judge you in meat, or in drink, or in respect of an holiday, or of the new moon, or of the sabbath days; which are a shadow of things to come; but the body is of Christ,"—ii. 16, 17. Now, while the Jews remained in Palestine, the two rival sects might maintain their separate creeds with proverbial tenacity; but when they were thrown together in foreign countries, their change of position must have brought them into more familiar contact, and led to the modification of their more distinctive tenets. Away from the hallowed soil and the temple, Pharisaism, unable to obey the ritual, must have lost somewhat of its love of externals, and been more ready to yield to the quiet speculations and self-restrictions of the Essene. Such modifications we may not be able to trace, though we cannot doubt of their existence, and therefore we need not wonder that a form of Christianized Judaism at Colosse should exhibit in combination some of those features which in Palestine characterized respectively Pharisee and Sadducee. Nor is it to be forgotten that while their peculiarities were mutually modified between themselves, both might receive another modification from the external world. The Jewish mind had come into contact with the East during the Babylonish captivity, and probably retained some permanent impressions. We may therefore surmise that it was infected with the atmosphere of Phrygia, and that as it met in that province with speculations kindred to its own, it would both impart and borrow. This appears, then, to be the true state of the case. While the errors seem to have sprung up with the Jewish converts, and to have retained not a little that belonged to the Mosaic ceremonial, they were at the same time in harmony with feelings and practices widely spread over the East, and of special attraction to the province of Phrygia. One might almost thus describe the heresy, that it was Essenic Judaism modified by introduction to the church; widening itself from a national into an Oriental system through sympathy with similar views around it; in the act of identifying its angels with Emanations, and placing Christ among them; and admitting or preparing to admit the sinfulness of what is material in man. We need not, therefore, with Hug,[1] ascribe the origin of the Colossian errors to the Magian philosophy directly: for it was rather the Jewish spirit influenced to some extent by this and other forms of theosophy with which it has been placed in juxtaposition. Nor should we, with Osiander, Kleuker, and Herder, deem the false teaching wholly Kabbalistic, though the germ of what was afterwards found in the Kabbala may be here detected. It is also a onesided view of Chemnitz, Storr, Credner, and Thiersch to regard the errorists simply as Christian Essenes, though in the Essene there was a strong and similar tendency. Nor can we, with Hammond and others, simply call them Gnostics, though there is no doubt that what was afterwards called Gnosticism appears here in its rudiments —especially that aspect of it which may be called Cerinthian Gnosticism. Similar errors are referred to in the Epistles to Timothy, who laboured in a neighbouring region. Cerinthus was but the creature of his age, bringing together into shape and system errors which were already showing themselves in the various Christian communities, so that he soon became identified with them, and now stands out as an early and great heresiarch. But it would seem to be beyond historic

[1] *Einleit.* Part ii. § 130, 4th edit.

evidence to fix on any precise party as holding those tenets. For the parties which afterwards did hold them were not then organized; nor were they known then by the names which they afterwards bore in the annals of the church. The errors which in a century became so prominent as elements of an organized system, were at this time only in germ. The winged seeds were floating in the atmosphere, and falling into a soil adapted to them, and waiting as if to receive them; in course of years they produced an ample harvest.

The apostle in the second chapter uniformly employs the singular number in speaking of the party holding the errors condemned by him. Either he marks out one noted leader, or he merely individualizes for the sake of emphasis. The apostle in Galatians generally uses the plural; but in v. 10 he employs the singular *ὁ ταράσσων*, "he that troubleth you," where the reference may not be to some special heretic, but to any of those whom the apostle's imagination singles out for the moment as engaged in the act of disturbing the church. But the plural is never employed in the epistle before us; though the invariable use of the singular may not fully or grammatically warrant the idea of one person being specially before the apostle's mind, since the singular occurs in admonitions, and these are rendered yet more pointed by its use.

V —CONTENTS OF THE EPISTLE

We present the contents of the epistle in the form of a translation, arranged under separate heads. Our translation is simply an easy rendering, claiming neither the exegetical lucidness of a free version nor the grammatical accuracy and purity of a literal one.

The Salutation

Paul, an apostle of Jesus Christ by the will of God, and Timothy the brother, to the saints in Colosse, and believing brethren in Christ: Grace to you, and peace from God our Father.

The Introduction.

Having heard of your faith in Christ Jesus, and the love which ye have to all the saints, we thank God, the Father of our Lord Jesus Christ always, when we pray for you; on account of the hope laid up for you in heaven, of which ye heard already in the word of the truth of the gospel, which has come to you, as it has also in all the world; and is bearing fruit, and growing, as indeed among you, from the day ye heard it and knew the grace of God in truth, just as ye learned it from Epaphras, our beloved fellow-servant, who is for your sakes a faithful minister of Christ, who has besides reported to us your love in the Spirit.

The Prayer

On this account we indeed, since the day we heard (such a report), cease not praying for you and asking that ye may be filled with the full knowledge of His will in all wisdom and spiritual insight, so as to walk worthy of the Lord in order to all well-pleasing[1]—being fruitful in every good work, and growing by means of the knowledge of God; strengthened with all strength after the measure of the might of His glory, in order to the possession of patience and long-suffering with joy; giving thanks to the Father, who has fitted us for sharing the inheritance of the saints in the light; who rescued us out of the power of darkness and transported us into the kingdom of the Son of His Love, in whom we have this redemption,—the forgiveness of sins.

Doctrine introduced—The Glory of Christ

Who is the image of the Invisible God, the First-born of the whole creation. For in Him were created all things—those in the heavens and those on the earth, the seen and the unseen, whether thrones or lordships, principalities or powers, the WHOLE by Him and for Him was created, and He is before all things, and all things in Him are upheld. And He is the Head of the Body, the church; He who is the Source, the

[1] "For general conciliation!" Turnbull's translation. London, 1854.

First-begotten from the dead; in order that in all things He might show Himself the First. Yea, God was pleased that all fulness should dwell in Him; and by Him having made peace by the blood of His cross; by Him (I repeat) to reconcile all things to himself, whether the things on earth, or the things in the heavens.

The Application of it

And you, who were formerly alienated and enemies in your mind by wicked works, yet now has He reconciled in the body of His (Christ's) flesh through death, so as to present you holy, and blameless, and unreprovable before Him. If, as is the case, ye continue in the faith grounded and fast, and not moved away from the hope of the gospel which you have heard, which has been preached to every creature under heaven, of which I, Paul, was made a prisoner.

The Apostle's own feelings and functions towards them

I now rejoice in my sufferings for you, and I fill up what is wanting of the afflictions of Christ in my flesh for His Body's sake, which is the church; of which I was made a minister according to the dispensation of God committed to me for you, to fulfil the word of God; to wit, the mystery which has been hid from ages and generations, but it is now revealed to his saints, to whom God wished to make known what are the riches of the glory of this mystery in the Gentiles, which is Christ in you, the hope of glory; whom we preach, reminding every man and teaching every man in all wisdom; in order that we may present every man perfect in Christ. To attain which end, I indeed labour, intensely struggling according to His inworking, which works mightily within me. For I would that ye knew what a struggle I have about you and those in Laodicea, and as many as have not seen my face in the flesh; that their hearts might be comforted, being knit together in love and unto the whole wealth of the full assurance of understanding, to the full knowledge of the mystery of God; in which all the treasures of wisdom and knowledge are laid up.

First and General Advice

Now this I say, lest any one should beguile you with enticing words. For though, indeed, in the flesh I am absent, yet in the spirit with you am I, joying and beholding your order and the steadiness of your faith on Christ. As then ye have received Christ Jesus the Lord, walk in Him, having been rooted in Him, and being built up in Him, and established in the faith as ye were taught, abounding in thanksgiving.

Second and Special Warning and Argument

Beware lest there be any one who may make a prey of you through philosophy and vain deceit, after the tradition of men, after the rudiments of the world, and not after Christ. For in Him dwells all the fulness of the Godhead bodily; and ye are filled up in Him, who is the Head of all principality and power. In whom also ye were circumcised with a circumcision not made with hands in the off-putting of the body of the flesh in the circumcision of Christ; having been buried with Him in baptism, in whom too you have been raised together by faith in the operation of God, who raised Him from the dead. And you being dead in the trespasses and the uncircumcision of your flesh, you hath He brought to life together with Him, having forgiven us all our trespasses; having blotted out the handwriting of ordinances which was against us, which was hostile to us, and He has taken it out of the way, having nailed it to the cross; having spoiled principalities and powers, He made a show of them openly, having triumphed over them in it. Let no one, therefore, judge you in eating or in drinking, or in the particular of a festival, or of a new moon, or of Sabbath days, which are a shadow of the things to come, but the body is Christ's. Let no one rob you of your reward, wishing to do it by his humility and worshipping of angels, penetrating into things which he has not seen, puffed up without reason by his fleshly mind, and not holding the Head, from whom the whole body through joints and bands supplied and compacted groweth the growth of God.

The consequent Reproof

Since with Christ ye have died off from the rudiments of the world, why, as yet living in the world, do ye suffer such ordinances to be published among you as "touch not, taste not, handle not," in reference to things which are meant to perish in the use—ordinances which have no higher authority than the commandments and the doctrines of men; which procedure, indeed, having a show of wisdom in will-worship, and humility, and neglecting of the body, not in any thing of value, only ministers to the gratification of the flesh[1] (or corrupt human nature).

Practical Portion.—Their Position and its Lessons

If, then, ye have been raised together with Christ, seek those things which are above, where Christ is, sitting on the right hand of God. Set your mind on things above, not on things on the earth; for you died, and your life has been hidden with Christ in God. When Christ, our Life, shall be manifested, then ye too shall be manifested with Him in glory.

Sins to be abandoned

Mortify, therefore, your members which are upon the earth, fornication, impurity, lust, evil concupiscence, and covetousness, which indeed is idolatry, on account of which sins cometh the wrath of God, in which sins ye verily once walked, when ye lived in them. But now do ye also put off all these —anger, rage, malice, calumny, scurrility—out of your mouth. Lie not to one another, having put off the old man with his deeds, and having put on the new man, who is renewed unto knowledge, after the image of Him who created him; where (in which sphere of renewal) there is not Greek and Jew, circumcised and uncircumcised, barbarian, Scythian, bond and free, but Christ is all and in all.

Virtues to be assumed

Put on, as the elect of God, holy and beloved, bowels of

[1] "Not to the credit of any one for personal appearance!"—Turnbull.

mercy, obligingness, humility, meekness, long-suffering, forbearing one another and forgiving one another, if any one has a fault against any, like as indeed Christ forgave you, so also do ye; and over and above all these, put on that love which is the bond of perfection.

What should be the Tenor of the Christian Life

And let the peace of Christ rule in your hearts, to which too ye were called in one body, and be thankful. Let the word of Christ dwell in you richly; in all wisdom teaching and counselling one another; in psalms, hymns, spiritual songs, singing with grace in your heart to God; and whatever ye do in word or deed, do all of it in the name of the Lord Jesus, giving thanks to God the Father by Him.

Inculcation of Domestic Duties

Wives, submit you to your husbands, as is fitting in the Lord. Husbands, love your wives, and be not bitter against them. Children, obey your parents in all things, for this is well-pleasing in the Lord. Fathers, chafe not your children, lest they be disheartened. Servants, in all things obey your masters according to the flesh, not with eye-service as men-pleasers, but with simplicity of heart, fearing the Lord. Whatever you are engaged in, work at it from the soul as to the Lord, and not to men, knowing that from the Lord you shall receive the reward of the inheritance: the Lord Christ serve ye: for the wrong-doer shall receive what he has wronged; and there is no respect of persons. Masters, afford ye on your part what is right and equal to your servants, in the knowledge that ye too have a master in heaven.

Parting Counsels

Continue in prayer, and watch in it with thanksgiving; praying at the same time also for us, that God would open to us a door of discourse to speak the mystery of Christ, for which yea I am bound, in order that I may make it manifest as it becomes me to speak it. Walk in wisdom toward those without, redeeming the time. Let your conversation be always with grace, seasoned with salt, that ye may know how you ought to answer every one.

Private Matters

Of all that concerns me, Tychicus shall inform you, the beloved brother and faithful minister and fellow-servant in the Lord, whom I have sent unto you for this very purpose, that ye might know our affairs, and that he might comfort your hearts; along with Onesimus, the faithful and beloved brother, one of yourselves; they shall inform you of all matters here.

Concluding Salutations and Signature

There salutes you Aristarchus my fellow-prisoner, and Mark, the cousin of Barnabas (about whom ye received instruction); if he come to you, receive him; and Jesus, surnamed Justus—who are of the circumcision: these alone (of their race) are my fellow-workers unto the kingdom of God, who have been an encouragement to me. Epaphras, one of yourselves, a servant of Christ, salutes you, always striving for you in his prayers, that ye may stand perfect and full assured in the whole will of God. For I bear him record that he has a great travail for you and them in Laodicea and them in Hierapolis. There salutes you Luke the beloved physician, and Demas. Salute the brethren in Laodicea, and Nymphas, and the church in his house. And when this epistle has been read among you, arrange that it be read also in the church of the Laodiceans, and that ye read too the epistle from Laodicea. And say to Archippus, See to the ministry which thou hast received in the Lord, that thou fulfil it. **The salutation by mine own hand of Paul. Remember my bonds. Grace be with you.**

VI.—TIME AND PLACE OF WRITING THE EPISTLE

What we have already said in Chapter V. of our Introduction to Ephesians may suffice. The arguments of Schulz, Böttger, Wiggers, Thiersch, and Meyer, do not convince us that the old and general opinion is wrong, and that this epistle was written at Cæsarea, not at Rome. Peter Lombard and others dream of an imprisonment at Ephesus, at which place they suppose that this epistle was written. The probability is that it was composed in Rome, and about the year 62. On its relation to the Epistle to the Ephesians the reader may also consult the fifth chapter of our Introduction to *Commentary* on the latter Epistle.

VII.—WORKS ON THE EPISTLE

The patristic and mediæval commentaries on Colossians are, with the exception of Jerome, the same as those we have enumerated under Ephesians. So it is with the expositors of the Reformation period and that which succeeded it. So it is with the editors of the New Testament, and the collectors of illustrations from the classics, Philo and Josephus. Among the more characteristic expositions, we have the French discourse of Daillé and the more academic Latin prelections of Davenant, the paraphrase and notes of Pierce, the sermons of Byfield (1615), Elton (1620), and the more recent popular volumes of Bishop Wilson, Gisborne, and Watson.

Among continental writers we may refer to Calvin, Melancthon, Beza, Erasmus, Zanchius, Zwingle, Crocius, Piscator, Hunnius, Baldwin, the Catholic Estius and a-Lapide (van Stein), and to Grotius, Heumann, Suicer, Röell, Bengel, Storr, Flatt, and Heinrichs.

Among later expositors we have the following:—

Historisch-kritischer und philologischer Commentar über den Brief Pauli an die Colosser; bearbeitet von Dr. Friederich Junker; Mannheim, 1828. *Commentar über den Brief Pauli an die Kolosser, mit steter Berücksichtigung der ältern und neuern Ausleger;* von Karl C. W. F. Bähr; Basel, 1833. *Theologische Auslegung des paulinischen Sendschreibens an die Colosser;* herausgegeben von Wilhelm Böhmer; Breslau, 1835. *Der Brief Pauli an die Kolosser;* Uebersetzung, Erklärung, einleitende und epikritische Abhandlungen von Wilhelm Steiger; Erlangen, 1835. *Commentar über den Brief Pauli an die Colosser;* von Joh. Ed. Huther; Hamburg, 1841. *Kurze Erklärung der Briefe an die Colosser, an Philemon, an die Epheser und Philipper;* von Dr. W. M. L. de Wette;

Leipzig, 1843. *Biblischer Commentar über sämmtliche Schriften des Neuen Testaments zunächst für Prediger und Studirende;* von Dr. Hermann Olshausen; Vierter Band; Königsberg, 1844. *Commentar über den Brief Pauli an die Epheser und Kolosser;* von L. F. O. Baumgarten-Crusius; Jena, 1847. *Kritisch exegetisches Handbuch über den Brief an die Kolosser und an Philemon;* von Hein. A. W. Meyer; Göttingen, 1848. *Auslegung der Epistel Pauli an die Colosser in 36 Betrachtungen;* von C. N. Kähler; Eisleben, 1853.

NOTE

In the following pages, when Buttmann, Matthiae, Kühner, Winer, Rost, Alt, Stuart, Green, Trollope, and Jelf are simply quoted, the reference is to their respective Greek grammars; and when Suidas, Passow, Robinson, Pape, Wilke, Wahl, Bretschneider, Liddell and Scott, are named, the reference is to their respective lexicons. If Hartung be found without any addition, we mean his *Lehre von den Partikeln der griechischen Sprache*, 2 vols.; Erlangen, 1832. In the same way, the mention of Bernhardy without any supplement represents his *Wissenschaftliche Syntax der griechischen Sprache;* Berlin, 1829. The majority of the other names are those of the commentators or philologists enumerated in the previous chapter. The references to Tischendorf's New Testament are to the second edition.

COMMENTARY ON COLOSSIANS

CHAPTER I

THE Epistle begins according to ancient custom. The writer introduces himself by name, and then salutes those to whom his letter is addressed, thus—

(Ver. 1.) *Παῦλος, ἀπόστολος Ἰησοῦ Χριστοῦ διὰ θελήματος Θεοῦ, καὶ Τιμόθεος ὁ ἀδελφός*—"Paul, an apostle of Jesus Christ by the will of God, and Timothy the brother." [Eph. i. 1, iv. 11.] Paul was an apostle of Jesus Christ, as he bore His commission, enjoyed His inspiration, did His work, and in all things sought His acceptance. His call to the apostleship was by a signal and unmistakeable summons of the Divine will. Since he uses similar phraseology in so many of his epistles, there is no foundation for the conjecture of Chrysostom, and some of his Greek imitators, that the apostle in here asserting his relation to Christ so decidedly, disclaims all mission from the inferior spirits that occupied so prominent place in the angelology of the false teachers who attempted to corrupt the Colossian church. The addition of the name of Timothy is found in the Second Epistle to the Corinthians, in that to the Philippians, and to Philemon, while it stands along with that of Silvanus in the salutations of both letters addressed to the church in Thessalonica. Though Timothy may have been the writer of this epistle, neither his name nor his pen gave any warrant or authority to the document, for he is only joined with the apostle in brotherly, but unofficial congratulations and prayers over the welfare of the Colossian believers. It is certainly rash on the part of Chrysostom and Theophylact[1] to infer that Timothy was to be honoured as an apostle,

[1] The conclusion of Theophylact is *ἄρα οὖν καὶ αὐτὸς ἀπόστολος.*

because his name stands in this connection. Were such an argument tenable, then Sosthenes and Silvanus might both be elevated to the apostolate. Paul styles him, however, "a minister of God, and our fellow-labourer in the gospel of Christ," 1 Thess. iii. 2.

Timothy, who received this Greek name from his father, though his mother was a Jewess, was in all probability a native of Lystra.[1] That he was one of the apostle's own converts is highly probable, as he has so fondly named him "son," "my own son," "my beloved son," "my dearly beloved son," 1 Tim. i. 18, i. 2; 1 Cor. iv. 17; 2 Tim. i. 2. The young disciple was "well reported of by the brethren," had enjoyed an early and sound religious education, the result of maternal and grand-maternal anxiety, and he possessed a "gift," so that Paul, after circumcising him, in order to allay Jewish prejudice, selected him to be his colleague, fellow-traveller, and work-fellow. At a later period the apostle bore him this high testimony—"he worketh the work of the Lord, as I also do"[2]—affirms at another time that both of them preached the same gospel of the Son of God;[3] nay, so much of a kindred spirit reigned within them, that he says to the church in Philippi, "I have no man like-minded, who will naturally care for your state," Phil. ii. 19, 20. Indications of Timothy's busy and ubiquitous career occur again and again, and he received himself, from his spiritual father, two solemn epistolary communications. In short, so well known was he as "the Brother," doing the apostle's work, carrying his messages, bringing correspondence to him, endeared to him in so many ways and representing him in his absence, that the church of Colosse could not wonder at his name being associated with that of Paul.

(Ver. 2.) *Τοῖς ἐν Κολοσσαῖς ἁγίοις καὶ πιστοῖς ἀδελφοῖς ἐν Χριστῷ*—"to the saints in Colosse and believing brethren in Christ." For the various forms of spelling the name of the city, see Introduction. According to the versions of Chrysostom, Œcumenius, De Wette, and others, the apostle thus addresses his letter: "to those in Colosse who are saints and believing brethren in Christ;" but, according to Meyer, "to the saints in Colosse, to wit, the believing brethren in Christ."

[1] Acts xvi. 1. [2] 1 Cor. xvi. 10. [3] 2 Cor. i. 19.

We incline to the latter interpretation, as the epithet ἅγιος came to have something of the force of a proper name, and did not need ἐν X. to qualify it. It, indeed, often stands by itself, as in Acts ix. 13, 32, 41, xxvi. 10; in Rom. i. 7, xii. 13, xv. 25, 26, 31, and in a great variety of instances in the other epistles. True, in Phil. i. 1, the words ἐν X. 'I. are added to it, and that probably because no other epithet is there subjoined. When these early disciples are named or referred to, the term ἅγιος, like the English "saint," was almost invariably used, not as an adjective, but as a noun. For the meaning of the word, and its application to members of the church, see under Eph. i. 1. The other terms of the clause are explanatory and supplemental. The adjective πιστοῖς, which occurs by itself in the twin epistle, is here joined to ἀδελφοῖς, and has the sense of believing, as we have shown it to have in the similar salutation, Eph. i. 1. The concluding words, ἐν Χριστῷ, belonging to the entire clause, describe the origin and circuit of the believing brotherhood. Their union to Him created this tender and reciprocal connection in Him. Out of Him there was neither faith nor fraternity, for He is the object of the one and the centre of the other. Thus πιστοῖς is not superfluous, as Steiger erroneously says, if it mean "believing;" for this faith was the very means of bringing them into a filial relation to God, and therefore into a brotherly relation with one another. (Gal. iii. 26.) Children of one Father by belief in Christ, the entire family are rightly named "believing brethren" in Him.

Χάρις ὑμῖν καὶ εἰρήνη ἀπὸ Θεοῦ Πατρὸς ἡμῶν—"grace to you, and peace, from God our Father." The additional clause of the Received Text, *καὶ κυρίου 'I. X.*, is not fully sustained by good authority, as it is wanting in B, D, E, J, K, while it is found in A, C, F, G. Many of the old versions also want it—as the Syriac, Ethiopic, and Vulgate. Chrysostom formally says: *καίτοι ἐν ταύτῃ τὸ τοῦ X. οὐ τίθησιν ὄνομα*—"yet in this place he does not insert the name of Christ." Theophylact, on repeating the sentiment, adds—*καίτοι εἰωθὸς αὐτῷ ὂν*—"although it is his usual way to insert it;" but he subjoins a silly reason for the omission, to wit, "Lest the apostle should revolt them at the outset, and turn their minds from his forthcoming argument." The clause is common in the other opening benedictions. We can account for its insertion in some Codices as being taken from these corresponding passages, but we cannot so well give a reason for its general omission, except on the suspicion that it was no portion of the original salutation. We dare not dictate to the apostle how he shall greet a church, nor insist that he shall send all his greetings in uniform terms. [Eph. i. 2.]

The apostle now expresses his thanks to God for the Colossian church, for their faith, love, and hope—the fruits of that gospel which Epaphras had so successfully taught them. Then he repeats the substance of that prayer which he had been wont to offer for them, a prayer that designedly culminates in a statement of their obligation to Christ and their connection with Him. But that Blessed Name suggests a magnificent description of the majesty of His person, and the glory of His work as Creator, Preserver, Redeemer, and Governor. The paragraph is without any formal polemical aspect, but under its broad and glowing statement of the truth error was detected and refuted. It was so placed in sunshine, that its hideousness was fully exposed, and it was seen to be "a profane medley."[1]

(Ver. 3.) *Εὐχαριστοῦμεν τῷ Θεῷ καὶ Πατρὶ τοῦ Κυρίου ἡμῶν Ἰησοῦ Χριστοῦ πάντοτε, περὶ ὑμῶν προσευχόμενοι*—"We bless God, the Father of our Lord Jesus Christ always, when praying for you." There are variations in the text, some of which may be noted. Some read *τῷ πατρί* on no great authority, and the Received Text inserts *καί* without conclusive evidence. Other MSS. read as if by correction *εὐχαριστῶ* in the singular, and *περί*, found in A, C, D[3], E[2], J, K, appears to have higher warrant than *ὑπέρ*, which is preferred by Lachmann and Griesbach. The distinctive meaning of *ὑπέρ* and *περί* in such a connection may be seen under Eph. vi. 19. We cannot agree with Bähr, Steiger, Baumgarten-Crusius, and Conybeare, who imagine that Paul simply means himself in the plural *εὐχαριστοῦμεν*. That he may occasionally use this style we do not deny. The apostle in the First Epistle to the Corinthians joins Sosthenes with himself in the salutation, but formally excludes him from any share in the communication, for he immediately subjoins

[1] "*Mélange profane.*"—Daillé.

the singular εὐχαριστῶ. The same avowed distinction is made with regard to Timothy himself in the Epistle to the Philippians i. 1–3. May we not infer, that if Paul had wished to exclude Timothy here, he would have done so by a similar use of the singular; and as he does afterwards employ the singular in sharp contrast, may not the plural here have been chosen to represent the share which Timothy had in those good reports, and the consequent prayers? There is no sentiment in the verses in which the plural is used, peculiar to inspiration. And we are the more confirmed in this view, because Paul formally disconnects himself from Timothy in verse 23, and by the emphatic words, ἐγὼ Παῦλος; and again a similar distinction occurs in verse 29, and in iv. 3. The phraseology of these three verses implies, that when he says "we," he means himself and Timothy, but that in cases where he states something special to himself, and not common to him and his colleague, he says "I," to prevent mistake. If the plural simply represented himself, he did not need to change the idiom. [Εὐχαριστοῦμεν, Eph. i. 16.] Under Eph. i. 3 we have shown that the genitive κυρίου 'Ι. is governed as well by θεός as by πατήρ. And if we read τῷ θεῷ καὶ πατρί, as in the Textus Receptus, the same construction would be vindicated here. But as the reading is either τῷ θεῷ τῷ πατρί, or rather τῷ θεῷ πατρί, it would seem that πατρί alone governs the following genitive. We thank God, the Father of our Lord Jesus Christ. [Πατρὶ τοῦ κ. Eph. i. 3.] Beza well says, *neque vero aliter a nobis considerari potest Deus in salutem nisi quatenus est Pater Christi.* It is God, in the character of the Father of Christ, that we thank, for He is in this relation our Father-God. The grateful heart pours itself forth in praises. Paul and Timothy, on hearing of the spiritual progress of the Colossians, did not congratulate one another, but both gave the glory to God. So much had Timothy of Paul's own spirit, that the apostle had no hesitation in saying, "We thank God."

It is a matter of dispute whether πάντοτε should be joined to εὐχαριστοῦμεν, or to προσευχόμενοι. Chrysostom, Theophylact, Grotius, Piscator, Beza, Luther, Calvin, Bengel, Suicer, Grotius, Böhmer, and Olshausen, hold the second view, and render with the English version, "praying always for you."

But if we follow the analogy of 1 Cor. i. 4, 1 Thess. i. 2, 2 Thess. i. 3, Philem. 4, Eph. i. 16, we shall join *πάντοτε* to the first verb. So think Bähr, Pierce, Meyer, De Wette, and Baumgarten-Crusius. The Syriac version follows the same exegesis—for it reads, "We give thanks for you always, and pray for you;" and Cranmer's Bible of 1539—"We give thanks to God alwayes for you in oure prayers." Besides, the declaration is, that the intelligence which he had received filled his heart with gratitude, and impelled him to give thanks. The Colossians did not need to be told that he prayed for them, but it was some comfort to be assured by him, that when he did pray for them such was his opinion of them, based on reports which he had received about them, that he gave thanks to God for them. He would have prayed for them, whatever their spiritual state, and the worse it was, the more importunate would have been his supplications, but he would not have given thanks for them unless he had been persuaded of their spiritual purity and progress. Therefore he adduces these reports as the grounds of his thanksgivings; and the spirit of his language is—"Whenever we pray about you, we always give thanks for you." So cheering was the intelligence communicated by Epaphras, that thanksgiving was uniformly mingled with his prayers for them, and the special contents of those prayers are mentioned for the first time in verse 9. This exegesis is far more natural than that of Olshausen, who says that the thanksgiving is offered at the moment, but the intercession is supposed to be going on, and to be based on the tidings which he had received. Now, those tidings did not create the prayer, but being so good, they naturally induced the thanksgiving. "We *always* give thanks to God, the Father of our Lord Jesus Christ, *as often as* we pray for you, because we have heard of your faith in Christ Jesus, and love to all the saints."

Περὶ ὑμῶν προσευχόμενοι—"praying for you." The apostle prayed for them—such was his interest in them, and sympathy with them, that he bore their names on his heart at the throne of grace. Nor could such an "effectual fervent prayer of a righteous man" be without its rich results. The suppliant in his far-off prison was like the prophet on Carmel, and as he prayed, the "little cloud" might be descried, which, as it gradually filled and darkened the horizon, brought with it the "sound of abundance of rain."

(Ver. 4.) *Ἀκούσαντες τὴν πίστιν ὑμῶν ἐν Χριστῷ Ἰησοῦ, καὶ τὴν ἀγάπην ἣν ἔχετε εἰς πάντας τοὺς ἁγίους.* The words *ἣν ἔχετε* are introduced into the text on the concurrent authority of A, C, D, E [1], F, G, the Vulgate, and other versions, with many of the Fathers. The apostle now expresses the reason why he gave thanks, the participle having a causal sense, Kühner, § 667; Stuart, § 169. Similar phraseology occurs in Eph. i. 15. The article is omitted before the proper names **Χ. Ἰ.** Winer, § 19, 2. In Ephesians, the apostle adds *κύριος*, and prefixes the article to the official epithet; but here the simple name **Χ. Ἰ.** from common usage, occurs without it. Gal. iii. 26. A different form of construction, inserting the article before the preposition—*πίστει τῇ ἐν* **Χ. Ἰ.** —occurs 1 Tim. iii. 13, and similarly 2 Tim. i. 13. That faith reposed in Christ Jesus—fixed and immoveable—for it felt satisfied in Him as a Divine Saviour. [Eph. i. 1.] Paul's heart had been gladdened by the news of their consistency and spiritual advancement, and in the fulness of his joy he offered thanks to God. It is not necessary, with Locke and Pierce, to take *πίστις* in the sense of fidelity, "sticking to the grace of God." And their love was universal in its sweep, not toward all men, but toward all the saints. [*ἅγιος*, Eph. i. 1.] In itself, this love is really only a form, or manifestation of love to the Divine object of their faith, for it is affection to Christ's image in the saints. As, though a mirror is broken, each fragment will still throw out the same reflection in miniature, and that perfectly, so the saints, as a body and individually, exhibit the same blessed and divine image of Christ enshrined with them, and are therefore the objects of Christian love. Who is not acquainted with the language of Tertullian?—*Sed ejusmodi vel maxime dilectionis operatio notam nobis inurit penes quosdam, vide, inquiunt, ut invicem se diligant.*[1]

(Ver. 5.) *Διὰ τὴν ἐλπίδα τὴν ἀποκειμένην ὑμῖν ἐν τοῖς οὐρανοῖς*—"On account of the hope laid up for you in heaven." It is not easy to fix precisely on the connection between this clause and the preceding statement. It is a lame and superficial exegesis simply to say that the apostle

[1] *Apologeticum*, xxxix. p. 260, Opera, Tom. 1; ed. Oehler, Lipsiae, 1853.

merely alludes to his three favourite graces, faith, love, and hope.

But 1. Grotius, Wolf, Davenant, Estius, Pierce, Olshausen, De Wette, Bähr, Heinrichs, and the Socinian expositors, Crellius and Slichting, connect it with the two preceding clauses, as if it told the reason why faith and love were formed and cherished within them—your faith in Christ, and love to all the saints—graces possessed and nurtured "in consequence of the hope laid up for you in heaven." With such a view, the connection appears to be elliptical, and not very clearly expressed in the language before us. Nor do we think it a Pauline sentiment. The apostle's references to future glory are not of this nature, and we cannot regard him as placing faith and love on so selfish a basis as the mere hope of a coming recompense; for Christ is worthy of that faith, and saints, from their very character, elicit that love. The evangelical expositors who hold this view have to maintain a stout protest against the idea that they favour the Popish doctrine of merit. Davenant formally proposes the question, "whether it be lawful to do good works with a view to, or for the reward laid up in heaven?"

2. A modified and more tenable view is held by Chrysostom, and some of the Greek Fathers, as well as Estius, Calvin, Macknight, Meyer, and Steiger, who refer διὰ τὴν ἐλπίδα solely to ἀγάπην, as if the meaning were, This love is not cherished under the expectation of any immediate return, but in the hope of ultimate remuneration. Still, under this hypothesis, the connection appears strained. If the apostle had said that they loved one another on account of the common hope which they had in heaven, or that the prospect of a joint inheritance deepened their attachments on their journey towards it, then the meaning might have been easily apprehended. But why the hope in itself should be selected as the prop of such love, we know not. Was their love to all the saints so selfish, that it could live only in expectation of a future reward? We do not deny the Christian doctrine of rewards, but we cannot put so selfish a valuation on Christian love as this exegesis implies; for of all the graces, it has the least of self in its nature, and its instinctive gratification is its own disinterested reward.

3. We incline, then, to take the words διὰ τὴν ἐλπίδα with the initial verb εὐχαριστοῦμεν. "Having heard of your faith in Christ Jesus, and the love which ye have to all the saints, as often as we pray for you, we thank God, the Father of our Lord Jesus Christ, on account of the hope laid up for you in heaven." That is to say, the report of their faith and love prompted him to give thanks; but as he gave thanks, the final issue and crown of those graces rose into prominence before him, and he adds, "on account of the hope laid up for you in heaven." Their faith and love, viewed not merely in present exercise, but also in their ultimate consummation and bliss, were the grounds of his thanksgiving. The hope, as Bengel suggests, shows *quanta sit causa gratias agendi pro dono fidei et amoris.* The fourth verse can scarcely be called a parenthesis. This view is, generally, that of Athanasius, Bullinger, Calixtus, Elsner, Cocceius, Storr, Zanchius, Bengel, Schrader, Peile, and Conybeare. Meyer objects that in the other epistles the foundations of thanksgiving are subjective in their nature. Nor is this phraseology, when properly viewed, any exception. For faith and love are not excluded from the grounds of thanksgiving, and hope laid up is not wholly objective, as it signifies a blessing so sure and attainable that it creates hope. Had the apostle said, "for the happiness laid up," the objection of Meyer might have applied, but he calls it "hope laid up"—a reality which excites and sustains the emotion of hope in the present state. It is further argued that εὐχαριστεῖν is never used in the New Testament with διά to express the ground of thanksgiving. It is so; but unless the objector can produce a parallel place to this, there is really no difficulty. If a writer means to express a different shade of idea, he will use a different preposition. Neither ὑπέρ nor ἐπί conveyed the precise idea of the clause before us. These prepositions would have denoted that the hope was in itself the great ground of gratitude; but the apostle, in using διά, says that the hope, while it is so noble and promising, has a special and ultimate connection with the faith and love, the report of which so cheered his heart. The hope was present to his mind when he said εὐχαριστοῦμεν, but other and subordinate thoughts intervene, and his idea is so far modified, that when he came to write ἐλπίδα, he prefixes διά.

'Ἐλπίς is the object hoped for—τὸ ἐλπιζόμενον. [Eph. i. 18.] In τὴν ἀποκειμένην is the idea of reservation and security. (Luke xix. 20; 2 Tim. iv. 8; 1 Pet. i. 4.)[1] It is not enjoyed now—but it exists now; it is kept in store, and will certainly be possessed. And it is laid up ἐν τοῖς οὐρανοῖς, "in the heavens"—in that high region of felicity and splendour—at God's right hand, which guards it, and in the presence of Christ, who won it, and will bestow it. And this heavenly glory is an object of hope to them who possess this faith and love for these good reasons:—1. It is future—as it is not yet enjoyed, but it is lying over; "hope that is seen is not hope." 2. It is future good, for it is in heaven, the scene of all that is fair and satisfying. Coming evil excites terror, but distant good creates hopeful desire and anticipation. For it is the unimagined glory of spiritual perfection, of living in the unshaded radiance of God's face, and in uninterrupted fellowship with Him, and the thronging myriads round about Him—the signet of eternity stamped on every enjoyment. 3. Such future good is attainable. Were it completely beyond reach, it might excite a romantic wish in one heart, and cover another with despair. But the apostle says it is laid up *for you*. It will therefore be enjoyed, for Christ has given His pledge. This faith, too, will elevate the spirit to heaven, and that love will prepare it for those supreme enjoyments,

"For love is heaven, and heaven is love."

Ἣν προηκούσατε ἐν τῷ λόγῳ τῆς ἀληθείας τοῦ εὐαγγελίου—"Of which ye have already heard in the word of the truth of the gospel." The verb occurs only in this place of the New Testament, but it is found in Herodotus, Xenophon, and Josephus.[2] In the προ compounded with the verb, De Wette and Olshausen think that the meaning is—they had heard of the hope in promise *before* the enjoyment of it. Such an exegesis is a species of truism, since they must have heard before they could cherish it. Therefore the interpretation of Meyer is equally objectionable—before ye had this hope, it was made known to you, it was communicated to you as a novelty. Nor can we say, generally, that the sense is—ye have heard of it

[1] Loesner, *Observ. ad N. T.* p. 360.

[2] Robinson, *Lexicon, sub voce.* Raphelius, *Annot. Sac.* vol. ii. p. 525.

before I now write it. But the meaning seems to be—that the hope laid up in heaven was, and had been, a prominent topic of preaching, and therefore an invariable topic of hearing in the Christian church. That *προ* has the sense of "already" we have shown fully under Eph. i. 12. It is as if he meant to say—I need not expatiate on this hope, bright and glorious though it be; you are not unacquainted with it, for in the earliest teachings of the gospel when it came to you, ye heard of it—heard of it—

Ἐν τῷ λόγῳ τῆς ἀληθείας. We cannot agree with Chrysostom, Erasmus, Heinrichs, Baumgarten-Crusius, Storr, and others, in giving the genitive an adjectival sense, as if the meaning were "the true and genuine gospel." The noun *ἀληθείας* is made prominent by the article prefixed to it, and the idiom denotes that "the truth" was the sum and substance of the *λόγος*, or oral communication made to them by the first teachers of Christianity. *Λόγος* refers to the fact that their first teaching was oral, and not epistolary, or by inspired manuscript; and this "word," or verbal tuition, had the truth for its pith and marrow. But the form of truth which had been presented to their minds was no common aspect of it. It belonged, not to philosophy or human speculation—it was the truth *τοῦ εὐαγγελίου*, "of the gospel." This genitive is not in apposition with *τῆς ἀληθείας*, as Calvin, Beza, Olshausen, De Wette, Böhmer, and Huther suppose, but it has its distinctive meaning—the truth which belongs to the gospel, or is its peculiar and characteristic message. [*ἀληθεία, εὐαγγέλιον*, Eph. i. 13.] "The word of the truth of the gospel" could alone reveal the nature and the certainty of future and celestial blessedness. The idea and expectation of spiritual felicity and glory in heaven are not connected with the sciences of earth, which deal so subtly with the properties and relations of mind and matter. These forms of knowledge and discovery lead but to the lip of the grave, and desert us amidst the dreary wail of dust to dust and ashes to ashes, but the truth contained in the gospel throws its radiance beyond the sepulchre, unvails the portals of eternity, and discloses the reality, magnitude, and character of "the hope laid up in heaven." And, therefore, every blessing which the gospel makes known has futurity in its eye—an eye that pierces beyond the present horizon; and the Christian life, in the meantime, is one as much of expectation as of positive enjoyment.

(Ver. 6.) *Τοῦ παρόντος εἰς ὑμᾶς καθὼς καὶ ἐν παντὶ τῷ κόσμῳ*—"Which has come to you, as it has come in all the world."[1] The verb is used with *πρός* in Acts xii. 20; 2 Cor. xi. 9; Gal. iv. 18, 20, in which instances the presence of persons is referred to, both in subject and object. Here it is followed by *εἰς* in the first clause, and *ἐν* in the second clause. In the one, by *εἰς*, the idea of travel prior to advent is implied; in the other, by *ἐν*, the notion of simple presence is affirmed, Kühner, § 622. The gospel had come to them, was brought to them, and was now with them, or in their possession. (2 Pet. i. 9.) Or, as Theophylact says, *οὐ παρεγένετό, φησιν, πρὸς ὑμᾶς, καὶ ἀπέστη, ἀλλὰ πάρεστι καὶ κρατεῖ ἐν ὑμῖν.* This idea suggested the Coptic rendering (*Phai etshop*)—"which abideth or dwelleth." And surely such a gift they would keep as their own, prize highly, love dearly, and never suffer it to be contaminated with popular errors, or exchange it for those mystical reveries which were broached among them. For while the errors which the apostle is about to reprobate were limited in their origin and popularity, this gospel was "in all the world." We see no necessity for choosing a new verb, and supplying the simple *ἔστιν*, while *πάρεστι* is suggested at once by the preceding clause. It was in all the world, because it had come to it. It was not indigenous in any country, but was there merely because it had been carried there. This expression is not to be scanned with narrow minuteness. We cannot, with Olshausen and Baumgarten-Crusius, look upon it as a prophetic or ideal statement; nor can we, with Michaelis, limit it to the Roman empire. The phrase is similarly used by Paul in Rom. i. 8. That world which lay all round about them—those countries which to them were the world, and were by them so named, had been brought into contact with the gospel. It arose in Judæa, but burst its narrow barriers, and came forth with world-wide adaptation, offers, and enterprise. The labours of the other apostles in so

[1] Raphelius, *Annotat.* ii. 525, 526; Krebs, *Observat.* 333: the former showing from the classics, and the latter from Josephus, that in *πάρειμι* is the notion of arrival. Passow, *sub voce.*

many countries of the east and west warranted the phraseology.

Καὶ ἔστιν καρποφορούμενον καὶ αὐξανόμενον.

Καί is omitted by Lachmann, and Griesbach is virtually of the same opinion. It is wanting in A, B, C, D¹, E¹, in several Minuscules, and in the Coptic and Sahidic versions; but it is found in D³, E², F, G, J, K, the Vulgate, and Syriac, and in the Greek Fathers. The authority of Codices against it is almost balanced by that of Codices in its favour. The words *καὶ αὐξαν.* are added to the Stephanic text on the evidence of A, B, C, D¹, E¹, F, G, J, and many other concurrent witnesses, such as almost all the Versions. Were the first *καί* not genuine, there would be a vital change of syntax. But with it there is only a common change. Kühner, § 863; Winer, § 64.[1] The reading we adopt frees the text from much entanglement of thought and diction. That gospel in all the world was no idle and barren speculation—a tinted cloud without rain, or a polished cistern without water. Or rather, it was as a tree—yielding his fruit in his season: whose leaf never fadeth. The gospel bore choice and noble clusters of fruit. It is not a ceremonial to be gazed at, or a congeries of opinions to be discussed. It is essentially a practical system, for its ethics are involved in its creed and worship. It makes the heart its home, and diffuses its control and its impulses over thought and action, over motive and life. That fruit is the assemblage of graces which adorn the Christian character.

The reference in *καὶ αὐξαν.* is variously understood. Grotius, Olshausen, and Steiger refer it to internal growth, or the growing and ripening of the fruits themselves. We prefer

[1] Olshausen thus states the case :—"Here the connection of the words is disputable, in consequence of the different readings ; St. Paul's discourse proceeds with *καθὼς καί* thrice repeated : it is true the *καί* is wanting in the third, in very many and important MSS., but the *omission* is far more explicable because it had already been put twice before, than the *addition* of it. But then A, C, D, read in the beginning of verse 6 *καθὼς καὶ ἐν παντὶ τῷ κόσμῳ ἔστι καρποφορούμενον.* By that reading the proposition *καθὼς—κόσμῳ* is separate from what precedes, and joined with what follows, which brings with it the great inconvenience that *then* the words *καθὼς καὶ ἐν ὑμῖν* do not fit the beginning of the proposition *καθὼς καὶ ἐν παντὶ τῷ κόσμῳ*, since the Colossians are to be conceived as included of course with the rest in the whole world. It is with reason, therefore, that Steiger, Bähr, and others have retained *καὶ ἔστι καρποφορούμενον*, and supplied *ἔστι* at *καθὼς καὶ ἐν παντὶ τῷ κόσμῳ.*"

the idea of the Greek Fathers, for Theodoret explains it thus —*αὔξησιν δὲ τῶν πιστευόντων τὸ πλῆθος*, that is, the growth is the external diffusion of the gospel. That fruit-bearing gospel was extending itself. To keep the figure of the apostle, it was like a tree, whose fruit, falling to the earth, germinated, so that there sprang up a youthful and healthy forest on all sides of it, or like the Eastern banyan, whose tall boughs, as they bend themselves in a graceful curve to the ground, enter it, and fastening into it a new root, rise up again in verdure, and on reaching the requisite height, stoop as before and repeat the same process of self-plantation till field upon field is covered with the progeny of its arches and alcoves. Thus did the gospel make progress—the disciples preached it around them, and their converts becoming preachers in turn, widened the circle of its influence and conquests. Acts xii. 24, xix. 20. *Καθὼς καὶ ἐν ὑμῖν*—"as indeed among you." What the gospel produced and achieved in the world, it produces and achieves among you. It exhibited the same vitality, fruitfulness, and power of self-diffusion in Colosse, as in the regions round about it. And those elements of the gospel had not been of slow production, or periodical manifestation—it, says Paul, had been so among you—

'Αφ' ἧς ἡμέρας ἠκούσατε καὶ ἐπέγνωτε τὴν χάριν τοῦ Θεοῦ ἐν ἀληθείᾳ—"From the day ye heard it, and knew the grace of God in truth." This peculiar form of elliptical construction by the incorporation of the noun into the relative clause is not uncommon; Winer, § 24; Bernhardy, p. 302. The accusative to the first verb *ἠκούσατε* is *εὐαγγέλιον*. It was the gospel which they had heard. This was the external and audible form of that grace which they had been privileged to know. It was by hearing it, or by verbal instruction about it, that they had become acquainted with it. The preposition *ἐπί*, with *γινώσκω*, has an intensive sense, as has been proved by us under Eph. i. 17. By hearing the gospel they had come to know fully the grace of God—for the grace of God is the essence of the gospel, or the glorious fact which it communicates. It is the good news that God has in His sovereign favour pitied and blessed the world, and conferred upon it an unmerited and unexpected salvation—that while He have might punished, He resolved to pardon—

that when He might have permitted the law to take its course, He has founded an economy of grace which man had no right to anticipate, and Himself was under no obligation to introduce. In every element of the gospel, in its pardon and purity, in its hope and life, in its means as well as in its offers of deliverance, in its application no less than its provision of saving blessings, in its precepts as much as in its privileges, there is felt and known in its peculiar ascendancy and fulness, "the grace of God." [χάρις, Eph. ii. 8.]

The last words, ἐν ἀληθ., are connected in various ways. 1. Some give the phrase the force of an adjectival epithet, and join it to χάρις—"the true grace" of God. Such is the view of Storr, Homberg, Pierce, Barnes, and Baumgarten-Crusius. This interpretation is without point. 2. Grotius and Musculus depart still farther from the true syntax by their paraphrase —"the grace of God revealed in the word of truth." 3. Beza, Crocius, Olshausen, Steiger, Huther, De Wette, Meyer, and Winer, join the phrase to the verb, "and truly or really" knew the grace of God. The knowledge possessed by the Colossians is thus supposed to be distinguished from a false or fictitious knowledge of the Divine grace. 4. We prefer, with Bähr and Calvin, a different shade of the same exegesis, giving to the phrase an objective meaning, as if the apostle meant to say—the grace which they knew had been presented to them "in its truth," for they had learned it from Epaphras. The preceding forms of exegesis are inferences from this. It was a correct interpretation of the scheme of grace which they had learned, or they possessed a true knowledge of the plan of mercy, because, as the next verse shows, Epaphras had taught them the gospel in its fulness and purity. This is also the idea of Œcumenius, though Theophylact and Chrysostom erroneously include the notion of miracles as confirming the truth. We understand the apostle to write thus—since the day ye heard it, and fully knew the grace of God in truth, as indeed in that true and complete form ye learned it from Epaphras; or, as Calvin explains, *testatus est sincere illis fuisse traditum.* The words ἐν ἀληθ. describe the teaching of Epaphras, or represent that genuine form, in which, by his preaching, the grace of God had been exhibited at Colosse. It is probable that in this statement there are various points of implied contrast with those corrupt representations which are mentioned and refuted in the subsequent chapter. Thus—the grace of God had been taught them without mutilation or admixture, but false philosophy shaded or curtailed its doctrines. The gospel was œcumenical, but the error which menaced them was only provincial in its sphere. The truth exhibited the basis and objects of a blessed hope, but falsehood darkened the horizon, and while the gospel yielded great abundance, such fictitious dogmas were barren and empty—a tree with leaves, but without fruit.

The apostle says—"since ye knew the grace of God in truth," or in its true form, "just as ye learned it from Epaphras"—

(Ver. 7.) ***Καθὼς ἐμάθετε ἀπὸ Ἐπαφρᾶ.*** The *καί* found in the Received Text after *καθώς*, is justly excluded on the authority of A, B, C, D[1], F, G, 17, 23, etc. It may have come into the text from its frequent employment in such an idiom by the apostle. It might be replied, however, that as, from an old tradition, Epaphras was supposed to be the only founder of the church, the *καί* was omitted, as seeming to militate against such a belief. Wiggers, indeed, has formally raised such an argument.[1] But even were *καί* genuine, might it not mean "really," or "indeed"—"as ye indeed learned of Epaphras"? The teaching of Epaphras is thus sealed and sanctioned by inspired authority. The apostle had no mean jealousy of a colleague who is further characterized as "our beloved fellow-servant"—

Τοῦ ἀγαπητοῦ συνδούλου ἡμῶν. The noun occurs again in iv. 7. Like ὁμόδουλος, the old Attic form, it signifies "fellow-servant." Conybeare and Macknight are found at opposite extremes about the term; the former rendering it "fellow-bondsman," with unnecessary emphasis, and the latter uttering the sentimental conjecture that Paul used the word because he did not wish to grieve the Colossian church by telling them that their Epaphras was in prison with him. Timothy, Paul, and Epaphras not only served a common master, but were engaged in the same service; and therefore this community of labour begat a special attachment. The heart of the apostle was knit in cordial affection to all his fellow-

[1] *Studien und Kritiken*, 1838, p. 185.

labourers. He had none of that ignoble rivalry which just "hints a fault and hesitates dislike." He felt no envy at their success, but was so identified with their work, that whatever gladdened them gladdened him; he shared in their triumphs and was saddened at their reverses. Still more, it is testified of Epaphras—

Ὅς ἐστι πιστὸς ὑπὲρ ὑμῶν διάκονος τοῦ Χριστοῦ—"who is for you a faithful minister of Christ." The noun διάκονος is used in a general sense, as may be seen under Eph. iii. 7. [πιστὸς διάκονος, Eph. vi. 21.] The reading ὑπὲρ ὑμῶν has been called in question, and ὑπὲρ ἡμῶν is adopted by Lachmann, Bengel, Olshausen, and Steiger. In favour of this last reading are A, B^1, D, G; and in favour of the former are C, D^3, E, F, G, K, and others, with almost all the versions and Fathers. Where external testimony is so decided, we cannot accede to Olshausen's pleading of any internal evidence. And the meaning attached to ὑπὲρ ἡμῶν—*vice apostoli*, in our stead—can scarcely be correct, since Epaphras was not simply an apostolical representative, for in ἡμῶν Timothy is included along with Paul. Nor is it necessary to give ὑπέρ the sense of "in room of," in Luke ix. 50, for there the phrase means "on our side." The phrase then ὑπὲρ ὑμῶν means "on your behalf." 2 Cor. iv. 5. The faithful labours of Epaphras were directed to the spiritual benefit of the Colossian church. For them he served, and served faithfully, in the gospel of Christ. A brief but noble eulogy. As he had devoted to them every energy, kept among them, and prayed with and for them, as he had presented to them a complete and symmetrical view of the gospel, and as their correct knowledge of Divine grace was based upon his teaching, and their spiritual eminence and fertility were the result of his patient and painstaking efforts, therefore were they to love him in his absence, and surely they would allow no false teacher to supplant him in their affection. Probably the encomium was a virtual warning, for, as Theodoret says, πολλοῖς δὲ αὐτὸν ἐκόμισεν ἐγκωμίοις—ἵνα αὐτοῖς πλείονος αἰδοῦς ἀξιώτερος γένηται. It is a faint view of Chrysostom to imagine that the faithful service here referred to, is but the truthful report of the spiritual condition of the Colossians, which Epaphras had brought to Rome. Such a slight message could scarce be called a service, and it is therefore to fidelity of ministerial labour at Colosse that the apostle refers. It is wholly a caricature of the words to suppose, with Calixtus, Michaelis, and Böhmer, that as Epaphras was the apostle's fellow-prisoner, he alludes to personal services done by the Colossian pastor to himself, as if he had said—"who is, in your room, a faithful servant of Christ to me."

(Ver. 8.) *Ὁ καὶ δηλώσας ἡμῖν τὴν ὑμῶν ἀγάπην ἐν πνεύματι*—"Who has besides made known to us your love in the Spirit." It narrows the meaning too much to restrict this love to the apostle himself and Timothy—"your love to us." Yet this is the view of the great majority of expositors, from Chrysostom in early times, and Erasmus and Grotius in later days, down to Bähr, Böhmer, Steiger, Huther, and Baumgarten-Crusius. But the language of the apostle does not warrant such a sense except by inference. Nor may the phrase be applied solely to brother-love, but, with Meyer, Theodoret, Heinrichs, and De Wette, we take it in a general sense as denoting the Christian grace of love. And the reason why this grace is selected and eulogized is evident from the concluding words—it was love "in the Spirit"—

Ἐν πνεύματι. To give this phrase, as in the opinion of Rosenmüller, a-Lapide, Trollope, and others, the mere sense of true Christian love, is a weak dilution. Nor can we with Wolf and others regard it as in tacit contrast to *ἐν σαρκί*, a love based on domestic or national ties; or as if the meaning were—a love to the absent apostle which must be spiritual, as they had never seen his face in the flesh. The words, as in Pauline usage, refer to the Holy Spirit, and point out the source and sphere of this gracious affection. Thus, Rom. xiv. 17, *χαρὰ ἐν πνεύματι.* Gal. v. 22; Rom. xv. 13. *Ἐν* will not stand for *διά*, as Grotius renders it. Not as if Epaphras had spoken only of their love, and had made no mention of their other spiritual attainments. But love is regarded as the crown and consequence of all the other graces, and the mention of it presupposed their lively and effective exercise. For this love is no affection based on common relations—such as human friendship or social instincts. It is the offspring of spiritual influence in a heart so full of antagonism by nature to what is good and pure. The Spirit of Him who is Love takes possession of the believing bosom, and exerts upon it His own assimilating power. And as love is at the same time the combined product or resulting fervour of the other graces, as it gives man his closest resemblance to God, as it is the life and glory of heaven; and as it is the great object of the gospel to create and perfect it in the church, it may be safely taken as the index of spiritual advancement. The more it is seen in its vivid sympathies with all that is fair and God-like, the more its genial harmonies pervade the churches, the more its chivalrous impulses are felt, the more token is there that the Spirit of God has been in powerful and characteristic operation, and therefore as the true summation or totality of its various spiritual gifts, a Christian community may be congratulated on its love. When Epaphras declared their "love in the Spirit," he spoke of the result, and from such a result it was at once inferred what a Divine change had been wrought, and how the elements of that change had been surely and successively developed and matured. "He that dwelleth in love, dwelleth in God, and God in him."

The reader will easily mark the course of thought. In verse 3, the apostle intimates that as he prayed, he gave thanks for them. Then naturally he tells the reason, but the telling of the reason in full prevents him from recording at once what formed the theme of his prayer. Now, however, in verse 9, he reverts to the contents of his supplications, and he says that he asked from God, for the Colossians, blessings fitted for mind, heart, and conduct,—a higher degree of knowledge, holiness, usefulness, persistence, and strength—all of them at once gifts of present possession, and elements of preparation too for future blessedness—all of them provided by the Father, and enjoyed by those who have been translated into the kingdom of His Son.

(Ver. 9.) *Διὰ τοῦτο καὶ ἡμεῖς, ἀφ' ἧς ἡμέρας ἠκούσαμεν, οὐ παυόμεθα ὑπὲρ ὑμῶν προσευχόμενοι, καὶ αἰτούμενοι*—"On this account, we too, since the day we heard of it, cease not praying and asking." *Διὰ τοῦτο*—on this account, because ye know the grace of God in truth—because such are your condition and prospects—because of the faith which sustains you, the love which glows within you, the blessed hope laid up for you, and the verdant fertility which characterizes you, and sets its seal on the genuineness of your Christianity. *Καὶ ἡμεῖς*—"we too," we on our part. There is no reason, with De Wette, for subjoining the *καί* to *διὰ τοῦτο* and rendering "on this account, indeed." The phrase *ἀφ' ἧς ἡμέρας* not only refers to verse 8, but carries us back to verse 4. The receipt of the intelligence produced immediate result, and led to prayer. The report did not lie in dormancy, or slowly wake up the reciprocal love of Paul and Timothy. The effect was instant—and it was not spent with a single impulse. From the day we heard it down to the period of our writing this letter—"we cease not." This continuous prayer is explained by the beautiful remark of Augustine on Psalm xxxvii.—*ipsum desiderium tuum oratio tua est, si continuum est desiderium—continua est oratio.*

The verb *παυόμεθα* is here followed by a participle, *προσευχόμενοι καὶ αἰτούμενοι*, and not by the infinitive. There is indeed a difference of meaning in the two usages, as the participle expresses an action which already exists. Winer, § 45, 4; Bernhardy, p. 477. [Eph. i. 16.] The distinction between the two participles has been variously understood. But the best mode of characterizing the difference is to regard the one as general, and the other as special; the first is prayer in its ordinary aspect, and the second is direct request. But it is an error on the part of Baumgarten-Crusius to say that *ἵνα* depends upon the last participle—for *προσεύχομαι* is followed by the conjunction in Matt. xxiv. 20; Mark xiii. 18; 1 Cor. xiv. 13. The phrase *ὑπὲρ ὑμῶν* belongs also to both participles. What the special object of supplication was is now made known. Praying—

Ἵνα πληρωθῆτε τὴν ἐπίγνωσιν τοῦ θελήματος αὐτοῦ—"that ye may be filled with the knowledge of His will." [As to this use of *ἵνα*, see Eph. i. 17.] The verb *πληροῦν*, like the correspondent term in Hebrew, governs two accusatives in the active conjugation, and may therefore govern one of them in the passive. The genitive is the case oftenest employed in the New Testament to denote the complement—that with which the action of the verb is realized. In this use of the accusative there is no need, with Beza and Erasmus, to supply *κατά*. Winer, § 32, 5.[1] We cannot agree with

[1] Moulton, p. 287, note 2.

Olshausen, that γνῶσις and ἐπίγνωσις have no distinction in the diction of the Apostle Paul. We have shown the true difference under Eph. i. 17. The vague definition of Steiger cannot be sustained; it is wrapt in uncertainty, and is at best but a metaphysical subtlety. The idea of Bähr, that ἐπίγνωσις is subjective, and γνῶσις is also objective, is only a partial view. Ἐπίγν. is full knowledge exhaustive of its object, and is especially meant for those who have already some little γνῶσις. The Colossians had γνῶσις, but the apostle wished them to be filled with additional and supplemental knowledge, not new knowledge, or a different form or section of Christian science, but a fuller development of the partial theological information which they already possessed. Had he gently wished them somewhat more of knowledge, he might have used γνῶσις, but as he prayed that they might be filled with more of that insight which they already enjoyed, such an accumulation was naturally expressed by ἐπίγνωσις.

That augmentation of knowledge had for its theme the Divine will. We apprehend that the principal fault of commentators has been to restrict too much the meaning of the phrase, "His will." Chrysostom, and the Greek Fathers Œcumenius and Theophylact, followed by Huther, refer it to the plan of redemption—especially salvation by Christ, not by angels—τουτέστι τὸ τὸν υἱὸν δοθῆναι ὑπὲρ ἡμῶν. Others refer it to the secret purpose of God—such as Suicer and Bähr, and that because it is elsewhere accompanied by μυστήριον. A third and numerous party understand the legislative will of God—the ethical feature of the Divine counsel, such as Theodoret, De Wette, and Meyer. We are inclined to take the phrase without any restriction—the Divine will as well in creed as in moral obligation; the one basis alike of what we ought to believe and of what we ought to do; the only rule of faith and manners. 1 Cor. i. 4, 5, 7, ii. 12, xii. 8; Eph. i. 17. The apostle implored for them a complete knowledge of the Divine Will in all its revealed aspects and elements—

Ἐν πάσῃ σοφίᾳ, καὶ συνέσει πνευματικῇ—"in all wisdom and spiritual insight." Some join the clause to the following verse, but without any necessity. The preposition does not signify "along with," nor does it, as Boehmer thinks, define the result. Nor does it mean, as Bähr takes it, "by means of;" nor does it, as Huther supposes, point out the quality of the knowledge. It seems to refer us to the mode of its acquisition—"in all wisdom and understanding." The prayer was not one for plenary inspiration—nor that God would by some dazzling self-discovery imbue them with a knowledge of His will, but that He would give them this higher spiritual science in the way of giving them all spiritual wisdom and understanding. These two nouns are not easily comprehended in their specific shades of difference. As a specimen of the scholastic forms of definition, we present that of Peter Lombard—*Sapientia est habitus infusus ad solius aeternae veritatis contemplationem et delectationem. Intelligentia ad Creatoris et creaturarum invisibilium speculationem.*[1] But,—

1. Not a few, such as Michaelis, Storr, Flatt, and Heinrichs, regard them as synonymous; a mode of interpretation too easy to be correct—too slovenly to be in accordance with accurate philology.

2. Many give *σοφία* the sense of theoretic wisdom, and *σύνεσις*, the meaning of practical discernment—such as Bähr, Heinsius, and Calvin.

3. Bengel, Meyer, and Baumgarten-Crusius, think the nouns related in the sense of general and special, while De Wette thinks the first term to be practical and general, and the second theoretical and special. We are inclined to take *σοφία* in a general sense, and to regard *σύνεσις πνευματική* as its characteristic form or peculiarity. For if God fill men with the knowledge of His will, it is usually by clearing their spiritual apprehension, and enlarging the sphere of their spiritual vision. The mind is trained and tutored to the study of Divine things; and as the horizon of its view is gradually expanded in such an exercise, it gathers in "wisdom"—and what is this wisdom but "spiritual insight"? Let there be intense practical application of the mental powers; prolonged reflection; devout and pensive contemplation; the inspection and comparison of premises; the solution of doubts; the ascent, step by step, slowly and surely, to first principles; the glimpse of ulterior relations based upon present realities, and conclusions drawn from recognized truths; and surely the

[1] Lib. iii. *Distinctio*, xxxv. 2, p. 318. Opera, ed. Migne, Paris, 1841.

mind so interested and occupied must feel all such acquisitions to be wisdom—wisdom, and not mere theory to be tested—wisdom, and not simple hypothesis that may be dismissed. And those fruits of diligent investigation are not like the coloured glimpses of a distant reverie which may be dimmed or exchanged, or may wholly fade away, as the whim of such imaginational pastime may lazily will it; but they bear at once upon the nearest of interests, and evince their immediate connection with the most momentous of relations. Of all forms of intellectual operation and enlightenment, this is the most practical—it is "wisdom." God fills the mind, not by the passive inpouring of transcendental truths, but by directing and upholding its energies, and so enabling it to work out the result which it makes its own, and recognizes as "all wisdom."

And this wisdom is really *σύνεσις πνευματική*—spiritual insight. As we have shown at length under Eph. i. 3, the prevailing meaning of *πνευματικός* in the New Testament, is "of, or belonging to the Holy Spirit." Spiritual is not opposed to carnal, and means not—in connection with the human spirit, but the phrase signifies discernment conferred and quickened by the Holy Ghost. This enjoyment of the Spirit of Light is the special privilege of believers. He dispels the mists which obscure the inner vision, fills the soul with an ardent relish for Divine truth and a fuller perception of it, enables it to see through a perfect medium, and thus confers upon it that power and perspicacity termed by the apostle "spiritual understanding." And where this purity and penetration of discernment are possessed, and the fruits of such wisdom are gleaned and garnered up, the mind, in the use of such a faculty, and the enjoyment of such acquisitions, cannot but be conscious that it has risen to an ampler knowledge of the Divine will. The apostle prefixes *πάσῃ*—"all." This wisdom and spiritual understanding are not limited or shrivelled, but may be enjoyed to their utmost bounds.

(Ver. 10.) *Περιπατῆσαι ὑμᾶς ἀξίως τοῦ Κυρίου*—"So that ye walk worthy of the Lord." *Ὑμᾶς* appears to be a spurious but natural supplement, and is omitted by A, B, C, D[1], F, G, though the authorities for it are of no mean value. The Syriac has a peculiar rendering. It reads in the last clause of the preceding verse—that ye walk "according to what is just," ܐܝܟ ܕܙܕܩ, and then adds—that ye may please God in all good works. The apostle, after the verb of prayer, first uses *ἵνα* with the subjunctive, as indicating the prime petition; then follows *περιπατῆσαι* as denoting a contemporaneous result, and this infinitive is succeeded by a series of dependent and explanatory participles. The figure implied in the verb is a common one, and is of Hebrew origin. It describes the general tenor of one's life, his peculiar gait and progress in his spiritual journey, what are his companions, and what are his haunts; whether he hold on his way with steady step, or is seduced into occasional aberrations. By *Κύριος* is meant Christ, and not God, as Anselm and Erasmus imagine; and the meaning and reasons of the name are fully detailed under Eph. i. 2. The adverb *ἀξίως* signifies "becomingly." [Eph. iv. 1.] Rom. xvi. 2; Phil. i. 27; 1 Thess. ii. 12. To walk worthy of the Lord, is to feel the solemn bond of redeeming blood, to enshrine the image of Him who shed it, to breathe His spirit and act in harmony with His example, to exhibit His temperament in its elements of purity, piety, and love, to be in the world as He was in the world, to be good and to do good, and to show by the whole demeanour that His law is the rule which governs, and His glory the aim which elevates and directs. No *meritum condigni* can be inferred from the passage, as Cameron shows against Bellarmine.[1]

Εἰς πᾶσαν ἀρέσκειαν—"In order to all-pleasing." The noun *ἀρέσκεια* has, in classic Greek, a bad sense, and means obsequiousness, but it has a purified meaning in Philo and in the New Testament.[2] The Lord is to be pleased and highly pleased in everything, for again the apostle prefixes *πᾶσαν*. This well-pleasing is not to be sectional, but uniform and unbounded; and it is not difficult to please Him. Men are not left in uncertainty to study the best method of ensuring His complacency, nor are there any moods or forms of caprice with Him. His highest pleasure is to see His own likeness in those who own His Lordship: in all their thoughts, purposes, and actions, there should be a pervading and paramount desire to walk so worthily of Him, as to secure His approval. Nor does this statement involve any subtle casuistry. What-

[1] *Myrothecium*, p. 263.

[2] Athenaeus, *Deipnos.* lib. vi.

ever is good in design, generous in sentiment, or noble in result, meets at once with His approbation. Whatever proximate motive leads the heart, this shonld be its pole star, the bright, prominent, and ultimate guide and director.

Ἐν παντὶ ἔργῳ ἀγαθῷ καρποφοροῦντες. The participles are in the nominative, and not accusative, as in Eph. iii. 18. Kühner, § 863; Winer, § 63, I. 2 a; Vigerus, De Idiotismis, p. 340. "Fruit-bearing in every good work." This clause is joined by Chrysostom, Theophylact, and Steiger, to *εἰς πᾶσαν ἀρέσκειαν.* But such a view is too narrow. It is an element of the worthy walk—and the first of four elements, each specified by a participle, *καρποφοροῦντες—αὐξανόμενοι—δυναμούμενοι—εὐχαριστοῦντες*; two of the participles preceded by a qualifying noun with *ἐν*; and two of them followed by *εἰς*, denoting purpose or result. The first two participles occur together in verse 6. Spiritual fruitfulness is the first characteristic. And those fruits are good works. 2 Cor. ix. 8; 2 Thess. ii. 17; Heb. xiii. 21; Gal. v. 22; Phil. i. 11. [*ἔργα ἀγαθά,* Eph. ii. 10.] Barrenness is deadness. The tree with sapless trunk and leafless branches is a melancholy object. The figure before us is that of a tree covered with dense foliage, and laden with goodly produce—its boughs bent with heavy clusters, its crops perennial—buds always bursting into blossoms, and blossoms forming into fruit. But the apostle says "every good work." For a third time he employs *παντί.* It is the want of this universality that is the chief mark of imperfection. This unique tree is omniferous. Other trees produce each only after its kind, unless altered by the artificial process of grafting. But this tree presents every variety of spiritual fruit without confusion or rivalry, as if it contained the stateliness of the palm, the fatness of the olive, and the exuberant fecundity of the vine. The graces of Christianity are, each in its place, adorning and adorned—none absent and none sickly, but the entire assemblage in perfect order and symmetry. Superabundance of one kind of fruit is no compensation for the absence of another. "Every good work" is inculcated and anticipated. It may be noble philanthropy, or more lowly beneficence—it may be the self-denial of a martyr, or the gift of a cup of water to the humble wayfarer—it may be a deed of magnanimity which startles the nations, or it may be the washing of a beggar's feet—teaching its first letters to a ragged orphan, or repeating the story of the cross in the hovel of poverty and distress. There is no exception—"every good work" which Christ did, and in which any of His disciples may imitate Him—every good work which the age needs, or circumstances warrant, or would benefit the church or the world. Such fruitfulness is not exhaustive. The tree grows healthfully while its fertility is so great. Its life is not spent, and its wealth is not impoverished in a single autumn, but other twigs are preparing for their burden, and other shoots are evincing the vitality of the parent stock—for the apostle adds—

Καὶ αὐξανόμενοι εἰς τὴν ἐπίγνωσιν τοῦ Θεοῦ—"And growing up to the knowledge of God." Other forms of reading are—*ἐν τῇ ἐπιγνώσει* and *τῇ ἐπιγνώσει*. The last seems to be the best supported by MSS.; the Versions seem to countenance the second; but the first is the most difficult form, and therefore has been preferred by Tischendorf. Meyer says that *εἰς* is necessary, because each of the two succeeding participles is followed by this preposition, and analogy demands it here. But what if we should reply—that to secure uniformity some have been tempted to write *εἰς* where another preposition originally stood? A, B, C, D[1], E, F, G, and some Minuscules, with the Syriac and Coptic versions, support the simple dative *τῇ ἐπιγνώσει*. If the accusative, with *εἰς*, be retained, various forms of exegesis may be proposed. Meyer renders *εἰς hinsichtlich*, in regard to. Theophylact paraphrases *κατὰ τὸ μέτρον*—"according to the measure" of the knowledge of God, an interpretation virtually adopted by Heinrichs and Böhmer. If the dative with *ἐν* be received, then the meaning may be, as Theodoret, the Peschito and Vulgate, Beza, Luther, and Junker, intimate—growing in the knowledge of God, that is, acquiring more and more of the knowledge of God. But with Olshausen, De Wette, and Huther, we regard the simple dative as instrumental—growing "by means of the knowledge of God,"—the knowledge of His essence, character, will, and dispensations. [See under Eph. i. 17.] This knowledge of God, the purest and loftiest of human acquisitions, is the only pabulum of spiritual growth. A God in shadow creates superstition, and the view of Him in only one phasis of His character, will, according to its colour, lead either to fanaticism or to mysticism. The more we know of His tenderness and majesty, the more conversant we are with His Divine procedure, either as we find Him in creation, or meet Him in providence; and especially the deeper the experience we have of the might of His arm and sympathy of His bosom in redemption, the more will the spirit confide in Him, and the more will it love the object of its living trust—in short, the more spiritual growth will it enjoy. This fruit-bearing and increase are the first features of the worthy and pleasing walk.

(Ver. 11.) The first clause, though its purpose is designated by the following εἰς, has a close connection with the preceding. It describes that peculiar spiritual condition in which believers bring forth fruit, and grow, and thus walk worthy of Christ. The power is not indigenous; the fertility is not the outburst of innate and essential vitality. It comes from imparted strength—the might of God lodged within us. As His own nature is for ever outworking in ceaseless acts of beneficence, so His strength, lodged in a believer, loses not its original and distinctive energy.

'Εν πάσῃ δυνάμει δυναμούμενοι. This verb occurs only here in the New Testament, though it is found in the Septuagint as the representative of two Hebrew verbs, Ps. lxviii. 29; Eccles. x. 10. Neither does it occur in the classical,[1] though it is used by the ecclesiastical writers. The common form in the New Testament is *ἐνδυναμόω.* The use of the correlate noun and participle intensifies the meaning. The apostle refers to the impartation of the Divine strength to believers. Fallen humanity is feeble, but rises under this gift into prowess and majesty. The semblance of moral omnipotence is communicated to it, and it easily surmounts frailty, pain, sorrow, and death, for the apostle a fourth time employs *πάσῃ.* Phil. iv. 13. And the measure of this gift is—

Κατὰ τὸ κράτος τῆς δόξης αὐτοῦ—"according to the might of His glory," that is, the might which is characteristic of His glory. Retaining with Meyer and others the full force of the syntax, we cannot, with Luther, Junker, Beza, Storr, Flatt, Bähr, and Davenant, resolve the idiom thus—His glorious or highest might; nor can we with Böhmer make the clause

[1] Phrynichus, ed. Lobeck, *Parerga*, p. 605.

mean—that might which is His glory; nor can we with Grotius and Valpy identify τῆς δόξης with the τῆς ἰσχύος of Eph. i. 19; nor, finally, can we with Thomas Aquinas and Peter Lombard understand by His glory "His Son Christ Jesus." The glory of God possesses a peculiar might, and that might is not love simply, as Huther imagines. [Eph. i. 19.] If we survey the glory of God in creation, the immensity of its architectural power overwhelms us; or in providence, its exhaustless and versatile energy perplexes us; or in redemption, its moral achievements delight and amaze us. If the spiritual strength given to believers be after the measure of the might of this glory, with what courage and ability shall they be armed? Will they not, with so much of God in them, realize the God-like in spiritual heroism, so as to resist evil, overcome temptation, banish fear, surmount difficulties, embrace opportunities of well-doing, obtain victory over death, and prove that they are able to rise above everything before which unaided humanity sinks and succumbs. "Strengthened"—

Εἰς πᾶσαν ὑπομονὴν καὶ μακροθυμίαν—"in order to all patience and long-suffering." These two nouns have been variously distinguished. The early definition of Chrysostom is fanciful—*μακροθυμεῖ γάρ τις πρὸς ἐκείνους οὓς δυνατὸν καὶ ἀμύνασθαι, ὑπομένει δὲ οὓς οὐ δύναται ἀμύνασθαι*—"Long-suffering is exercised toward those whom we can punish, patience toward those whom we are unable to punish," wherefore he adds, "patience is never ascribed to God, but long-suffering often." Others refer the first noun to feeling under what God sends; and the second, to feeling under what man inflicts. A third class understand by the one term the state of temper under difficulties; and, by the other, mental calmness under suffering. But, not to notice other varieties of opinion,[1] we incline to give the words a more extended signification than to resignation, or quietness under injury. Both of them and their correspondent verbs are used not simply in reference to the pressure of present evil, but also to the prospect of coming deliverance, and as adjuncts or qualities of faith, or the life of faith. The following examples may suffice:—"Bring forth fruit," ἐν ὑπομονῇ, Luke viii. 15; "Possess ye your souls," ἐν ὑπομ., Luke xxi. 19; "Well-

[1] Tittmann, *De Synon. N. T.* p. 194.

doing," καθ' ὑπομ., Rom. ii. 7; "Let us run the race," δι' ὑπομ., Heb. xii. 1; or again, Heb. x. 36, "Ye have need of patience." The word in such places denotes that tenacity of spirit which still holds on, and perseveres, and waits God's time for reward or dismissal. There is similar usage also of the second noun. Its verb is used to denote the same exercise of mind, Matt. xviii. 26, 29, Heb. vi. 15, Jas. v. 7, 8; and the substantive in Heb. vi. 12, 2 Tim. iv. 2. There is no reference in this epistle either to persecution or to coming calamity. But believers in the present state are not perfect, they have not arrived at the ultimate goal. Impatience would lead to defection, and fretfulness to apostasy. There is rest set before them, but they have not reached it; hopes held out, but their fruition has not come. It is more trying to virtue to bear than to act: or, as a-Lapide says, *fortia agere Romanum est, aiebat Scaevola, sed fortia pati Christianum est.* Now, Christians are apt to faint under such discouragements, to lose heart and despond. Therefore do they need "patience and long-mindedness;" and because these graces dwell not in their unassisted nature, the apostle prays that the strength of God be for this purpose imparted to them. Even in their beneficent fruitfulness there may be a long and trying process ere the result be witnessed. In the midst of apparent anomaly and contradiction, with so much to distress and disappoint, so much to try and provoke, so much to tempt a prayer for the immediate substitution of sight for faith, there is surely great necessity for perseverance and unruffled equanimity; and because temper fails under such irritation, as it did with Moses and Elisha, and there are dark and inconsistent questionings and surmises, as if He were "slack concerning His promise," a higher power is vouchsafed, even the strength of Him whose patience and long-suffering transcend all measurement and description. And thus "all patience and long-suffering" are possessed, and for a fifth time, in the fulness of his heart, the apostle writes πᾶσαν. As the Colossian church was pestered with insidious errorists, whose speculations might occasionally perplex and confound them, immobility was the more requisite for them; and such, therefore, is the apostle's supplication in common with the sentiment of the prophet—"In quietness and confidence shall be your strength."

Μετὰ χαρᾶς—"with joy." A large number of expositors join these words to the following participle—*εὐχαριστοῦντες*. Of this opinion are Chrysostom, Œcumenius, and Theophylact, Estius, Böhmer, Huther, and Meyer, the Syriac version, and the editors Lachmann and Tischendorf. But we do not see any propriety in such a connection, for the participle carries the idea of joy along with it. The preposition, moreover, indicates a connection with the preceding nouns, or shows the concomitant of this imparted power; and therefore, with Luther, Grotius, Zanchius, Hyperius, Gomarus, De Wette, Bähr, Baumgarten-Crusius, Junker, Steiger, and Olshausen, we keep the words as they stand in the Received Text. This joy characterizes, or rather accompanies, as the preposition implies,[1] the graces of patience and long-suffering. That peculiar position which necessitates the exercise of patience and long-suffering should not induce despondency, or cast a gloom over the heart as if it were inevitable fate, to be sullenly submitted to, but rather should there be joy that this Divine power is communicated, and that the mind is upborne in triumph, and enabled to hope and wait in quiet expectation. And there are abundant reasons of joy.

(Ver. 12.) *Εὐχαριστοῦντες τῷ πατρί.* There are some variations of reading which need not be noted or analyzed. Codices D[1] and G read *καλέσαντι* instead of *ἱκανώσαντι*, perhaps from 1 Thess. ii. 12; while B reads *καλέσαντι καὶ ἱκανώσαντι*, a form erroneously adopted by Lachmann.

But with what portion of the previous context should this verse be connected? Chrysostom, Theodoret, Calvin, Calovius, Böhmer, and Baumgarten-Crusius, refer the connection to *οὐ παυόμεθα*, as if *εὐχαρ.* referred to Paul and Timothy, the writers of this epistle and the offerers of this prayer. "Since the day we heard it we cease not to pray for you . . . giving thanks to the Father." But such a connection is wholly capricious and unwarranted, and would make the two preceding verses a species of parenthesis. The natural order is to regard *εὐχαριστοῦντες* as co-ordinate with the preceding participles *καρποφοροῦντες*, *αὐξανόμενοι*, *δυναμούμενοι*, and as all four dependent on the infinitive *περιπατῆσαι*—that ye may walk, fruit-bearing, growing, strengthened, and giving thanks.

[1] *Commentary on Ephesians*, vi. 23.

And there is a beautiful sequence of thought. The apostle prayed that they might walk in immediate spiritual fertility and growth; amidst difficulties, strengthened into patience with joy; and such joy is no romantic enthusiasm, for it is based upon experience, inasmuch as even during this imperfect and unsatisfactory state, they were warranted to thank Him who was qualifying them all the while for the heavenly inheritance. From the visible and outward manifestation of fruit as a present and characteristic duty, the apostle ascends to internal and sustaining sentiment, and rises yet higher to that gratitude, which, based upon a growing maturity for heavenly blessedness, expresses its ardour in thanksgiving to the Father. The future is thus linked with the present, and sheds its lustre over it; and though the believer be now in a condition whose intermediate nature necessitates the possession of patience and long-suffering, his mind feels at the same time within it the elements of accelerating preparation for a nobler and purer state of existence.

In the participle *ἱκανώσαντι*, connected with *ἵκω*—"I reach, or arrive at," is the idea of fitness—"who hath fitted us," 2 Cor. iii. 6. The pronoun *ἡμᾶς* includes the writer of the epistle and his readers, and the aorist may denote repeated action, continued during a past period. The object to which this fitness relates is described—

Εἰς τὴν μερίδα τοῦ κλήρου τῶν ἁγίων ἐν τῷ φωτί—"For the share of the inheritance of the saints in light." The noun *μερίς* denotes a portion or share which one is to enjoy, and that share is in the *κλῆρος*, or inheritance, so designated from an allusion to the division and allotment of the land of Canaan. [Eph. i. 11.] Both words represent a Hebrew phrase—חֵלֶק, חֶבֶל, Deut. xxxii. 9. That inheritance has a peculiar proprietary, or population—it belongs to the saints.[1] The saints are neither Jews nor believers of an early date, but the company of those who are Christ's. [Eph. ii. 19, iii. 18.]

The meaning and connection of the remaining phrase have been variously understood. We merely notice, without dwell-

[1] As specimens of eccentric etymology may be quoted two attempts to theologize upon *ἅγιος* and *sanctus*—the former, according to Adam Clarke, being compounded of *α*, privative, and *γῆ*, "the earth;" and of the latter, Isidore the Pelusiot says—*sanctum dici quasi* sanguine tinctum.

ing on it, the opinion of some of the Fathers, that by φῶς is meant baptism; that of Aretius, that Christ Himself is indicated by the term; that of Grotius, that the syntax may be thus filled—ἁγίων τῶν ἐν φωτί; that of Bengel, that ἐν τῷ φωτί should be joined to μερίδα—participation in the kingdom of light, *in hoc regno partem beatam.*

1. Meyer and others, after Chrysostom, Œcumenius, and Theophylact, with Vatablus and Schrader, take ἐν as instrumental, and join it to ἱκανώσαντι, and then the meaning will be—who fits us by means of the light—the illumination of the gospel, τῇ γνώσει.

2. Others, as Macknight, give the same meaning to the term φῶς, but with a different connection, the inheritance of the saints which consists of light, to wit, their present evangelical state as in contrast with the darkness of their previous condition.

To both these forms of exegesis we have objections. 1. The position of ἐν τῷ φωτί at the end of the verse seems to connect it with the κλῆρος, as descriptive of it. 2. The language of the next verse speaks of a kingdom of darkness, out of which the Colossians had been translated. Now, the appropriate contrast is, out of a kingdom of darkness into one of light—light not being the instrument of translation, but the special property of the second realm. 3. Κλῆρος is often followed by ἐν to signify what it consists in. Thus, in the Septuagint—Wisd. v. 5, ὁ κλῆρος ἐν ἁγίοις; also Job xxx. 19, ἡ μερὶς ἐν γῇ; and in the New Testament, Acts viii. 21, xxvi. 18; Rev. xx. 6. This "light," however, though enjoyed here, is not meant to describe their present, but their future state. For the inheritance, though given on earth, is finally enjoyed in heaven, and therefore in Eph. i. 14 the Holy Ghost is called the "earnest of our inheritance;" and in the same chapter, the apostle prays that the Ephesians may comprehend the riches of the glory of God's inheritance among His saints. Again he specifies, in the same epistle, v. 5, certain classes of men who have no inheritance in the kingdom of Christ and God. In Acts xx. 32, xxvi. 18, 1 Pet. i. 4, the inheritance is future glory. We apprehend, then, that the apostle means to say, that God has fitted them for the future inheritance of the saints, which consists in light. It is too restricted a view of Böhmer and Huther, to find in φῶς simply the glory of heaven—and of Beza and Storr, to confine it to the happiness of heaven. The expressive epithet suggests both the one and the other, suggests that knowledge is the concomitant of happiness, and purity the basis of glory.

For heaven is a region of light. The radiance of Him who is Light streams through it and envelopes all the children of the light who live and walk in its lustre. A happy and unfailing intuition, sustained by its vicinity to the Uncreated Mind, is the source of unchequered and perfect knowledge. Intellectual refinement is robed "in the beauty of holiness." The brilliancy of the Divine image is reflected from every stainless heart, and the material glory of the residence is only surpassed by its spiritual splendour. That "light" is liable to no revolution and suffers no eclipse; it glows with unchanging permanence, and meeting with no obstruction creates no shadow. For they are "saints," who dwell in this kingdom—adorned with purity and perfection. Now such being the nature of the inheritance, it is not difficult to discover what are the elements of meetness for it. Man is incapable of enjoying it by nature; for darkness covers his mind, and impurity has seized upon his heart, and he must needs be changed. John iii. 3. He has no loyalty to its God, no love to its Saviour, no relish for its pursuits, and no sympathy with its inhabitants. His nature must be brought into harmony with the scene, and into congeniality with the occupations of such a world of light. So that every element of mental obscurity, all that tends to the dark and dismal in temperament, and all that vails the nobility of an heir of God, is dissolved, and fades away in the superior glory. The "saints" possess it—therefore their sanctification is complete. No taint of sin remains, no trace of previous corruption can be discerned. The language of prayer is superseded by that of praise, and the tongue shall be a stranger for ever to moaning and confession. None but the saints, as being "light in the Lord," can dwell in that light. An unregenerate spirit would feel itself so solitary and so unhappy, especially as it saw its hideousness mirrored in that sea of glass which sleeps before the throne, that it would rather plunge for relief into the gloom of hell, and there for a moment feel itself at ease among others so like it in punishment and crime.

Again, the one inheritance is shared by *many* participants, and they who are to enjoy it are made meet for *social* intercourse. Selfishness vanishes before universal love, the intense yearnings of a spiritual brotherhood are developed and perfected, for the entire assemblage is so united as if only one heart thrilled in their bosom, while one song bursts from their lips.

In fine, all this moral fitness is a paternal process, the work of the Father, qualifying His children for their patrimony. They do not infuse this maturity into themselves—this transformation is not a natural process, nor do they ripen of necessity into purity and love. The Father meetens them: and from Him are the blood that pardons, the Spirit that purifies, the truth which nourishes, the hope which sustains, the charter which secures—the whole preparation which meetens for the heavenly inheritance. He, therefore, is to be thanked, by all whose experience assures them of this auspicious training. If they are sensible of growth in truth, holiness, and affection—if they feel that they are travelling from stage to stage of spiritual assimilation—if their sanctified instincts and susceptibilities are finding congruous satisfaction and luxury in spiritual exercises, then, in spite of every drawback which is inseparable from their present condition in its trials and wants—they are only giving utterance to irrepressible emotion when they are giving thanks "unto the Father."[1] Nay, more, the very fact that a renewal is requisite, and that the present state, by its ills and emptiness, renders imperative the exercise of patience and long-suffering, gives a purer relish to celestial enjoyments. So sudden and vast is the change from expectation to enjoyment, and from pain to rapture, that the translated saint will feel a zest on entering heaven which cannot be tasted by those who have never had experience of any other state or sphere of existence. Nor do we deny that in the present state the inheritance of light is partially enjoyed, for heaven begins on earth, or as Chrysostom says, the apostle speaks "of things present and things to come." The translation out of darkness is effected here, and the dawning of the perfect day is already enjoyed, though cloud and gloom are often inter-

[1] Chrysostom well says—*Οὐ μόνον ἡμῖν ἔδωκε τὴν τιμὴν, ἀλλὰ καὶ ἰσχυροὺς πρὸς τὸ λαβεῖν ἐποίησε.*

mingled with it, and vail its beams. And when the inheritance is reached, the spirit of this thanksgiving shall still rule the heart. Conscious of its meetness, it shall pour itself out in hearty and prolonged halleluiahs. The world of perfection is a world of universal happiness and song, for no tongue is ever mute, no harp ever unstrung, and the harmony is never disturbed by the mournful echo of a plaintive strain.

The apostle glides insensibly out of the language of prayer into that of direct theological statement. Still, the statement is virtually a portion of the prayer, as it describes Him who in His redeeming love and power imparts the knowledge of Himself and His revealed will, who confers His own might upon His people, and prepares them for glory—the very God who has delivered us out of the kingdom of darkness.

(Ver. 13.) *Ὃς ἐρρύσατο ἡμᾶς ἐκ τῆς ἐξουσίας τοῦ σκότους*—"Who rescued us out of the kingdom of darkness." This verse does not describe the entire process of preparation, as Meyer seems to think; it rather gives us a vivid glance of the two termini—the one of departure, and the other of arrival. The unregenerate state is described as the kingdom of darkness.[1] It is one of spiritual gloom in its government, essence, pursuits, and subjects. In its administration it is named—"the power of Satan," in itself it is darkness—its actions are "works of darkness," and its population are "children of disobedience and wrath." Luke xxii. 53; Acts xxvi. 18. It is needless, with Augustine,[2] Zanchius, Bloomfield, and others, to regard *ἐξουσία* as personified, and as meaning Satan. [*Σκότος*, Eph. iv. 18, v. 8.] This principality is named "darkness" on account of its prevailing ethical element. Above it the heaven is shrouded in dismal eclipse, around it lies dense and impervious gloom, and before it stretches out the shadow of death. What men should believe and what they should do, what they should rest on and what they should hope for, what the mind should fasten

[1] Blackwall, *Sacred Classics*, vol. ii. 134, proposes to read verses 9–12 in a parenthesis, and as the result of such an arrangement, he exclaims—"How round the period, how vigorous and Divine the sense!" But such a parenthesis would be a miserable invention, as it leaves *ὅς* without an antecedent at all, or absurdly gives it *πνεύματι* in verse 8.

[2] Vol. ii. p. 1216, Op. ed. Bened. Paris, 1836.

on as truth and what the heart should gather in upon itself as a portion, what the spirit should present as acceptable worship and what the conscience should venerate as a rule of duty—all had been a matter of deep perplexity or hopeless uncertainty to the Colossians prior to their spiritual translation. There were occasionally in the heathen world shrewd guesses at truth—incidental approximations, when some brighter intellect unfolded its cogitations and longings. But the masses were involved in obscurity, and scarcely observed the fitful glimmer of the meteor which had shot over them. Ignorance, vice, and misery, the triple shades of this darkness, held possession of them. This "kingdom of darkness" stands in contrast to the sainted heritage in light. The deponent verb, from an obsolete form,[1] signifies, first, to draw to oneself, then to rescue, to pluck out of danger. The act of deliverance is still ascribed to the Father, for He alone can achieve the spiritual transportation described in the following clause.

Καὶ μετέστησεν εἰς τὴν βασιλείαν τοῦ υἱοῦ τῆς ἀγάπης αὐτοῦ—"And translated us into the kingdom of the Son of His love." The verb is often employed by the classical writers to signify the deportation of a body of men, or the removal of them to form a colony.[2] The term is therefore an expressive one. The Colossians had been lifted out of the realm of darkness, their original seat and habitation, and they had been carried into the kingdom of His Son, and colonized in it. They were not as emigrants in search of a home, nor as a company of dissatisfied exiles, but they were marched out of the one territory and settled in the other expressly by Divine guidance. *βασιλεία* stands in contrast with *ἐξουσία*, but there appears to be no ground for Wetstein's affirmation, that in such a contrast the latter word means a tyranny,[3] for in Rev. xii. 10 the one term is referred to God, and the other to Christ. "The kingdom of His Son" is plainly that kingdom which has Christ for its Head and Founder—which is partially developed on earth, and shall be finally perfected in heaven. [Eph. v. 5.] The word "kingdom" is used in harmony with the action indicated by the verb. As a church, men meet together in its sacred assemblies; as a kingdom, they

[1] Passow, *sub voce;* Buttmann, *Lexilogus*, p. 305, ed. Fishlake, London, 1840.
[2] Josephus, *Antiq.* ix. 2, 1. [3] Raphel. *Annot.* ii. p. 527.

are located as citizens in it. It belongs of right to "His Son." He founded it, organized it, and rules over it—prescribes its laws, regulates its usages, protects its subjects, and crowns them with blessings. It is therefore a kingdom of light, whose prismatic rays are truth, purity, and happiness. We cannot say, with Olshausen, that the kingdom is regarded in its subjective aspect, for the language is that of objective transference—change of condition, implying, however, change of character. This kingdom is one in which the Colossians were, at the period of Paul's writing to them. It is not the future heaven, ideally, as Meyer takes it, and in which they were placed only *spe et jure*, as Gesner, Keil, Koppe, and others have it. It is a present state—but one which is intimately connected with futurity. The one kingdom of God has an earthly and a celestial phasis. It resembles a city divided by a river, but still under the same municipal administration, and having one common franchise. The head of this kingdom is named—

Τοῦ υἱοῦ τῆς ἀγάπης αὐτοῦ—"The Son of His love." This is a solitary appellation. The apostle is about to descant upon the glory of the Saviour, and therefore he here introduces Him as the Son. [Eph. i. 3.] The phrase itself does not really differ from *υἱὸς ἀγαπητός*, Matt. iii. 17, xii. 18, xvii. 5; or from the similar idiom in Eph. i. 6, *υἱὸς ἠγαπημένος*. It signifies the Son who possesses His love—or who excites it in the Divine heart. The meaning is the same in either case, for He who possesses the love is the cause of it towards Himself. Sustaining such a relation to the Father, He is the object of boundless and unchanging affection. This love corresponds to the nature at once of Him who manifests it and Him who enjoys it. The love of God to one who is His own Image will be in harmony with the Divine nature of both—infinite as its object, and eternal and majestic as the bosom in which it dwells. This love of the Father to the Son prompted Him to give that Son as Saviour, and then to exalt Him to Universal Empire. John iii. 35. Two metaphysical and antagonistic deductions from this clause may be noted. The first extreme is that of Theodore of Mopsuestia,[1] who affirms that we are here taught that Christ

[1] Ὅθεν καὶ "υἱὸν ἀγάπης" αὐτὸν ἐκάλεσεν· ὡς οὐ φύσει τοῦ Πατρὸς ὄντα υἱὸν ἀλλ' ἀγάπῃ τῆς υἱοθεσίας ἀξιωθέντα τούτων.—*Catena*, ed. Cramer, p. 302.

is Son, not by nature, but by adoption. But the apostle is not speaking of the essential relation of the Son to the Father, but of the emotion which such a relationship has created. He does not say how He became the Son; he only says, that as the Son, He is the object of intense affection on the part of the Father. The other extreme is that of Augustine,[1] who argues that love indicates the essence or substance of Deity, out of which the Son sprang. But Love is an attribute, and not an essence; it belongs to character, and not to substance; it prompts, and does not produce. It is the radiance of the sun, but not the orb itself—the current of the stream, but not the water which forms it. Olshausen's modification of the same hypothesis is liable to similar objections. Nor do we find sufficient ground for the inference deduced by Huther and De Wette, that the phrase "kingdom of His Son" implies that the blessing of sonship, or adoption, is conferred on all its members, or that they become sons; for believers are, in the context, and in harmony with its imagery, regarded as subjects, and not as children. Nor is God named *our* Father in verse 12. Lastly, our rescue and subsequent settlement are ascribed to God the Father, for His sovereign grace and power alone are equal to the enterprise—and thanks again are due to Him.

(Ver. 14.) *Ἐν ᾧ ἔχομεν τὴν ἀπολύτρωσιν, τὴν ἄφεσιν τῶν ἁμαρτιῶν*—"In whom we have redemption—the forgiveness of sins." The words *διὰ τοῦ αἵματος αὐτοῦ* of the Received Text rest on no good authority, for the entire preponderance of authorities, manuscripts, versions, and quotations, is against them. The phrase is an imitation of Eph. i. 7. Lachmann reads *ἔσχομεν* in the aorist, without sufficient grounds. The apostle could not speak of the Son without a reference to His redeeming work. The work of the Father has its own aspect, and so has the work of the Son. Our direct change of condition is ascribed to the Father, as the almighty and powerful dispenser of blessing; but we are said to be united to the

[1] Quod autem dictum est filii caritatis suæ, nihil aliud intelligatur, quam filii sui dilecti quam filii postremo substantiæ suæ. Caritas quippe patris, quæ in natura ejus est ineffabiliter simplici, nihil aliud est, quam ejus ipsa natura, atque substantia. Ac per hoc filius caritatis ejus nullus alius est, quam qui de substantia est genitus.—Opera, ed. Bened. vol. viii. p. 1501, Paris, 1836.

Son, and so to be in Him as to obtain redemption in the union—for by the price He paid forgiveness of sins is secured and conferred. This verse, then, does not merely describe a blessing—the enjoyment of which is indispensable to our preparation for heaven, and our removal from the realm of darkness, but it also and especially characterizes a continuous gift enjoyed by those who are settled in the kingdom of the Son. The subjects of His kingdom are in vital union with Him—in Him they are having redemption. Their translation out of the tyranny of darkness—their place in the new kingdom, and their growing maturity for heavenly bliss, are implied in this redemption, though its special element is the forgiveness of sins. Their first condition was one of guilt as well as gloom, and forgiveness was enjoyed in their emigration from it. Nor are they perfect under the benign reign of the Son, and as a state of imperfection is so far one of sin, it is in daily need of repeated pardon. The results of Christ's work are fully enjoyed only in heaven—the process of redemption is there completed, and thus we are said still to be having it as long as we are on earth. The entire verse has been fully illustrated under Eph. i. 7. The difference of diction is unessential, *ἁμαρτιῶν* being employed in Colossians, and *παραπτωμάτων* in the Epistle to the Ephesians. One question not alluded to there may be here noticed, and that is, why forgiveness occupies in both places so prominent a place? It stands as an explanation of redemption, not as if it included the whole of it, but because—

1. It is a first and prominent blessing. So soon as faith springs up in the heart the pardon of sin is enjoyed—the results of expiation are conferred. This doctrine was placed in the front of apostolic preaching: Acts v. 31, xiii. 38, xxvi. 18; and among the Divine declarations and promises of the Old Testament, it occurs with cheering emphasis and repetition: Ex. xxxiv. 7; Isa. xl. 2, lv. 7; Jer. xxxiii. 8; Mic. vii. 18; Ps. lxxxv. 2, ciii. 3; and again and again it is announced as the result of accepted sacrifice in the Levitical law. And no wonder. So deep is man's guilt, and so tremendous is the penalty; so agonized is his conscience, and so terrible are his forebodings; so utterly helpless and hopeless is his awful state without Divine interposition, that

a free and perfect absolution from the sentence stands out not only as a blessing of indescribable grandeur and necessity, but as the first and welcome offer and characteristic of the gospel of Christ. And it is no sectional or partial blessing. It makes no distinction among sins, no discrimination among transgressors. Its circuit is complete, for every sin is included, and it is offered with unbounded freedom and invitation. No previous qualification is requisite, and no subsequent merit is anticipated. And as it is the act of the sovereign judge, who shall arraign its equity, or by what other authority can it be revoked or cancelled? Rom. viii. 33, 34.

2. Forgiveness is more closely connected with redemption than any other blessing, as it is the only blessing enjoyed immediately from Christ, and as the direct result of His expiation. It springs at once from the *λύτρον* which forms the centre and basis of the *ἀπολύτρωσις*. Other blessings obtained for Christ's sake are given through some appointed and dependent medium. Thus, peace is the effect of pardon; and holiness is the product of the Spirit and the word, as agent and instrument. But forgiveness passes through no intervention—it comes at once from the cross to the believing soul.

3. It is essentially bound up with subsequent gifts. Forgiveness precedes purity—there is change of state before there is change of heart. The Holy Ghost did not come down till Christ was glorified—till His expiatory oblation had been accepted. Being justified, believers are sanctified. The imputation of righteousness is a necessary pre-requisite to the infusion of holiness. The Spirit will not take up His abode in an unpardoned soul, and the sinner's relation to the law must be changed ere his nature be renovated. At the same time, pardon and holiness are inseparably associated, and the remission of trespasses is the precursor of peace and joy, hope and life. So that, such being its nature, origin, and results, the apostle naturally places "forgiveness of sins" in apposition with redemption in Christ Jesus.

Having now spoken of Christ and the blessings secured by union to Him, the apostle, for obvious reasons, lingers on that Name round which crystallized all the doctrines he taught —all the truths of that theology which it was the one business of his life to proclaim.

The next verse begins a lofty and comprehensive paragraph, in which the dignity and rank of Christ are described in linked clauses of marvellous terseness and harmony. The apostle introduces the name of the Son on purpose, and then details in sweeping completeness the glory of His person and work. There is no doubt that the verses were composed in reference to modes of error prevalent at Colosse, and the forms of expression have their special origin, shape, and edge in this polemical reference. While the writer states absolute truth in rich and glowing accumulation of sentences, still, the thought and diction are so moulded as to bear against false dogmas which were in circulation. It is strange that in any system of theology the person of Christ should be depreciated, and His mediatorial work vailed and slighted. The spectacle, however, is not an uncommon one. Yet the apostles can scarcely find language of sufficient energy and lustre to tell in it the honour and majesty of the Redeemer. The sentences in which Paul describes the rank and prerogative of Christ are like a bursting torrent, dashing away every barrier in its impetuous race. How he exults in the precious theme, and how his soul swells into impassioned panegyric!

We do not know in what precise way the dignity of Jesus was vilified by the Colossian errorists. It would seem, indeed, that the germs of Gnosticism and Ebionitism were to be found in Colosse—denial of Christ's actual humanity, and of His supreme divinity. The apostle, therefore, holds Him out as the one Supreme Creator, not only of the world, but of the universe, and declares that reconciliation is secured in the body of His flesh through death. Confused notions of the spirit-world appear also to have prevailed. Jesus was discrowned. The Lord of the angels was placed among the angels, as if he had been a selected delegate out of many illustrious compeers. That He was superhuman may not have been denied—but that He was truly human was more than questioned. That there had been a being of superior order upon earth was allowed, but whether as a veritable man he had blood to shed, and a soul and body to be severed in death and re-united in resurrection, appears to have been doubted or denied. Ascetic austerities, and mystical speculations, took the place of reliance on an objective atonement.[1] The gospel was shorn of its simplicity, and mutilated in its adaptations, in order to be fitted in to the dogmas and announced in the specious nomenclature of a vain theosophy. That Jesus, as a celestial being, stood in a certain relation to God, and bore some similitude to Him, might be granted—but the likeness was thought to be faint and distant. The apostle affirms of Him in choice and expressive terms, on the other hand, "Who is the image of the invisible God"—

(Ver. 15.) *Ὅς ἐστιν εἰκὼν τοῦ Θεοῦ τοῦ ἀοράτου.* 2 Cor. iv. 4. The clause dazzles by its brightness, and awes by its mystery. We feel the warning—"Draw not nigh hither, for the place is holy ground." One trembles to subject such a declaration to the scrutiny of human reason, and feels as if he were rudely profaning it by the appliances of earthly erudition. The invisible God—how dark and dreadful the impenetrable vail! Christ His image—how perfect in its resemblance, and overpowering in its brilliance! We must worship whilst we construe; and our exegesis must be penetrated by a profound devotion.

The relative *ὅς* carries us back at once to *υἱός*, in verse 13, and in its connection with the intermediate verse it may bear a causal signification, "inasmuch as He is," etc. Bernhardy, p. 292. The noun *εἰκών* does not require the article, being clearly defined by the following genitive. Winer, § 19, 2, (*b*).[2] That this term was a current one in the Jewish theosophy, is plain from many citations.[3] Hesychius defines *εἰκών* by *χαρακτήρ* and *τύπος*. Chrysostom speaks of it as *τὸ κατὰ πᾶν ἴσον καὶ ὅμοιον*, "a faithful likeness in every thing;" and Theophylact describes it as *ἀπαραλλάκτος*, "without change."

The epithet *ἀόρατος*, as applied to God, refers not, perhaps, to the fact that He is and has been unseen, but to His invisibility, or to the fact that He cannot and will not be seen. John i. 18; Rom. i. 20; 1 Tim. i. 17. Perhaps the Great

[1] See Introduction. [2] Moulton, p. 155, note 6.

[3] Philo, *De Opificio*, λόγον εἰκόνα θεοῦ, p. 12, Opera i. ed. Pfeiffer, λόγος δέ ἐστιν εἰκὼν θεοῦ, *De Monarch.* Similar expressions are found among the Kabbalists, and among oriental theosophists, and seem to embody in various forms of disguise and error a truth which appears to have descended with other fragments of an early patriarchal time. Kleuker, *Zendavesta*, i. p. 4. Usteri, *Paulin. Lehrb.* p. 308.

God remains concealed for ever in the unfathomable depths of His own essence which, to every created vision, is so dazzling as to be "dark with excess of light." There needs, therefore, a medium of representation, which must be His exact similitude. But where shall this be found? Can any creature bear upon him the full impress of Divinity, and shine out in God's stead to the universe without contraction of person or diminution of splendour? Could the Infinite dwarf itself into the finite, or the Eternal shrink into a limited cycle? May we not, therefore, anticipate a medium in harmony with the original? The lunar reflection is but a feeble resemblance of the solar glory. So that the image of God must be Divine as well as visible—must be *ὁμοούσιος*—of the same essence with the original. A visible God can alone be the image of God, possessing all the elements and attributes of His nature. The Divine can be fully pictured only in the Divine. The universe mirrors the glory of God, but does not circumscribe it. His "invisible things" assume a palpable form and aspect in the objects and laws of creation. Man is made in the image of God—in his headship over the earth around him, he is "the image and glory of God"—but he was only a faint and fractional miniature, even in his first and best estate, and now it is sadly dimmed and effaced. But Christ is the image of God—not *σκία*—a shadowy or evanescent sketch which cannot be caught or copied, but *εἰκών*, a real and perfect likeness—no feature absent, none misplaced, and none impaired in fulness or dimmed in lustre. The very counterpart of God He is.

Now, this Image of God is not Christ in His Divine nature, or as the eternal Logos, as Olshausen, Huther, Bähr, Usteri, and Adam Clarke, and many of the Fathers, suppose, for the apostle is speaking of the Son, and of that Son as the author of redemption and forgiveness of sin. It is therefore Jesus in His mediatorial person that the apostle characterizes as being the image of God. For it is a strange notion of Chrysostom, and some of his followers, such as Clarius, that as invisibility is a property of God, it must also be a property of His image, if that image be an undeviating similitude.[1] Our Lord Himself said, even when He dwelt upon earth robed in

[1] Bengel says—Invisbilis *imago secundum naturam divinam;* visibilis *secundum humanam.*

no mantle of light, and with no nimbus surrounding His brow, "He who hath seen me hath seen the Father." Visibility is implied in the very notion of an image. The spirit of the statement is, that our only vision or knowledge of the Father is in His Son. "No man knoweth the Father but the Son, and he to whom the Son shall reveal Him." The Socinian hypothesis, advocated even by Grotius and Heinrichs, that only because He revealed so fully the will of God is He called the image of God, is far short of the full meaning,[1] though as the "image" shines upon us we look and learn. To Him, as "Angel of the Presence," we are indebted for those glimpses of the "eternal power and Godhead" which creation discloses—those glimpses of sovereignty throned upon boundless power, fathomless wisdom, and unwearying goodness, which are presented by the universe above us and around us. The elements of the Divine nature and character which are mirrored out to us in providence are derived from the same source. Christ, as Creator and Preserver, is the palpable image of God. In this aspect, it is not visibility of person that can be maintained, but the embodiment of attribute in visible result, as in Rom. i. 20, where it is said, "the invisible things" of the Creator are "clearly seen."

But especially in Himself and as Redeemer is He the representative of God. His prophetic epithet was "Immanuel, God with us." In His incarnate state He brought God so near us as to place Him under the cognizance of our very senses—men saw, and heard, and handled Him—a speaking, acting, weeping, and suffering God; He was, as Basil terms it, *εἰκὼν ζῶσα*,[2] a living image. He held out an image of God in the love He displayed, which was too tender and fervent, too noble and self-denying, to have had its home in any created bosom—in the power He put forth, which was too vast to be lodged in other than a Divine arm, and also in His wisdom and holiness, and in those blessed results which sprang from His presence. When he moved on the surface of the billows, did not the disciples see a realization of the unapproachable prerogative of Him "who treadeth upon the

[1] Dr. Owen says—"Were He not the *essential* image of the Father in His own Divine person, He could not be the *representative* image of God unto us as He is incarnate."—*Christologia*, p. 78, *Works*, vol. i. Edin. 1850.

[2] *Contra Eunom.* p. 28.

waves of the sea"? When the crested waves were hushed into quiet, as He looked out upon the storm and spoke to it, His fellow-voyagers felt that they had heard the voice of Divinity. When the dead were evoked by His touch and word from their slumbers, the spectators beheld the energy and prerogative of Him who says of Himself, "I kill, and I make alive; I wound, and I heal." When the hungry were satisfied with an immediate banquet in the desert, the abundance proved the presence of the Lord of the Seasons, who, in the process of vegetation, multiplies the seed cast into the furrow "in some thirty, in some sixty, and in some an hundred fold." In those daily miracles of healing was there not manifest the soft and effective hand of Him who is "abundant in goodness"? and in those words of wondrous penetration which touched the heart of the auditor was there not an irresistible demonstration of the Divine omniscience? Still, too, at the right hand of the Majesty on high, is He the visible administrator and object of worship. Thus, "the Son of His love" is a visible image of the invisible Father, not the "copy of an image"[1]—distinct from Him, and yet so like Him, making God in all His glorious fulness apparent to us—showing us in Himself and His works the bright contour and likeness of the invisible Jehovah. This glory is not merely official, but it is also essential, not won, but possessed from eternity. O the grandeur of that redemption of which He is the author, and the magnificence of that kingdom of which He is head! Not only is He the image of God—but the apostle adds—

Πρωτότοκος πάσης κτίσεως—"The first-born of every creature." [*πάσης*, Eph. ii. 21.] The meaning of this remarkable phrase is not easily discovered to our entire satisfaction. Only, it is clear, from the previous clause, and from the succeeding verse, that the apostle cannot mean to class Jesus Himself among created things. It is an awkward expedient on the part of Isidore,[2] Erasmus, Fleming,[3] and Michaelis, to propose to change the accentuation *πρωτο-*

[1] Παράδειγμα εἰκόνος, Epiphanius, *Haeres.*, lxv. See also Dorner, *Lehre von der Person Christi*, etc., Berlin, 1852.

[2] Ep. iii. 31—Οὐ πρῶτον τῆς κτίσεως . . . ἀλλὰ πρῶτον τετοκέναι . . . ἵνα ἡ τρίτης συλλαβῆς ὀξυμένης, ὡς πρωτοκτίστης.

[3] *Christology*, i. p. 216.

τόκος, and by making it a paroxyton, to give it the sense of first-producer. But the term, with such a meaning, has only a feminine application,[1] and it cannot bear such a sense in the eighteenth verse.

1. Many of the Fathers, and not a few of the moderns, understand the epithet as denotive of the generation of the Logos, or Divine Son. Thus, in Œcumenius occurs the phrase *γεννηθεὶς συναΐδιος*, "begotten co-eternally," and Chrysostom says of Him—*θεὸς γὰρ καὶ θεοῦ υἱός*. Athanasius describes Him—*ἄτρεπτος ἐξ ἀτρέπτου*, "the unchangeable from the unchangeable," a statement preceded by another to this effect—*ὁ δὲ υἱὸς νόμος ἐκ τοῦ πατρὸς ἀΐδιος ἐγενήθη*.[2] Theophylact puts the question—"first-born of every creature, how?" and *διὰ γεννήσεως* is his reply. Tertullian, too, uses similar phraseology—*primogenitus ut ante omnia genitus;* and again, *primogenitus conditionis, i.e. conditorum a Deo.*[3] Ambrose writes—*primogenitus, quia nemo ante ipsum, unigenitus quia nemo post ipsum.*[4] We cannot readily accept the interpretation, though defended by Calovius, Aretius, Bähr, Böhmer, von Gerlach, and Bloomfield, etc. As Bengel admits, it makes the genitive *πάσης κτίσεως* depend on *πρῶτος* in composition. The syntax is not impossible, as with the simple adjective, John i. 15, 30, but the following similar phrase—*πρωτότοκος ἐκ τῶν νεκρῶν*, shows that such an exegesis cannot here be adopted, for it is plain that it cannot mean "begotten before all the dead." The comparison there is not one of time even, as Meyer erroneously takes it—but one of rank. The sense assigned by this class of critics is, that Christ was the begotten of the Father, and became His Son prior to the work of creation. But we doubt if this be the form of truth intended by the apostle, for we should have expected the noun *υἱός*, or some other term denoting relationship, to have occurred in the clause. Christ is called *πρωτότοκος* in reference to His mother, but never in connection with His Divine Father, in any place where any semblance

[1] Homer, *Iliad*, xvii. 5. So Thomas Magister—*Πρωτότοκος ὁ πρώτως τεχθείς, πρωτοτόκος δὲ μήτηρ, ἡ πρώτως τίξασα.*

[2] *Expositio fidei*, i. p. 242. Vide Suicer's *Thesaurus, sub voce πρωτότοκος.*

[3] *Adversus Prax.* c. 7; *Adversus Marc.* v. 19, pp. 660, 330, vol. ii. Opera, ed. Oehler, Lipsiae, 1854.

[4] *De Fide*, xiv. 89, Opera, vol. ii. p. 550, ed. Migne, Paris, 1845.

of the doctrine of eternal filiation is referred to, and in such a word derived from *τίκτω*, the reference is to maternal, not to paternal origin.

2. The antagonist exegesis is that of the Arians and Socinians, which presumes that Christ is, in this phrase, classed as a portion of creation. Even Athanasius, in his second discourse against the Arians, admits that Christ has got the name *διὰ τὴν πολλῶν ἀδελφοποίησιν*. A common argument in favour of this exegesis is, that where this epithet is used, it is implied that he who bears it is not only compared with others, but is one of them. Thus, in the phrase "first-born among many brethren," the inference is, that the first-born is one of the family, though his rank be pre-eminent; and in the phrase "first-born from the dead," Jesus is plainly regarded as having been one of the dead Himself, though He now be exalted above them. So that the deduction is, if He is called the "first-born of every creature," then He is, in the comparison, and from a necessary *ὁμογένεια*, regarded as one of the creatures. Why then, it is confidently asked, shrink from such a conclusion?

We might give the reply of Basil to Eunomius,[1] who had adopted such an exegesis—"if He be called the first-born of the dead, because He is the cause of their resurrection, then, by parity of argument, he is the First-born of the whole creation, because He is the cause of its existence." Theodoret puts the question—if He is only-begotten, how can He be first-begotten: and if first-begotten, how can He be only-begotten? And he guards against the Arian inference by adding—*πρωτότοκος οὐχ ὡς ἀδελφὴν ἔχων τὴν κτίσιν*, that is, He cannot have a brotherly relation to the creation, and be at the same time its maker. The ancient critics also observe that the epithet employed by the apostle is not *πρωτόκτιστος*, first-created. Besides, in the cases in which the term *πρωτότοκος* marks him who bears it, as one of a class referred to, such a class is usually expressed in the plural number, as in the 10th verse, and Rom. viii. 29, Rev. i. 5, but the apostle does not here say *τῶν κτισμάτων*.

[1] *Εἰ δὲ πρωτότοκος νεκρῶν εἴρηται, διὰ τὸ αἴτιος εἶναι τῆς ἐκ νεκρῶν ἀναστάσεως, οὕτω καὶ πρωτότοκος κτίσεως, διὰ τὸ αἴτιος εἶναι τοῦ ἐξ οὐκ ὄντων εἰς τὸ εἶναι παραγαγεῖν τὴν κτίσιν.*—Lib. iv. Opera ii. p. 204.

Yet, even assuming for a moment the Socinian hypothesis, we would not be nonplussed. We reckon it very wrong on the part of Usteri[1] to translate the Pauline term by *Erstgeschaffene*, "first-created," and it is easy to see what must be the theological conclusions drawn from such a rendering. Anselm explains that the words apply to Jesus only as man, for as God He is *unigenitus non primogenitus*. Now, we have shown that the preceding clause, "image of the invisible God," implies Christ's divinity, and we might say with Anselm that this refers to His humanity. That body was *created* by the Holy Ghost—it was a creature, and still is so, as we believe. Though on the throne, it is not deified—is not so covered nor interpenetrated with divinity as to cease to be a humanity. Nay, the last and loftiest prerogative is to be exercised by the "MAN whom He hath ordained," so that even with this construction we are under no necessity to adopt the Arian or Socinian hypothesis. If in the former clause there is express proof of Christ's divinity, in the latter there is no less assertion of His real humanity, a humanity which stands out in special pre-eminence over the entire creation, as its Lord and proprietor.

3. Our own view is a modified form of that which takes πρωτότοκος in its figurative meaning of chief or Lord—"begotten before all creation." This view is held by Melancthon, Cameron, Piscator, Hammond, Röell, Suicer, Cocceius, Storr, Flatt, De Wette, Pye Smith, Robinson, and Whitby. Theodore of Mopsuestia[2] held the same opinion—οὐκ ἐπὶ χρόνου λέγεται μόνον· ἀλλὰ γὰρ καὶ ἐπὶ προτιμήσεως—but he understood by κτίσις the new creation. The famous Photius, of the ninth century, in the 192nd question of his *Amphilochia*, has given a similar view, referring, however, the phrase to His human nature, and His resurrection from the dead.[3] Some critics conjoin both the first and second views. We apprehend that the apostle selects the unusual word for a special reason. It seems to have been a prime term in the nomenclature of the Colossian errorists, and the apostle takes the epithet and gives it to Him to whom alone it rightfully belongs. Traces of the same idiom are found in the Jewish

[1] *Lehrb.* p. 315. Holzhausen, in his reply to Schleiermacher in the *Tübing. Zeitschrift*, 1833, uses similar unguarded language.

[2] *Catena*, ed. Cramer, p. 306.

[3] Wolf, *Curae*, vol. v. 800.

Kabbala—in which Jehovah Himself is called the "first-born of the world," that is, in all probability, the Divine representative of essential and immanent perfection to the world.[1] Thus the first heavenly man was called Adam Kadmon—the first-begotten of God—He who is Messiah and the Metatron of the burning bush. Not that Paul merely borrowed his language, but the terms which the errorists were perverting he refers to Jesus in their full truth and legitimate application. In a similar theological dialect, Philo names the λόγος by the epithet πρωτόγονος.[2] The diction of the Old Testament in reference to the Hebrew בְּכוֹר is in harmony, and is based upon the familiar rights and prerogatives of human primogeniture. The Hebrew adjective is applied to what is primary, prominent, and the most illustrious of its classis, Job xviii. 13; "first-born of death"—alarming and fatal malady, Isa. xiv. 30; "first-born of the poor"—a pauper of paupers. Still more, we find the term in the Messianic oracle of the 89th Psalm—"I will make him my first-born"—will invest him with royal dignity, and clothe him with pre-eminent splendour, so as that he shall tower in majesty above all his kingly compeers. Israel elevated above the other nations, brought into a covenant relation, and reflecting so much of the Divine glory, is Jehovah's first-born, Ex. iv. 22, Jer. xxxi. 9. The church of Christ, blessed and beloved, and placed nearer the throne than angels, is the "church of the first-born," Heb. xii. 23. And when believers are regarded as sons—as a vast and happy brotherhood—He who loved them, and died for them, who has won for Himself special renown in their adoption, and has imprinted His image on all the children, stands out as chief in the family, and is "the first-born among many brethren," Rom. viii. 29. Again, in Heb i. 6, Jesus receives the same appellation, inasmuch as the spirits of the heavenly world are solemnly summoned to do Him homage as His Father's representative.[3] Moreover, when He is styled, as in the 18th verse,

[1] Schoettgen, *Horae Heb.* i. 922.

[2] *De Confusione Ling.* p. 381, vol. ii. Opera, ed. Pfeiffer.

[3] Bleek, *in loc.* *Der Brief an die Hebräer erläutert*, Berlin, 1836. It may be added that under the Roman law, *haeres* and *dominus* were interchangeable terms, and to compare great things with small, in one of the Hebrides it was the custom for the head of the clan to abdicate when his son came of age.—Boswell's *Tour*, p. 261.

and in Rev. i. 5, "the first-born of the dead," the reference is not to mere time or priority, but to prerogative, for He is not simply the first who rose, "no more to return to corruption," but His immortal primogeniture secures the resurrection of His people, and is at once the pledge and the pattern of it. The genitive then may be taken as that of reference. Bernhardy, p. 139. The meaning therefore is, "first-born in reference to the whole creation." The phrase so understood is only another aspect of the former clause. The first-born was his father's representative, and acted in his father's name. Christ stands out as the First-born, all transactions are with Him, and they are equivalent to transactions with the Sovereign Father. The Father is invisible, but the universe is not left without a palpable God. Its existence and arrangements are His, and the supervision of it belongs to Him. He is the God who busies Himself in its affairs, and with whom it has to do. He is its First-born, its chief and governor. As the first-born of the house is he to whom its management is entrusted, so the First-born of the whole creation is He who is its governor and Lord, and whose prerogative it is to exhibit to the universe the image and attributes of the unseen Jehovah. He is manifested Deity, appearing, speaking, working, ruling, as in patriarchal times when He descended in a temporary humanity, and held familiar discourse with the world's "grey fathers," and as under the Mosaic economy, of whose theocracy He was the head, of whose temple He was the God, and of whose oracles He was the inspirer. Now He is exalted to unbounded sovereignty, as "Lord of all," rolling onwards the mighty and mysterious wheels of a universal providence, without halting or confusion; seated as His Father's deputy on a throne of unbounded dominion, which to this world is its tribunal of judgment—wearing the name at which every knee bows, "of things in heaven, and things in earth, and things under the earth"—the acting President of the universe, and therefore "the First-born of every creature." His Father's love to Him has given Him this pre-eminence, this "double portion,"[1] "Thou art my Son, this day have I begotten Thee." It is plainly implied at the same time that He existed before all creatures, for He has never stood in any other or secondary relation

[1] Deut. xxi. 17.

to the universe — to the many mansions of His Father's house.

(Ver. 16.) Ὅτι ἐν αὐτῷ ἐκτίσθη τὰ πάντα, τὰ ἐν τοῖς οὐρανοῖς καὶ τὰ ἐπὶ τῆς γῆς. The conjunction ὅτι assigns the reason of the preceding statement. He is first-born of the whole creation, for by Him "all things" were created—and He is the image of God, for as Creator He shines out in the "brightness of His Father's glory," so that we apprehend it to be a narrow and confined view to restrict the reference of ὅτι to the last clause of the previous verse. The phrase τὰ πάντα means "the all"—the universe, the whole that exists. Winer, § 18, 8. The aorist characterizes creation as a past and perfect work. Creation is here in the fullest and most unqualified sense ascribed to Christ, and the doctrine is in perfect harmony with the theology of the beloved disciple, John i. 3. The work of the six days displayed vast creative energy, but it was to a great extent the inbringing of furniture and population to a planet already made and in diurnal revolution, for it comprehended the formation of a balanced atmosphere, the enclosure of the ocean within proper limits, the clothing of the soil with verdure, shrubs, trees, and cereal grasses—the exhibition of sun, moon, and stars, as lights in the firmament—the introduction of bird, beast, reptile, and fish, into their appropriate haunts and elements—and the organization and endowment of man, with Eden for his heritage, and the world for his home. But this demiurgical process implied the previous exercise of Divine omnipotence, for "in the beginning God created the heaven and the earth." It is not, therefore, the wise and tasteful arrangement of pre-existent materials or the reduction of chaos to order, beauty, and life, which is here ascribed to Jesus, but the summoning of universal nature into original existence. What had no being before was brought into being by Him. The universe was not till He commanded it to be. "He spake and it was done." Every form of matter and life owes its origin to the Son of God, no matter in what sphere it may be found, or with what qualities it may be invested. "In heaven or on earth." Christ's creative work was no local or limited operation; it was not bounded by this little orb; its sweep surrounds the universe which is named in Jewish diction and according to a natural division—"heaven and earth." Every form and kind of matter, simple or complex—the atom and the star, the sun and the clod—every grade of life from the worm to the angel—every order of intellect and being around and above us, the splendours of heaven and the nearer phenomena of earth, are the product of the First-born.[1]

Τὰ ὁρατὰ καὶ τὰ ἀόρατα—"The visible and the invisible." This distinction seems to have been common in the Eastern philosophy:[2] the latter epithet being referred to the abode of angels and blessed spirits. The meaning is greatly lowered by some of the Greek Fathers, who thought the term was applicable to the souls of men, and by not a few of the moderns, who include under it the souls of the dead. The meaning is, what exists within the reach of vision, and what exists beyond it. The object of which the eye can take cognizance, and the glory which "eye hath not seen," are equally the "handiwork" of Jesus. The assertion is true, not only in reference to the limited conceptions of the universe current in the apostle's days, but true in the widest sense. The visible portion of the creation consisting of some myriads of stars, is but a mere section or stratum of the great fabric. In proportion as power is given to the telescopic glass, are new bodies brought into view. Nothing like a limit to creation can be descried. The farther we penetrate into space, the luminaries are neither dimmer nor scarcer, but worlds of singular beauty and variety burst upon us, and the distant star-dust is found to consist of orbs so dense and crowded as to appear one blended mass of sparkling radiance. Rays of light from the remotest nebulæ must have been two millions of years on their inconceivably swift journey to our world. The nearest fixed star is twenty-one billions of miles from us, so that between it and us there is room in one straight line for 12,000 solar systems, each as large as our own. From the seraph that burns nearest the throne, through the innumerable suns and planets which are so thickly strewn in the firmament, and outwards to the unseen orbs which sentinel the verge of space—all is the result of Christ's omnipotence and love.

It is probable, however, that the apostle thought of heaven proper when he spoke of things invisible, for he adds, as if in

[1] See also on p. 54. [2] Gesenius, *de Theolog. Samaritana*, p. 20.

special reference to its population—"whether they be thrones, or dominions, or principalities, or powers"—

Εἴτε θρόνοι εἴτε κυριότητες εἴτε ἀρχαὶ εἴτε ἐξουσίαι. These epithets refer to celestial dignities. In Eph. i. 21, he says —*ὑπεράνω πάσης ἀρχῆς καὶ ἐξουσίας καὶ δυνάμεως καὶ κυριότητος.* The arrangement is different—the two last terms of the one are the two first in the other, and *κυριότης*, which is second here, is last in Ephesians. *Θρόνοι* occurs here, but *δυνάμεως* is excluded. The "thrones" appear to be the highest, —chairs of state in humble and distant imitation of the Divine imperial throne. We need not repeat our remarks made on this subject under Eph. i. 21. If we may credit Irenæus,[1] the Gnostics held that another power than Divine created the celestial hierarchy. Simon Magus said—*Ennoian generare angelos et potestates, a quibus et mundum hunc factum.* The object of the apostle is to show that Jesus is the creator, not simply of lower modes of being, but of the higher Essences of the Universe. Yes, those Beings, so illustrious as to be seated on "thrones;" so noble as to be styled "dominions;" so elevated as to be greeted with the title of "principalities;" and so mighty as to merit the appellation of "powers:" these, so like God as to be called "gods" themselves,[2] bow to the Son of God as the one author of their existence, position, and prerogative. As no atom is too minute, so no creature is too gigantic for His plastic hand. What a reproof to that "worshipping of angels" afterwards reprobated by the apostle —beings who are only creatures, and who themselves are summoned to do suit and service to the First-born. The sentence is at this point concluded, but the apostle reiterates—

Τὰ πάντα δι' αὐτοῦ καὶ εἰς αὐτὸν ἔκτισται—"All things by Him and for Him were created." Already the apostle had said—*ἐν αὐτῷ ἐκτίσθη τὰ πάντα.* The change of preposition and tense can scarcely be regarded as accidental, or as introduced for the mere sake of varied diction. Chrysostom, indeed, and many after him, regard *ἐν* and *διά* as synonymous. Indeed, this Father says, *τὸ ἐν αὐτῷ, δι' αὐτοῦ ἐστι*; and Usteri repeats the blunder; while De Wette finds compacted into *ἐν* the double sense of *δι' αὐτοῦ* and *εἰς αὐτόν.* The old school

[1] *Cont. Haer.* i. 23, § 2; vol. i. 238, ed. Stieren.
[2] Ps. xcvii. 7.

of Jewish interpretation, represented by Philo and some of the Kabbalists, held a theory which was adopted by several of the Fathers, as Origen, Athanasius, and Hilary; by the mediæval divines; and virtually by Neander, Bähr, Böhmer, Kleuker, Olshausen, and Kähler. Their notion is, that in the Logos, and by Him, was the world created—the idea was in Him, and its working out was by Him. He is both *causa exemplaris* and *causa effectiva.* "In Him," says Olshausen, "are all things created, *i.e.* the Son of God is the intelligible world, the *κόσμος νοητός*, *i.e.* things themselves according to the idea of them, He carries their essentiality in Himself; in the creation they come forth from Him to an independent existence, in the completion of all things they return to Him." We cannot, with Cocceius and others, take ἐν as bringing out the idea that the universe was created by the Father, in the Son. No mention is made of the Father in the context. We rather hold, with Meyer, "that the act of creation rests in Christ originally, and its completion is grounded in Him." He is not simply instrumental cause, but He is also primary cause. The impulse to create came upon Him from no co-ordinate power of which He was either the conscious or the passive organ. All things were created in Him—the source of motive, desire, and energy was in Him. He was not, as a builder, working out the plans of an architect—but the design is His own conception, and the execution is His own unaided enterprise. He did not need to go beyond Himself, either to find space on which to lay the foundation of the fabric, or to receive assistance in its erection. On the other hand, the extrinsic aspect is represented by διά—the universe is the result of the exercise of His omnipotence, or as the Syriac renders, "by His hand." It still stands out as having been brought into existence by Him. The aorist carries us back to the act of creation, which had all its elements in Him, and the perfect tense exhibits the universe as still remaining the monument and proof of His creative might. The first clause depicts creation in its origin, and the second refers to it as an existing effect. In the former, it is an act embodying plan and power, which are alike "in Him"—in the latter, it is a phenomenon caused and still continued "by Him." Winer, § 50, 6.

Καὶ εἰς αὐτόν. Not *in ipso*, as the Vulgate renders, but "and for Him." This clause marks out His final purpose in creation. It means not "for Him" as the middle point of creation, as Bähr and Huther imagine; nor simply "for His plan," as Baumgarten-Crusius holds; nor merely "for His glory," as Böhmer explains it; nor with a main view to His Incarnation, as Melancthon regards it; nor yet with an express reference to His Universal Headship, as Grotius and Storr have maintained. The phrase "for Him" seems to mean for Him in every aspect of His Being, and every purpose of His Heart. He is, as Clement of Alexandria says, *τέλος* as well as *ἀρχή*. Not only is the universe His sole and unhelped work, but it is a work done by Himself, and especially for Himself,—for every end contemplated in His infinite wisdom and love. A man of taste and skill may construct a magnificent palace, but it is for His sovereign as a royal habitation. On the contrary, Christ is uncontrolled, meeting with no interference, for His is no subordinate agency defined and guided by a superior power for which it labours and to which it is responsible. No licence of this nature could be permitted to any creature, for it would be ruinous to the universe and fatal to himself. Such a path of uncurbed operation would astonish all heaven, and soon surprise all hell. He only "of whom, to whom, and for whom are all things," can have this freedom of action in Himself and for Himself.

Had the Divine Being remained alone, His glory would have been unseen and His praises unsung. But He longed to impart of His own happiness to creatures fitted to possess it—to fill so many vessels out of that "fountain of life" which wells out from His bosom. Therefore Christ fitted up these "all things" "for Himself," in order that He might exhibit His glory while He diffused happiness through creatures of innumerable worlds, and enabled them to behold His mirrored brightness and reflect it; that He might occupy a throne of supreme and unapproachable sovereignty; and show to the universe His indescribable grace, which, in stooping to save one of its worlds, has thrown a new lustre over the Divine holiness, and proved the unshaken harmony and stability of the Divine administration. For this Creator is He "in whom we have redemption," and this noblest of His works was in certain prospect when for Himself all things were created—a platform of no stinted proportions prepared for Him and by Him. Creation in itself presents an imperfect aspect of God, opens up a glimpse of only one side of His nature—His brightest and holiest phase lying under an eclipse; but redemption exhibits Him in His fulness of essence and symmetry of character. And did not Christ contemplate such a manifestation when He brought into existence so vast an empire to enjoy and adore the august and ennobling spectacle? Thus His all-sided relation to the universe is depicted—it is "in Him," "by Him," and "for Him." Let no one say, He is an inferior agent—the universe was created "in Him;" let no one surmise, He is but a latent source—it is "by Him;" let no one look on Him as another's deputy—it is "for Him." In every sense He is the sovereign creator—His is the conception, and Himself the agent and end.

(Ver. 17.) *Καὶ αὐτός ἐστιν πρὸ πάντων*—"And He is before all." The pronoun in the nominative has an emphatic sense—"and this one"—the creator of all, is before all. Two meanings have been assigned to the preposition *πρό*.

1. Many take it in the sense of order, or eminence—such as Noesselt, Heinrichs, Baumgarten-Crusius, Schleiermacher, and, of necessity, the Socinian expositors. There is no need of this secondary meaning, and the phrase as it occurs in Jas. v. 12, 1 Pet. iv. 8, does not warrant such an exegesis, for it occurs in those places as a kind of adverbial emphasis.

2. It naturally means "before all" in point of time—as Böhmer, Meyer, De Wette, and Huther take it. John i. 30. When connected with persons, *πρό* bears such a primary meaning always in the New Testament, John v. 7; Rom. xvi. 7; Gal. i. 17. Priority of existence belongs to the great First Cause. He who made all necessarily existed before all. Prior to His creative work, He had filled the unmeasured periods of an unbeginning eternity. Matter is not eternal—is not the dark and necessary circumference of His bright Essence. He pre-existed it, and called it into being. Everything is posterior to Him, and nothing coeval with Him. And the present tense is employed—"He is," not "He was." John viii. 58. His is unchanging being. At every point of His existence it may be said of Him, He is. He is all that

He was, and all that He will be—and comprises in Him the birth and end of time. Were His existence measured by human epochs, you might say of Him at some bygone period, "He was"—but the apostle, glancing at His immutability of nature, simply says, "He is." Œcumenius rightly remarks, that the apostle writes not *ἐγένετο πρὸ πάντων, ἀλλ' ἔστι πρὸ πάντων.*

Καὶ τὰ πάντα ἐν αὐτῷ συνέστηκε—"And all things in Him are upheld." Not only is He the creator, but He is also preserver. Heb. i. 3. The verb sometimes signifies to arrange, to constitute, to create, but it also denotes to maintain in existence what has been created. 2 Pet. iii. 5.[1] Such is the view of the Fathers; as Œcumenius paraphrases—*δι' αὐτοῦ τὴν γένεσιν καὶ τὴν διαμονὴν ἔχει. Προμηθεῖται ὧν ἐποίησε.* The perfect tense seems to point us to this signification. What has been created has still been preserved. The two meanings of the verb meet and merge in its perfect tense. The *τὰ πάντα,* in this verse, are those of the preceding clauses, and not simply the church, as some in timidity and error restrict it. All things were brought together, and are still held together in Him. The energy which created is alone competent to sustain, every successive moment of providence being, as it were, a successive act of creation. In Him this sustentation of all things reposes. He is the condition of their primary and prolonged being. What a vast view of Christ's dignity! His arm upholds the universe, and if it were withdrawn, all things would fade into their original non-existence. His great empire depends upon Him in all its provinces—life, mind, sensation and matter; atoms beneath us to which geology has not descended, and stars beyond us to which astronomy has never penetrated. He feeds the sun with fuel, and vails the moon in beauty. He guides the planets on their journey, and keeps them from collision and disorder. Those secret forms of existence which the unaided eye cannot detect are receiving from Him "their meat in due season." The rain

[1] Thus we find—*Herodotus*, vii. 225, στράτευμα συνεστηκός, a standing army; τὰ συνεστηκότα, things as at present. Again, Aristotle, *de Mund.* 6, ἐκ τοῦ θεοῦ τὰ πάντα καὶ διὰ θεοῦ ἡμῖν συνέστηκε. So Plato, *Pol.* 7, etc.; *Timaeus*, p. 29. In Philo, too, the same meaning is often found, as may be seen in the collected examples of Elsner, Krebs, Loesner, and Kypke.

out of His reservoirs nourishes "grass for the cattle, and herb for the service of man." The vitiated atmosphere discharged from animal lungs becomes in His laboratory the source of special nutrition to vegetable life, and the foul breathings of forges and manufactories supply with strength and colour the tall and gorgeous plants of the torrid zone. Thus that universal balance is preserved, the derangement of which would throw around the globe the pall of death. Order is never violated, the tree yields fruit "after his kind," and according to the original edict. Evening and morning alternate in sure and swift succession. The mighty and minute are alike to Him whose supervision embraces the extinction of a world and the fall of a sparrow. The "creeping things innumerable in the great and wide sea" look up to Him, and He opens His hand and "they are filled with good;" as well the leviathan who is "made to play therein," as the insect that builds its coral cell—first its dwelling and then its tomb. Every pulsation of our heart depends on His sovereign beneficence who feeds us and clothes us. The intellect of the cherub reflects His light, and the fire of the seraph is but the glow of His love. All things which He has evoked into being have their continued subsistence in Him.

Are we not entranced with the dignity of our Redeemer, and are we not amazed at His condescension and love? That the creator and upholder of the universe should come down to such a world as this, and clothe Himself in the inferior nature of its race, and in that nature die to forgive and save it, is the most amazing of revelations. Dare we lift our hearts to contemplate and credit it? And yet it is truth, most glorious truth; truth sealed with the blood of Calvary. What sublimity is shed around the gospel! The God of the first chapter of Genesis is the babe of the first chapter of Matthew. He whom Isaiah depicts as "the Lord God, the creator of the ends of the earth," "who hath measured the waters in the hollow of His hand, and meted out heaven with the span," is the Christ crucified of evangelical story and apostolic preaching. He who, in the pages of Jeremiah, is "the true God, the living God, and an everlasting King," is in the pages of John the Word made flesh—the weeping Jesus—the master girded with a towel and washing His disciples' feet—the sufferer crowned with thorns and nailed in nakedness to the cross. He who is depicted in Ezekiel as seated on the sapphire throne, with the rainbow for its canopy, and the cherubim for its bearers and guardians, is none other than He whose garments were divided by His executioners, yea, whose corpse was pierced by the barbarous arm of a Roman soldier, and probed to the very heart to prove the reality of His death. He who warned the ancient people that they "saw no manner of similitude in the day when He spake to them in Horeb," says at length to a group standing around Him, "Behold my hands and my feet, that it is I myself, handle me and see." He by whom all things were made had not "where to lay His head." What faith in power and extent should not be reposed in such a Saviour-God! Surely He who made and who sustains the universe is able to keep that we "have committed to Him," and will not, from inability or oversight, suffer a confiding spirit to sink into perdition.

We have not chosen to interrupt the course of exegesis by taking notice of the non-natural interpretation which has been sometimes put upon these verses. The deniers of the Redeemer's deity, and of necessity such as Crellius, Slichting, and the editors of the "Improved Version,"[1] hold that the creation referred to is not the physical, but a moral creation,—an exegesis acquiesced in, in some of its parts, by Grotius, Wetstein, Ernesti, Noesselt, Heinrichs, Schrader, Baumgarten-Crusius, and Schleiermacher. But, as Whitby remarks, it is a "flat and mean" exposition; or, as Daillé calls it, "*chicaneuse glosse.*" For—

1. It is contradicted by the paragraph which afterwards, and that formally, introduces the new or spiritual creation, and connects it as a sequel with that other creation which in these verses the apostle ascribes to Christ. This mode of connection is a plain proof that two distinct acts, or provinces of operation and government, are referred to Christ.

2. The obvious meaning of the terms employed is against the Socinian hypothesis. Had the words occurred in any

[1] The views of Photinus, a disciple of Marcellus, in the fourth century, were similar, and were condemned even by an Arian Council at Sirmium, in 351. It is strange to find Lampe adopting the Socinian exegesis, as in his Commentary on the 45th Psalm, p. 573.

common paragraph, their meaning would never have been doubted. Had the Father been spoken of, the reference to creation, in its proper sense, would never have been impugned. Why then, when the reference is to the Son, should not the first and most natural interpretation be put upon the language? Pierce remarks, that the exegesis which adopts the notion of a spiritual creation would never have been espoused "but for the sake of an hypothesis." The language in its words and spirit—its minuteness and universality—leads us to the first or physical creation. It is a miserable shift of the editors of the Improved Version to argue "the apostle does not say by Him were created heaven and earth, but things in heaven and things on earth." The inspired language is, the universe—"the all" was created by Him without exception; "things in heaven," comprising heaven and its population; and "things on earth," meaning earth and all that it contains. One is apt to wonder at the hardihood of such an exegesis, and to pause and ask with Whitby, "Do the angels need this moral creation, or are they a part of this spiritual creation?" And how jejune to say, that by "things in heaven" are meant the Jews, and by "things on earth," the Gentiles! Besides, if we adopt the hypothesis, that a moral renovation is described by these words, the paragraph would lead us to suppose that it had been already effected, and that it still subsisted, whereas in reality it had only commenced.

3. Such phraseology cannot signify a moral creation. The verb *κτίζω* has sometimes a secondary sense, and refers to the new creation. In such cases not only is the meaning obvious from the context, as in Eph. ii. 10, 2 Cor. v. 17, Eph. iv. 24, Col. iii. 10, but also the subjects of the renovation are living men already in physical existence; and there can be therefore no mistake in calling the mighty moral change that passes over them a creation. In the paragraph before us, on the other hand, no such previous condition exists; all things are said to be created, that is, brought into existence, by Christ Jesus. The passages of similar meaning in the Old Testament, as Ps. li. 10, Isa. xlv. 8, Jer. xxxi. 22, etc., present no difficulty, for they carry with them the principle of their own solution. Such phraseology as that before us occurs not in any of these places; and in one of them

where there is similar diction, ambiguity is guarded against by the addition of the epithet "new,"—"I create new heavens and a new earth."

Lastly, as Whitby,[1] Dr. Pye Smith,[2] and Burton [3] have shown, the early Greek Fathers unanimously understood the passage of a "proper and physical creation." The Socinian interpretation, in short, is as repugnant to sound exegesis as the transparent trick of Marcion was to ordinary honesty, when, according to Tertullian, he omitted in his edition the verses altogether. The perversion of them is not better than the exclusion of them; nay, the latter has the merit of a direct avowal of inability or reluctance to explain them. They, however, survive as a bright and glorious testimony to Him who is the "true God and eternal life."

A similar assault upon the natural meaning of the paragraph, and which created no small stir, was made by Schleiermacher [4] in the third number of the *Studien und Kritiken*, 1832. His exegesis in its general principles and minute details is opposed alike to sound philology and to the context. His affirmation that κτίζειν is never used in Hellenistic Greek of creation proper, is contradicted by Wisd. i. 14, etc.; Rev. iv. 11, x. 6. His attempt to connect πρωτότοκος as an adjective with the preceding εἰκών is another failure clearly proved by the verbal arrangement. How frigid to confine the phrase, "visible and invisible," to the last half of the previous clause—"things on earth"! Somewhat more spiritual and ingenious than the Socinian hypothesis, this exegesis of Schleiermacher leads to the same unsatisfactory result. It was answered by Osiander in the same journal, 1833; and by Holzhausen in the *Tübing. Zeitschrift*, 1833; by Bähr in an appendix to his *Commentary;* and by Bleek in his *Exposition of Hebrews*, i. 3.

[1] See also *Pearson on the Creed*, p. 156, vol. i. ed. Oxford, 1847.

[2] *Scripture Testimony*, iii. 273.

[3] *Testimony of the Ante-Nicene Fathers to the Divinity of Christ* (passim), Oxford, 1837.

[4] Thus he says, "Christus ist in dem gesammten Umfang der geistigen Menschenwelt das *erstgeborne* Bild Gottes, das ursprüngliche Abbild Gottes; alle Gläubigen sollten in das Bild Christi gestaltet werden, woraus ebenfalls das Bild Gottes in ihnen entstehen müsse, ein Bild zweiter Ordnung."—*Stud. u. Krit.* 1832, 3, S. 521 ff.

(Ver. 18.) *Καὶ αὐτός ἐστιν ἡ κεφαλὴ τοῦ σώματος τῆς ἐκκλησίας.*—"And He is the head of the body—the Church.' The latter genitive is in apposition. The apostle now commences the second portion of the paragraph, and portrays Christ's relation to the Church. As Theodoret says, He passes *ἀπὸ τῆς θεολογίας εἰς τὴν οἰκονομίαν.* Still He stands out supreme—the one guardian and benefactor—the one Saviour and president—*καὶ αὐτός*—He and none other. The meaning of the phrase, "head of the body—the church," has been given under Eph. i. 22, 23, and iv. 15, 16. The probability is that Christ's headship was impugned by the false teachers, in consequence of their theory of emanations and other fantastic reveries about the spirit-world. The church is not, as Noesselt[1] says, the whole family in heaven and in earth, —nor yet the human race, one of whom Christ became;— but the company of the redeemed, the body of the faithful in Christ Jesus. The previous verses show His qualification for such a headship,—His possession of a Divine nature—His supremacy over the universe, and His creation and support of all things. Any creature would be deified were he so highly exalted; for he would, from his position, become the god of the Christian people, as their blesser, protector, and object of worship. But the church and the universe are under one administration, that of Him who is "King of kings and Lord of lords." The king of the universe is able to be Head of the church, and He has won the Headship in His blood. It is no eminence to which he is not entitled, no function which he cannot worthily discharge. For the apostle subjoins the following statement as proof—

Ὅς ἐστιν ἀρχή—"Who is the beginning." This term has been variously understood. Storr and Flatt reduce its significance by making it mean governor of the world; Calvin comes near the true view in his paraphrase—*initium secundae et novae creationis;* Baumgarten, nearer still, when he defines it by *Urheber*, originator. Meyer, De Wette, Huther, Bähr, Steiger, and others, join it to the following words, as if the full clause were—*ἀρχὴ . . . τῶν νεκρῶν.* Meyer and De Wette take it simply in a temporal sense (*πρὸ πάντων ἀναστάς*, as Theophylact has it), and as if it were equivalent to *ἀπαρχή*, which some

[1] *Opuscula*, vol. ii. p. 231.

MSS. even have,[1] while the other expositors give the sense of *principium*. Such a construction is certainly very strange, especially when we consider that ἐκ precedes τῶν νεκρῶν. We incline to keep the word by itself, and to regard it as being much the same as in the phrase, Rev. iii. 14—ἡ ἀρχὴ τῆς κτίσεως τοῦ Θεοῦ—the cause or source of the creation of God. Wisdom of Solomon, xii. 16, xiv. 27. The noun, standing by itself, would seem to point out Christ in His solitary grandeur as the prime source of all the blessings and honours detailed in the subsequent verses. The relative has plainly a causal sense, so that the connection is "He is Head of the body,—the church,—inasmuch as He is the one source of its existence and blessings;" and He is so, as being "the first-begotten from the dead," and, as verse 20 shows, the Reconciler of men to God by the blood of His cross. This exegesis gives a special dignity to the epithet—Christ, the first source of existence and blessing. But for His gracious intervention, no church had ever existed, and no salvation been ever enjoyed. Having ransomed the church by His blood, may He not rule it by His power, and be "the Head"?

And no matter what blessing is enjoyed, what its kind or amount, He is its author. There may be subordinate supplies —wells of water; but His rain from heaven fills them. Conviction of sin and repentance unto life are produced by a glimpse of Christ. "They shall look on me whom they have pierced, and mourn." The pardon of guilt comes directly from Him; and His death provides for the sanctification of the heart; His Spirit the agent, and His word the instrument. Every grace may be traced to Him, and it bears the heart away to Him as the source of saving influence. He has originated salvation, and He gives it. He is in the most unlimited sense —ἀρχή—"the beginning." And we are the more confirmed in this view of keeping ἀρχή separated from the following clause and giving it an absolute meaning, from the fact that, in the Philonic vocabulary,[2] it is the name of Logos, and was pro-

[1] Such as 17, 46, 63; Chrysostom's text, and that of Œcumenius.

[2] Καὶ γὰρ ἀρχὴ . . . καὶ λόγος. *De Confus. Ling.* p. 380, vol. iii. ed. Pfeiffer. The first source of all was named by Cerinthus, as in the Latin of Irenaeus, *principalitas*. *Adver. Haeres.* p. 253, Opera, vol. i. ed. Stieren, 1853. As to the question whether the Logos of Philo be a person, or only the personification of an attribute, a question both sides of which are discussed by Gfrörer, Lücke,

bably introduced by the apostle with a special reference to current and insidious errors. The description proceeds—

Πρωτότοκος ἐκ τῶν νεκρῶν—"First-begotten from the dead." In Rev. i. 5 we find but the simple genitive. It is out of the question, on the part of Bullinger, Keuchenius, Aretius, Erasmus, and Schleiermacher, to connect *ἀρχή* with *πρωτότοκος*—an abstract with a concrete. We must take this word as in the former clause—"first-begotten of every creature," and regard it as referring, not to the priority of time, but to dignity and station. He was not the first that rose in absolute priority, nor simply the first who rose, no more to die. But He was among the dead; and as He rose from the midst of them, He became their chief, or Lord—"the first-fruits of them that sleep." From Him the dead will get deliverance, for He rose in their name, and came—*ἐκ*—out from among them as their representative. In this character He destroyed "him that had the power of death." Not only when He was "cut off, but not for Himself," did He "finish transgression and make an end of sin," but He "abolished death." Nay, He has the keys of death and Hades. His people rise in virtue of His power. The instances of resurrection prior to His own were only proofs that the dead might be raised, but His resurrection was a pledge that they should be raised. The Lord Himself shall descend; the trump shall sound, and myriads of sleepers shall start into life; no soul shall lose, and none mistake its partner; neither earth nor sea shall retain one occupant. But He is not only the pledge, He is also the pattern. His people shall be raised in immortal youth and beauty; their vile bodies fashioned like unto His glorious body, and therefore no longer animal frames, but so etherealized and attempered as to be able to dwell in a world which

Dorner, Dahne, Pye Smith, and other distinguished scholars, we quite agree with the view of Schaff (*Church History*, i. p. 213), that Philo himself vibrated between the two opinions, and took each as it served his turn. There is no doubt, that when he calls his Logos, archangel, interpreter, High Priest, the first-born Son of God, he seems to give Him a personal existence; and there is little doubt that he appears to regard Him only as a species of personification, when he names Him the reflection of God, the ideal world, the medium of the sensible world, the summation of those ideas which are the archetypes of all being.—Dorner, *Entwickelungeschichte der Lehre von der Person Christi*, 2nd ed. vol. i. pp. 24, 25, Also, Lücke, *Commentar über das Evang. Johannis*, i. 249 *et seq.*, Bonn, 1840.

"flesh and blood cannot inherit"—to see God and yet live, to bear upon them without exhaustion the exceeding weight of glory, and to serve, love, and enjoy the unvailed Divinity without end.

Ἵνα γένηται ἐν πᾶσιν αὐτὸς πρωτεύων—"In order that in all things He should have the pre-eminence." The conjunction appears to be telic, and not merely ecbatic, as Bähr supposes. It indicates, not the resnlt, but the final purpose of the entire economy. And we cannot, with Meyer and others, connect this clause solely with the one that goes before it, as if His pre-eminence rested merely upon the fact that He was the first-born from the dead. The clause has its root in the entire paragraph, as we shall immediately endeavour to show. The emphatic verb *πρωτεύω* does not occur anywhere else in the New Testament, but we find it in the Septuagint, 2 Macc. vi. 18; Esth. v. 11; Xenophon, *Cyrop.* 8, 2, 28; Joseph. *Antiq.* 9, 8, 3; Plutarch, *De Educat. lib.* c. 13, where this very phrase occurs;[1] Plato, *Leges*, 692, p. 54, vol. vii. Opera, ed. Bekker, 1826. Two distinct meanings have been assigned to *ἐν πᾶσιν*. 1. It may be taken as masculine, "among all persons," as is the opinion of Anselm, Beza, Cocceius, Heinrichs, Piscator, and Usteri. If the clause referred simply to the *νεκροί*, of which Jesus is the first-born, then we should have expected the article—*ἐν τοῖς πᾶσιν*. That *ἐν* following *πρωτεύω* may refer to persons, Kypke has shown in his note on this verse, though *παρά* is the preposition as frequently employed, and more usually the simple genitive. 2. The phrase *ἐν πᾶσιν* is more naturally taken by the majority in a neuter sense, "in every thing," or "in all respects." This is the ordinary meaning of the phrase in the New Testament. 2 Cor. xi. 6; Eph. i. 23; 1 Tim. iii. 11; 2 Tim. ii. 7; Tit. ii. 9; 1 Pet. iv. 11. The *usus loquendi* is therefore in favour of this interpretation, "first in all points;" or as Theophylact says, in all things—*τοῖς περὶ αὐτὸν θεωρουμένοις*—"in all things which have reference to Himself;" as Chrysostom has it, *πανταχοῦ πρῶτος*. The verb *γένηται* is not to be confounded with the verb of simple existence. The meaning is not that He might be, but that "He might become." Acts x. 4; Rom. iii. 19; Heb. v. 12. The verb in such cases denotes the manifestation

[1] See Wetstein, *in loc.*

of result—that He may show Himself to be in all things FIRST. We do not say, with Meyer and Huther, that this pre-eminence is looked upon as wholly future, and as only to be realized at the resurrection. If we held the close and sole connection of *πρωτεύων* with *πρωτότοκος*, we should be obliged to keep this view partially, but not to its full extent; for, in respect to the dead, as now dead, Jesus stands out as the First who has so risen from a similar state. The meaning, then, is, that in consequence of His being what the apostle has just described Him to be, He has in all things the primacy; that He stands out as FIRST to the universe, for He is its visible God, its Creator and Preserver; and He is the Head of the Church, the fount of spiritual blessing, the "Resurrection and the Life."

As the image—*εἰκών*—of the invisible God He has the pre-eminence. For He is without date of origin or epoch of conclusion. No eclipse shall sully the splendours of His nature. What He has been, He is, and He shall be. Nor is His essence bounded by any circumference, but it is everywhere, undiluted by boundless extension. His mind comprises all probabilities, and has decided all certainties. His power knows no limit of operation, and is unexhausted by effort. His truth is pure as the solar beam, and the fulness of infinite love dwells in His heart. But such Divine glory is common to the Godhead, and He shares it equally with Father and Spirit. Even here, however, He is First; for He has visibility, which the Father and Spirit have not; and He is the God of the universe whom it sees, recognizes, and adores. Nay, more, He has cast a new lustre over His original glory by His incarnation and death. He has won for Himself an imperishable renown. This dignity so earned by Him is specially called His own, in contradistinction from His prior and essential glory, and it is His peculiar and valued possession. Robed in His native majesty, which has been augmented by the mediatorial crown, is He not the most glorious being in the universe? Matt. xxv. 31; John xvii. 24.

And He has pre-eminence as Creator, for creation is His special work. It existed in idea in the mind of God, but it was brought into existence by the power of Christ. These worlds on worlds, which in their number and vastness confound us, have Him as artificer, for He "telleth the number of the stars, and calleth them by their names." Creation owns Him as Lord. The natural impulse is to reason from effect upwards to cause—"from nature up to nature's God:" but the God whom such instinctive logic discovers, and whose might and wisdom, science and philosophy illustrate with rich, varied, profound, and increasing, nay, interminable examples, is none other than this "First-born of every creature." On His arm hangs the universe, and He receives its homage. Above all, there is matchless grandeur in the constitution of His person as the Head of the Church. The Father is pure Divinity, and so is the Spirit: the wisest, greatest, and best; infinite, eternal, and unchangeable in essence, attributes, and character. But the Son has another nature, one in person with His Deity. The divine is not dwarfed into the human, nor has the human been absorbed into the divine, but both co-exist without mixture or confusion. The incarnation of Jesus illuminates the Old Testament as a promise, and fills the New Testament as a fact. Possessed of this composite nature, Christ is distinguished from every being: none like Him in unapproachable mystery—as the God-man who has gained His capital supremacy by His agony and cross. Was ever suffering like His in origin, intensity, nature, or design?

Again, as the source of blessing, has He not primal rank? These spiritual gifts possess a special value, as springing from His blood, and as being applied by His Spirit. He is seated in eminence as the dispenser of common gifts to His universe, but He is throned in pre-eminence as the provider and bestower of spiritual blessings to His Church. Are not His instructions without a rival in adaptation, amount, and power? What parallel can be found to His example, so perfect and so fascinating, that of a man that men may see, and admire, and imitate; while it contains in itself, at the same time, the secret might of Divinity to mould into its blessed resemblance the heart of all His followers who are "changed into the same image from glory to glory"? In short, there is such wondrous singularity in the glory of Christ's person and work, so much that gives Him a radiance all His own, and an elevation high and apart, that it may be truly said, that in all things He has the pre-eminence. None like Christ is the decision of faith:

none but Christ is the motto of love. The apostle assigns another or additional reason—

(Ver. 19.) *Ὅτι ἐν αὐτῷ εὐδόκησεν.* A different spelling of the word is exhibited in some of the MSS. such as A, D, E, —*ηὐδόκησεν*, but without authority. Schmid supposes that *πλήρωμα* is the nominative; and he understands it thus—the entire Godhead was pleased to dwell in Christ. We believe, with the majority of expositors, that *ὁ θεός* is to be supplied as the nominative, and not *τῷ θεῷ*, in the dative. Matt. iii. 17; Luke iii. 22. The full syntax is found in 1 Cor. i. 21; Gal. i. 15. But we cannot hold, with some, that the pronoun *αὐτῷ* refers to God, for we take it as still pointing to Him who has been the prime subject of discourse. To make *ὁ Χριστός* the nominative, as Conybeare does, implies the sense that Christ is not only the means, but the end in this reconciliation, for the reading would plainly be in the next verse—"and by Himself to reconcile all things unto Himself," a mode of speech not in accordance with Pauline usage. Christ reconciles, not to Himself, but to God. We incline also to connect the clause immediately with the preceding one, and not generally with the previous paragraph. "That in all things He might have the pre-eminence;" for, in order to this, "it pleased God—it was His good purpose—that in Him should all fulness dwell." The pre-eminence, therefore, could not but be His. The verb does not mean that it was God's desire that all fulness should dwell in Christ, but that it was His resolve, as being His pleasure.[1]

Πᾶν τὸ πλήρωμα κατοικῆσαι. On the meaning of *πλήρωμα* we have spoken at length under Eph. i. 23. In the verb the idea of past and continued residence is presented. We see no reason to deviate here from the meaning assigned to the noun in the place referred to, so that we must hold, against Bähr and Steiger, that the word has a passive, and not an active signification, denoting, not that which fills up, but the state of fulness, or the contents of it. But to what does this fulness refer?

1. It is a most extraordinary exegesis of Theodoret and Severianus,[2] followed by Baumgarten-Crusius, Heinrichs, Wahl,

[1] In reference to the meaning and derivation of the verb, there is an elaborate note of Fritzsche, *Comment. in Ep. ad Roman.* ii. 369. See also *Sturz*, p. 168; *Lobeck ad Phryn.* p. 456.

[2] *Catena*, p. 310.

and Schleiermacher, that πλήρωμα signifies the multitude which compose the church. This view has been exposed by us under Eph. i. 23. Here it would yield no tolerable meaning, and would not be in harmony at all with the context. Pierce follows the rendering of Castalio—" it seemed good to God the Father to inhabit all fulness by Christ."

2. Some limit the meaning of the clause by basing their interpretation of it on a following verse in ii. 9, "all the fulness of the Godhead." But there is no reason to subjoin the genitive τῆς θεότητος in this place, the meaning here being more general and sweeping in its nature.

3. This fulness is referred by Œcumenius, Huther, and others, to the Divine essence. Servetus based, according to Beza, a species of Pantheism on this declaration. But such an idea cannot be entertained, because the Divine essence dwelt in Christ unchangeably, and not by the Father's consent or purpose. It is His in His own right, and not by paternal pleasure. Whatever dwells in Christ by the Father's pleasure is official, and not essential; relational, and not absolute in its nature.

4. The proper exegesis, then, is, that all fulness of grace, or saving blessings, dwells in Christ—a species of fulness, the contents of which are described in the following verse. John i. 14–16. We do not exclude the work of creation as a result of this fulness laid up in the Image and First-born, but the apostle seems to connect it more with the process and results of redemption. Whatever is needed to save a fallen world, and restore harmony to the universe, is treasured up in Him—is in Him. It was indispensable that the law should be magnified while its violators were forgiven, lest the circuit of the Divine jurisdiction should be narrowed, or its influence counteracted; and there is a fulness of merit in the sufferings of Jesus which has shed an imperishable lustre on the nature and government of God. That copious variety of gifts connected with the Christian economy has its source in Jesus. Knowledge and faith, pardon and life, purity and hope, comfort and strength, impulse and check, all that quickens and all that sustains, each in its place and connection, is but an emanation of this unexhausted plenty. And there is "all" fulness; abundance of

blessing, and of every species of blessing, in proper time and order. As the bounties of providence are scattered around us with rich munificence, and consist not of one kind of gift which might become fatal in its monotony, but of an immense variety, which is essential, singly and in combination, to the sustenance of life; so the blessings which spring out of this fulness are not only vast in number and special in adaptation, by themselves, but in their mutual relations and dependence they supply every necessity, and fill the entire nature with increasing satisfaction and delight. The impartation of knowledge, though it grew to the "riches of the full assurance of understanding," could not of itself minister to every want; nor yet could the pardon of sin severed from the benefits which flow from it. Therefore there is secured for us peace as well as enlightenment; renovation along with forgiveness: condition and character are equally changed; the tear of penitence glistens in the radiance of spiritual joy, and the germs of perfection ingrafted now are destined for ever to mature and expand. Provision, moreover, would be inadequate without application. Man is not merely informed that God is merciful, and that he may come to Him and live; or that Christ has died, and that he may believe and be saved; or that heaven is open, and that he may enter and be happy. Not only is provision ample, but in this fulness appliance is secured. Not only has salvation been purchased, but it is placed within an available reach, for while the cross is erected, the eye is opened, and the vision carried towards its bleeding victim; not only has atoning blood been shed, but it is sprinkled upon the heart; not only is there the promise of a heavenly inheritance, but the soul is purified, yea, and "kept by the power of God through faith." In short, every grace, as it is needed, and when it is needed, in every variety of phasis and operation; every grace, either to nurse the babe or sustain the perfect man, to excite the new life or to foster it, to give pardon and the sense of it, faith and the full assurance of it, purity and the felt possession of it; every blessing, in short, for health or sickness, for duty or trial, for life or death, for body or soul, for earth or heaven, for time or eternity, is wrapt up in that fulness which dwells in Christ.

It may be that *πλήρωμα* was a term employed by the heretics who disturbed the Colossian church, but we cannot lay such stress upon this circumstance as is done by Bähr and Steiger, nor safely deduce from it an inevitable exegesis. There is no doubt that *πλήρωμα* was a distinctive epithet in the vocabulary of the heretics of a later age, such as Valentinus, and in the teaching ascribed to Cerinthus. It is found also among the peculiar terms of the Kabbalists. But it would be rash to affirm that the apostle used the word because these heretics abused it, for in his days the germ of that theosophy and mysticism had only found existence, and neither the system nor the nomenclature was fully developed.

(Ver. 20.) *Καὶ δι' αὐτοῦ ἀποκαταλλάξαι τὰ πάντα εἰς αὐτόν*—"And by Him to reconcile all things to Himself." This sentence still hangs upon the verb *εὐδόκησε*. *Εἰρηνοποιήσας* agrees with *θεός*, the understood nominative to *εὐδόκησε*. God having made peace by the blood of His cross (Christ's), was pleased to reconcile by Him (Christ) all things to Himself. If the participle *εἰρηνο.* referred to Jesus, we should have expected it to be in the accusative before the infinitive. The instances adduced by Steiger, who holds this view, to prove the occurrence here of a species of anacoluthon, are not in point. On the meaning of *ἀποκαταλ.* we have spoken under Eph. ii. 16, and need not repeat our remarks. The phrase *τὰ πάντα*, in this verse, must be identical in meaning with *τὰ πάντα* in the 16th verse—created by Jesus and for Him; and *τὰ πάντα* in the 17th verse—preserved by Him. The meaning is further developed and specified in the last clause—*εἴτε τὰ ἐπὶ τῆς γῆς, εἴτε τὰ ἐν τοῖς οὐρανοῖς*—all things, "whether they be things on earth, or things in heaven." The apostle seems thus to refer to the universe—specially the intelligent universe. The reconciliation is effected through Christ, an idea repeated by the apostle in the 22nd and 23rd verses.

1. It is surely a low and pointless interpretation of the words to refer them, with Junker, Heinrichs, Schleusner, and others, to Jew and Gentile, for the passage is widely different from the paragraph in the 2nd chapter of Ephesians; or with Beza, Crocius, and Wolf, to understand "things in heaven" of the happy souls of the departed; or with Schleiermacher, to suppose the apostle to refer to earthly and ecclesiastical

relationships. The previous context plainly condemns such a narrow and groundless interpretation.

2. On the other hand, it is going beyond the record to base upon the words the dogma of universal restoration. Evil spirits, and finally impenitent men, are left in unrelieved gloom. Those who reject this reconciliation, and depart from the world in unbelief, fall into the hands of a God "who is clear when He judges."

On this passage, Davenant says truly—*torquet interpretes et vicissim ab illis torquetur.* De Wette, indeed, referring to Job iv. 18 and xv. 15, imagines that angels need some process of peacemaking, or rather of perfecting—a notion akin to Calvin's,[1] that they were in want of confirmation.

But supposing that by "things in heaven" we understand angels and all other holy intelligences, in what sense can it be said that they need or receive reconciliation? Some elude the difficulty, and argue that the reconciliation is not between God and perfect spirits, but between them and redeemed humanity. Thus Theodoret—*συνῆψε τοῖς ἐπιγείοις τὰ ἐπουράνια*: and such is the view of Chrysostom, Augustine, and Pelagius, of Cameron, Dickson, and perhaps the majority. This is a truth, but perhaps not the whole truth intended. The language implies more than this exegesis contains, for all things in heaven are not merely reconciled to all things on earth, but both are at the same time reconciled to God. And we cannot espouse the opinion of Huther, Bähr, and Olshausen, who make the reference in *εἰς αὐτόν* to Christ, regarding Him as both means and end. The idea is not in

[1] Inter Deum et Angelos longe diversa ratio, illic enim nulla defectio, nullum peccatum, ideoque nullum divortium. Sed tamen duabus de causis Angelos quoque oportuit cum Deo pacificari: nam quum creaturae sint, extra lapsus periculum non erant, nisi Christi gratia fuissent confirmati. Hoc autem non parvum est momentum ad pacis cum Deo perpetuitatem, fixum habere statum in iustitia, ne casum aut defectionem amplius timeat. Deinde in hac ipsa obedientia, quam praestant Deo, non est tam exquisita perfectio, ut Deo omni ex parte et citra veniam satisfaciat. Atque huc procul dubio spectat sententia ista ex libro Iob (4, 18.), In Angelis suis reperiet iniquitatem: nam si de diabolo exponitur, quid magnum? pronuntiat autem illic Spiritus summam puritatem sordere, si ad Dei iustitiam exigatur. Constituendum igitur, non esse tantum in Angelis iustitiae, quod ad plenam cum Deo coniunctionem sufficiat, itaque pacificatore opus habent, per cuius gratiam penitus Deo adhaereant. *In loc.*

unison with Pauline phraseology, for God is usually regarded as the ultimate end. But the idea in this case would be, that all beings are brought by the death of Christ to obey Him, and to find in Him their common centre. The dative, indeed, is commonly employed, as in Eph. ii. 16, Rom. v. 10; but the employment here of the accusative with εἰς may indicate something unusual in the verb—may denote to reconcile for, or in reference to Himself, that is, God, He being regarded generally as the end of this reconciliation. Reconciliation to God is thus predicated of the "things in heaven," though they had never revolted. Nor can we simply declare, with Melancthon, Cameron, and Bähr, that the sentiment of this verse is identical with that found in Eph. i. 10, and that *ἀποκαταλλάξαι* is of the same meaning as *ἀνακεφαλαιώσασθαι*. Indeed, as Meyer well suggests, the bringing together under one head is the result of the reconciliation which is here described. The verb *ἀποκατ.* is defined by Suidas as meaning *φιλοποιῆσαι*—to make friends; and Fritzsche renders it *prorsus* reconciliare.[1] The *ἀπό*, in composition, does not signify "again," as Passow erroneously gives it. [Eph. ii. 16.] This reconciliation we understand in its result—εἰς—and as denoting unalterable union,—that he might reconcile all things and unite them so reconciled to Himself. Such a pregnant meaning of verbs is no uncommon occurrence. 2 Tim. iv. 18—*σώσει εἰς τὴν βασιλείαν*, will save *and translate* us to His kingdom. Mark viii. 19—*ὅτε τοὺς πέντε ἄρτους ἔκλασα εἰς τοὺς πεντακισχιλίους*, when I broke *and distributed* the five loaves to the five thousand. Acts xxiii. 24, etc.; Winer, § 66, 2, d; Xenophon, *Anab.* 11, 3, 11; *Polyb.* 8, 11; *Odyss.* ii. 14. There needed no atonement for innocent creatures, but they must have felt the disruption of sin, and seen the terrible anger of God against it. May they not have trembled at the bare idea of apostasy, and may not the very suspicion of it have made them stand before God with more of awe than love? When the angels beheld their fellows sin so grievously, when they mourned over the tarnished brightness of their lost and exiled natures, might not the memory of the melancholy spectacle fill them with terror, and as they felt themselves placed in a jeopardous

[1] *Comment. in Ep. ad Rom.* i. 278.

crisis, might they not shrink as they gazed upon the unsullied justice and inexorable vengeance of Jehovah-king? Might not holiness unrelieved by an act of grace, be ever impressing the conviction that "it is a fearful thing to fall into the hands of the living God"? For sin was possible to them, and what had happened might again take place, while the penalty of sin was as swift in its descent as it was unspeakable in its burden, and irremediable in its effects. The flashing majesty of the throne might still the pulse of the universe, or cause it to throb in subdued and solemn alarm. The radiance of grace had not been seen to play upon the sceptre of righteousness. Acquiescence in the Divine rectitude might not conquer trepidation, and the love which encircled them might not cast out all fear of lapse and punishment. But when they found out the ineffable stores of the Divine benignity towards man—in the mission and death of Jesus, in the untold abundance and fulness of blessings conferred upon him, in a vast salvation secured at a vast expense, and in a happy alliance concluded between them and the ransomed church—did they not share in the same reconciliation and feel themselves drawn nearer a God of grace, whom they can now love with a higher thrill and praise with a more rapturous hallelujah? In being re-united with man they feel themselves brought closer to God, and though they sing of a salvation which they did not require, still they experience the Saviour's tenderness, and are charmed with the reign of His crowned humanity. The gloom that sin had thrown over them is dispelled; and creation as one united whole rejoices in the presence of God. The one Reconciler is the head of these vast dominions, and in Him meet and merge the discordant elements which sin had introduced. The breach is healed. Gabriel embraces Adam, and both enjoy a vicinity to God, which but for the reconciliation of the cross would never have been vouchsafed to either. The humanity of Jesus bringing all creatures around it, unites them to God in a bond which never before existed—a bond which has its origin in the mystery of redemption. Thus all things in heaven and earth feel the effect of man's renovation; unnumbered worlds, so thickly strewn as to appear but dim and nebulous masses, are pervaded by its harmonizing influence; a new attraction binds them to the throne. Blessings which naked Deity might not be able to bestow are poured out upon them by the incarnate Lord "who filleth all in all;" and the exhibition of love in the agonies of Christ may have secured what unalloyed equity could not, may have placed the universe for ever beyond the reach of apostasy and revolt. Then at length starts into view the blessed kingdom—"the new heavens and new earth, wherein dwelleth righteousness."

Nor need we wonder at the infinite results of the death of Christ, when we reflect that, as the apostle has described Him, He is Creator, Preserver, and End of all things. Creation, to its farthest verge, could not but be affected by the grace and the death of Him who gave to it its original being and still supplies the means of its continued existence. When He laid aside the splendours of the Godhead, and walked a man upon the footstool, and died on a world and for a world which He had made, to satisfy Divine justice, and glorify the principles of the Divine administration, it might be anticipated that the effect of that stupendous enterprise should be felt everywhere, diffusing the attractive power of a new spiritual gravitation among all things, "whether they be things on earth or things in heaven."

Εἰρηνοποιήσας διὰ τοῦ αἵματος τοῦ σταυροῦ αὐτοῦ—"Having made peace by the blood of His cross." We understand the participle to be in agreement with *θεός*, as the nominative to *εὐδόκησε*, and not with *Χριστός*, as the Greek Fathers, and even Storr and Steiger, construe the clause. The aorist participle here is of the same tense with the aorist infinitive in the preceding clause, and it points out the method by which reconciliation has been secured. The blood of His, that is, Christ's cross, was the source of peace—the reference being to the atoning sacrifice presented on Calvary. Blood shed on earth creates feuds to be extinguished only by other blood; it calls up the avenging kinsman to wait, watch, pursue, and retaliate; but the blood of Christ's violent and vicarious death brings peace, restores alliance between heaven and earth. While we look on the paternal aspect of God's character, we must not overlook His position as moral governor—bound to inflict the penalty annexed to the violation of His statutes. [Eph. ii. 16.] He must visit the sinner with His judicial displeasure; or as the scholastic theology of Bede phrased it, "in every one of us He hated what we had done, He loved what He Himself had done." The justice of God, as Nitzsch[1] says, is a necessary and inseparable idea of His love. The antithesis of mercy and justice is no longer unresolved, nor do they neutralize one another. Sin at the same time creates enmity in the human heart towards God, an enmity removed also by faith in the great propitiation. Thus the cross is the symbol of peace. He who died on it possessed God's nature, the offended party, and man's nature, the offending party; and thus being qualified to mediate between them, His blood was poured out as a peace-offering. The law is satisfied, and guilty sinners are freed from the curse: an amnesty is proclaimed; God reconciles the world unto Himself, and justified man has peace with God.

The apostle repeats δι' αὐτοῦ to give prominence to the efficacious agency of His Son. "By Him," that is, by His blood, and by all the work which His mediatorial person is so well fitted to carry on and consummate. The last clause explains the preceding πάντα. As if there might be doubt in some minds; or as if some ascribed a limited influence to a Jewish death upon Jewish soil, the apostle exclaims "all"—"whether they be things in earth," which is first and specially interested; or whether they be "things in heaven." Chrysostom, to support his view, erroneously and ungrammatically connects this clause with the one immediately before it, as if the peace made by the blood of the cross was simply and solely peace between things in heaven and things on earth. In fine, the entire process, as the connection of this verse with the preceding one shows, springs from the Divine pleasure—it so "pleased" Him.

Now, if there was a tendency among the false teachers in Colosse to depreciate Jesus, lower the value and restrict the extent of His saving work; if they derogated either from His personal dignity or official prerogative, the apostle applies a mighty and sufficient counteractive. That Saviour whom the apostles preached was no creature, but Himself the Creator; was invested with no provincial government, but ruled and preserved the wide realms of space; was no subordinate spirit

[1] *System der Christlichen Lehre*, § 80, 5th Auflage, Bonn, 1844.

in the celestial crowd, but one who is the end as well as author of all things; is supreme Lord of His Church, as is most due; and as He possesses all fulness within Himself, and has by the shedding of His blood restored harmony to the universe, therefore, now, in every point He has an unchallenged pre-eminence. On the dark background of an old theosophic heresy there shines out this starry halo of mediatorial merit and renown.

(Ver. 21.) *Καὶ ὑμᾶς, ποτὲ ὄντας ἀπηλλοτριωμένους καὶ ἐχθροὺς τῇ διανοίᾳ ἐν τοῖς ἔργοις τοῖς πονηροῖς, νυνὶ δὲ ἀποκατήλλαξεν*—"And yet now He has reconciled you who were once alienated and enemies in your mind by wicked works." The apostle turns directly to the Colossians, and applies to their experience the results of these more general statements. And he does not disguise the truth when he describes their past condition—*ποτέ*. *Καὶ ὑμᾶς*, "you even." Hartung, p. 125. The participle *ὄντας* occurs before *ἀπηλλ.* Jelf, § 375, 4. [*Ἀπηλλοτ.* Eph. ii. 12, iv. 18.] It here denotes that spiritual alienation from God which characterized the heathen world. Though the term God is not expressed, the idea is plainly implied. They had strayed so far from God, that they had lost all view of His unity and spirituality, His holiness and His love, and felt no longer the hallowing influence of His existence, majesty, and government. This severance from God was the early fruit of sin, for when the Divine Being descended to paradise, as was His wont, the guilty Adam acknowledged the impulse of this alienation when he attempted to "hide himself from the presence of the Lord God among the trees of the garden." So severed, they needed re-union. Nay, not only were they aliens, but enemies—*ἐχθρούς*. We see no reason to adopt Meyer's view, and take the adjective in a passive sense—objects of the Divine enmity, a meaning which it does not bear in Rom. v. 10. We prefer the usual and active sense, as seen in the common phrase *ὁ ἐχθρός*; and it is superfluous on the part of Calovius to unite both acceptations. That enmity had its seat *τῇ διανοίᾳ*, which Meyer is obliged to render, with Luther, "on account of your mind"—hated on account of your corrupt mind. This enmity toward God was in the mind. [*διάνοια*, Eph. ii. 3.] The noun represents the seat of thought, or rather of disposition. Luke i. 51; 1 Chron. xxix. 18.

The connection of this with the next clause has been variously understood. Michaelis gratuitously renders "enmity in consequence of pre-eminence in evil works." Erasmus is as wide of the mark in his explanation—*inimici, cui? menti, etenim qui carni servit, repugnat rationi.* Bähr, relying on the usage of *διανοεῖν* being followed by *ἐν*, connects the two clauses very closely—*operibus malis intenta, peccatorum studiosa.* We incline to take the clauses as separate statements in order, the first as describing the seat of enmity, and the second as marking the sphere of its development. It is lodged in the mind, but it embodies itself in deeds; and those deeds are "wicked," are in harmony with the source of activity. The apostle charges them not merely with spiritual and latent hostility to God, but with the manifestation of that hostility in open acts of unnatural rebellion. It is not a neutral alienation, but one characterized by positive enmity. The charge may be easily substantiated. No thoughts are more unwelcome to men, none less frequently in their mind, than God. Men may like an ideal God of their own creation, such an one as themselves have invested with a fictitious divinity, but the God of the gospel stirs up opposition; His holiness alarms them; and their heart is filled with prejudice against His scheme of salvation, because it so humbles the creature by pressing on him as a ruined and helpless sinner a gratuitous pardon which he could never win; and because, in urging him to the possession of holiness, it necessitates a total revolution in all his habits and desires. It is a melancholy indictment: antagonism to infinite purity and love: sins committed in violation of a law "holy, and just, and good." It was true of the heathen world, and it is true generally of fallen humanity, that there is alienation, that such alienation creates enmity, and that this enmity proves its virulence and disloyalty in repeated transgressions.[1] Some of the Fathers, such as Tertullian, Ambrose, and Jerome, following an unwarranted reading found in D^1, E^1, *τῆς διανοίας αὐτοῦ*, render—enemies to His, that is, God's mind.

Νυνὶ δὲ ἀποκατήλλαξεν. This reading of the verb has the high authority of A, C, D^{111}, E, J, K, almost all the Versions,

[1] As Photius says, they were enemies, for they were seen—*τὰ ἐχθρῶν πράττοντες* Apud Œcumen. *in loc.*

and many of the Fathers. Codex B has ἀποκατηλλάγητε, a form which Lachmann follows; while D[1], F, G, and some of the Latin Fathers, have the participle ἀποκαταλλαγέντες. The peculiarity of construction has apparently given rise to these various lections, but the Textus Receptus is best supported. The order adopted by Lachmann gives us this connection —"It pleased God that in Him should all fulness dwell, and that He should reconcile all things to Himself; and even you, once aliens and enemies (but ye are now reconciled), even you it pleased Him to present, holy and perfect, before Him." The same parenthetical connection might be maintained by keeping the verb in the active. Or the first clause may form a pendant to the preceding verse—"It pleased Him to reconcile all things to Himself, and you too, though ye were enemies in your mind by wicked works." But these forms of construction are intricate and needless. We prefer beginning a new sentence with καὶ ὑμᾶς ποτέ, and then παραστῆσαι, in the following verse, becomes the infinitive of design. Nor do we perceive any grounds for changing the nominative, God being still the subject, as is the view of Zanchius, Bengel, Bähr, Boehmer, Huther, Meyer, against that of the Greek Fathers, with Beza, Calvin, Crocius, Estius, Heinrichs, and De Wette, which refers the nominative to Christ. The work of reconciliation is God's. Man does not win his way back to the Divine favour by either costly offering or profound penitence. God reunites him to Himself; has not only provided for such an alliance, but actually forms and cements it.

The apostle has dwelt at length on the dignity and majesty of Jesus, but without hesitation he speaks here of His incarnate state, for in Him there was a union of extremes, of God and man—of earth and heaven. Indeed, the incarnation, rightly understood, enhances the Redeemer's greatness. The spiritually sublime is truly seen in His condescension and death. So, he adds—

(Ver. 22.) Ἐν τῷ σώματι τῆς σαρκὸς αὐτοῦ διὰ τοῦ θανάτου —"In the body of His (Christ's) flesh through death." Sirach xxiii. 16. The clause has a remarkable distinctness. Reconciliation is effected in His body; that body is a genuine physical frame, for it is the body of His flesh; and there was an actual decease, as by His death peace was secured. They were reconciled in His body and by His death, a difference of relation being indicated by the prepositions ἐν and διά; the latter pointing out the instrumental cause, and the former describing the inner sphere of uniting operation which preceded that death. Without that fleshly body there could have been no death, and the assumption of humanity brought Jesus into a fraternal relationship with all His people. The apostle thus cautions against a spurious spiritualism, which seems to have endangered the Colossian church—as if without an atonement man could be redeemed. Marcion, in his quotation of the verse, omitted the words τῆς σαρκός.

We need not say, with Bengel, Schrader, and Olshausen, that the apostle writes "the body of His flesh," lest any one should imagine that He might mean His body, the church;[1] nor need we suppose, with Beza, Huther, Böhmer, and Steiger, that there is an express polemical reference to Doketism, or the denial of a real humanity to our Lord, though the germs of such a heresy might be in existence. Jerome, in one of his letters to Pammachius, says of the apostle and the language of this verse — *apostolus volens corpus Christi carneum et non spirituale, aëreum, tenue, demonstrare.* There is no such emphasis in the phrase as Estius and Grotius find when they speak of such vast results flowing from so feeble an instrument, nor is there that contrast between the earthly and glorified body of Christ as is suggested by Flatt, Röell, and von Gerlach. The purpose of reconciliation is next described.

Παραστῆσαι ὑμᾶς ἁγίους καὶ ἀμώμους καὶ ἀνεγκλήτους κατενώπιον αὐτοῦ.—"To present you holy and blameless, and unreproveable before Him." This is the infinitive of design. Winer, § 44, 1; Matthiae, ii. p. 1234. [Eph. i. 3.] The three adjectives express generally the same idea, but in different and consecutive aspects. [*Ἁγίους καὶ ἀμώμους κατενώπιον αὐτοῦ*, Eph. i. 4.] There is no ground for the hypothesis of Bähr and Bengel, that the three epithets may be thus characterized—the first as having reference to God, the second to ourselves, and the third to our fellow-men. The first term refers to inner

[1] Yet Pierce inclines to such a notion, though he says, "I am not positive in this interpretation."

consecration, and the purity which it creates and fosters; the second shows the development of this purity in the life; and the third expresses the result, that heart and life are therefore alike unchallengeable, and that neither against the one nor the other can any charge be preferred. It cannot be alleged against the life that its holiness is but hypocrisy, since that has its root in the sanctified spirit; neither can the sanctity of the heart be arraigned as inoperative and dead, for it exhibits itself in actions of heavenly worth and resemblance. God presents them before Himself, not before Christ, as Meyer supposes, ἑαυτοῦ not being required. This we take to be the connection, though some connect the words *κατενώπιον αὐτοῦ* with the three epithets, as if it described their genuineness or reality. Such is the connection in Eph. i. 4, but here the phrase seems most naturally connected with the verb—to present before Him. The allusion is to the ultimate consummation: to no period on earth, but to final acceptance before the throne—when the saint shall have come to maturity, and his spiritual development shall have been crowned and perfected. [Eph. v. 27.] The question has been raised, whether the apostle refers, in this last clause, to the righteousness of justification, or the holiness of sanctification; to *justitia imputata*, as Huther supposes; or to *justitia inhaerens*, as Chrysostom, Theophylact, and Calvin maintain; or to both, as is held by Theodoret, Zanchius, Crocius, Calovius, De Wette, and Meyer. [Eph. i. 4.] Besides that the terms employed by the apostle are inapplicable to justifying righteousness, it may be remarked that the reconciliation which the apostle represents as having already taken place is but another form of expressing the blessing of justification—pardon, and acceptance with God. This privilege was past, but the ultimate result which flows from it was still to come. Therefore, as this change of state is only a prelude to a change of character—as this justification is a step towards such an end, it follows that the holiness realized in that end is that of sanctification, the maturity of which is acknowledged in the presentation of the saint to God. 1 Cor. i. 8; 1 Thess. iii. 13, v. 23.

(Ver. 23.) *Εἴ γε ἐπιμένετε τῇ πίστει τεθεμελιωμένοι καὶ ἑδραῖοι, καὶ μὴ μετακινούμενοι ἀπὸ τῆς ἐλπίδος τοῦ εὐαγγελίου* οὗ ἠκούσατε[1]—"If ye continue in the faith, grounded and fast, and not moved away from the hope of the gospel which ye have heard." The clause depends, not, as Bengel intimates, on ἀποκατήλλαξεν, but on the nearer verb παραστῆσαι. The attainment of spiritual perfection, and the honour of presentation to God, are dependent on the fact specified in this verse. Εἴγε does not imply doubt [Eph. iii. 2], and so far differs from εἴπερ, but there is no reason to render it, with Pierce, "because." "If, as is the case, ye continue in the faith;" for τῇ πίστει is connected with ἐπιμένετε, as in Rom. vi. 1, xi. 23, 1 Tim. iv. 16;[2] whereas τεθεμελ. would require ἐπί, as in Matt vii. 25, or ἐν, as in Eph. iii. 18. Continuance in the faith is essential to salvation: loss of faith would be forfeiture of life. The blessings of Christianity are given without interruption only to continuous belief. And that perpetuity of faith was not to be a vibratory and superficial state. They were to remain in the faith, or saving belief of the truth, ἑδραῖοι καὶ τεθεμελιωμένοι—"grounded and settled." [Eph. iii. 18.] 1 Pet. v. 10; 1 Cor. vii. 37, xv. 58. The first epithet alludes to the cause, and the second to its effect, for what is founded becomes fixed: while the third clause depicts a general result—καὶ μὴ μετακινούμενοι, "and therefore not shaken away," as the use of μή seems to indicate. The adverb μή has such a connection of dependence, Kühner, § 708; Hartung, ii. pp. 113, 114; Winer, § 55, 1, a. If they were founded, they were fixed, and if both they could not be moved—ἀπὸ τῆς ἐλπίδος τοῦ εὐαγγελίου οὗ ἠκούσατε. [Eph. i. 18.] See also verse fifth of this chapter. The hope is that blessed life revealed by the gospel as its distinctive prospect. That gospel is further characterized as "having been preached to every creature which is under heaven"—

Τοῦ κηρυχθέντος ἐν πάσῃ κτίσει τῇ ὑπὸ τὸν οὐρανόν. The article τῇ before πάσῃ is probably to be expunged, on the authority of A, B, C, D[1], F, G. The general meaning of this hyperbole will be found under verse 6. Thomas Aquinas was so hard pressed[3] as to propose a future rendering—*praedica-*

[1] Ἠκούσατε is spelt, by an oversight, with a spiritus asper in Tischendorf's second edition.

[2] Aelian, *Hist. var.* x. 15. Joseph. *Antiq.* viii. 7, 5.

[3] *De Praescrip. Haer.* iii. vol. ii. p. 5, Opera, ed. Oehler, 1754.

bitur. Perhaps, as Meyer proposes, these words are a species of confirmation. Apostasy was all the more blameable, for they had *heard* the gospel—a gospel of no *narrow* diffusion and value—a gospel, also, which numbered among its adherents and preachers, the great *name* of Paul. There is thus a warning in these words of coming danger and seductive influence. It is an extraordinary reason which Anselm, after Gregory, proposes—that every creature must mean man, because man has something in common with every creature; existence with stones, living growth with trees, sense and motion with the lower animals, and reason and intellect with the angels.

Thus a life of faith is one of hope, and leads to glory. This belief has a conservative power; for it keeps in a justified state, and it secures augmenting holiness. While, therefore, the perseverance of the saints is a prominent doctrine of Scripture, and a perennial source of consolation, it is inconsistent with exhortations to permanence of faith, and not warnings of the sad results of deviation and apostasy. He who stops short in the race, and does not reach the goal, cannot obtain the prize. He who abandons the refuge into which he fled for a season, is swept away when the hurricane breaks upon him. The loss of faith is the knell of hope. "There is a way to hell even from the gate of heaven." As Tertullian says: "While the straws of light faith fly away, the mass of corn is laid up the purer in the garden of God." For man is not acted on mechanically by the grace of God, but his whole spiritual nature is excited to earnest prayer and anxious effort. Its continuance in the faith is not the unconscious impress of an irresistible law, but the result of a diligent use of every means by which belief may be fostered and deepened. The fact that God keeps believers makes them, therefore, distrustful of themselves and dependent upon Him. And the confidence of success inspirits them. "Many a man, from having been persuaded that he is destined to attain some great object, instead of being lulled into carelessness by this belief, has been excited to the most laborious and unwearied efforts, such as perhaps, otherwise, he would not have thought of making for the attainment of his object."[1] Thus, as rational

[1] Whately, quoted in Wood's *Theology*, iii. 238.

beings are wrought upon by motives, so warnings and appeals are addressed to them, and these appliances form a special feature of God's plan of preserving them. The apostle thus shows them how much is suspended on their perseverance.

Οὗ ἐγενόμην ἐγὼ Παῦλος διάκονος—"Of which I Paul was constituted a minister." [Eph. iii. 7.] The apostle reverts to his solemn inauguration, his past course of active service, and the authority under which he had acted. This brief and distinct intimation forms a special introduction to the second section of the epistle, and the warning against seduction by false teachers.

(Ver. 24.) *Νῦν χαίρω ἐν τοῖς παθήμασιν ὑπὲρ ὑμῶν*—"Now I rejoice in my sufferings for you." The MSS. D[1], E[1], F, G, with the Vulgate, and many of the Latin Fathers, prefix *ὅς*. The reading probably arose from a homoioteleuton or repetition of the last syllable of the previous word—*διάκον ος ὅς*. *Νῦν* is not a particle of transition, as Bähr and Lücke[1] make it, but means "at the present time;" with the chain upon my wrist, I rejoice; not, however, as if he had been sorrowful at a previous period. The apostle felt that his sufferings had their source in his diaconate, and therefore he gloried in them. The simple dative, or a participial nominative, is more frequently used to express the cause of joy; the preposition *ἐπί* sometimes employed, and occasionally *ἐν*, as in Phil i. 18, Luke x. 20, and in the clause before us. To rejoice in them is not very different from to rejoice over, or upon, or for them, only, that in the latter case, the afflictions are regarded as external causes of joy, whereas, in the former case, the writer represents himself as immersed in them, and rejoicing in them. The Stephanic Text adds *μου* after *παθήμασιν*, but on no great authority. The words *ὑπὲρ ὑμῶν*, which we connect with *ἐν παθ.* and not with *χαίρω*, have been variously interpreted. They cannot mean "in your stead," though Steiger adopts such a view; and yet in some sense Paul might be regarded as the representative of the churches in heathendom. Nor can the words mean, on the other hand, merely "for your good," as Meyer, De Wette, and Huther suppose; or as Œcumenius gives it, *ἵνα ὑμᾶς ὠφελῆσαι δυνηθῶ*, for this was

[1] *Programm*, 1833.

an ultimate effect, and not the immediate cause of the apostle's sufferings. We prefer, with Heinrichs and Stolz, the ordinary sense of "on your account," as we may suppose the apostle to refer especially to the Gentile portion of the church. His preaching to the Gentiles was the real and proximate cause of his incarceration. He had, in Jerusalem, declared his mission to the Gentiles, but the mob broke upon him in fury. He was confined for safety, and having on his trial appealed to Cæsar, he was carried to Rome, and pending the investigation kept a prisoner there. Paul does sometimes refer to the good results of his sufferings, as in Phil. i. 12, but he here alludes to the cause of them.

Καὶ ἀνταναπληρῶ τὰ ὑστερήματα τῶν θλίψεων τοῦ Χριστοῦ—"And fill up what is wanting of the afflictions of Christ." *Καί* is simply connective, not ἀλλά, as Bengel imagines; nor καὶ γάρ, as Bähr explains it. It does not render a reason, as Calvin supposes, but simply begins an explanatory statement. This is peculiar language, and its peculiarity has given rise to many forms of exegesis. Chrysostom says:—"It appears a great thing which he utters, but not one of arrogance"—ἀλλ' οὐκ ἀπονοίας. The noun ὑστέρημα denotes what is yet lacking, 1 Cor. xvi. 17, 1 Thess. iii. 10, Phil. ii. 30; and is rendered by Theodoret λειπόμενον; and θλῖψις is pressure from evil, violent suffering. The general sense of the verb is to fill up; and the question is, in what sense did the apostle fill up what was wanting of the sufferings of Christ?

1. Many of the mediæval Catholic interpreters understood the clause as referring to the atonement, and that its defects may be supplied by the sufferings of the saints. This was a proof-text for the doctrine of indulgences which Bellarmine, Cajetan, Salmeron, Suarez, the Rhemish annotators, and others, laid hold of, as if the merits of Paul's sufferings supplemented those of Christ, and were to be dispensed so as to procure the remission of penalty. This inference, which a-Lapide characterizes as *non male*, is in direct antagonism to the whole tenor of Scripture, which represents the sacrifice of Jesus as perfect in obedience and suffering, so perfect as to need neither supplement nor repetition.

2. Not a few get rid of the difficulty by giving the genitive

Χριστοῦ an unwonted and unwarrantable meaning, and rendering the phrase—"sufferings on account of Christ." The idea may be in itself a correct one, but it is not the shade of idea which the genitive expresses. This exegesis is supported by Tertullian, Schoettgen, Elsner, Storr, Pierce, Rosenmüller, Flatt, Böhmer, Burton, and Trollope, but it cannot be grammatically defended.

3. Calovius, Carpzovius, and Seb. Schmid, understand the phrase as signifying "sufferings meted out to His people by Christ;" a meaning not very different from that adopted by Lücke—*afflictiones, quae Paulo apostolo, Christo auctore et auspice Christo, perferendae erant.* This mode of explanation does not fix upon the pointed meaning of the genitive, which, when following *θλῖψις*, denotes the suffering person; Eph. iii. 13; 2 Cor. i. 4; Jas. i. 27.

4. Yet more remote is the view of Photius, adopted by Junker and Heinrichs, that the clause denotes such sufferings as Christ would have endured, had He remained longer on the earth. The words of Photius are—*ἀλλ' ὅσα . . . ἔπαθεν ἂν καὶ ὑπέστη, καθ' ὃν τρόπον καὶ πρὶν κηρύσσων καὶ εὐαγγελιζόμενος τὴν βασιλείαν τῶν οὐρανῶν.*[1]

5. Some able and accomplished scholars take this view—that the sufferings of Paul are styled by him the afflictions of Christ, because they were similar in nature. Such is the view of Theodoret, Meyer, Schleiermacher, Huther, and Winer. Fergusson says—"the great wave of affliction did first beat on Him, and being thereby broken, some small sparks of it only do light upon us." The idea is a striking one, yet it is not universally true. The distinctive element in Christ's sufferings had and could have no parallel in those of the apostle—to wit, vicarious agony: Divine infliction and desertion—endurance of penalty to free others from bearing it. There were general points of similarity, indeed, between the sufferings of Christ and those of the apostle, so that he might, though at an awful distance, compare his afflictions to those of his Divine Master. Both suffered at the hand of man, and both suffered in innocence. Rom. viii. 17; 1 Pet. iv. 13. But though such a thought may occur in other parts of Scripture, it does not occur in connection with such

[1] *Amphilochia*, 143.

phraseology as is found in the clause before us. An apostle may say that he endures afflictions like those of Christ; but here Paul says that he supplements the afflictions of Christ. There is an idea in the phrase above and beyond that of mere similarity. Similarity is not of itself supplement, nor does it of necessity imply it.

And thus, in the last place, we are brought to the common interpretation—that these sufferings are named the afflictions of Christ because He really endured them; they were His, for He really felt them. The genitive is naturally that of possession. Such is the view of Chrysostom and Theophylact, Augustine and Anselm, of Calvin and Beza, Luther and Melancthon, Zanchius and Grotius, Vitringa[1] and Michaelis, of Bähr and Steiger, of the Catholics Estius and a-Lapide, Davenant, Whitby, Conybeare, Doddridge, De Wette and Olshausen. Thus, Augustine on Ps. lxi. exclaims of Christ—*qui passus est in capite nostro et patitur in membris suis, id est nobis ipsis.* And Leo, quoted by Böhmer, says—*passio Christi perducitur ad finem mundi, in omnibus qui pro justitia adversa tolerant, ipse compatitur.* Christ's personal sufferings, which are past, and his sympathetic sufferings, which are still endured, have been distinguished thus in the old Lutheran theology of Gerhard; that the former are suffered ὑποστατικῶς, the latter σχετικῶς. The Rabbins, in their special dialect, attached a similar meaning to the phrase חבלי משיח[2]—sufferings of Messiah—distributing them through various generations. The church is in the next clause called the body of Christ: and the Head suffers in all His members. The apostle's sufferings were those of Christ, for Christ is identified with all His people. The scene of the apostle's conversion impressed this truth upon his mind too deeply ever to be forgotten by him: the startling challenge yet rang in his ear—"Saul, Saul, why persecutest thou me?" The Redeemer was one with the poor flock at Damascus, so soon, in Saul's imagination, to be "scattered and peeled;" for the errand of blood was directed against Him as really as against them. On the other hand, but in accordance with this truth, apostates who resile from their profession, and virtually proclaim that they have discovered faith in Christ to be a dream and a delusion, are said

[1] *Observat. Sacrae*, p. 144. [2] Buxtorf, *Lex. Tal.* p. 700.

to "crucify to themselves the Son of God afresh, and put Him to an open shame." Again, in 2 Cor. i. 5, the apostle says —"The sufferings of Christ abound in us," that is, sufferings endured by Christ in us; and therefore, such being the sympathetic affinity between us, our consolation also aboundeth by Christ.[1] Again, in Heb. xiii. 13, Christians are exhorted to "go forth unto Him without the camp, bearing His reproach;" not reproach on His account, but the reproach which is His, and which He still bears in us, through our living connection with Him. 2 Cor. ii. 10. Nay, more, we are informed in Heb. xi. 26, that Moses esteemed "the reproach of Christ greater riches than the treasures in Egypt." Now, according to the Old Testament, the God of the theocracy, the Jehovah of the burning bush, the Angel of the covenant, is none other than He who became incarnate; so that, while Moses, as His representative, incurred special and ungrateful obloquy, that obloquy is termed the reproach of Christ, of Him who sent him, and who was personated by him. And there is ample foundation laid for the language before us in our Lord's pathetic and solemn discourse, recorded in Mathew, in which He declares His oneness with His people, that He lives in them, endures in them the pangs of hunger and thirst, and in them is fed and refreshed, is shut up when they are imprisoned, and welcomes the step of benevolence—is conscious, with them, when they are in a foreign land, of the desolation and solitude of a stranger, and is thankful for the shelter and fellowship of hospitality—feels the shame of their nakedness when they are bereft of clothing, and accepts with joy the proffered gift of a compassionate friend—suffers in them in their sickness, and enjoys a kind look and deed.

The personal sufferings of Jesus are over, but His sufferings in His people still continue. They are still defective; for much remains to be endured in this world. The apostle, in suffering for the sake of the church, felt that he was filling up the measure of those afflictions.

The double compound verb ἀνταναπληρῶ denotes "to fill up in relation to." Some, like Olshausen[2] and Elsner, lay no peculiar stress on the preposition; but we cannot suppose

[1] Alford, *in loc.*

[2] Fischer, *Animadver. ad Welleri Gram.* p. 369.

it to be used without some special purpose. The verb ἀναπληρῶ has a simple sense, but ἀνταναπληρῶ has a relative one. What the relation is, has been disputed. Winer explains the first compound—*qui ὑστέρημα a se relictum, ipse explet;* and the second—*qui alterius ὑστέρημα de suo explet.* Robinson and Schrader give ἀντί a reference to the Colossians—who "in your room fill up;" while Fritzsche, in a note under Rom. xv. 19, suggests the notion of accumulation—*in malis perferendis aemulans.* Some give the first preposition the sense of *vicissim*—"in turn," as is done by E. Schmid, Beza, Macknight, and Le Clerc,[1] who render—*ille ego qui olim ecclesiam Christi vexaveram, nunc vicissim in ejus utilitatem pergo multa mala perpeti.* Others, as Œcumenius, give it the sense of equivalent repayment for the sufferings which Jesus endured for us; or, as Gerhard has it, quoted in Bähr—"as Christ suffered for my redemption, it is but fitting that I should, in my turn, *vicissim,* suffer for the advancement of His glory." This view is also held by Bähr, Böhmer, and Tittmann.[2] We cannot adopt this view, for we do not see it fully sustained by the passages adduced in support of it. The passages from Dio Cassius, Apollonius Alexandrinus, and Demosthenes, do not bear it out; for in them the ἀντί of the verb may bear an objective sense—may denote the correspondence between the supplement and the defect. So Conybeare, in the passage before us—"the ἀντί is introduced into ἀνταναπληρῶ, by the antithesis between the notions of πληροῦσθαι and ὑστερεῖσθαι." Meyer's view is similar, and it is, we believe, the correct one. The verb denotes to fill up with something which meets the exigence, or is equivalent to the want. The apostle filled up the sufferings of Christ not with some foreign agony that had no *relation* to the defect; but the process of supplement consisted of sufferings which met the deficiency, in quality and amount. It was not a piece of new cloth on an old garment, or new wine in old bottles—an antagonism which would have happened had Paul suffered "as a murderer, or as a thief, or as an evil-doer, or as a busybody in other men's matters;" but the apostle filled up what was yet wanting in the Saviour's sympathetic sorrows, for he adds, they were endured—

[1] *Ars. Crit.* p. 134, London, 1698. [2] *De Synon.* p. 230.

Ἐν τῇ σαρκί μου ὑπὲρ τοῦ σώματος αὐτοῦ—"In my flesh for his body's sake." Storr, Bähr, Böhmer, Steiger, and Huther, connect the first clause with *τῶν θλίψεων τοῦ Χ.*—sufferings which are in my flesh. But more naturally, with Meyer and De Wette, we join the words to the verb, and believe them to represent the mode or circumstances in which the apostle filled up what was left of the afflictions of Christ. It was in his present fleshly state, and as a suffering man. 2 Cor. iv. 11; Gal. iv. 14. The next clause points out the cause of suffering—"for his body's sake;" and this fact gave his sufferings their mysterious and supplemental value. Suffering for His body, implies the fellow-suffering of the Head. Steiger and Lücke's connection—"sufferings of Christ for His body's sake"—is wholly against the spirit of the interpretation. [*Τοῦ σώματος αὐτοῦ ὅ ἐστιν ἡ ἐκκλησία.* Eph. i. 23.]

(Ver. 25.) *Ἧς ἐγενόμην ἐγὼ διάκονος*—"Of which church I was made a minister." [*Διάκονος*, Eph. iii. 7.] In the passage in the Epistle to the Ephesians, the apostle speaks of his diaconate in reference to the gospel; but here in connection with the church. And truly the church never had such a servant as Paul—of such industry and heroism—such enthusiasm and perseverance—such sufferings and travels—such opposition and success. He had no leisure even when in chains. The artistic beauties of Athens served but to give point to his orations; and the Prætorium at Rome furnished him with occasion to describe the armour and weapons of the sacramental host of God's elect. His service stands out in superlative eminence, whether you measure it by the miles he journeyed, by the sermons he preached, by the stripes and stonings he endured, by the privations he encountered,—"in hunger and thirst, in cold and nakedness," and by the shipwrecks he suffered, or by the souls he converted, the churches he planted or watered, the epistles he wrote, and the death which crowned a life of such earnestness and triumph.

Κατὰ τὴν οἰκονομίαν τοῦ Θεοῦ, τὴν δοθεῖσάν μοι εἰς ὑμᾶς—"According to the dispensation of God committed to me for you." [*Οἰκονομία*, etc., Eph. i. 10, iii. 2.] In the Divine arrangement of the spiritual house, the apostle held a function which had special reference to the members of the Gentile churches. Paul regarded this as his distinctive office, and how he gloried in it! It had a breadth which suited his mighty mind, and it necessitated the preaching of an unconditioned gospel, which specially delighted his ample heart. He would not be confined within the narrow circuit of Judaism; the field on which his soul set itself was the world.

Πληρῶσαι τὸν λόγον τοῦ Θεοῦ—"To fulfil the word of God." Rom. xv. 19. The meaning is not altered, whether you connect these words with the first or second clause of the verse, either—"of which I was made a servant, to fulfil the word of God," or—"according to the dispensation given in charge to me, to fulfil the word of God." The last is the more natural, and is in accordance with the usual style of the apostle. In either case *πληρῶσαι* is the infinitive of design. The verb has various meanings in the New Testament, and has therefore been variously understood here.

Vitringa,[1] as was natural to such a Hebraist, seeks the meaning of the term from Jewish usage, and compares *πληρόω* to גָּמַר, which signified to teach. Flatt and Bähr follow him in their exegesis; but such a method has no warrant, and we are not forced to it by the impossibility of discovering another. Cornelius a-Lapide ekes out a meaning in this way—to fulfil what Christ began; Steiger, following Tholuck,[2] adopts the subjective idea—to realize and experience its fulness. One class of interpreters, represented by Calixtus and Heinrichs, apply it to the fulfilment of the Divine promises and prophecies of the admission of Gentiles into the church; and another class, headed by Theodoret, regard the clause as pointing out the diffusion of the gospel—the filling of all places with its preaching. Calvin takes the special idea of fulfilling or giving effect to the gospel—*ut efficax sit Dei sermo*, virtually the interpretation of some of the Greek Fathers; while Luther renders *reichlich predigen*, to preach fully—a notion adopted by Olshausen, that is, to declare the gospel in all its fulness and extent. Fritzsche has a conjecture of his own—that the apostle uses this term as if his instructions were a supplementary continuation of those of

[1] *Observat.* i. p. 207. [2] *Berg-pred.* p. 135.

their teacher Epaphras;[1] and De Wette, by a metonymy, regards the gospel as a service or decree which Paul wrought out, a notion also held by some of the Lexicographers. In assigning a meaning to the verb, much depends on the signification given to the noun. Now, we regard the following verse as explanatory—the λόγος being the mystery hid from ages and generations—not the gospel in itself, but that gospel in its adaptation to the Gentiles, and its reception by them. The apostle says of himself that he did not preach, but that he *fulfilled the gospel.* He carried out its design—held it up as the balm of the world—proclaimed it without distinction of blood or race. He did not narrow its purpose, or confine it to a limited sphere of influence; but, as the apostle of the Gentiles, he opened for it a sweep and circuit adapted to its magnificence of aim, and its universality of fitness and sufficiency. He carried it beyond the frontiers of Judæa, lifted it above the walls of the synagogue, and held it up to the nations. The gospel, since the apostle's time, has received no fuller expansion, nor have any wider susceptibilities been detected or developed in it. As an instrument of human regeneration, he brought it to perfection. Whether you regard the purpose of its author, its own genius or adequacy, its unlimited offers, indiscriminate invitations, and tested efficacy; the apostle, in preaching it everywhere, and to all classes without reserve, laboured "to fulfil the word of God." Luke vii. 1, ix. 31; Acts xiii. 25, xiv. 26.

(Ver. 26.) *Τὸ μυστήριον τὸ ἀποκεκρυμμένον ἀπὸ τῶν αἰώνων καὶ ἀπὸ τῶν γενεῶν, νυνὶ δὲ ἐφανερώθη τοῖς ἁγίοις αὐτοῦ.* This verse, as we have said, defines what is meant by the "word" which Paul fulfilled. The meaning of "the mystery hid from ages and from generations," has been explained under Eph. iii. 3, 6. [*μυστήριον,* Eph. i. 9, *αἰών, γενεά,* Eph. iii. 9, 21.] *Αἰών* is age or lifetime, and *γενεά* is the space of one generation. In all past time, this mystery was concealed. The apostle does not say, as has been remarked—*πρὸ τῶν αἰώνων,* as if the mystery had been hidden from eternity; but only that it was wrapt in obscurity during the entire past historical epoch. It is a strange conceit of Bengel—*Aeones referuntur ad angelos, generationes ad homines.* The mystery

[1] *Comment. in Ep. ad Rom.* vol. iii. 257.

is not the gospel generally, as Calvin and Davenant erroneously suppose; but the preaching of it to the Gentiles, and their incorporation into the church, or, as the apostle here describes it—"Christ in you, the hope of glory." Nay, so little was it understood, that it required a special revelation to make it known to the reluctant mind of the Apostle Peter.

In the next clause the syntax is changed, and therefore, as might naturally be expected, we find various readings devised to amend the grammar, such as *φανερωθέν* in D and E, and *ὃ νῦν ἐφανερώθη* in other Codices. The participial construction is suddenly departed from, and the verb is employed. The anacoluthon gives a sharpness to the contrast. Winer, § 64; Bernhardy, p. 473. [Eph. i. 20.] The adverb *νυνί*, supported by A, D, E, J, K, is the strengthened form of *νῦν*, Buttmann, § 80; and *δέ* points out the contrast. The verb employed to denote the disclosure of a mystery is *ἀποκαλύπτω* in Eph. iii. 5; but this verb occurs in a similar connection, Rom. xvi. 26; Tit. i. 3; Mark iv. 22. The word denotes manifestation by Divine power, as the inspired history so plainly relates. But what is meant by *τοῖς ἁγίοις*? Because the apostle, in the parallel passage in the Epistle to the Ephesians, adds *ἀποστόλοις καὶ προφήταις*, many think that the same addition is to be understood here. Such is the view of Theodoret, Estius, Bähr, Böhmer, Steiger, Olshausen, and others. F, G, add, without warrant, *ἀποστόλοις* to the text. There is no reason to depart from the meaning which the epithet bears in the first verse of the epistle; and so Chrysostom, Calvin, Meyer, and De Wette rightly take it.

(Ver. 27.) *Οἷς ἠθέλησεν ὁ Θεὸς γνωρίσαι, τίς ὁ πλοῦτος τῆς δόξης τοῦ μυστηρίου τούτου ἐν τοῖς ἔθνεσιν*—"To whom," or, as being persons, "to whom God wished to make known what are the riches of the glory of this mystery among the Gentiles." Some suppose that *γνωρίσαι* has a broader and more definite meaning than *ἐφανερώθη*, though without good foundation. [*γνωρίσαι*, Eph. i. 9.] It is wrong on the part of many expositors to press a theological meaning upon the verb *ἠθέλησεν*, as if it contained a special reference to free grace. It merely intimates that the Divine intention was not necessitated, and that it was God's pleasure to instruct His people in the full bearings and adaptation of the gospel. The saints did not discover the mystery: the development of Christianity sprang neither from their philanthropy nor their ingenuity, but it was God who unfolded the mystery in all wisdom and prudence. The apostle now illustrates the character of the disclosure—*τί τὸ πλοῦτος τῆς δόξης* (for such seems to be the preferable reading)—"what is the wealth of the glory" of this mystery. There is no ground for resolving the phrase into a Hebraism, and rendering it with Chrysostom, *πολλὴ δόξα*; nor with Erasmus, *gloriosa opulentia;* or with Beza and Davenant, *gloriosae divitiae.* [Eph. i. 6.] Both terms, *πλοῦτος* and *δόξα*, are favourites of the apostle, and are employed to represent what is bright, substantial, and permanent. That mystery is enveloped in glory, and that glory has at once a solid basis and an unfading lustre. It is no halo which glimmers and disappears—no gilding which is easily effaced; but it is rich, having the weight, value, and brilliancy of gold. There is no authority for rendering, with Vatablus and Heinrichs, the interrogative by *quantus.* And that such wealth of glory may be appreciated, the apostle adds, in explanation—

Ὅς ἐστιν Χριστὸς ἐν ὑμῖν, ἡ ἐλπὶς τῆς δόξης—"Which is Christ in you, the hope of glory." There are various readings —the neuter *ὅ* being found in A, B, F, G, the Vulgate, and Latin Fathers—a reading suggested by the gender of the preceding noun. The masculine is preferable — the gender being caused by that of the following substantive *Χριστός.* Winer, § 24; Kühner, § 786, 3; Mark xv. 16; Gal. iii. 16. The meaning depends very much on precision of view as to the antecedent. It is not *μυστήριον*, as Chrysostom, a-Lapide, Kistmacher, Junker, and others suppose—a supposition which yields but a bald interpretation; for it is not the mystery in itself, but the wealth of the glory of the mystery which God had disclosed to the saints. It is not the fact that Christ was among the Gentiles, but the character and relations of that fact that the apostle dwells on. Nor is the antecedent merely *πλοῦτος*, as many maintain, among whom are Theodoret and Œcumenius, Meyer and Böhmer; nor simply *δόξα*, as Schmid holds; for the reference is not to the riches of the glory by themselves, but to those riches possessed and enjoyed by the Gentile converts. The one idea is at the same time involved in the other; the glory is not an abstraction, for it resides in the mystery, and the mystery cannot appear in nakedness, for it always exhibits this pure and imperishable lustre. The antecedent is rather the complex idea of the entire clause—not Christ in Himself, but in His novel and gracious relation to the Gentile world, as a developed and illustrious mystery. The term Christ is not to be explained away, as if it merely meant the doctrine of Christ, as is proved by the subsequent clause—"whom we preach." The words ἐν ὑμῖν are rendered by many "among you," that is, in the midst of you, as in the preceding clause and in the margin of our English Bibles. But the meaning "in you" is virtually implied; for Christ, as the hope of glory, was not contemplated merely, but possessed. He was not merely before them to be beheld, but in them to be felt. Pierce and Macknight render, loosely and incorrectly—Christ to you the hope of glory. This frequent allusion to the Redeemer by name—to His power and work, as the Divine source of blessing, seems to have had a reference to the views of some among the Colossians, who would have had a church without a Christ and salvation without a Saviour.

The clause ἡ ἐλπὶς τῆς δόξης is in apposition with Χριστός. It is out of all rule, on the part of Erasmus, Menochius, and others, apparently following Theophylact, to render τῆς δόξης by the adjective ἔνδοξος. Nor is this glory simply that of God, nor is it the moral worth and dignity of Christians, nor yet the glory obtained in disclosing the mystery. The "glory" is the future blessedness of believers, as in Rom. ii. 7, 10, viii. 18; 1 Cor. ii. 7; 2 Cor. iv. 17; 1 Thess. ii. 12; Heb. ii. 10; Rom. v. 2. The noun ἐλπίς is not hope as an emotion, but the foundation of it, as in 1 Tim. i. 1, and it is followed by the genitive of the thing hoped for, or the object of hope. The clause is well explained by Theophylact—διότι δι' αὐτοῦ ἐλπίζομεν τῆς δόξης τυχεῖν αἰωνίου. The life of glory rests on Christ as its author and basis—such is the blessed statement of the apostle. Let us pause for a moment over this glory, and its connection with Christ, and then we shall be able to know with the saints—"what are the riches of the glory of this mystery among the Gentiles."

The glory of Christians is yet to come, but it is certain. What they so earnestly pray for, and so heartily long and labour for, shall be revealed over and beyond their anticipations. Deliverance from all evil is followed by introduction into all good. What is partially and progressively enjoyed in time, is fully and for ever possessed in heaven. The spirit in its present feebleness would bow and faint beneath the pressure of it, nay, it might die in delirious agony; but then it shall have power and stateliness not only to bear, but to enjoy the "far more exceeding and eternal weight of glory." Now, no man can see Him and live—our frail humanity would be consumed by the terrible vision; but the saint is prepared to gaze with unmingled rapture on His majesty, and to live, walk, and be happy in its lustre. The mind shall be filled with light from the face of God, and the heart shall pulsate with love in eternal and undivided empire. The image of God, in all its loveliness and brilliance, shall be restored to every heart, and that heart shall enjoy uninterrupted fellowship with Him who sits upon the throne. Nothing can happen to mar or modify this communion; for though an angel were to pass between him and the throne, he could cast no shadow upon the rapt and adoring saint. Every man shall be as perfect as Christ—in soul, body, and spirit, and beyond the possibility of forfeit or relapse. The burden of sin is removed, and to the sense of oppression there shall succeed the consciousness of spiritual buoyancy and elevation; the taint of depravity is wiped away, and the joy of salvation shall mingle its aromatic fragrance with the "new wine" in the kingdom of our Father. The body, too, shall be raised an ethereal vehicle, no longer the prey of disease, languor, and death, but clothed in immortal youth and vigour, and so assimilated to the blessed spirit within it, as neither to cramp its movements nor confine its energies. No pain there—no throbbing brow there—no tear on the cheek there—no sepulchre there—no symbol of mourning there—no spectacle like the apparition of Rachel weeping for her children—or like the widow of Nain following the bier of a lost and loved one. "Death is swallowed up of life"—the graves have been opened—they that dwell in the dust have awakened to endless minstrelsy. Nor do they dwell in a paradise restored amidst the lovely bowers, shady groves, and exuberant fruits of a second Eden. Such glory is too bright for earth, and is therefore to be enjoyed in a scene which shall be in harmony with it. See under verse 12.

Now, Christ is the hope of this glory. Glory had been forfeited, but Jesus interposed for its restoration. When the Saviour is received by faith, the hope of glory springs up in the bosom—a hope as strange aforetime to it as the pine and the box-tree in the desert. Christians are by nature sinners doomed to die, yet, through Christ, they exult in the promise of life. Though, in their physical frame, they are of the earth earthy, their treasure is in heaven. They can look on the Divine Judge, who must, but for Christ, have condemned them, and call him, in Jesus, their Father-God; and they can gaze on the home of angels, so far above them, and say of it, in confidence—that, too, is our home. The basis of this life is Jesus. If it be asked, why have his sins not borne down the evil-doer, and crushed him beneath the intolerable load? why has the lightning slumbered beneath the throne, and not swiftly descended on his head? why are the angry passions within him hushed, and his gloomy thoughts dissipated? whence such a change in relation and character?—the problem is solved by the statement—"Christ within you." This hope rests on His objective work—for "it was Christ that died." Who shall reverse the sentence of our justification, or pronounce it inconsistent with sovereign equity? And who shall condemn us? Shall sin raise its head?—He has made an end of it. Shall Satan accuse?—he has been cast out. Shall conscience alarm?—it has been purged from dead works. Or shall death frown horribly on us?—even it has been abolished. The basis of this hope of glory is also the subjective work of Christ—by His Spirit within the saint. Not only has he the title to heaven, but he gets maturity for it. The process of sanctification begets at once the idea and the hope of perfection. If one sees the block of marble assuming gradually, under the chisel, the semblance of humanity, he infers at once what form of sculpture the artist intends. So, if there be felt within us the transforming influence of the Holy Ghost, bringing out the Divine image with more and more fulness and distinctness, can we doubt the ultimate result? Rom. xv. 13. Such consciousness inspires vivid expectation. In short, in whatever aspect the saints view their hope, they see it in connection with Christ. If they look behind them, the earliest dawning of it sprang from faith in His cross; if they look around them, it is sustained by the promises of Him who sealed these pledges in His blood; if they look forward and upward, it is strengthened by the nearing proximity of realization in Him who is "in the midst of the throne." What a blessed change to the Gentile world! They had been described as once "without Christ," but now Christ was in them; once they had no hope, but now, they had in them Him who was the hope of glory. No wonder that the apostle rejoiced in suffering for the Gentile churches, and thanked God for that arrangement which enabled him to carry out the gospel to its widest susceptibility of application, and thus develop a doctrine which had been concealed for ages. Is his language too gorgeous, when, surveying the wondrous process and the stupendous results, he speaks of the "riches of the glory of this mystery among the Gentiles —Christ in you, the hope of glory"? And that glory is not to be under eclipse—that Saviour is not to be selfishly concealed. No; the apostle adds, as characteristic of his grand commission and daily labour—

(Ver. 28.) *Ὃν ἡμεῖς καταγγέλλομεν*—"Whom we preach." Acts xvii. 3; Phil. i. 17. Chrysostom and Theophylact lay undue stress on the *κατά*, as if the idea of down—*deorsum*, were implied in the verb, and the inference were, that they delivered a message which had descended from heaven. This Christ, so glorious in person and perfect in work—the incarnate God—the bleeding peacemaker—the imperial governor of the universe—it is He, none else, and none besides Him, whom we preach. Not simply His doctrine, but Himself; and He was preached, not by Paul alone, but by all his colleagues. This Christ is the one and undivided object of proclamation; and if He be the hope of glory, no wonder that they rejoice to proclaim Him wide and far, and on every possible occasion. The apostolic preaching was precise and definite. It contained no reveries about the heavenly hierarchy. It was overlaid by no tasteless and tawdry declamation about invisible and worthless mysteries. It dealt not in ascetic distinctions of meats and drinks. There was about it none of those abstruse transcendentalisms in which the Colossian heresiarchs seem to have indulged. It did not gratify the morbid and curious, by prying into celestial arcana. It did not nourish a carnal pride under the delusion of a "voluntary humility." Nor did it dethrone a Saviour-God, and substitute the worshipping of angels for the faith, love, and homage due to Him. The one theme was Christ—"Him first, Him last, Him midst." Christ, as the one deliverer, conferring pardon by His blood, purity by His Spirit, and perfection by His pledge and presence, securing defence by His power, comfort by His sympathy, and the hope of glory by His residence in the believing heart; this Christ, as the only source of such multifarious and connected gifts, we preach, and we preach with special tenderness and anxiety. For he characterizes his preaching thus—

Νουθετοῦντες πάντα ἄνθρωπον, καὶ διδάσκοντες πάντα ἄνθρωπον ἐν πάσῃ σοφίᾳ—"Reminding every man, and teaching every man in all wisdom." iii. 16. The two participles, as might be expected, have been variously distinguished. [*Νουθεσία*, Eph. vi. 4.] There is no warrant in the context for translating this first term by the Latin *corripientes*—as in the Vulgate; as if the apostle meant to say, either that men in sin needed to be rebuked, or that false teachers were subjected by himself to severe and merited castigation. Theophylact, followed by De Wette and Olshausen, refers the first term to practice—*ἐπὶ τῆς πράξεως*, and the second to doctrine—*ἐπὶ δογμάτων*. According to Steiger, the one marks the early communication of Christian truth, and the latter characterizes fuller instruction. By Huther the heart is supposed to be concerned in *νουθετοῦντες*, and the intellect in *διδάσκοντες*. Meyer affirms that the two words correspond to the cardinal injunction of the gospel—*μετανοεῖτε* and *πιστεύετε*—repent and believe. We are inclined to be somewhat eclectic among these opinions, and to regard the first term as the more general, and the second as the more special—the one as describing the means employed to arouse the soul and stimulate it to reflection, and the other as the definite form of instruction which was communicated to the anxious and inquiring spirit.[1] The apostle warned every man—any one,

[1] Thus Clement says,—*ἡ νουθέτησις οὖν οἱονεὶ δίαιτα ἐστι νοσούσης ψυχῆς*, etc.—"Counsel is the prescribed diet of a diseased soul, advising it to take what is salutary, and warning it against what is pernicious."

every one,—urged him as a sinner to bethink himself, to consider his danger, as the victim of a broken law—and apprehending the certainty of safety alone in Christ, to look at the adaptation of the gospel and the glory of its evidence, and to submit to its paramount claims. And he taught "every man"—gave him full instruction—left him in no dubiety, but presented him with a correct and glowing sketch of redemption by the cross. And this was done—

Ἐν πάσῃ σοφίᾳ—"In all wisdom." Estius and Rosenmüller, Pierce and A. Clarke, following the Latin Fathers, blunder when they take these words to denote the object of the teaching; for in the New Testament that object is governed in the accusative. Mark vi. 30, xii. 14; Luke xx. 21; John xiv. 26; 1 Tim. iv. 11; Tit. i. 11. Röell combines both this view and the following one. Chrysostom rightly renders *ἐν* by *μετά*. See the phrase explained under Eph. i. 8. It is probably to be joined to the latter or principal participle, and points out the mode or spirit of the apostle's teaching. 1 Cor. iii. 10. The apostle rejects, indeed, one species of wisdom—that which so often assumed the self-satisfied name of philosophy; but still he felt the necessity of employing the highest skill and prudence in discharging the duties of his office. 1 Cor. ii. 4. To preach the gospel so as to guide the wandering sinner to Christ—to drive him from all refuges of lies, and urge him to embrace a free and full salvation—to enlighten, comfort, strengthen, and refresh the children of God, is seen to be a task demanding consummate wisdom, when we consider the endless varieties of character and temperament, the innumerable sophistries of the human heart, and the ever-changing condition and events of our brief existence. Yet, while Christ crucified is the theme of every address, such uniformity of doctrine does not imply sameness of argument or tedious monotony of imagery and illustration. There may be, and there will be, in this wisdom, circumstantial variety in the midst of essential oneness—for the truth, though old, is ever new.

And the apostle dwells on the individualizing character of the gospel, and repeats the words "every man." There is in this probably a special reference to the partial views of those who were disturbing the Colossian church. The apostle felt an undying interest in every man, whatever his character or creed—every man, whatever his race or lineage—every man, whatever his colour or language—every man, whatever his class or station; every living man on earth shared in his sympathies, had a place in his prayers, and, so far as the sphere of his personal teaching extended, might receive the impress of his counsels, and the benefit of his instructions. The motive of his effort is then described—

Ἵνα παραστήσωμεν πάντα ἄνθρωπον τέλειον ἐν Χριστῷ—"In order that we may present every man perfect in Christ." A glorious aim—*ἵνα*—the noblest that can stimulate enthusiasm, or sustain perseverance in suffering or toil. The *Ἰησοῦ* of the Textus Receptus is not supported by full authority. The phrase "perfect in Christ" does not simply mean perfect in knowledge, because of this previous teaching, as Chrysostom and Calvin supposed; for the effect of such knowledge is moral in its nature, and sanctifying in its effect. John xvii. 3. Such perfection is "in Christ," in fellowship with Him, is derived from Him, and consists in likeness to Him. The verb occurs in verse 22, and in a clause of similar import. The time of presentation is described under Eph. v. 27. The object of his preaching was to save every man. He was contented with nothing less than this, and nothing else than this was his absorbing motive. Not that every man was perfected whom he had endeavoured to instruct, but such was his avowed object. Theophylact thus writes—*τί λέγεις; πάντα ἄνθρωπον; ναί, φησι, τοῦτο σπουδάζομεν· εἰ δὲ μὴ γένηται, οὐδὲν πρὸς ἡμᾶς.* Clement of Alexandria takes *πάντα* in the sense of *ὅλον*—the man entire—soul, body, and spirit. And the gaining of that object cost the apostle no small pains and labour, for he adds—

(Ver. 29.) *Εἰς ὃ καὶ κοπιῶ*—"For which I also labour." To attain this blessed end, I also toil—*ἀγωνιζόμενος*—"intensely struggling," or as Wycliffe renders—*I traueile in stryuynge.* It was no light work, no pastime; it made a demand upon every faculty and every moment. 1 Tim. iv. 10. Since the apostle had many adversaries to contend with, as is evident from numerous allusions in his epistles, Phil. i. 29, 30, 1 Tim. vi. 5, 2 Thess. iii. 2, many suppose that such struggles are either prominently alluded to here, or at least are distinctly implied in the use of the participle. But the context does not favour such a hypothesis. It would seem from the following verses, that it is to an agony of spiritual earnestness that the apostle refers—to that profound yearning which occasioned so many wrestlings in prayer, and drew from him so many tears; *μετὰ πολλῆς τῆς σπουδῆς*, as Chrysostom paraphrases it. When we reflect upon the motive—the presentation of perfect men to God, and upon the instrument—the preaching of the cross, we cease to wonder at the apostle's zeal and toils. For there is no function so momentous,—not that which studies the constitution of man, in order to ascertain his diseases and remove them; nor that which labours for social improvement, and the promotion of science and civilization; nor that which unfolds the resources of a nation, and secures it a free and patriotic government—far more important than all, is the function of the Christian ministry. What in other spheres is enthusiasm, is in it but sobriety. Barnes well says—"In such a work it is a privilege to exhaust our strength; in the performance of the duties of such an office, it is an honour to be permitted to wear out life itself."

It was, indeed, no sluggish heart that beat in the apostle's bosom. His was no torpid temperament. There was such a keenness in all its emotions and anxieties, that its resolve and action were simultaneous movements. But though he laboured so industriously, and suffered so bravely in the aim of winning souls to Christ and glory, still he owned that all was owing to Divine power lodged within him—

> The work to be perform'd is ours,
> The strength is all His own;
>
> 'Tis He that works to will,
> 'Tis He that works to do;
> His is the power by which we act,
> His be the glory too.

Therefore the apostle thus concludes—

Κατὰ τὴν ἐνέργειαν αὐτοῦ τὴν ἐνεργουμένην ἐν ἐμοὶ ἐν δυνάμει—"According to His working, that worketh in me with might." The preposition *κατά* expresses the measure of Paul's apostolical labour. He laboured not only under the prompting of the Divine energy, but he laboured just so far as that imparted energy enabled him. 1 Cor. xv. 10. "By the grace of God I am what I am: and His grace which was bestowed upon me was not in vain; but I laboured more abundantly than they all: yet not I, but the grace of God which was with me." The pronoun *αὐτοῦ* refers not to God, as many imagine, but to Christ. The participle is not in the passive, but the middle voice, as in Gal. v. 6. [Eph. iii. 20.] Winer, § 38, 6. The phrase *ἐν δυνάμει* does not, as Vatablus and Michaelis suggest, refer to miracles, but has an adverbial sense, specifying the mode of operation. Rom. i. 4; 2 Thess. i. 11. The occurrence of the noun and a correlate verb intensifies the meaning. Winer, § 32, 2. [Eph. i. 5, 6.] It was no feeble manifestation of Divine power that showed itself in the great apostle of the Gentiles. Its ample energies clothed him with a species of moral omnipotence. Phil. iv. 13. The sublime motive to present every man perfect in Christ, through the preaching of Christ, could only be realized by the conferment of Divine qualification and assistance. Mere human influence cannot reach it, though the faculties be kept in full tension, and the mind be disciplined into symmetrical operation. Learning, industry, and genius, are of little avail, without piety and spiritual support. "Our sufficiency is of God." 2 Cor. iii. 5, 6.

CHAPTER II

THE apostle had just spoken of his sufferings for the church, and his conflicts for the realization of the one grand aim of the Christian ministry. That aim filled his spirit and nerved his energies. It made him what he was—a preacher, and at length a martyr. The value of souls and the glory of Christ wrapt themselves up in one burning thought, and created and sustained one dominant and living impulse within him. It was his heart's desire that the gospel should be preserved in its purity and simplicity, free from all admixtures of Judaism and false philosoply. He knew that the introduction of error imperilled the salvation of sinners, hindered the diffusion of the word, and robbed the cross of its special adaptations to a lost world. And his affection was not wholly set upon churches where he had preached in person. He had no little jealousies and no favouritism, but all the believing communities, whatever their age, place, or origin, found in him immediate sympathy and co-operation. The churches which he had not visited in person might scarcely be inclined to believe this fully, and might naturally imagine that their neighbours which had been honoured by his presence had a deeper hold on his affection. But the apostle seeks to dispel this illusion, and says in earnest exhortitude [1]—

(Ver. 1.) *Θέλω γὰρ ὑμᾶς εἰδέναι, ἡλίκον ἀγῶνα ἔχω περὶ ὑμῶν καὶ τῶν ἐν Λαοδικείᾳ, καὶ ὅσοι οὐχ ἑωράκασι τὸ πρόσωπόν μου ἐν σαρκί*—"For I wish that you knew what a great conflict I have about you and them in Laodicea, and as many as have not seen my face in the flesh." It is disputed whether *περί* or *ὑπέρ* be the better reading—A, B, C, D†††, declare for

[1] "From the construction of this Exordium, I venture to assert, that there is no rule laid down by Aristotle, Cicero, and other masters of eloquence, concerning the framing of introductions, which is not adhered to in this brief opening. For three things are required by them in a legitimate Exordium: That it be adapted to render the hearer *attentive*, and *docile*, and to *conciliate his affection.*" —Davenant, *in loc.*

the latter; while the former is supported by D[1], E, F, G, J, K, and the Greek Fathers; Lachmann and Tischendorf are divided. Perhaps περί is the right reading, and ὑπέρ was suggested from iv. 12 and i. 24. The reading ἑώρακαν—the Alexandrian form—is also preferable to that of the Textus Receptus—ἑωράκασι. Winer, § 13, 2 *c*.

The division of chapters is here unhappy, for this verse is but a supplementary explanation of the preceding one. "I am in an agony," he had said, and now he adds, "I would ye knew what an agony I am in about you." The noun ἀγών means deep and earnest solicitude,[1] accompanied with toil and peril. Phil. i. 30; 1 Thess. ii. 2; 1 Tim. vi. 12. It points out that intense and painful anxiety which preyed upon him, now in occasional terror, and now in reviving hopes—that ceaseless conflict which filled his waking hours with effort, and relieved with prayer the watches of the night. His soul was in a perpetual distress for them: every suspicion about them left a pang behind it—the bare possibility of their relapse or apostasy brought with it unutterable dismay and sorrow. Therefore he says, ἡλίκον ἀγῶνα—"How great a struggle." Hesychius gives, as synonyms for the adjective, ὁποῖον, ποταπόν. Jas. iii. 5. It was no easy or supine struggle. He knew what was at stake. They were in danger, and he could not be in the midst of them. The seducer might have been pictured out to him, but he was not privileged to confront him. How the Colossians stood he knew not. He was aware of the hazard they were in generally—but the shiftings of the crisis and its individual results could only be faintly apprehended. Like the caged bird beating its bared and bleeding breast against the wires of its prison, as it hears the repeated cry of its unseen young ones, the apostle turned ever and anon toward those churches, painted to himself their danger and their need of help, and strained his eager spirit to the utmost as he sighed over the possible desolation which might come upon them. Nor did he idly chafe in his confinement, —but he wrote this letter, and he wished them to know the depth of the love which he cherished toward them. "I would that ye knew." Similar construction is found in 1 Cor. xi. 3; Phil. i. 12; Rom. xi. 25. If they knew it, they would listen

[1] Πολλὴ φρόντις—as Theodoret explains it.

all the more readily to his suggestions and counsels. Laodicea is also mentioned, from its proximity to Colosse, and perhaps because it was exposed to similar seductions. A few Codices, with the Philoxenian Syriac, add *καὶ τῶν ἐν Ἱεραπόλει*, a gloss evidently taken from iv. 13. The apostle says, besides, "and as many as have not seen my face in the flesh." This mode of expression is a popular one, and is not therefore to be pressed as if "in the flesh" was opposed to "in the Spirit," or as if, as Olshausen suggests, it puts "the bodily countenance in contrast to the spiritual physiognomy." The reference in *ὅσοι* has been keenly disputed—whether it alludes to a class different from the Christians in Colosse and Laodicea; or whether it characterizes them also as persons unknown to the apostle and unvisited by him. This question has been fully treated in the Introduction, to which the reader is referred. The point of the apostle's agony is thus described—

(Ver. 2.) *Ἵνα παρακληθῶσιν αἱ καρδίαι αὐτῶν*—"That their hearts might be comforted." In the violent effort described in *ἀγών*, there is implied a definite design expressed by *ἵνα*. The pronoun *αὐτῶν*, in the third person, comprehends all the classes of persons mentioned in the preceding verse. We agree with Meyer that there is no reason to depart from the ordinary sense of the verb, which plainly means to comfort, in 1 Thess. iii. 2; 2 Thess. ii. 17; Eph. vi. 22; Matt. ii. 18, v. 4; 2 Cor. i. 4. The addition of *καρδία* renders such a meaning more certain. It appears to us that there is in this earnest wish an allusion to that discomfort which the introduction of error creates, as indeed is more plainly shown by the concluding phraseology of the verse. The conflict of error with truth could not but lead to distraction and mental turmoil; and in proportion to their misconception of the gospel, or their confusion of idea with regard to its spirit, contents, and aim, would be their loss of that peace and solace which the new religion had imparted to them.

Συμβιβασθέντες ἐν ἀγάπῃ—"United together in love." [Eph. iv. 16.] The Elzevir Text reads *συμβιβασθέντων* on very slight authority. The reading is an evident emendation with reference to the preceding *αὐτῶν*. The masculine form and nominative case of the participle presents no real difficulty. [Eph. iv. 2.] The Vulgate translation—*instructi*—is based upon the usage of the Septuagint, in which this verb represents several Hebrew verbs, the principal of which are portions of either יָדַע or יָרָה, and signifying to instruct.[1] Isa. xl. 13; Ex. xviii. 16; Lev. x. 11, etc. It is used with a similar secondary sense in Acts xvi. 10, ix. 22, where it means to gather up the lessons presented, and knit them together in the form of inference or demonstration. Hesychius defines *συμβιβάζει* by *εἰς φιλίαν ἄγει*; and the Scholiast, quoted by Wetstein, has it, *συμβιβασθέντες, οἷον ἑνωθέντες*; this last term being that also employed in explanation by Theophylact.[2] But the natural sense here is, "being compacted together," love being the element of union; *ἐν* pointing not simply to its bond, as if it were *διά*. In the peculiar condition of the Colossian church, this virtual prayer was very necessary. The entrance of error naturally begets suspicion and alienation. One wonders if his neighbour be infected, and how far; and that neighbour reciprocates similar curiosity and doubts. Expressions are too carefully weighed, and a man is made "an offender for a word." A sinister construction is apt to be put upon the slightest actions; nay, caution defeats its very purpose, and fails to secure good understanding. But the apostle was anxious that these churches should feel no such disaster, should be shivered into repellent fragments by none of those evil influences, but that they should remain in mutual and affectionate oneness—bound together in love—proof alike against the invasion of heresy, and the secret upspringing of internal mistrusts and dislikes.

Καὶ εἰς πάντα πλοῦτον τῆς πληροφορίας τῆς συνέσεως—"And unto the whole wealth of the full assurance of understanding." But with which of the preceding clauses is this one to be joined? It seems preferable to connect it with the last—"knit together"—*ἐν . . . καὶ εἰς*—"in love and in order to the wealth." The two prepositions are closely united by *καί*—*ἐν* pointing out the element of union, and *εἰς* denoting its purpose. This syntax seems preferable to connecting the phrase with the *ἡλίκον ἀγῶνα* of the first verse, as is done by

[1] So also Ambrosiaster and Hilary, as well as Bretschneider, who, in his *Lexicon*, *sub voce*, renders this clause *bene edocti ad amorem mutuum.*

[2] Herodotus, i. 74, and Thucydides, ii. 29, where it is said of Nymphodorus, that he reconciled Perdiccas to the Athenians—*ξυνεβίβασε.*

Calovius, or even with *παρακληθῶσιν* of the first clause of this verse, as is proposed by Storr and Flatt; for in this last connection *καί* would seem to be superfluous, or it must begin a new clause and receive another than its merely copulative signification. Luther, in his version, wrongly omits *καί*, and renders—*in der Liebe zu allem Reichthum;* and this is also the rendering of the Peschito ܒܚܘܒܐ ܠܟܠܗ ܥܘܬܪܐ. The two things have, indeed, a close connection. Pascal remarks, "In order to love human things, it is necessary to know them; in order to know those that are divine, it is necessary to love them." The conjunction *καί* is simply copulative, and *εἰς* points out the purpose or design, which might have been expressed by *ἵνα*, with a verb. The noun *πληροφορία* is full certainty or assurance. 1 Thess. i. 5; Heb. vi. 11, x. 22. "The full assurance of understanding" is the fixed persuasion that you comprehend the truth, and that it is the truth which you comprehend. It is not merely the vivid belief, that what occupies the mind is the Divine verity, but that this verity is fully understood. The mind which has reached this elevation, is confident that it does not misconceive the statements of the gospel, or attach to them a meaning which they do not bear. Believing them to be of God, it is certain that it apprehends the mind of God in His message. If a man possesses not this certainty—if the view he now cherishes differ from that adopted by him again—if what he holds to-day be modified or explained away to-morrow—if new impressions chase away other convictions, and are themselves as rapidly exiled in turn—if, in short, he is "ever learning and never able to come to the knowledge of the truth," then such dubiety and fluctuation present a soil most propitious to the growth and progress of error. And as the mental energy is frittered away by such indecision, the mind becomes specially susceptible of foreign influence and impression. It was the apostle's earnest desire that the Colossian church, and the members of the other churches referred to, should assuredly understand the new religion—its facts and their evidence—its doctrines and their connections—its promises and their basis—its precepts and their adaptation—its ordinances and their simplicity and power. The fixed knowledge of those things would fortify their minds against the seductive insinuations of false teachers, who mix just so much truth with their fallacies as often to give them the fascinations of honesty and candour, and who impose them as the result of superior enlightenment, and of an extended and advantageous research. The mind most liable to be seduced is that which, having reached only an imperfect and onesided view, is continually disturbed and perplexed by opposite and conflicting ideas which from its position it is unable to reconcile, but is forced to wonder whether really it has attained to just conceptions of the truth. The traveller who has already made some progress, but who begins gradually to doubt and debate, to lose faith in himself, and wonder whether he be in the right way after all, is prepared to listen to the suggestions of any one who, under semblance of disinterested friendship, may advise to a path of danger and ruin. No wonder that the apostle describes the value of the full assurance of understanding by his favourite term—"riches"—for it is a precious form of intellectual wealth, and no wonder that he yearns for the Colossian Christians to possess it in no scanty measure, but in all its opulence. *Σύνεσις* has been explained under i. 9.

Εἰς ἐπίγνωσιν τοῦ μυστηρίου τοῦ Θεοῦ καὶ Πατρὸς καὶ τοῦ Χριστοῦ—"To the full knowledge of the mystery of God, and of the Father, and of Christ." So reads the Received Text. The connection of this clause has been variously understood. It is needless to make the preceding clause a parenthesis, and join this one to *παρακληθῶσιν*. Bähr takes it as denoting the end, while the clause before it specifies the means—"unto all riches of the full assurance of understanding, so that ye may know the mystery." But perhaps the clause is merely parallel with the preceding one, or rather, is a farther development of it. The noun *ἐπίγνωσις* is plainly shown here to mean "full knowledge," as, indeed, we have argued under Eph. i. 18, and in this epistle, i. 9. The idea of a mystery is taken from verses 26 and 27 of the former chapter. The mystery, he says, had been long hid; but God had chosen to reveal the riches of its glory, and therefore he desires that his readers should not only distinctly recognize it, and highly value it, but specially, that they should fully comprehend its contents and lessons. The reading of the concluding portion of the clause is sadly perplexed and uncertain. The difficulty relates to the words of the Received Text—*καὶ πατρὸς καὶ τοῦ Χριστοῦ*. These have on their side D[111], E, J, K, and several of the Fathers; Codices 47, 73, with Chrysostom and Pelagius, who have—*πατρὸς καὶ τοῦ Χριστοῦ*, followed by the Syriac, Vulgate, and Coptic Versions. Codices A, C, 4, read —*τοῦ Θεοῦ πατρὸς τοῦ Χριστοῦ*, while Codices 41 and 61 have—*τοῦ Θεοῦ καὶ πατρὸς τοῦ Χριστοῦ*. The word *πατρός* is omitted by some MSS., while Codex 17 reads—*τοῦ Θεοῦ τοῦ ἐν Χριστῷ*. D[1] presents the clause thus—*τοῦ Θεοῦ ὅ ἐστι Χριστός*, but B has—*τοῦ Θεοῦ Χριστοῦ*. Hilary follows the last reading, but Clement and Ambrosiaster quote—*τοῦ Θεοῦ ἐν Χριστῷ*. The shorter reading, ending with *Θεοῦ*, is found in 37, 67[2], 71, 80[1], and 116. For the short reading without the clause, Tischendorf, in his second edition, Griesbach, Scholz, Heinrichs, Bähr, Olshausen, De Wette, and Rinck, have declared themselves. The reading—*τοῦ Θεοῦ Χριστοῦ* has advocates in Lachmann, Meyer, and Steiger. It is plain, on the one hand, that many of these readings are nothing but glosses to escape or solve a difficulty; and it is as clear, on the other, that none of them possesses preponderating authority. For A, B, and D read differently, and the older Fathers and Versions agree with none of them, since Cyril has, for example —*τοῦ Θεοῦ καὶ Χριστοῦ*, and Theophylact cites—*τοῦ Θεοῦ πατρὸς ἐν Χριστῷ*, while Hilary explains, by adding, *Deus Christus sacramentum est.*

(Ver. 3.) *Ἐν ᾧ εἰσι πάντες οἱ θησαυροὶ τῆς σοφίας καὶ τῆς γνώσεως ἀπόκρυφοι*—"In which are hidden all the treasures of wisdom and knowledge." The reference in the relative is supposed, by the great majority of interpreters, from Chrysostom down to Baumgarten-Crusius, to be to Christ. The margin of our English version gives "wherein," that is, in which mystery; and this, we apprehend, is the right construction. Such is the view of Suicer, Cocceius, Röel, Lange, Grotius, Bengel, Huther, Bähr, Böhmer, De Wette, etc. If the short reading of the previous clause be adopted, then there is no mention of Christ in the last verse at all. But especially the apostle is speaking of the mystery, and he here eulogizes it as worthy of fuller and farther insight. Nay, he places it in sharp contrast with the false and hollow error which was insinuating itself among them. That system which was "not after Christ," might boast of its stores of philosophy, but they were not to be captivated by its pretences. They needed not to go in quest of higher truth and loftier science; for in that mystery proclaimed among them were deposited all the treasures of wisdom and knowledge. The nouns *σοφια* and *γνῶσις* are, perhaps, not to be carefully distinguished, as the words seem to be used in reference to the terminology of the false teachers. The words appear to have been favourite epithets with them—were, in fact, a sample of the enticing words referred to in the next verse, for they imagined themselves in possession of the only genuine wisdom and knowledge. But the apostle affirms, in opposition, that only in this mystery are they to be discovered in reality, and that all else bearing the name is but hollow semblance and counterfeit. Whatever distinction may be made, as in Rom. xi. 33, 1 Cor. xii. 8, such seems to us the preferable exegesis in the verse before us. Augustine makes a distinction, by referring to the Vulgate translation of Job xxviii. 28—"Behold, piety is wisdom—*sapientia*, and to abstain from evil is knowledge—*scientia*."[1] Calvin says—*inter sapientiam et intelligentiam non porro magnum discrimen, quia duplicatio ad augendum valet;* but this statement is scarcely correct. The two substantives may refer to the same thing, but under different aspects. Not that the first comprehends *res humanae*, and the other *res divinae;* or, that the one is practical sagacity, and the other theoretic knowledge of God. This latter distinction, though it be commonly held, and may be true of the English terms wisdom and knowledge, is not warranted by Scripture usage. Col. i. 9; 1 Cor. i. 17, 21, ii. 6, viii. 1. Meyer says *σοφία* is the more general, and *γνῶσις* the more special. The latter term is divine science, and the first is that enlightenment which springs from it. So that the first noun is subjective, and the second objective. The study of the *γνῶσις* brings the *σοφία*. Wisdom results from penetration into this knowledge. Knowledge is the study, and wisdom its fruit.

The verse before us is thus a high encomium on the mystery, and an inducement to the apostle's readers to value it, to cling to it, to study it, and to enthrone it in a niche so lofty and

[1] *Enarratio in Psal.* cxxxv. Op. vol. 4, ed. Paris, 1835.

inaccessible, that it could neither be rivalled nor dethroned. We quite agree, with Robinson, that ἀπόκρυφοι does not denote "hid" in its literal sense, for the apostle says that God had made known the mystery; but "hid" in the secondary sense of being laid or treasured up, as in Septuagint, Isa. xlv. 3; 1 Macc. i. 23. So that there is no need to adopt the suggestion of Bengel and Meyer, which denies that ἀπόκρυφοι is the predicate, and would render—"in whom all the hidden treasures are laid up." Bähr objects to the same mode of construction, that the article should precede ἀπόκρυφοι; but the objection is not based upon an invariable rule or practice. And we are also, by the exegesis which we propose, saved all the perplexity which the idea of concealment originates. For those treasures are hidden, according to Böhmer and Davenant, from the unbelieving world; according to Olshausen, from the unassisted intellect; and, according to Calvin, they are said to be hidden because the preaching of the cross is always foolishness to the world. *Abditam sapientiam*, says Melancthon, *quia mundus non eam intelligit*, as is said in 1 Cor. ii. 7, 8; Matt. xi. 25; 2 Cor. iv. 3, 4. Θησαυρός has a similar tropical meaning, as well in the classics as in the New Testament. Xenophon, *Memor.* i. 6, 14; Hesiod, *Op.* 715; Eurip. *Ion*, 923; Plato, *Phil.* 15, e; Matt. vi. 20; Mark x. 21; 2 Cor. iv. 7. The meaning of the apostle then is, that in this mystery are stored up all the treasures of wisdom and knowledge; not a few scanty fragments of faded wealth, but the entire amount without alloy or defalcation. Here, and not in the vaunted theosophy of the false teachers, might a man become wise, by being initiated into the true knowledge. Let it be the knowledge of God which he yearns after—the comprehension of the essence, character, attributes, and works of the invisible Majesty—then he will obtain full satisfaction neither from the palpable limnings of nature—for they present but a shaded profile, nor yet from the subtleties of a spiritualistic philosophy—for it can only bring out a dim and impersonal abstraction. But God as He is—in every element and relation—in the fulness of His being and glory—is revealed in the gospel, and there may we find Him out, not by searching, but by looking on Him as portrayed not only in His power and wisdom, His eternity and infinitude, but also in

His grace and love, His condescension and mercy—those properties of His nature which creation could not have disclosed, nor human ingenuity have either imagined or anticipated.

The highest conceptions of the Divine polity are to be learned, also, from this mystery. By means of the atonement, it achieves what to human administration is utter impossibility. It pardons without weakening the authority of law, or bringing prerogative in conflict with enactment. Earthly governments proclaim the ordinance, and then apprehend, convict, and punish offenders; and when they do commute a sentence or grant a respite, they are usually prompted to such clemency because the penalty is felt to be too severe in the circumstances, and then so-called mercy is only equity correcting inequalities of law. Were they not to punish, they would dissolve the bonds of society and speed their own extinction. The sphere of the tribunal is that of indictment and proof, and according to the evidence so are the verdict and sentence. But God, the Legislator, is not under such restraint, for while He proclaims a universal amnesty to all who will avail themselves of it, He neither by this anomaly repeals the code, nor declares it superseded for the crisis, nor suffers it to fall into contempt; but, charging sinners with their atrocious guilt, and convincing them that they are most justly liable to the menaced punishment, He at once absolves them, without encouraging them to sin with hope of impunity, or weakening the allegiance of the universe by the apparent reversal of those righteous principles which are the habitation of His throne, and which have guided and glorified His past procedure. By the dignity of His nature and the extent of His humiliation, the perfection of His obedience and the substitutionary efficacy of His death, that Christ whom the false teachers depreciated had glorified the law more than if man had never sinned, or having fallen, had himself suffered the unmitigated penalty. No philosophy ever dreamed of such an awful expedient as God robed in humanity, and in that nature dying to redeem His guilty creatures—whose name, nature, and legal liabilities He had assumed; and such a scheme never found a place in any system of jurisprudence. Such knowledge was too wonderful for them, it was high, they could not attain unto it.

On the other hand, the false preachers laboured in inculcating asceticism, penance, and neglect of the body, as a means of weaning the spirit from earth, and bringing it into fellowship with God. They also gave unwarranted functions to angels and higher spirits, as if they could shield the soul from guilt, and as if contact with them spiritualized it, and helped to raise it to blessedness. They put mysticism in room of the atonement, and ascribed to the hosts of God that guardian power which belongs to faith and the Divine Spirit. Theirs was a temple without an altar or a propitiation, though it was crowded with genii and tutelar subordinates. It was vain philosophy and out of place; for it fell short of heaven, and could secure no benefit upon earth. It was wrong about God, and erring about man—it gave him a stone for bread.

But "wisdom and knowledge" were in the evangelical mystery—the veritable and coveted γνῶσις was there. There might be discovered the truest theosophy—no gaudy vision, but blessed fact—God in Christ, and our God; there would also be found the richest philosophy, in which antagonisms were reconciled, and all the relations of the universe were harmonized by the cross, the mystery of man's origin, nature, and destiny, cleared up; while the noblest ethics were propounded, in unison with all our aspirations and spiritual instincts—plainly showing what man may be, ought to be, and will be, through the influence and operations of the Holy Ghost—the crowning and permanent gift of the Christian dispensation. What men have sought in deep and perplexing speculations on the order and origin of all things, they will find in this mystery. What they have striven in daring adventure to reach about the existence and issue of evil, they will get here laid to their hand. The intricacies and anomalies of their own mental and moral nature, on which they have constructed so many conflicting and self-destructive theories—which still have repeated themselves in successive generations, are here solved by Him who knows our frame. The interminable discussions on man's chief end, which ended only in fatigue and disappointment, are silenced here by the "still small voice." "Where is the wise? where is the scribe? where is the disputer of this world?" Let them come and see, and learn, and they will find that, in the Divine plan of redemption are manifested the noblest elements of reflection, and the purest objects of spiritual faith and attachment. For theology transcends all the sciences in circuit and splendour. It brings us into immediate communion with Infinitude and Eternity. Its theme is the Essence and Attributes of Jehovah, with the truth He has published, and the works He has wrought. It tells us of the unity and spirituality of His nature, the majesty of His law, the infinitude of His love, and the might and triumph of His Son, as the conqueror of sin and death. The intellect is unable to comprehend all its mysteries by superior subtlety and penetration, and the imagination only fatigues itself in the attempt to grasp and realize its destiny. Its fields of thought can never be exhausted, even though the slower processes of understanding were superseded by the eager and rapid discoveries of unwearied intuition. "Who can, by searching, find out God; who can find out the Almighty unto perfection?" And after those combinations of wisdom, power, and love, which characterize the counsels and government of God, have attracted and engaged the inquiring soul through innumerable ages, there will still remain heights to be scanned, and depths to be explored, facts to be weighed, and wonders to be admired. [Eph. iii. 10.]

The apostle approaches nearer and nearer his subject—the seductions of a false and pretentious philosophy.

(Ver. 4.) *Τοῦτο δὲ λέγω*—"Now, this I say." This present tense some regard as future in its look, as if the apostle meant —"what I am about to utter is intended to prevent your being led astray." But the clause has evidently a retrospective reference to the preceding statement, and not exclusively either to the first or third verse. "What I am saying, or have just said, as to my anxiety for you, and as to the treasury of genuine science in the gospel, has this purpose—to put you on your guard. Do not listen to those specious harangues about their boasted possession of the only or the inner *σοφία* and *γνῶσις*. It is all a delusion intended to impose upon you Purest wisdom and loftiest knowledge are not in their keeping but in yours; for in that mystery into which you have been now so fully initiated, are hidden all the treasures of wisdom and of knowledge." *Quaerendum est,* says Tertullian, *donec invenias, et credendum ubi inveneris, et nihil amplius, nisi custodiendum quod credidisti.*[1]

Ἵνα μή τις ὑμᾶς παραλογίζηται ἐν πιθανολογίᾳ—"Lest any man should beguile you with enticing words." The reading μηδείς, though unusual, is supported by A, B, C, D, E, while the reading μή τις of the Stephanic Text rests on inferior authorities. The deponent verb used by the apostle occurs only again in Jas. i. 22; but is found in the Seventy, 1 Sam. xix. 17. It is found also in Demosthenes,[2] where it signifies to miscount. Here it denotes to delude by false reasoning, as in Æschines, p. 53 (ed. Dobson, vol. xii.); Polyb. 16, 10, 3; Gen. xxix. 25; Josh. ix. 22 (28). The means of deception are characterized by one pithy and expressive compound—πιθανολογίᾳ. The word occurs only in this place. The cognate verb which is found in the classical writers,[3] is defined by Passow to mean—to bring forward reasons in order to prove anything likely or probable; or, as we might say in English—"to talk so as to talk one over." The substantive occurs in Plato;[4] and the word, in its separate parts, πιθανοὶ λόγοι, is found in Josephus and Philo.[5] The term is here employed in a bad sense,—to characterize that teaching which aimed to fascinate their mind and debauch their conscience, by its specious sophistry. This is a common accompaniment of heretical novelty. It professes, by a process of dilution or elimination, to simplify what is obscure, unravel what is intricate, reconcile what is involved in discrepancy, or adapt to reason what seems to be above it. Or it deals in mystery, and seeks to charm by a pretence of occult wisdom, and the discovery of recondite senses and harmonies. It was a form of similar mysticism, priding itself in intimate communion with the invisible and the spiritual, that seems to

[1] *De Praescrip. Haeret.* cap. ix. Opera, vol. ii. p. 12, ed. Oehler.

[2] 822, 25; 1037, 15, ed. Reisk; or vol. vii. p. 413; vol. viii. p. 43, of *Oratores Attici*, ed. Dobson.

[3] Arist. *Eth.* i. 1. Diodorus Sic. i. 39, xiii. 95. Diogenes L. 10, 87, ed. Hübner.

[4] *Theaet.* § 52, vol. iii. p. 440, ed. Bekker, London. In this place it is joined with εἰκός, and denotes deception; probability being opposed to ἀπόδειξιν καὶ ἀνάγκην—conclusive demonstration. Fabric. *Cod. Apoc.* iii. 694.

[5] Joseph. *Antiq.* viii. 9. Philo, *de Migratione Ab.* vol. iii. p. 490, ed. Pfeiffer.

have been introduced at Colosse. How much need, therefore, they had of that "full assurance of understanding" which the apostle so earnestly wished them to possess. Such illumination was a perfect shield against this delusive rhetoric, with which they might be so artfully and vigorously plied.

(Ver. 5.) *Εἰ γὰρ καὶ τῇ σαρκὶ ἄπειμι, ἀλλὰ τῷ πνεύματι σὺν ὑμῖν εἰμι*—"For though indeed in the flesh I be absent, yet in the spirit with you am I." *Γάρ* gives the reason why the writer so warns them. It is refinement on the part of Theophylact to make the sense—"I see in spirit the false teachers, and therefore bid you be on your guard." The meaning is very plain. Personally the apostle was not, and could not be, at Colosse; but mentally he was there. In 1 Cor. v. 3, 4, the apostle employs *τῷ σώματι*—a more Hellenic phrase. It is in opposition to the plain sense to refer *πνεῦμα*, with Ambrosiaster, Grotius, and Lord Barrington, to the Holy Spirit; as if a special inspiration had kept the apostle cognizant of what was transacting at Colosse. When one takes a very deep and continuous interest in a distant community, he is not only ever picturing them to his imagination, but he so transports himself, in idea, to their locality, that he walks and speaks with them, is an inmate of their dwellings and a guest at their table, is engaged in all their occupations, and feels himself for the moment to be one of themselves. So it was with the apostle and the absent church in Asia Minor. *Σύν* is similarly employed in Phil. i. 23; 1 Thess. iv. 17. That this language does not by any means imply a previous residence in Colosse, as Wiggers supposes, has been shown in the Introduction to this volume. The particle *ἀλλά* is rendered "yet"—*doch*, by Huther; *attamen*, by Bähr—a translation which it may often bear after *εἰ* or *ἐάν*.[1] There is no need at all for supposing such an ellipsis as the following,—I am absent, still not wholly ignorant of you, or uninterested in you, *ἀλλά*, but I am with you in spirit. Hartung, ii. p. 40; Kühner, § 741, 1, 3; Klotz, *Devarius*, vol. ii. 18; and Devarius, vol. i. 7.

Χαίρων καὶ βλέπων ὑμῶν τὴν τάξιν—"Joying and beholding your order." One would naturally expect the apostle to say—seeing and rejoicing; that is, rejoicing because he saw.

[1] See Bähr, *in loc.* Kypke, *apud* 1 Cor. iv. 15.

Bähr adduces Josephus as expressing himself similarly—*ὑμᾶς εὖ ἔχοντας χαίρω καὶ βλέπω.* But the German commentator misquotes the Jewish historian, or rather the best MSS. show that he uses the participle *βλέπων*, as does the apostle, and not the verb. De Wette adopts this form—"with joy seeing your order." Calvin and Estius have it—"rejoicing because I see your order," and others — "*gaudeo videns.*" Winer, followed by Olshausen, takes *καί* in the sense of *scilicet*— "I am with you rejoicing, inasmuch as I see your order."[1] Fritzsche is nearer our view when he solves the difficulty thus—rejoicing *over you, ἐφ' ὑμῖν*—*laetans de vobis*—and seeing your array.[2] Dismissing the idea of a hendiadys and a zeugma —taking *καί* in its ordinary sense, and neither as causal nor explicative; and seeing *τάξιν* can belong only to one of the verbs *βλέπω*, we come to the conclusion of Meyer, that the first participle qualifies the clause—"present with you." The meaning is—I am present with you in spirit, rejoicing in this ideal fellowship, and viewing your order. His spiritual presence with them was a source of joy, and it enabled him to see their orderly array and consistency. The sentiment is somewhat similar to that contained in i. 3, 4. There he says, that the accounts which he had received about them prompted him, as often as he prayed, to thank God for them; here he tells them that his being with them in spirit was a source of joy, and neither of doubt, disquietude, nor sorrow. And the verb *βλέπων* is used with special appropriateness, as the apostle supposes himself to be among them, looking around him and taking a survey of their condition. 2 Cor. vii. 8; Rom. vii. 23. Schleusner, referring to a common trope, indeed says quaintly, of the verb — *de omnibus reliquis sensibus corporis usurpatur, ut adeo βλέπειν saepe sit audire*, as in Matt. xv. 31, where it is said that the people saw the dumb speak. But the meaning there is not, that they heard them speak, but that they saw the whole phenomenon of the restoration of hearing. The Lexicographer instances also the verse before us, as if the apostle meant to say, that he knew of their order from hearing the reports of others. But such an exegesis is truly bathos, and robs the sentiment of its spirit and beauty.

While the noun *τάξις*, among its other uses, is often found

[1] § 54, 5. [2] *Comm. in Ep. ad Rom.* ii. p. 425.

as a military term,[1] denoting the result of that discipline to which an army is subjected, and also sometimes describing the symmetry and arrangement of society;[2] it has besides the emphatic signification of good order.[3] Thus Chrysostom uses, in explanation, *εὐταξία*. In the latter significant sense, the apostle here employs the term—"seeing your good order." What the writer refers to, we may learn from his own usage. And first, the apostle accuses certain members of the church of Thessalonica of a breach of order—that they walked *ἀτάκτως*—"disorderly;" whereas of himself and coadjutors he says—*ὅτι οὐκ ἠτακτήσαμεν ἐν ὑμῖν*—"for we were not disorderly among you," and again, he adds—*ἀκούομεν γάρ τινας περιπατοῦντας ἐν ὑμῖν ἀτάκτως*—"for we hear that some among you walk disorderly." 2 Thess. iii. 6, 7, 11. The disorder referred to in this passage, was the strong and vicious tendency to idleness which had been manifested in Thessalonica—some refusing to work and earn a subsistence, and aiming to throw themselves on the liberality of the richer brethren in the church. This breach of order was private and personal. 1 Thess. v. 14. And secondly, after rebuking the church in Corinth, for the turbulence and confusion caused by the display of spiritual gifts, he sums up by saying—"let all things be done decently and in order,—*καὶ κατὰ τάξιν*." There had been a social or ecclesiastical breach of order. Perhaps to both kinds of order does the apostle here refer. In their individual consistency and purity of character, in their unshaken attachment to the truth in the midst of seduction, and in all the arrangements and forms of their worship and discipline, such good order was observed, as that error was excluded, unity preserved, and edification promoted. It is a meagre explanation of Michaelis and Heinrichs, to represent this order in the vulgar sense of subjection to the office-bearers, and as opposed to insubordination. Theophylact and Huther are more correct in referring it to love, which at least was the bond of union, and one principal support of order.

Καὶ τὸ στερέωμα τῆς εἰς Χριστὸν πίστεως ὑμῶν—"And the solidity of your faith in Christ." The noun *στερέωμα* is not

[1] Suidas, *sub voce*. Josephus, *B. Jud.* iii. 9, 2. Xen. *Cyrop.* viii. 3, 6.
[2] Dem. 200, *Orat. At.* vol. v. p. 308, ed. Dobson. Plato, *Crit.* 109.
[3] Plato, *Gorg.* 504, *Leg.* 875. Polybius, i. 4.

found elsewhere in the New Testament. Representing, in the first chapter of Genesis, the Hebrew רָקִיעַ, and rendered in the Vulgate *firmamentum*, it signifies something solid or compact, such as the foundation of a building. It naturally came to signify not the object, but the quality which characterizes it—firmness or hardness. Ps. lxxiii. 4. So that it here points out that feature in the faith of the Colossians which specially commended it to the notice and eulogy of the apostle, to wit, its unyielding nature, or the stiffness of its adherence to its one object—Christ. In such a crisis as that, when fluctuation would have been incipient ruin, it was not the elevation of their faith, nor its growth, nor any of its fruits, but this one feature of it—its unshaken constancy—which the watchful eye of the apostle so carefully noted, and so joyously recorded. Acts xvi. 5; 1 Pet. v. 9. The very position of the words is emphatic—τῆς εἰς Χριστὸν πίστεως, as if εἰς X. distinguished and glorified the faith. [Eph. i. 1.] It reposed on Christ—as unshaken as its object. His love never wavers, His power never fails, His fidelity never resiles from its pledge. And those unseen blessings which faith surveys are unchanging in their certainty and glory. The portals of heaven are never barred—its living stream is never dried up; the pearls of its gates are unsoiled, nor is the gold of its pavement ever worn through. Surely, then, faith ought to be as stedfast as the foundation on which it rests, and the object which it contemplates and secures. It is out of place, with Bengel and others, to make this noun a species of adjective to πίστεως, as if the meaning were *firma fides non patitur quicquam ex ordine suo moveri.* Nor is it warrantable on the part of Olshausen and Meyer, to take τάξις in its military sense, and to make στερέωμα the power which strengthens for the fight, or a species of fortification by which they were defended. Στερέωμα is, indeed, employed to represent the Hebrew סֶלַע in Ps. xviii. 2, but the Greek translation is according to the general sense of the Hebrew term,—the proverbial firmness of a rock. In 1 Macc. ix. 14, quoted by Meyer, στερέωμα τῆς παρεμβολῆς is not the fortification of the camp, but the strength of the army, that portion which could be relied upon for its prowess. In the Version of Symmachus, Isa. xxvi. 1, it represents the Hebrew חֵל, which the Seventy render περίτειχος; the principal idea of the original term being strength, while bulwark, *antemurale*, is only a secondary and technical application. It is a curious reading of the clause which occurs in Augustine and Ambrosiaster—the former having *id quod deest fidei vestrae in Christo*, and the latter, *supplens id quod deest utilitati fidei vestrae in Christum*—implying that they both read *ὑστέρημα* for *στερέωμα*.

(Ver. 6.) *Ὡς οὖν παρελάβετε τὸν Χριστὸν Ἰησοῦν τὸν Κύριον, ἐν αὐτῷ περιπατεῖτε*—"As then ye have received Christ Jesus the Lord, walk in Him." The particle *οὖν* turns us to the preceding verse, and to the fact of their order and stedfast faith. Calvin rightly says—*laudi attexit exhortationem*. He has commended them for their order and stedfast faith, and he now adds a word of warning and counsel. Gradually does he approach the main end of his writing. Ever as he comes near it does he utter some sentiment which delays his full admonition. He wishes by his previous allusions and warnings to prepare their minds for the final and thorough exposure and condemnation. And thus he has intimated—what thanks he offers for them, what prayers he presents for their deeper illumination and persistency in the truth—what sufferings he has endured for them, and what sympathies he has with them—what joy he felt in being mentally present with them, and surveying their good order and unswerving faith. And he has eulogized that gospel which they had received—as the truth—as a fruit-bearing principle—as a disclosure of the Divine person, exalted dignity, and saving work of the Son of God; and as a mystery long hidden, but at length revealed, and comprising in it the deep and inexhaustible treasures of all spiritual science. Since, therefore, they had received Christ Jesus, the Lord, the giver and subject of that gospel, it surely became them to walk in Him.

The verb *παραλαμβάνω*, signifying to take to oneself, is used emphatically to appropriate wisdom or instruction—much as in Scotland the faculty of acquiring knowledge is termed *uptake*. 1 Cor. xi. 23, xv. 1, 3; Gal. i. 9, 12; Phil. iv. 9; 1 Thess. ii. 13. They had received him, in the way of being taught about Him—verse 7. They had been instructed, and they had apprehended the lesson. It is a superficial exegesis on the part of Theophylact, Grotius, and others, to make the proper name *X. 'I.* mean merely the doctrine of Christ. For it was Christ Himself whom they had received —the sum and life of all evangelical instruction. Nay, more, the repetition and structure of the sentence show that the full meaning is—ye have received Christ Jesus as the Lord. In the character of Lord they had accepted Him. This was the testing element of their reception. The Anointed Jesus is now "Lord of all," and to acknowledge His Lordship is to own the success of His atoning work as well as to bow to His sovereign authority. Thus we understand the apostle when he says, 1 Cor. xii. 3, "Wherefore I give you to understand, that no man speaking by the Spirit of God calleth Jesus accursed; and that no man can say that Jesus is the Lord, but by the Holy Ghost." On the special meaning and use of the terms see Eph. i. 2. The form of error introduced among them, which would rob the Saviour of His dignity, led to the denial of the Messiahship in its true sense; and in its spiritualism, it would, at the same time, explain away His humanity.

These expressive terms are thus the symbols of a vast amount of instruction. Whatever men receive in the gospel, it is Christ. He is the soul of doctrine—for prophets foretold Him, and apostles preached Him; and the oracles of the one and the sermons of the other had no splendour but from Him, and no vitality but in Him. Ethical teaching has as close a connection with Him, for it expounds His law, defers to His authority, and exhibits the means of obedience and fertility in His imparted Spirit and strength. Promise is based upon His veracity, and sealed in His blood, and suffering looks for sympathy to Him who bled and wept. The great mystery of the Divine government is solved in Him, and in Him alone is the enigma of man's history and destiny comprehended. Spiritual life has its root in Him—the growth of the Divine image, and the repose of the soul in the bosom of Him who made it. In believing the gospel, men receive no impersonal abstraction, but Christ Himself—light, safety, love, pattern, power, and life. And they receive Him as "the Lord." He won the Lordship by His death. He rose from the sepulchre to the throne. To Him the universe bends in awful homage, and the church worships Him in grateful allegiance. The Colossians had received Him as the Lord, and surely no seduction would ever lead them to discrown Him, and transfer their fealty to one of the crowded and spectral myriads which composed the celestial hierarchy—one of a dim and cloudy mass which was indistinct from its very number, surrounding the throne, but never daring to depute any of its members to ascend it.

"As ye have received Him, walk in Him." The particle ὡς denotes something more than a reason, for it indicates manner —"according as." Matt. viii. 13; Luke xiv. 22; 1 Cor. iii. 5; Tit. i. 5. The demonstrative adverb which follows ὡς, in sense, is here as often omitted. *Ἐν αὐτῷ περιπατεῖτε*—"Walk in Him." The verb is often used to describe manner of life, or visible conduct; and that life is to be enjoyed in union with Christ. If reception of Christ the Lord refer to inner life, then this walk refers to its outer manifestation. It was to be no inert or latent principle. Christ was not merely a theme to be idly contemplated or admired in a supine and listless reverie; nor a creed to be carelessly laid up as in a distant and inaccessible deposit; nor an impulse which might produce a passing and periodical vibration, and then sink into abeyance and exhaustion; but a power, which, in diffusing itself over mind and heart, provided for its own palpable manifestation and recognition in the daily life. For there could be no walking in Him, without the previous reception of Him. The outer life is but the expression of the inner. Ability to walk is the result of communicated animation. Nay, more, if they received Him, they could not but walk in Him. The reception of such truth necessitates a change of heart. It is a belief which, from its very nature, produces immediate results. In Him, and in Him according to the character in which they had received Him, were they to walk. And they would not walk in Him as they received Him, if they were tempted to reject His functions and qualifications as the *Christ*, or in any form, or on any pretext, to modify, depreciate, or set aside His claims; or if they were prompted to deny or explain away His true humanity as *Jesus*—taking from His life its reality, and from His death its atoning value; or if they were induced to withhold their allegiance from Him as *Lord*, the one rightful governor, proprietor, and judge. There must therefore be faith in Him as the Christ, the consciousness of a near and living relation to Him as Jesus, the kinsman, the brother-man; and deep and loyal obedience to Him as Lord. "He is thy Lord, worship thou Him." "In Him" presupposes the reception of Him; and to "walk in Him," is to have life in Him and from Him, with thought and emotion shaped and inspired by His presence. The hallowed sphere of walk is in Him, but beyond this barrier are sin and danger, false philosophies, and mazy entanglements. If they walked in Christ, they would be fortified against those doubts which the pernicious teachings of error, with their show of wisdom, were so apt to superinduce.

(Ver. 7.) *Ἐῤῥιζωμένοι καὶ ἐποικοδομούμενοι ἐν αὐτῷ*—"Having been rooted, and being built up in Him." [*Ἐῤῥιζωμένοι*, Eph. iii. 17. *Ἐποικοδ.* Eph. ii. 20.] The participles are used in a tropical sense, and are connected with the preceding clause—"walk in Him." The figures, as Meyer remarks, neither agree with the preceding verb, nor with one another. But the main ideas are stability and growth—the root, "in Him," beyond the possibility of eradication; and the growth that of a symmetrical structure, which, "in Him," has its unshaken foundation. The first participle, by its tense, indicates a previous state, and the second a present condition. They had already been rooted, but they were still to be making progress. Were such their character, were they rooted in Christ, and not simply adhering to Him by some superficial tie, and were they being built up, or growing in gracious attainment, then might they defy all the efforts of the false teachers to detach them from the truth.

Καὶ βεβαιούμενοι ἐν τῇ πίστει καθὼς ἐδιδάχθητε—"And stablished in the faith, as ye have been taught." The preposition is omitted in some Codices, and by Lachmann and Tischendorf. If this reading be adopted, we should be inclined, with Meyer, to take the dative in an instrumental sense—"stablished by means of the faith;" but if *ἐν* be retained, perhaps the common rendering is preferable. See under i. 7. They were to be confirmed in the faith which had been taught them—that system of belief which Epaphras had preached to them. We should agree with Olshausen, against Meyer, that *πίστις* is faith in the objective sense, were it not for *ἐν αὐτῇ* in the following clause, which we believe to be genuine, though it is wanting in A and C. For the apostle says—*περισσεύοντες ἐν αὐτῇ*. This abounding bids us take faith in a subjective sense—the conscious belief of the truth—and in that belief they were not to be stinted, cautious, or timid, but they were to abound. Their faith was not to be scanty as a rivulet in summer, but like the Jordan in harvest, overflowing its banks. And they were to abound in it—

'Εν εὐχαριστίᾳ—"With thanksgiving." A similar construction is found in Rom. xv. 13; 2 Cor. iii. 9, viii. 7. They could not but be thankful that the truth had been brought to them, and that by the Divine grace they had been induced fully and unreservedly to believe it. Two other and opposing forms of construction have been proposed. Grotius renders *per gratiarum actionem crescentes in fide*, as if the thanks were the means of abounding in faith; while Storr, Flatt, Böhmer, and Huther take it thus—abounding by means of the same in thanksgiving, as if faith were the means of thanksgiving. But the connection, as we have first given it, is more in harmony with the sequence and position of the words. The entire verse is at once a precept and a warning, and were the precept obeyed and the warning listened to, then "philosophy and vain deceit" would ply their machinations in vain.

Having again and again approached his subject by indirect allusions, the apostle now boldly and fully brings it out. "Beware lest any man spoil you through philosophy and vain deceit." And we may remark in introduction, that the sentiment of the verse has been sometimes greatly abused. The apostle has been quoted in condemnation of philosophy in general, though he expressly identifies the philosophy which he reprobates with "vain deceit." Philosophy, science, or the pursuit and love of wisdom, cannot be stigmatized, as in itself hostile to faith. The apostle himself has employed philosophy to prove the existence of the Creator, and show the sin and folly of polytheism and idolatry. Rom. i. 19–23. The attributes of the Divine nature—not in themselves cognizable by the senses—have assumed a visible embodiment in the works of creation, and he who fails to discover the one God in His productions is "without excuse."[1] So that the

[1] "God, whom the wisest men acknowledge to bee a Power uneffable, and Vertue infinite, a Light by abundant claritie invisible; and Understanding which

teaching of Natural Theology is not erroneous, but defective —it needs not to be corrected, but only to be supplemented. Why should the love of wisdom be reckoned vanity, when the page on which man is invited to study is wide as the universe, and rolls back to creation? Wherever he turns his eye, on himself or beyond himself—above, around, or beneath him, ten thousand things invite his examination. Earth and heaven, mind and matter, past and present, summon him to wake up his faculties, and scrutinize and reflect on the universe around him. Let him look down on the sands and rocks of his home, and he enters into Geology. Let him know this ball to be one of many similar orbs in the sky, and Astronomy entrances him. Let him gaze at the munificent plenty around him, spread over zone and continent in the shape of trees, flowers, and animals, and he is introduced into Geography, Botany, and Zoology. Let him survey the relations of matter—its forms, quantities, and laws of mixture and motion, and at once he finds himself among Mathematics, Optics, Mechanics, and Chemistry. Let him turn his vision upon himself, and observe the attributes and functions of his physical life, and he dips into the mysteries of Anatomy and Physiology. Let him strive to learn what has happened before him, and in what connection he stands to brethren of other tongues and countries, and he is brought into acquaintanceship with History, Philology, and Political Economy. And, in fine, let his own conscious mind make itself the theme of reflection—in its

it selfe can onely comprehend, an Essence eternall and spirituall, of absolute purenesse and simplicity: was, and is pleased to make himselfe knowne by the worke of the World: in the wonderfull magnitude whereof, (all which He imbraceth, filleth and sustaineth) we behold the Image of that glory, which cannot be measured, and withall that one, and yet universall Nature, which cannot be defined. In the glorious Lights of Heaven, we perceive a shadow of his divine Countenance; in his mercifull provision for all that live, his manifold goodnesse: and lastly, in creating and making existent the World universall, by the absolute Art of his owne Word, his Power and Almightinesse; which Power, Light, Vertue, Wisdome, and Goodnesse, being all but attributes of one simple Essence, and one God, we in all admire, and in part discerne *per speculum creaturarum*, that is, in the disposition, order, and variety of Celestiall and Terrestriall bodies: Terrestriall, in their strange and manifold diversities; Celestiall, in their beauty and magnitude; which in their continuall and contrary motions, are neither repugnant, intermixt, nor confounded. By these potent effects, we approach to the knowledge of the Omnipotent cause, and by these motions, their Almighty Mover."—Sir Walter Raleigh, p. 1, *History of the World*, London, 1614.

powers and aspirations, its faculties and emotions, its obligations and destiny, and he is initiated into the subtleties and wonders of Metaphysics and Morals, Legislation and Theology. Thus, Strabo, in the first chapter of his *Geography*,[1] says—"That acquaintance with Divine and human things constitutes what is called philosophy."

Again, not only is philosophy a necessary result of our being and condition, but it is full of benefit, for the more a man knows his own nature, the more will he feel the adaptation of Christianity to it, and be persuaded of its Divine origin. The inner nature has its religious instincts and susceptibilities, which are not grafted upon it, but are of its very essence. As the eye is fitted for the reception of light, and light alone can enable it to fulfil its functions—as it is made for the light and the light for it—so religious truth alone is fitted to satisfy those yearnings and aspirations. There is a perfect harmony between God's inner revelation of Himself in man, and His external revelation of Himself in Scripture. Wrong belief may be against reason, but unbelief is against nature. A sound philosophy comes to this conclusion—that Christianity fulfils every condition—that in its God and its incarnate Jesus—its revelation and its atonement—its sanctifying agency and its future heaven—it responds to every want and hope of humanity. Man must have some God—it gives him the true one. He seeks to some revelation, and it sends him the genuine oracle. He relies on some sacrifice, and it shows the perfect atonement. He anticipates a heaven, and it provides him with such a home, and enables him to reach it. This philosophy develops what Tertullian has happily called *testimonium animae* naturaliter *Christianae.*

But it is not such philosophy, or such use of philosophy, that the apostle condemns—"Philosophy was, in its first descent, a generous, noble thing; a virgin beauty, a pure light, born of the Father of lights."[2] At the same time, it is not to be denied that the greater portion of heresies have been

[1] Ἤ τοῦ τὰ θεῖα καὶ τὰ ἀνθρώπεια ἐπιβλέποντος ὥνπερ τὴν φιλοσοφίαν ἐπιστήμην φασίν. Vol. i. p. 4, ed. Cramer, Berlin, 1844. Justin also characterizes philosophers thus—Καὶ οἱ φιλόσοφοι οἱ τὴν ἀληθῆ καὶ θείαν εἰδέναι ἐπαγγελλόμενοι γνῶσιν. *Cohort. ad Graecos*, p. 14, vol. i. Opera, ed. Otto, 1842.

[2] Gale, *Court of the Gentiles*, Part ii. Preface. Clement, *Strom.* i. p. 282.

allied to a false philosophy. Tertullian, in the seventh chapter of his *De Praescriptione Haereticorum*, says—*ipsae denique haereses a philosophia subornantur.*[1] Platonism and Aristotelianism had each in turn the ascendency, and Christianity has suffered from the four great forms of philosophy—Sensationalism, Idealism, Scepticism, and Mysticism, the error of each of which lies in pushing to extravagance some important truth. And in modern times, has not Hegelian Pantheism clothed itself in biblical phraseology? Its doctrine, that "the consciousness which man has of himself is the consciousness which God has of Himself," finds its appropriate mythical representation in the mediatorial person of the God-man; while "eternal life" is but the symbol of an immortality without individual existence. Have not men in their wildness invoked "the stars in their courses" to fight against Him who, enthroned above them, has not forgotten that distant and insignificant planet on which sin and misery dwell? Have they not called to them the rocks and fossils of the early

[1] The Father justifies his accusation in the following strains:—Inde aeones, et formae nescio quae infinitae, et trinitas hominis apud Valentinum; Platonicus fuerat: inde Marcionis deus melior de tranquillitate; a Stoicis venerat: et ut anima interire dicatur, ab Epicureis observatur: et ut carnis restitutio negetur, de una omnium philosophorum schola sumitur: et ubi materia cum deo aequatur, Zenonis disciplina est: et ubi aliquid de igneo deo allegatur, Heracletus intervenit. Eadem materia apud haereticos et philosophos volutatur, idem retractatus implicantur: unde malum, et quare? et unde homo, et quomodo? et, quod proxime Valentinus proposuit, unde deus? scilicet de enthymesi et ectromate. Miserum Aristotelem! qui illis dialecticam instituit, artificem struendi et destruendi, versipellem in sententiis, coactam in coniecturis, duram in argumentis, operariam contentionum, molestam etiam sibi ipsi, omnia retractantem, ne quid omnino tractaverit. Hinc illae fabulae et genealogiae interminabiles, et quaestiones infructuosae, et sermones serpentes velut cancer, a quibus nos apostolus refrenans nominatim philosophiam contestatur caveri oportere, scribens ad Colossenses, Videte, ne qui sit circumveniens vos per philosophiam et inanem seductionem, secundum traditionem hominum, praeter providentiam spiritus sancti. Fuerat Athenis, et istam sapientiam humanam, affectatricem et interpolatricem veritatis, de congressibus noverat, ipsam quoque in suas haereses multipartitam varietate sectarum invicem repugnantium. Quid ergo Athenis et Hierosolymis? quid academiae et ecclesiae? quid haereticis et Christianis? Nostra institutio de porticu Solomonis est, qui et ipse tradiderat dominum in simplicitate cordis esse quaerendum. Viderint qui Stoicum et Platonicum et dialecticum Christianismum protulerunt. Nobis curiositate opus non est post Christum Iesum, nec inquisitione post evangelium. Cum credimus, nihil desideramus ultra credere. Hoc enim prius credimus, non esse quod ultra credere debeamus.—*De Praescr. Haeret.* p. 8, Opera, vol. ii., Lipsiae, 1854.

infancy of the globe to prove that the record of creation was not furnished by the Creator? Are there not those at the present time who regard inspiration as but the "fine frenzy" of an Oriental temperament, or look upon it as being "as wide as the world, as common as God," and who, therefore, take from the biblical records their sole, infallible, and supreme authority, leaving us an Old Testament without prophecies, and a New Testament without miracles and redemption? These are, verily, abuses of philosophy—"oppositions of science, falsely so called." We do not, therefore, object to philosophy, or to the philosophical treatment of Christianity. We can have no horror at free thoughts and bold inquiry, so long as men indicate their desire to submit to the decisions of Evidence. There is a legitimate province for philosophy to work in, and "faith is the synthesis of reason and the individual will."[1]

But the system condemned by the apostle was something which assumed the name of philosophy, yet had nothing of its spirit. It sprang from a wrong motive. So far from being the love of wisdom, it was the fondness of folly. It was nursed in a fantastic imagination, and intruded into a supersensuous sphere. It did not deal with nature around it, but with the supernatural beyond it. It did not investigate its own constitution, but it pryed into the arcana of the spirit-world. It was wholly spectral and baseless. It developed superstition and crossed the path of the gospel. It lived in a cloud-land which it had created, and withdrew itself from the influence and faith of apostolical Christianity. The plain truths of redemption did not satisfy its prurient appetite, nor could it content itself with the "manifold wisdom" of the cross. It longed for something more ethereal than historical facts, something more recondite than the mystery of godliness. It forestalled the Rosicrucian vanities. It peopled the spheres with imaginary Essences, to which it assigned both names and functions. It laboured to purge itself from the vulgarities of physical life, in order to enter this spiritual circle. It battled with the flesh, till the crazy nerves gave it such sights and sounds as it longed to enjoy. The ordinances of the New Testament were too tame for it, and it

[1] "Essay on Faith," in Coleridge's *Confessions of an Inquiring Spirit*, p. 120.

created a new and emaciating ritual for itself. It was, in short, an eccentric union of Judaism with the Gnostic Theosophy—a mixture of Jewish ritualism with Oriental mysticism. It took from Moses those special parts of his economy, which "sanctified to the purifying of the flesh," and it seems to have deepened and exaggerated them. It selected from the Eastern Theosophy its armies of Æons, its array of principalities and powers, whom it marshalled as its mediators, and to whom it inculcated homage. It was smitten with the disease of him who will look into the sun, and who soon mistakes for realities the gaudy images that float before him. Such was the visionary science which had special charms for the inhabitants of Phrygia, and which in after years produced unmistakeable results. That the apostle means such philosophy is evident, for in no other way could his warning be appropriate. It was of a present, and not a future danger—a real, and not an imaginary jeopardy that he so earnestly cautioned them. It was not, as Tertullian imagines, the whole Greek philosophy, for that lay not in his way; nor yet any special form of it, as Grotius and others have held, for the philosophy of the Academy and the Porch, of Epicurus and Pythagoras, was not the source of immediate danger to the Colossian church.

(Ver. 8.) *Βλέπετε, μή τις ὑμᾶς ἔσται ὁ συλαγωγῶν διὰ τῆς φιλοσοφίας καὶ κενῆς ἀπάτης*—"Be on your guard lest any one make a spoil of you through philosophy and vain deceit." The verb *βλέπω*, in this sense, is sometimes followed by the accusative of the persons to be guarded against, occasionally by the genitive preceded by *ἀπό*, sometimes also by *ἵνα*; but most usually by *μή*, and its compounds with the aorist subjunctive. Here, however, we have the future indicative, *ἔσται*, as in Heb. iii. 12. The apostle therefore does not say that the evil had happened, but he expresses his fear that it would happen—his misgiving, that what he apprehended would take place. Winer, § 56, 2 (b), *a*; Bernhardy, p. 402; Hartung, vol. ii. 139. He saw the attractive subtlety, and he could not withhold the warning and pre-intimation. The expression, too, is pointed and emphatic—*τις ὁ συλαγωγῶν*—more so than if he had employed the subjunctive, *συλαγωγῇ*. It individualizes the spoiler—represents him as at his work

—associates vividly the actor with the action. Gal. i. 7. When some infer from the language that the apostle had only one person specially in his eye—one restless and attractive heresiarch, we would not contradict, though we are not prepared to come decidedly to the same conclusion. The participle, which occurs only here, belongs to the later Greek,[1] and denotes—making a prey of—driving off as booty, though it is finical on the part of Meyer to base the latter signification upon the expression of the 6th verse, walk in Him, as if they might be caught when not in that walk, and forced away as a spoil. The expression shows the strong feeling of the apostle, and how he regarded their capture by that philosophy as fatal, almost beyond recovery, to their faith and peace. It is not in accordance with the language to think of the false teacher or teachers taking faith, mind, or purity, or anything else as a prey from the Colossians, for the Colossians themselves are the booty. The means employed were—

Διὰ τῆς φιλοσοφίας καὶ κενῆς ἀπάτης—"By philosophy and empty delusion." This philosophy is none other than the theme of the *πιθανολογία* of verse 4, and is nothing else in essence than "vain deceit." For the second clause, where neither preposition nor article is repeated, explains the first —philosophy which was expressed in "vain words," is identical with "vain deceit." There is no reality about it. It is out and out a delusion, a tissue of airy figments. The term philosophy was a favourite one in the Greek world, but it was extended in course of time to portions and objects of Jewish study by the affectation of Philo[2] and Josephus.[3] Tittmann, in his very one-sided essay,[4] restricts the term solely to Jewish doctrine, and Heinrichs no less narrowly to Jewish worship. Perhaps the apostle would not have given any mere Jewish system such an appellation, but he uses the term because there might be in it some mixture of Gentile

[1] Heliodorus, 10, p. 512. Aristaenet. ii. ep. 22.

[2] *De Somniis*, Opera, vol. v. p. 160, ed. Pfeiffer. [3] *Cont. Ap.* ii. 4.

[4] *De Vestigiis Gnost. in N. T. frustra quaesitis*, etc., Lipsiae, 1773. Compare, on the other hand, Neander, *Geschichte der Pflanzung*, etc., vol. i. p. 512. Vaughan's *Causes of the Corruption of Christianity*, p. 167, etc. Brucker, *Histor. Crit. Phil.* ii. p. 40, etc.

lore, and especially because the false teachers dignified their views by such a title.

Κατὰ τὴν παράδοσιν τῶν ἀνθρώπων—"After the tradition of men." The preposition does not connect this with the first clause of the verse, as Meyer construes, and as if it showed the direction in which they were seduced, but it is to be joined with the immediately preceding words. It points out, not so much, as Storr supposes, the authority of that philosophy, as its general source and character. It is according to the tradition of men, and not according to Divine revelation. In 2 Thess. iii. 6, the construction is fully expressed. Elements of the tradition here referred to are found in Matt. xv. 2; Mark vii. 3, 5, 8, 9, 13; Gal. i. 14. It is not simply doctrine, as Olshausen and Huther take it; nor perhaps Græco-Jewish doctrine, as others supposed. It was, to a great extent, that tangled mass of oral teaching, which, age after age, the Jews had unwarrantably engrafted on the written law. That farrago of unwritten statute and ritual is contrasted by Jesus with the "commands of God." It was solely of man, and partook largely of his vanity and weakness. As in the instance adduced by Christ, it explained away the obligation of the fifth commandment by a mean quibble, which added impiety to filial neglect, and permitted a son to starve his parent under a pretence of superior liberality to God. It taught the payment "of mint, anise, and cumin," but forgot "the weightier matters of the law, judgment, mercy, and faith." It scrupled to eat with unwashed hands, but was forward to worship with an unregenerate heart. It was eloquent and precise about cleaning of cups, but vague and dumb about the purifying of conscience. It converted religion into a complicated routine, with a superstitious and perplexing ritual, as if man were to be saved by the observance of ceremonies as puerile as they were cumbrous—a series of postures, ablutions, amulets, and vain repetitions. It lost sight of the spirituality of worship, but enjoined a careful genuflexion. It buried ethics under a system of miserable and tedious casuistry. It attempted to place everything under formal regulation, and was now busied in solemn trifling, and now lost in utter indecency. It was mighty about the letter, and oblivious of the spirit. It rejoiced in the oblation of a ram, but had no sympathy with the "sacrifice of a broken and contrite heart." It drew water every year from the well at Siloam with a pompous procession, but had no thirst for the living stream which its prophets had predicted and described. It would drill man into a fatiguing devotion. It trained to the mere mummery of worship when it prescribed the movement of eye and foot, of head and arm. It intruded its precepts into every relation, and attempted to fill out the Divine law by laying down directions for every supposable case. It was not content with leading principles, but added innumerable supplements. It surrounded the rite of circumcision with many ridiculous minutiae. It professed to guard the sanctity of the Sabbath by a host of trifling injunctions, descending to the needle of the tailor, the pen of the scribe, and the wallet of the beggar. The craftsman was told that he was guilty if he tied a camel-driver's knot, or a sailor's knot, on that day, but not guilty if he merely tied a knot which he could loose with one of his hands; and that he might leap over a ditch, but not wade through the water that lay in it. It declared by what instrument the paschal lamb should be roasted, and how a jar of wine must be carried during a festival; with what gestures a phylactery was to be put on, and with what scrupulous order it was to be laid aside. It left nothing to the impulse of a living piety. It was ignorant that a sanctified spirit needed no such prescriptions; that the "due order" could only be learned from the inner oracle; and that obedience to all its ramified code, apart from the spirit of genuine faith and devotion, was only acting a part in a heartless pantomime.

And these traditions proved that they were from man, not only from their character, but from their verbiage and appended sanctions. If the Mishna be, as we believe it to be, on the whole, a faithful record of many such traditions, then, that they were of men is a fact inscribed on their very front. The recurring formula is—Rabbi Eleazar said this, but Rabbi Gamaliel said that; this was the opinion of Rabbi Meir, but that of Rabbi Jehudah; Hillel was of this mind, but Beth Shammai of that; Rabbi Tarphon pronounced in this way, but Rabbi Akivah in that; thus thought Ben Azai on the one hand, but thus thought Rabbi Nathan on the other;

such was the decision of Jochanan Ben Saacchai, but such was the opposite conclusion of Matthias Ben Harash. It never rose above a mere human dictum, and it armed its jurists with supreme authority. It never shook the mire off its wings, or soared into that pure and lofty empyrean which envelopes the Divine tribunal, so that in His light it might see light. What had been thus conceived in the dry frivolity of one age, was handed down to another, and the mass was swiftly multiplied in its long descent. The Pharisee selected one portion and practised it, and the Essene chose another and made it his rule of life. It was carried in one or other of these shapes to other lands, and though it commingled with other opinions of similar source and tendency, it never belied its parentage as the TRADITIONS OF MEN.

Κατὰ τὰ στοιχεῖα τοῦ κόσμου—"After the rudiments of the world." The reference is somewhat obscure. The noun *στοιχεῖον* is employed in 2 Pet. iii. 10, 12,[1] to denote the elements of physical nature, while in Heb. v. 12 it signifies the simple lessons and truths of Christianity, and is opposed to *τελειότης*. In the former sense it frequently occurs in the ancient philosophy, as comprising fire, air, earth, and water. It is amusing to observe with what ingenuity some of the Greek Fathers[2] give it such a sense in the passage before us, because, forsooth, all the elements are employed in the Jewish service—water for purification and fire for sacrifice, earth for the erection of altars, and the revolution of the aerial bodies for the determination of the sacred festivals. The noun sometimes signifies an elementary sound, or a letter, and so came to denote what is rudimentary—what is suited to the tuition of infancy. In this sense we understand the apostle to use it in Gal. iv. 3, 9, and with special reference to the Jewish ritual and worship. The churches in Galatia had a strong and wayward tendency to revert to Judaism, or at least to incorporate it, or a portion of it, into the new religion. And as they had embraced a system which was spiritual and mature—which was not embodied in types and ceremonies, but in pure, simple, universal truths—the apostle wonders why, with their higher and manly privilege, they should go

[1] Wisdom vii. 17, xix. 17. Plato, *Timaeus*, 48. Vitruvius, 1, 4.
[2] Especially Genadius, quoted by Œcumenius, *in loc.*

back to "the weak and beggarly elements;" why, when they had been reading the book of Divine instruction with its complete and lasting lessons, they should revert and descend again to the mere alphabet. It was as if one who was able to sweep the heavens, and tell the sizes, distances, and revolutions of its luminaries, should forswear this noble exercise, and seat himself in an infant school, and find the highest pleasure among the first and trite axioms and diagrams of geometry.

The term *κόσμος* marks the nature of these elements. It is said that the Jewish economy had *ἅγιον κοσμικόν*—"a worldly sanctuary," an epithet placed in contrast with *τὰ ἐπουράνια*, and with *σκηνὴ οὐ χειροποίητος*. Our opinion is, that in the clause under discussion, the apostle refers to the Jewish worship. Some interpreters, such as Meyer and Böhmer, think this exposition too restricted, and give the meaning as referring both to the ritual of the Jewish and the heathen world, supposing the "world" to signify, as it often does, the non-Christian portion of its population. Huther also gives it a similar extension of meaning—*Elemente des ethischen Lebens in der Welt.* His objections to the common interpretation are fully set aside by De Wette, and are not in themselves of any weight. But the phrase before us has a definite meaning affixed to it in the Epistle to the Galatians, and there it denotes simply the Jewish system. There was in the Galatian churches no attempt to heathenize, but only to Judaize; no endeavour to engraft heathenism, but only Judaism on the new dispensation.

That the Mosaic economy should receive the name of elements is easily understood, but why should such a genitive as *κόσμου* be added? It belonged to the world in a special sense, not to the world or age in the Jewish sense of the term, as if, as Wahl supposes, the meaning were—adapted to the men of this age. It was of the world, as being like it, evident to the senses, visible, and material, in contrast with what is spiritual and invisible. In this sense, the whole economy was mundane, for it was sensuous; it pictured itself to the eye in the stones of its edifice, the robes of its priests, the victims of its altars, its restrictions on diet, its frequent washings, the blood of its initiatory rite, and the periods of its sacred festivals. It was a worldly panorama, and it portrayed but the elements of spiritual truth. It set before its votaries the merest first principles, which were indeed often expounded and developed by its prophets. It was "a shadow of things to come," not even a full and vivid picture. Under the 17th verse the exposition will be more fully given. The party at Colosse, who attempted to seduce, presented some elements of the Mosaic ritual and worship as a special instrument of spiritual elevation and ascetic discipline. They inculcated a philosophy which, whatever might be its mysticism or its metaphysical or heathen features, was in essence an adaptation of Judaism, not as found in the Mosaic writings, but as overlaid and disfigured by a mass of accumulated traditions.

Καὶ οὐ κατὰ Χριστόν—"And not after Christ." That philosophy was not according to Christ. It is a needless dilution of the sense, on the part of Erasmus and Röell, etc., to render—"not according to the doctrine of Christ." It was not based upon Christ, but was in contrariety to His person and work. It depreciated Him, and undervalued His mediation. But true Christian science has Him for its centre, and Him for its object. It bows to His authority, and ever seeks to exalt Him. Any new doctrine may be safely tested by the estimation in which it holds Christ; for all that is false and dangerous in speculation, invariably strives to lower His rank and official dignity, and therefore is neither in source, spirit, substance, nor tendency, according to Him.[1] And they were to be on their guard against such dangerous deceptions, which were not according to Christ. Though the apostle says—"not after Christ"—it must not be inferred that the errorist or errorists made no profession of Christianity, or were openly hostile to it. Had this been the case, their non-Christian character would have been boldly and distinctly pointed out by the apostle. They seem to have been disciples in name. Nor did they come like mere Judaizers and make an open assault, or insist in plain terms that Christian Gentiles should be circumcised and keep the law. Then they would have been confronted like the Judaizers in Galatia. But they were

[1] "My design all alongst this discourse, butts at this one principle, that speculations in religion are not so necessary, and are more dangerous than sincere practice. It is in religion as in heraldry, the simpler the bearing be, it is so much the purer and ancienter."—Sir George Mackenzie's *Religio Stoici*, p. 141, Edinburgh, 1665.

more insidious in their attack—boasted the possession of an inner and a higher knowledge, and preached an ideal system of specious pretensions, and made up apparently of Judaism and Gnosticism,[1] — or Judaism deeply imbued with that mysticism which distinguished the Essenes, and that kind of theosophy which is found in Philo.[2]

(Ver. 9.) *Ὅτι ἐν αὐτῷ κατοικεῖ πᾶν τὸ πλήρωμα τῆς θεότητος σωματικῶς.* This is an irresistible argument. Any system not after Christ must be human and wrong—"for in Him dwells all the fulness of the Godhead bodily." The noun *πλήρωμα* has been fully explained under Eph. i. 23. The substantive *θεότης* is an abstract term, like Deity, in which God is viewed in essence rather than personality. The word is quite different in meaning from *θειότης*, Rom. i. 20—a term which describes quality rather than being. The words differ as *divinitas* and *deitas*—divineness and Deity; or, as the Germans express it—*Göttlichkeit* and *Gottheit.* The Syriac uses the expressive term ܕܐܠܗܘܬܐ. The fulness of the Godhead is a fulness filled up by it—is that Godhead in all its native attributes and prerogatives. And it is the whole fulness—not one cycle of Divine perfections—a single cluster of Divine properties—not a partial possession of isolated glories—nor a handful of meted and fractional resources, but the entire assemblage of all in existence and character that constitutes the Divinity. What He is, and as He is, in being, mode, and manifestation, dwells in Christ. See under i. 15. One blushes to mention the Socinian misinterpretation, which so reduces this sublime statement as to make it signify merely, that the whole will of God was manifested by Him—an attempt which Calovius well names *detorsio mera.* Nor are we less confounded with the capricious and baseless exposition of Heinrichs, Baumgarten-Crusius, Schleusner, Gerhard, and Junker, that *πλήρωμα* can mean the church gathered without distinction from all nations, and that the apostle intends to say—that the whole church has its existence, wellbeing, or

[1] See also Matter, *Histoire Critique du Gnosticisme*, etc., Paris, 1828; Burton, *An Inquiry into the Heresies of the Apostolic Age*, Works, vol. iii.; the Bampton Lecture for 1829.

[2] Davidson, *Introduction*, vol. ii. p. 411.

instruction in Christ. Nor is the singularly ungrammatical exegesis of some early expositors less wonderful—that "in Him" means in the church, and that in this church dwells the fulness of the Godhead. Bähr ably refutes the view of Noesselt, which, though a little more ingenious than the Socinian hypothesis, does not essentially differ from it in result. The sense naturally suggested by the terms is the correct one. Nor are we to search for any recondite meaning, as if πλήρωμα must be taken in a Gnostic sense; or as if in the verb κατοικεῖ there were a necessary allusion to the so-named Shechinah—in which dwelt the Divinity. Whatever be the polemical reference, the ordinary meaning of the verb cannot be set aside, as denoting actual and prolonged habitation.

The mode of this mysterious inhabitation is declared to be σωματικῶς—"in a bodily form," for such is the first and plain meaning of the adverb. Other and vaguer ideas have been attached to it. It is a necessary result of the interpretation which takes πλήρωμα to signify the church, that it must regard σωματικῶς as intense and hyperbolical, and therefore we have the dilution of a *quasi*. The church dwells in Christ, *as if* in a bodily form—as if it formed His body. But—

1. The least plausible hypothesis is that of Capellus and Heumann, who look upon the term as equivalent to ὅλως, and as signifying "altogether." Such a translation makes the clause tautological, for πᾶν is already employed, and besides it cannot be borne out by any legitimate examples. Why resort to a rare and technical use of the word, as peculiar as in our familiar phrase, *a body of divinity*, meaning a full course of theological instruction?

2. Others, again, under the influence of the previous contrast between the law and the gospel, imagine an antithesis in the word, as if it stood in antagonism to τυπικῶς. There was a symbolical residence in the temple, but an actual one in Christ Jesus. The polemical Augustine first broached the idea. *Non ideo corporaliter quia corporeus est Deus, sed aut verbo translato usus est, tanquam in templo manufacto non corporaliter sed umbratiliter habitaverit, id est, praefigurantibus signis, nam illas omnes observationes umbras futurorum vocat, etiam ipso translato vocabulo, ... aut certe corporaliter dictum est, quia et in Christi corpore, quod assumpsit ex virgine,*

tanquam in templo habitat Deus.[1] Augustine has been followed by Vatablus, a-Lapide, Grotius, Glassius, Hackspann, Vitringa, Röell, Crellius, Schoettgen, Noesselt, Michaelis, Bengel, and Bretschneider. But there is no such implied contrast in this verse as between *σῶμα* and *σκιά* in verse 17, and there is therefore no just ground of departure from the common and absolute signification. Christ is held up as the grand centre and source of true philosophy, and the reason is that Godhead was incarnate in Him, and that therefore His claims are paramount, both in person and function. He is not only the Wonder of wonders in Himself, but creation and redemption—the two prime books of study—trace themselves to Him as their one author.

3. A large number of critics give to *σωματικῶς* the meaning of *essentialiter*, that is, the Godhead dwells in Christ really, or in substance — *οὐσιωδῶς*. Names of high authority are leagued in favour of this interpretation. Theophylact and Œcumenius, and Isidore the Pelusiot, among the Fathers; Calvin, Beza, and Melancthon, among the reformers; with Steiger, Huther, Olshausen, and Usteri,[2] among the more recent expositors. The ground of this interpretation lies again in a supposed polemical contrast, which certainly does not appear in the context. Melancthon says—*est oppositum inhabitationi separabili ut habitat Deus in sanctis*, that is, the union of Divinity with Christ is a personal union—not like the influential indwelling of God in a believing heart. Huther supposes such a contrast as this, that the Deity did not dwell in Christ as it dwelt in the old prophets who preceded Him. Olshausen again gives prominence to a Gnostic antagonism, as if the apostle meant to distinguish between a merely temporary influence of a higher spirit, and a permanent union of the Godhead—an idea as naturally brought out by giving to the adverb its usual signification. To fall back for defence upon any uses of the Hebrew word עֶצֶם, is all but to surrender the cause. The Hebrew noun does signify *ipse*, but never in connection with persons—*de rebus tantummodo*, as Gesenius, *sub voce*, remarks. The noun *σῶμα* does signify person in the New Testament, though Bähr

[1] *Ep.* 187, vol. ii. p. 1036, ed. Ben., Paris, 1836.
[2] *Lehrb.* p. 234. See also Hammond, *in loc.*

denies it. Davenant says—"the Hebrew put souls for persons, and the Greek put bodies;" but the instances of the latter usage adduced by him will not bear him out; for in them there is usually distinct reference to the corporeal part of the person. In those instances in the New Testament in which σῶμα appears to signify person, it is not only followed with a genitive of person, but there is always some special reason why the term should be so employed—some implied contrast, some contextual point, or some tacit reference to the body or external person. Thus, among the classics, it is appropriately used of soldiers and slaves, whose bodies are in special request. As in the New Testament it is used in connection with the eye, Matt. vi. 22; with marriage—a union characterized as "one flesh," Eph. v. 28; with the idea of death, Phil. i. 20; and the notion of a living sacrifice, in which the dead bodies of victims were offered, Rom. xii. 1. Indeed, in Homeric usage σῶμα always denotes a corpse. So that, absolutely, the noun does not signify person; and such a sense is never given to the cognate adjective or adverb. This exegesis seems to have arisen from an attempt to define by it the nature of that union which subsisted between Divinity and humanity in the person of Christ.

4. The last and best interpretation is that which takes *σωματικῶς* in its literal and only meaning—in a bodily shape, and not as Theodoret paraphrases—ὡς ἐν σώματι. Such is also the view of Calovius, Estius, Storr, De Wette, Bähr, Böhmer, and Meyer. Yet Steiger calls it—*abgeschmackt*—insipid, and Olshausen regards it as tautological, because the words "in Him" occur in the same clause. But the words "in Him" are the general reference, and the adverb specifies the mode in which He possessed the Divine fulness. The fulness of the Godhead was embodied in Him, or dwelt in Him—in no invisible shape, and by no unappreciable contact. It assumed a bodily form. It abode in Him as a man. It made its residence the humanity of Jesus. Divinity was incarnated in Christ. It shrank not from taking upon it our nature, and realizing the prophetic title—"Immanuel, God with us." The same idea is contained in John i. 14—"the Word was made flesh, and dwelt among us." The Logos, yet

unfleshed, was God, and was with God, Divine and yet distinct from the Father; but the fulness of Godhead was only spiritually within Him. Now, it has made its abode in his humanity without consuming it or deifying it, or changing any of its essential properties. It hungered and it ate, it thirsted and it drank, it grieved and it wept, it watched and prayed, it wearied itself and it lay down, it was exhausted and it slept, it bled and it died. That body so filled and honoured was no phantom, as many even in the apostolic age imagined, for it had "flesh and bones," and, after its resurrection, it bore the scar of its recent wounds. It was therefore no vehicle which Divinity assumed by any singular process, but in the same way as the children become "partakers of flesh and blood," so did Christ partake of them. He was born as children are born, and the infant was wrapt "in swaddling bands." He was nursed as children are nursed, for "butter and honey should he eat." His young soul grew in wisdom as His physical frame grew in stature. It was easily seen that Godhead dwelt in that humanity, for glimpses of its glory flashed again and again through its earthly covering. The radiance was vailed, but never entirely eclipsed. His disciples "beheld His glory, the glory indeed of the only begotten of the Father." Peter felt impressed by it, and urged his own sinfulness as the reason why intercourse should be suspended; while Thomas, under the impulse of wonder and faith, cried out—"My Lord, and my God." Jesus prayed for others, and bade others pray on their own behalf; but He never solicited their prayers for Himself. When suppliants bowed the knee to Him, He never said—"See thou do it not;" never thought it to be idolatry on their part to offer Him homage, or felt it to be "robbery" on His part to accept it. His second coming is "the glorious appearing of the great God." At His baptism and transfiguration, the voice from the excellent glory hailed Him as God's beloved Son. He detected the inmost thoughts and enmities of the multitude, for he possessed a species of intuition which lies far above humanity. "He knew what was in man." "The wind bloweth where it listeth," but it listened to Him; and He who trod upon the waves of the Sea of Galilee, made them a path which God marks as His own. He wrought miracles at discretion, and wielded at pleasure the prerogative of forgiving sins. He assumed a co-ordinate power with the Father, and claimed with Him an equal right of dispensing with those obligations of the sabbatic law, which had been enacted for men by Divine authority. The most ordinary eye discovered something extraordinary about Him. The crowd that heard Him said—"He speaketh as one having authority;" for He spoke in the tones of conscious Divinity. "We have seen strange things to-day," shouted the spectators; and no wonder, those strange things were the characteristic acts of the strangest of Beings—the only Being who is God-man. A perfection not of earth belonged to His nature; for "the prince of this world," who finds so much to work upon in common humanity, could find nothing in Him; and the demons, whose appetite for evil leads them ever to detect it and vaunt over it, acknowledged Him to be "the Holy One of God." Referring to His death as the destruction of a temple, He asserted Himself able in three days to raise it again—a task that could be achieved only by the Divine Creator and Life-giver. While He walked on earth, He spoke of Himself as one "who is in heaven." Born centuries after Abraham, He yet pre-existed the great father of His nation. Lowly and humble—the son of Mary, He was the Image of the invisible God; and so close was His likeness to Him who sent Him, that He said—"He who hath seen me, hath seen the Father." And the apostle uses the present tense—the Divine fulness still "dwells" in Him. It was no temporary union, but an abiding possession. His glorious body has in it the same fulness of the Godhead, as had the body of His humiliation. The mode of inhabitation the apostle does not specify. What may be inferred is, that the union is a personal union of His natures—not a simple concord of will, so that there are two persons; nor such an absorption of the one element into the other, that there is only one nature. We know not whether Docetic views prevailed at that early period in the Colossian church, but it is certain that Christ was undervalued and His person misunderstood, in the false philosophy. Therefore the apostle affirms, in this brief but weighty clause, the great mystery of His mediatorial nature—the personal union in Him of Divinity and manhood. Any philosophy not "after Christ," must be earthly and delusive. It has missed the central truth—is amused with the stars, but forgetful of the sun. "For in Him dwells all the fulness of the Godhead bodily;" and, with singular congruity, the apostle adds—

(Ver. 10.) ***Καί ἐστε ἐν αὐτῷ πεπληρωμένοι***—"And ye are made full in Him." The clause is still in continuation of the warning, and crowns the argument. It is in entire opposition to the *usus loquendi* of the New Testament, on the part of Grotius, Bos, and Heumann, to make ἐστέ an imperative, for it emphasizes their present state. The phrase ἐν αὐτῷ has a meaning found with peculiar frequency—in Him—in union with Him; and it is wrong in Erasmus to render it—"by, or by means of Him." The participle πεπληρωμένοι is evidently used with a reference to the πλήρωμα of the preceding verse —ye are filled out of Christ's fulness, or are full in His fulness.

Opinions on the sense or reference of the participle are modified by the view entertained of the meaning of the preceding verse. Schoettgen narrows the meaning by far too much, and gives but one aspect of the sense, which he renders —*per istum estis perfecte edocti;* for though the apostle has been referring to instruction, yet far more is here implied. The exegesis of Grotius is rather an inference—*illo contenti estote;* for if they were complete in Jesus, it followed that they needed no supplemental endowments from any other quarter. The meaning of the clause is much the same as that found in Eph. iii. 19, to the exposition of which the reader may turn. Meyer says that nothing is to be supplied after πεπληρ., neither τῆς θεότητος with Theophylact, nor τοῦ πληρώματος τῆς θεότητος with De Wette. But the question recurs, of what elements is this fulness composed? or, if the participle be rendered "perfect"—"ye are perfect in Him," of what elements is this perfection made up? The clause has a very close connection with the foregoing verse, and with the phrase—"all the fulness of the Godhead." It is because that fulness dwells in Christ that they are filled up in Him. Being in Him, they are brought into contact with what is in Him; and that fulness of God contains a life whose pulsations create a responsive throbbing within them. There is in Christ complete provision, and what is so furnished is pledged to be conferred. There needs, therefore, be no want, and no casting about for any other source of supply. Believers have actual and present completeness of provided blessing, and there is the guaranteed completeness of prospective gifts. "Ye ARE complete in Him," for the scriptural view of Christ's person meets the deepest necessities of our spiritual nature. "What does it mean?" asks Chrysostom, "that you have nothing less than Him"—τὶ οὖν ἐστιν; ὅτι οὐδὲν ἔλαττον ἔχετε αὐτοῦ. The apostle adds another and striking clause—

Ὅς ἐστιν ἡ κεφαλὴ πάσης ἀρχῆς καὶ ἐξουσίας—"Who is the head of all principality and power." On the authority of B, D, E, F, G, Lachmann reads ὅ, but ὅς is retained on the authority of A, C, J, K, and that of the Greek Fathers. Lachmann's choice is vindicated by Steiger and Böhmer, though it appears to have sprung from a grammatical fondness for πλήρωμα as the principal preceding noun. If this reading be adopted, the foregoing clause must be placed in a parenthesis. "In Him, and that bodily, dwells all the Godhead's fulness . . . which is the Head of all principalities and powers." The authorities are nearly balanced, but the reading ὅς is most in analogy with the apostle's style of thought and expression. Besides, with the reading ὅ, the words ἐν ᾧ in verse 11 must refer also to πλήρωμα, and no tolerable sense could be extracted from such a connection. The terms ἀρχή and ἐξουσία are abstract ones, having reference to celestial dignities, and to such as were unfallen. The relative, as in i. 18, may be rendered—"as being He who is;" or, perhaps, "inasmuch as He is." Jelf, § 836, 3. The Head of principalities and powers. Eph. i. 21. There is no exception; the entire hierarchy, even its mightiest and noblest chieftains and dignities, own submission to Christ, and form a portion of His spiritual dominions. i. 16. There was some special reason why he intimates Christ's headship not generally over the church or the universe, but specially over the angelic hosts. If we can rely on accounts of the teaching ascribed to Simon Magus, we might find in them an illustration of the apostle's statement. Epiphanius relates, that Simon Magus invented names of principalities and powers, and insisted that the learning of such names was essential to salvation. Similar bizarrerie is ascribed to Cerinthus. See Whitby, *in loc.* Whatever be its source, there is no doubt that the apostle alludes to some prevalent error—which interposed angels, in some sense, as mediators—and so far derogated from the personal glory and saving merit of Christ. That theosophy which was invading them seems to have dealt largely in idle and delusive speculation on the rank and office of angels—assigning to them provinces of operation which belong to the Son of God—looking to them as guardians or saviours, and forgetting that they are but His servants, executing His commission and doing Him homage. Why rely upon the courtiers, when access may be had at once to the King? why be taken up with our fellow-servants, who are only stewards of limited resources, when the Master has not only the fulness of Divinity, but has it in a human shape—has the heart of a brother to love you, and the arm of a God to protect and bless you? Alas! that saints so called have the usurped place of principalities and powers in the Church of Rome.

If they were complete in Christ, they had no need to go beyond Christ, and to resort to any ceremonies imposed upon them by the Judaizers. They had everything which it was alleged they wanted, and everything already in Christ. The heretical preceptors had enjoined upon them the rite of circumcision, but the apostle shows that it would be really a superfluous ceremony, since they had already experienced a nobler circumcision than that of the knife—for it was executed by no material hand. They were, in short, the "true circumcision"—for the apostle proceeds—

(Ver. 11.) Ἐν ᾧ καὶ περιετμήθητε περιτομῇ ἀχειροποιήτῳ —"In whom, too, ye were circumcised with a circumcision not made with hands." There is no need to suppose, with Olshausen, that in these words there is expressed an ideal unity of all His people in Christ in His death and resurrection. Though such an idea may be found in other parts of Scripture, it cannot be found here—save in the exercise of a refined ingenuity. For, first, the formula ἐν ᾧ has its usual significance—union with Him—union created by the Spirit, and effected by faith; and, secondly, the blessing described in the verse had been already enjoyed, for they were and had been believers in Him in whom they are complete. Through their living union with Christ, they had enjoyed the privilege, and were enjoying the results of a spiritual circumcision. Why then should they suffer the incision of a sharp flint or a glittering knife—in itself, at best, but a sign—when they had already experienced the blessing of a circumcision that drew no blood, and gave no pain—a circumcision "not made with hands"? The meaning of the adjective *ἀχειροποίητος* is very apparent. Mark xiv. 58, and 2 Cor. v. 1. The circumcision made without hands is plainly opposed to that which is made with hands—*χειροποίητος*. [Eph. ii. 11.] This idea of a spiritual circumcision was no novel one, for it occurs in the Old Testament in different forms.[1] When Israel was yet in the wilderness, the Divine command was given—"Circumcise the foreskin of your heart," and at the same period the Divine promise was made—"And the Lord thy God will circumcise thine heart and the heart of thy seed, to love the Lord thy God with all thine heart and with all thy soul, that thou mayest live." The prophet Jeremiah repeats the injunction—"Circumcise yourselves to the Lord, and take away the foreskins of your heart, ye men of Judah and inhabitants of Jerusalem." He also describes a part of the population thus—"Behold, their ear is uncircumcised;" nay, he declares that the whole house of Israel are "uncircumcised in the heart." Ezekiel speaks of men "uncircumcised in heart and uncircumcised in flesh." Stephen, in his address, used this ancient phraseology, and calls his audience "uncircumcised in hearts and ears."[2] The Apostle Paul in other places has similar ideas and language.[3] Schoettgen has adduced like quotations from the Rabbis, and Philo, as is his wont, spiritualizes the ordinance[4]—as *ἡδονῶν ἐκτομήν*; *παθῶν πάντων ἐκτομήν*. So that the kind of circumcision referred to was easily understood, and could not be misinterpreted. It was besides an invaluable blessing, for it lay—

Ἐν τῇ ἀπεκδύσει[5] *τοῦ σώματος τῆς σαρκός*—"In the putting off of the body of the flesh." The noun *ἀπέκδυσις* occurs only here—the verb is found in the 15th verse. The MSS., A, B, C, D[1], E[1], F, G, etc., omit the words *τῶν ἁμαρτιῶν*, found in the Received Text. Flesh is corrupted humanity,

[1] Deut. x. 16, xxx. 6; Jer. iv. 4, vi. 10, ix. 26; Ezek. xliv. 7.

[2] Acts vii. 51.

[3] Rom. ii. 29.

[4] *De Migrat. Abr.* Oper. vol. iii. p. 454.

[5] ἐπεκδύσει erroneously in Tischendorf.

Rom. vii. 23; Gal. v. 16. [Eph. ii. 3.] We cannot take σῶμα in any other than its usual signification, though Calvin, Grotius, Zanchius, Crocius, Bähr, and Steiger, take it in the sense of totality or mass. See under verse 9. But the spirit of this exegesis is plainly implied. It is in harmony with the idea of circumcision, that the peculiar phrase—"body of the flesh," is used; and the contrast seems to be this, that in the manual circumcision only a portion of one member of the material body was cut off; but in the spiritual circumcision, the whole flesh which is the seat and habitation of sin is cast away and laid aside. The entire slough which encircles the spirit and enslaves it is rolled off, newness of life is felt, and the believer walks no longer after the flesh, is no longer carnal, or does its deeds. As Meyer well says, "He who is so circumcised is no more ἐν τῇ σαρκί, as heretofore, when concupiscence ἐνηργεῖτο ἐν τοῖς μέλεσιν; he is no longer σάρκινος, πεπραμένος ὑπὸ τὴν ἁμαρτίαν, and walks no longer κατὰ σάρκα, but in newness of spirit." It is plain that the spiritual circumcision is not different from regeneration, or the putting off the old man and putting on the new man. The apostle adds a further explanation of this marvellous change, when he says—

Ἐν τῇ περιτομῇ τοῦ Χριστοῦ—"In the circumcision of Christ." Some have regarded the genitive as that of agent, as if the apostle meant—the circumcision which Christ performs. Such is the virtual view of Theophylact, when he says of Christ—ὅλον ἄνθρωπον περιτέμνει. Schoettgen, again, regards the phrase as an allusion to the personal circumcision of Jesus, as if that sufficed for all His people. Neither view is in harmony with the language and context. The circumcision of Christ is that circumcision which belongs to Him, in contradistinction to that which belonged to Moses or to the law. The spiritual circumcision is a blessing which specially belongs to Christ—is of His providing, and is to be enjoyed only in fellowship with Him. That of Moses was made with hands, and was a seal of the Abrahamic or national covenant—that of Christ is no chirurgical process, but is spiritual and effectual in its nature. The mark in the foreskin was the token of being a Jew, but the off-thrown body of the flesh was the index of one's being a Christian.

Though the scar of circumcision might attest a nationality, it was no certificate of personal character—"all are not Israel who are of Israel;" but, wherever "the flesh" was parted with, there was the guarantee of individual purity and progress. The charter of Canaan was limited to the manual circumcision, but the "true circumcision" are thereby infefted in a heavenly inheritance. The Hebrew statute was for the man-child eight days old, but the Christian privilege has no distinction of age, or sex, or nation; for it belongs to every one in Christ. And it was, and is, a chief blessing—the death of sinful principle and the infusion of a higher life—the possession of a new nature, which has Christ for its source, ay, and Christ for its pattern. Thus the flesh is thrown off, and the spirit assumes the predominance, with its quickened susceptibilities, its healthful activities, and its intense aspirations—thinking, feeling, and acting, in harmony with its sphere and destiny. And if such a collection of spiritual blessings has been received, why be subjected to a legal ceremony which could be at best but a faint type of them? Surely if they had received the thing signified, they need not now degrade themselves by submitting to a sign, which was in itself only a painful and bloody symbol of the Hebrew nationality and covenant. For a new sign has been appointed—

(Ver. 12.) *Συνταφέντες αὐτῷ ἐν τῷ βαπτίσματι*—"Having been buried with Him in baptism." The state described in this past participle precedes or is coincident with the action of the verb *περιετμήθητε*. "Having been buried, they were circumcised." The burial and the circumcision only differ in form and circumstance. The circumcision was seen to be effected when the burial was completed. Burial implies a previous death; and what is that death, but the off-casting of the body of the flesh? The reality of death is evinced by burial, for this body of sin which once lived with us is slain and sepulchred. This point of burial they had reached—when they were baptized—for then they personally professed a faith which implied the death of sin within them. Why then does the apostle use the figure of a burial? for the burial is as really without hands as is the circumcision—since no knife was employed at the one, and no bier or shroud was deposited in the other. The apostle employs the figure, first, to show the reality of the death which the old man had undergone; and, secondly, to connect the process by harmony of symbol or parallel with the resurrection of Christ, which was at once a sign and pledge of the resuscitation. Those two ideas, the excision of the body of the flesh, which is equivalent to its death, and the raising of Christ as the typal life and the Life-giver, seem to have suggested to the apostle the notion of an intervening process—a burial with Christ. When you were baptized, you were so placed as if you had been laid with Christ in His tomb—"all old things passed away;" you were in respect to the old man what the dead Christ was in respect to His first physical life—dead to it and done with it. Only, He died for sin, and you die to it; He died for it in His body, while you die to it in your souls. But this burial is not a final state, it is simply one of transition—"In whom also ye are raised by faith."

The reference is plainly to the ordinance of baptism, and to its spiritual meaning. We scarcely suppose that there is any reference to the mode of it; for whatever may be otherwise said in favour of immersion, it is plain that here the burial is wholly ideal—not a scenic and visible descent into an earthy or a watery tomb, but of such a nature entirely as the circumcision with which it is identified, and the resurrection which invariably succeeds it. Thus, in the apostolic conception, men may be buried in baptism without being *submerged* in water, in the same way as they may be circumcised without the spilling of blood. The entire statement is spiritual in its nature—the death, the burial, and the resurrection; the circumcision, and the off-putting of the body of the flesh. The apostle looks on circumcision and baptism as being closely connected—the spiritual blessing symbolized by both being of a similar nature; though, probably, it would be straining this connection to allege it as a proof that baptism has been in all points ordained for the church in room of circumcision.

It is not within our province to enter on the question whether apostolical baptism was by immersion, sprinkling, or affusion. What we say is,—granting that immersion had been the early and authorized form of baptism, we are not prepared to admit any allusion to that form in the clause before us.

It does not advance the opposite argument to say, that the immersion of a believer resembles a burial. This has been a favourite idea from very early times. And not only so, but trine immersion was often practised—one reason assigned being a reference to the Trinity, but another argument being that it was a symbolic allusion to the three days—*τὴν τριήμερον*—of Christ's abode in the tomb.[1] Still, to many minds there is manifest incongruity in the symbol. Where, in Scripture, is water the symbol of the world of death, or of the grave? It is always the means of washing—the instrument of purification. At what point of baptism is death symbolized—for it precedes burial? Means of imitating the death and resurrection of Jesus could be easily devised—for they were physical facts that could with no difficulty be pictured out. But a believer's death and resurrection with Christ are spiritual events; and the same process cannot surely be the emblem of both classes of truths—cannot be at the same time the figure of a fact, and the figure of a figure. Death, burial, and resurrection, are truths not portrayed by gesture and position in baptism, but only recognized in it—not acted out, or represented in visible form, but only experienced and professed. Believers are buried in baptism, but even in immersion they do not go through a process having any resemblance to the burial and resurrection of Christ. The Colossians did not personate death and burial in baptism any more than they imitated the circumcision of Moses. In a similar sense, though without reference to any sacramental institute, believers are crucified with Christ, though no nail pierce their hands; they are enthroned with Him, while they wear no symbol of royalty; and they have an unction from the Holy One, but no material oil is poured upon their heads.

'Εν ᾧ καὶ συνηγέρθητε—"In whom too ye were raised together." Beza, and after him Calixtus, Suicer, Steiger, Böhmer, De Wette, and Baumgarten-Crusius, refer the relative to *βαπτίσματι*. But the language would, in such a case, be inapt, as "out of baptism" would appear to be the natural

[1] Gregor. Nyss. *Opera*, vol. iii. p. 372. Cyril. Hieros. *Catech.* ii. 4. Joannes Damas. *Expositio fidei Ortho.* 10. The works of Vossius, Gale, Wall, Carson, Wilson, Beecher, and Halley, may also be referred to.

expression. There appears to be no formal resemblance between baptism and burial in the apostle's mind, and so he says not ἐξ οὗ, but simply ἐν ᾧ—"in whom," that is, in Christ. Justinian and Davenant, Meyer and Huther, thus refer the pronoun—"With Him" they are buried—"in Him" they rise again; for union with Him is the one efficacious principle. The verb is explained and its meaning defended under Eph. ii. 6. It is not an ideal or potential spiritual resurrection secured for them, but one now and actually enjoyed by believers. The vivification of the soul involves in it, as a necessary result, the resurrection of the body—a result essential to the development of the new life in its highest sphere; but it is wrong in Theophylact to give this aorist verb a future meaning, or rather to mix up the two significations. While union with Christ is the bond of security, the instrumental cause is next described—

Διὰ τῆς πίστεως—"By the faith." A similar use of ἐν and διά is found in Eph. i. 7, each preposition retaining its distinctive signification. It is faith which achieves this spiritual resurrection—belief in the Divine testimony is the vehicle which the Divine resurrectionary power employs. The apostle, Eph. i. 19, 20, prays that the Ephesians might know "what is the exceeding greatness of God's power to us-ward *who believe*," and the kind of power referred to is, as here, that which raised Christ from the dead, and which also quickens and raises up believers who had been "dead in trespasses and sins." Thus it is faith—

Τῆς ἐνεργείας τοῦ Θεοῦ τοῦ ἐγείραντος αὐτὸν ἐκ νεκρῶν—"Of the operation of God who raised Him from the dead." Many interpreters take the genitive as that of agency—"faith inwrought by God." Such is the view of Flacius, Calixtus, the older interpreters, Luther, Melancthon, as also of Storr, Flatt, Bengel, Bähr, Böhmer, De Wette, Huther, Olshausen, and Conybeare. Luther renders—*den Gott wirket;* and Melancthon draws the lesson—*non igitur potest suis viribus ratio fidem in nobis efficere.* Whatever truth may be in this doctrine, and whatever may be the proof of it in other parts of Scripture, it is not the doctrine which the apostle here delivers. For according to usage in such a case, the genitive is that of object. So with regard to *Θεοῦ,* Mark xi. 22: *'Ονόματος,* Acts iii. 16;

'Ιησοῦ Χ., etc., Rom. iii. 22; Gal. ii. 16, 20, iii. 22; Eph. iii. 12; Phil. iii. 9; Jas. ii. 1; Rev. ii. 13: *Εὐαγγελίου*, Phil. i. 27: '*Αληθείας*, 2 Thess. ii. 13. The genitive thus denotes the object of faith, or the thing believed. Such is the view of the mass of interpreters, of the Greek Fathers, of Calvin and Beza, of Grotius and Erasmus, of Meyer, Bloomfield, etc. The object of this vivifying faith is the Divine power which raised up Christ from the dead. The construction which the apostle employs in Eph. i. 19—*εἰς ἡμᾶς τοὺς πιστεύοντας κατὰ τὴν ἐνέργειαν κ-τ-α*, is no argument against this view, for, as we have there said, *κατά* does not point out the source of faith, but turns attention to the model after which the Divine power operates in quickening the spiritually dead. A description of the Divine power, as showing itself in the resurrection of Christ, more naturally allies itself with the idea of spiritual resuscitation, which it resembles, than with that of the production of faith.

The sinner is raised out of death. United to Christ by the Spirit, and exercising a belief in God, he is justified and obtains legal life—exemption from the penalty of law; and he is also sanctified, or is endowed with spiritual life—comes to the conscious enjoyment of God's favour, and the possession of His image. This faith has special reference to the Divine power in one of its manifestations, the raising of Jesus Christ from the dead. Power is evinced most strikingly in a resurrection—the restoration of a dead body to life is the work of Omnipotence. Love may pity, but power restores—a power which the apostle calls exceeding great and mighty. Eph. i. 19. Faith lays hold on this phasis of omnipotence, and on this act of its achievement, because it feels that spiritual quickening is at once the result which springs from the one and is pledged by the other. The nature of this power and its relation to believers have been fully explained under a similar passage—Eph. i. 20. The resurrection of Christ proves the acceptance of his atonement on the part of the Father, "who raised His Son from the dead, and gave Him glory that our faith and hope might be in God." It therefore showed that the way of salvation was open, that the majesty of the law had been vindicated, and that the blessings of redemption might therefore be conferred in all their fulness and without restraint. Blood had been shed, and might now be sprinkled; and the Saviour being glorified, the Spirit might now descend. If I believe in that power which raised Jesus Christ from the dead, I believe in a power which might righteously have crushed me, but is now mercifully wielded to save me; which has set its seal on the work of Christ, and will now distribute and apply its rich results; and which, having exalted the Redeemer, has placed itself under a solemn stipulation to reward Him with a numerous seed, so that He shall "see of the travail of His soul and shall be satisfied." Thus, this power working out the purposes of Divine Love and the devices of Infinite Wisdom, stands out so employed as the object of saving faith.

But the apostle now appeals to the Colossian believers.

(Ver. 13.) **Καὶ ὑμᾶς νεκροὺς ὄντας ἐν τοῖς παραπτώμασιν καὶ τῇ ἀκροβυστίᾳ τῆς σαρκὸς ὑμῶν, συνεζωοποίησεν ὑμᾶς σὺν αὐτῷ**—"And you, being dead in trespasses and the uncircumcision of your flesh, you He quickened with Him." Any differences of reading are too trivial to be noted save that which repeats *ὑμᾶς* on the authority of A, C, J, K. The apostle still continues the general thought without any formal and specific connection. The connection proposed by Steiger, namely, to join the first clause to the participle *ἐγείραντος*, is utterly untenable. It would create tautology, and the repetition of *ὑμᾶς* does not render it necessary. Bernhardy, p. 275. We far prefer connecting *νεκρούς* with the verb *συνεζωοποίησεν*. Though we admire the acuteness and general soundness of Meyer, yet we wonder how here, and in Eph. ii. 1, he comes to the conclusion that *νεκρός* refers to physical death. For the dead condition was one of reality, though it be past. It was not a liability to death; they were not, as he phrases it—*so gut wie todt*—*certo morituri*, they were *mortui*. Besides, the liability to physical death is not removed by faith in Christ. And the quickening and upraising are already experienced, they are not blessings to be enjoyed uncounted years afterwards. The apostle does not surely say—that believers were soon and certainly to die, and that when the Saviour came again, they should all be summoned out of their graves to the possession of eternal life. But he appeals to present enjoyments already conferred—to a death which had bound them, and a life which the Divine energy had infused into them. Meyer argues for the ideal possession of life now, and its full realization at the second coming. But if such ideal possession leave the dreadful reality untouched, it brings with it no good. If, instead of ideal possession, he had said partial possession, he would have come nearer the truth. For the life now enjoyed is, alas, too often faint and languid in its pulsations, and the fulness of its strength is a future bestowment. We therefore take the tenses in their simple significance, and not in any proleptic sense, as even Chrysostom takes them, and we regard the preposition ἐν before παραπτώμασιν, as denoting that condition in which spiritual death exists. When Meyer insists that the life to which believers are raised is eternal life, and that nothing less can be meant by the apostle, he forgets that present spiritual life precedes —that glory is only the consummation of grace, and that eternal life is but the crown and perfect development of emotions already felt, occupations already begun, and pleasures already experienced. The life implanted now is brought to maturity in a sphere where all is congenial to its tastes and instincts, its susceptibilities and powers. The Colossians had been really and spiritually dead, they were now as really and spiritually alive. They had been not only exposed to death on account of sin, but had been dead in sin. Now they are not simply gifted with the charter of a life yet to be reached, but they are actually living in faith and holiness. The nature of this death, and its connection with sin, along with the meaning of παραπτώμασιν, will be found explained in the parallel place, Eph. ii. 1, etc. There is no ground for Olshausen's notion, that the prior clause has a general meaning, and that this verse begins a practical application; for the same appeal runs throughout, only it may be more pointed and intense in the verse before us.

Καὶ τῇ ἀκροβυστίᾳ τῆς σαρκὸς ὑμῶν—"And in the uncircumcision of your flesh." The apostle here alludes to their Gentile extraction. They wanted in their flesh the seal of the Abrahamic covenant. We incline to take the words in their literal sense. Uncircumcision had, indeed, sometimes a spiritual meaning. Deut. x. 16; Jer. iv. 4. Theodoret adopts such a sense here—*ἀκροβ. τ. σαρκὸς τὴν πονηρίαν ἐκάλεσεν*; so also

Beza, Grotius, Bähr, Steiger. But such an interpretation rather takes up the result than gives the meaning. Thus, the Gentiles were uncircumcised, and in consequence were "aliens from the commonwealth of Israel, and strangers from the covenants of promise, having no hope, and without God." Their degraded, miserable, idolatrous, and dead state was the effect of their uncircumcision. Calvin says—*sed tamen Paulus hic loqueretur de contumacia cordis humani adversus Deum, et natura pravis affectionibus inquinata.* But there is no occasion to take σάρξ in other than its physical meaning. Beza takes the genitive as one of apposition—flesh, which is uncircumcision, a thing abominable to God; while others render it—*praeputium nempe vitiositas.* That "uncircumcision" and "flesh" are to be taken in their ordinary physical sense, is also apparent from the change of person in the last clause. Did the term simply signify natural corruption, then the apostle himself was once in such a state. But he does not feel or say so. On the contrary, he makes the distinction *you* Gentiles were dead in the uncircumcision of your flesh—but *we*, Jew and Gentile alike, are *forgiven our trespasses.* See under next clause. Uncircumcision of the flesh was the physical mark of a heathen state, and that heathen state was in consequence of this want, and in itself, one of degradation, impurity and death. The flesh which had not the seal was truly corrupted and sinful. It is pressing the clause too much to bring out of it a proof of original sin, as is done by Zanchius and Bengel; the latter calls it—*exquisita appellatio peccati originalis.* The false teachers insisted strenuously on the necessity of circumcision—a theory very common in those times, for believing Jews were zealous of the law.[1] But the apostle naturally says—True, ye were uncircumcised; your flesh had not been wounded so as to bear the sign of the Divine covenant, but ye have been circumcised, not with a manual operation, but with the circumcision of Christ. The apostle admits that they were uncircumcised, for they did not belong to Israel, but he has already contended that such a

[1] In a pamphlet named *Israel's Ordinances*, the late Charlotte Elizabeth, addressing a Jewish convert, Bishop Alexander of Jerusalem, rebukes him for not circumcising his sons—"Call you what we will, my Lord, you are a Jew—a circumcised Jew. My dear Lord, bear with me, while I respectfully and affectionately put once more the query—*why are not your sons also Jews?*"

circumcision as that which of old disabled the Shechemites from self-defence, and kept the Israelites after they crossed the Jordan from commencing the conquest, did not become them, and was in their case wholly superfluous, for they had been spiritually initiated, and had put off the body of flesh. They had been dead in sins—this was their real moral state; dead too in the uncircumcision of their flesh, and this was their external and heathen condition. Looking at them as men, they were dead in sins—looking at them as heathen men, they were dead also in the uncircumcision of their flesh.

Συνεζωοποίησεν ὑμᾶς σὺν αὐτῷ—"You He brought to life together with Him." The nominative is still God—not Christ, as Heinrichs would have it. The work of quickening is God's prerogative. This process of life-giving is not simply redemption, as De Wette gives it, but rather one special aspect or blessing of it. It is used with perfect propriety, for life is the blessing appropriate to the dead. Some wonder why *συνηγέρθητε* should have occurred before it, since the idea of resurrection so naturally follows that of life-giving. But in both places the verbs are in harmony with the figure; the apostle, in verse 12, speaks of burial, and therefore he employs the term resurrection, while here he speaks simply of death, and so he places life in correspondence and contrast with it. But not only so, there is also a difference of allusion and meaning. The burial there is a voluntary renunciation of sin, and off-casting of its body—the completing point of the process of death to sin; but here it is a death in sin which the apostle describes, and out of which the Colossians had been raised by the power of God, and through their union with Christ. The former is a series of acts in which the believer in the enjoyment of vivifying energy dies unto sin—and puts off the flesh. Nay, the more he lives, the more he dies; and in proportion to the growth and development of life are the extent and progress of death. It is a special view of the work of sanctification, in which, according to the measure of life to God, there is death to sin. But the death described in this verse is very different. It is a death which pre-exists life, and does not co-exist with it—death in sin—in consequence of its fatal reign and power. The one is dying—a conscious state; the other is death—a condition of insensibility and danger. In the one, the decay of love to sin may be registered; in the other, the mastery of sin is spiritual paralysis and death. The nature of this life, and its connection with Christ, are illustrated under Eph. ii. 5.

Χαρισάμενος ἡμῖν πάντα τὰ παραπτώματα—"Having forgiven us all our trespasses." The reading *ἡμῖν* is on largely preponderant authority preferred to the *ὑμῖν* of the Received Text. It is easy to see how *ὑμῖν* should have been inserted, as *ὑμᾶς* precedes. Nor is it difficult to apprehend why the apostle should say "us" instead of "you." He speaks in one clause of a distinctive feature of their past spiritual state—"dead in the uncircumcision of your flesh." That was peculiar to them, but death in sin was common both to him and to them, and they were now both partakers of the "common salvation." They both had enjoyed forgiveness, and so he says—"having forgiven *us* our trespasses." The aorist participle points to forgiveness as something past, and yet preceding the act of life-giving. Having forgiven your trespasses, He has quickened you. The pardoning and life-giving are scarcely synonymous, as some would argue. But this dead state is a guilty state, for it is a sinful state, and all sin brings down upon itself the Divine displeasure and penalty. Having forgiven them these trepasses, which were the source and means of death, He brings them out of it. To have given them spiritual life, and yet kept them under the penalty of sin, which is legal death, would have been a process in which one gift neutralized its fellow. The restoration to life is thus the token and result of a prior forgiveness. The welcome to the prodigal son was a proof that he had been pardoned. The death was one in trespasses; and those very trepasses, yea "all" of them, are blotted out. The reader is requested to turn to what is said under chap. i. 14, and under Eph. i. 7. The life is not, as Böhmer imagines, subsequent to this forgiveness, because the pardon is God's special act, whereas the life originates in man's co-operation and response. This doctrine is neither stated nor implied. Nor is it true. For all life is God's immediate gift, from its lowest to its highest forms. No human chemistry can produce it beneath us—no suasion nor art can create it within us. It is a drop out of the Fountain of Life. [Eph. i. 20.] The apostle proceeds to describe the process through which sin was forgiven—or that work which God had done, the result of which had been to them life and forgiveness.

(Ver. 14.) Ἐξαλείψας τὸ καθ' ἡμῶν χειρόγραφον—"Having blotted out the handwriting against us." This verse is so curt and compact, that its analysis is not without difficulty. It is to be borne in mind that "God" is still the subject, and the alteration for which Heinrichs contends cannot for a moment be admitted. It will not do to say, with Trollope, that "the apostle, in the ardour of his mind, has not attended to the syntax." What in other places is ascribed to Christ, may be here without any impropriety ascribed to God; for Christ's suffering and death were of His sanction, and with His co-operation. What Christ did, God did by Him. Nor is there any argument here, as Bähr insinuates, against the *satisfactio vicaria*. For the satisfaction was offered by Christ, and God, having accepted it, did the act described in the participle ἐξαλείψας. This verb[1] signifies to smear, or plaster over, and then it is used to denote the act by which a law or deed of obligation is cancelled. It is found with another signification, Rev. vii. 17, xxi. 4. It occurs also in Rev. iii. 5; but it is used in a sense not very different from what it bears in this verse in Acts iii. 19; and in Sept. Ps. l. 1, 9, cviii. 13; Isa. xliii. 25. In these places it describes the forgiveness of sin, where sin as a debt is supposed to be wiped out. The word occurs in Demosthenes[2]—σκοπεῖσθε εἰ χρὴ τοῦτον [νόμον] ἐξαλεῖψαι. Its technical signification may be gathered from the fact that it stands opposed to ἀναγράφω, and sometimes to ἐγγράφω. Liddell and Scott, *sub voce*. The word, then, means here, to expunge. That to which the process of obliteration is applied is appropriately termed a handwriting—χειρόγραφον, a note of hand, a written bond. The term occurs only here in the New Testament, but is found in Tobit v. 3, ix. 5; Josephus xvii. 14, 2; Polybius, *Excerpta Legat.* 98. Schoettgen and Vitringa take it as corresponding to the Hebrew שטר חוב, and as denoting *tabula debiti*. But as it

[1] From the root λιπ that runs through so many of the Indo-Germanic tongues.—Benfey, *Wurzel-Lex.* ii. 122.

[2] *Oratores Attici*, vol. vi. p. 429, ed. Dobson; also vol. vii. p. 378, viii. p. 15, etc. Also Lysias, do. vol. ii. p. 182, and p. 588. Ἀναιρεῖν is more frequently used with χειρόγ. or συγγραφή.

signifies a claim of unpaid debt, it is therefore also one of punishment, for it was καθ' ἡμῶν—"against us."

Both the connection and meaning of τοῖς δόγμασιν have been variously taken. That it is to be joined with χειρόγραφον we have no manner of doubt.

1. Some, such as Erasmus, Storr, Flatt, Conybeare, and Olshausen, divide the verse thus—τὸ καθ' ἡμῶν χειρόγ. τοῖς δόγμασιν, ὃ ἦν ὑπεναντίον ἡμῖν—"The handwriting, which, by its ordinances, was against us." Olshausen admits that, with such a construction, the position of the dative is not quite natural, and he quotes, along with Winer, Acts i. 3, with which this verse has little analogy. The admittedly natural reference of the dative is to χειρόγραφον.

2. Others attach δόγμασιν to the participle ἐξαλείψας, and understand it as describing the means by which the blotting has been effected. This is the view of the Greek expositors, of Grotius, Estius, Bengel, Fritzsche,[1] and Böhmer. The explanation of δόγμασιν, by Theodoret, is ἡ εὐαγγελικὴ διδασκαλία; and by Theophylact—τουτέστι τῇ πίστει. To this we answer as we have done to the similar exegesis of Eph. ii. 15, that such a sense given to δόγμα is wholly unbiblical—that the declaration of Scripture is, that the handwriting against man, which we here understand to be the Mosaic law, is abrogated, not by any opposing or modifying enactments, but by the death of Christ. Besides, and more convincingly still, we learn from verse 20 that these δόγματα are no longer law, for the apostle says—τί δογματίζεσθε; why do ye suffer such δόγματα to be published or imposed? That is—these ordinances are abolished, and it is now the height of folly for others to re-enact them, or for you to observe them. The cognate verb of the 20th verse is used with special reference to the noun of this verse. Whatever these ordinances are, they belong to an obsolete economy, and are no longer of any obligation, for they were on the handwriting which has been wiped out.

3. Steiger joins δόγμασιν with the participle in this verse. He understands the phrase as defining one special phase of the handwriting—"the handwriting in respect of its ordinances." Having blotted out the handwriting in this aspect

[1] *Dissert.* ii. p. 168.

of it, viz. its enactments—plainly implying that in some other aspect of it it still stands unrepealed. See on this view, also, our comment on Eph. ii. 15.

4. Bähr, Huther, and De Wette understand δόγμασιν as belonging to the whole clause, or rather as explaining how it came that the handwriting was against us. It is because of its δόγματα that it is against us; De Wette renders—*durch die Satzungen.* Calovius and Gieseler supply the participle ὄν—the handwriting which is, or being in its ordinances against us.

5. But keeping the words in their natural position and connection with χειρόγραφον, there is variety of view. Calvin, Beza, Vitringa, Wolf, Camerarius, Heinsius, and others, eke out the construction from the parallel passage of the Epistle to the Ephesians, and would supply at discretion either ἐν or σύν[1]—the handwriting consisting in ordinances, or the handwriting along with its ordinances; or taking the dative for the genitive, the handwriting of ordinances.

6. Meyer takes the dative as that of instrument. The δόγματα, in his view, as a constituent portion of the law, are that with which the handwriting is made out. We prefer calling the simple dative that of form, that distinctive and well-known form which the handwriting assumed. In this way, the dative is governed by the verbal portion of the noun, γραφον—that is γεγραμμένον. The apostle thus describes the handwriting as of a special shape, it assumed the form of ordinances. Had the apostle said ἐν δόγμασιν, the meaning would have been—which consisted of ordinances; a meaning which, however, is not materially different from that to which we incline, as the form is but the index to the substance. Our view also embraces inferentially that given under No. 4. We do not say that the handwriting is against us because of its δόγματα, but we say more largely, that the handwriting whose form of structure was that of δόγματα, is against us. For the meaning of δόγματα, see under Eph. ii. 15. This handwriting was καθ' ἡμῶν—"directed against us." After verbs, and in phrases implying hostility in word or action, κατά denotes against, and points out the direction of the hostility. And to explain more fully his meaning, the apostle adds—

[1] Bishop Middleton on Greek article, *in loc.*

Ὃ ἦν ὑπεναντιον ἡμῖν—"Which was inimical to us." It is a needless refinement on the part of Beza, Böhmer, and Robinson, to lay stress upon the ὑπό, as if a covert or *under*-hand hostility were implied, or as if it had been unnoticed, or as if, as Suicer and Witsius think, it is only in some sense contrary to us, because in another sense it was a symbol of coming grace. None of these meanings are sustained by biblical usage. Sept. Gen. xxii. 17; Lev. xxvi. 17; Ex. xxiii. 27; Num. x. 9; Deut. xxxii. 27; Josh. v. 13; in which places it represents one or other of the two Hebrew terms—אוֹיֵב, or צַר. The word is one of those frequent compounds which characterize the later Greek, and mark it as a period of decay. Thus we do not, like many expositors, take καθ' ἡμῶν and ὑπεναντίον ἡμῖν as synonyms, or the latter as explanatory of the former, but we regard the two statements as giving two distinct ideas. Bengel compares the first to a *status belli*, and the second to *ipsa pugna*. It has a hostile attitude—it has also in it a deep and active antagonism. The question then recurs, what is the hostile handwriting?

1. A strange exposition is found in ancient times—that the handwriting is man's corporeal frame. Theodoret expressly says—ἡγοῦμαι τοίνυν καὶ τὸ σῶμα ἡμῶν καλεῖσθαι χειρόγραφον. That is, probably, our body, as represented by Christ's humanity, which was nailed to the cross. This is, to some extent, the view of Steiger, given both in his Commentary on 1 Pet. ii. 24, and in this place. In the first comment referred to, he says—"Our sin adhered to Him until it was legally destroyed in His body, and His body was in this respect like a handwriting over our guilt." Again, he adds, "That by the appointment of His Son to be our sacrifice, God set out a corporeal document of our guilt." On the verse before us he writes:—"The body of Christ, as a body, is no handwriting; but it is that body, destined to be a sin-offering, which is at once a document exhibiting our guilt, and representing the law, in so far as the latter serves the purpose of an indictment." The image, however, is not very distinct, and the sacrificial body of the Lord was rather a witness of our sin, than a handwriting against us. But the idea is, that something different from Christ, and yet closely associated with Him, was obliterated in His death. Steiger's notion is evidently

based upon a literal interpretation of the last clause of the verse, yet it is wholly out of harmony with the entire phraseology. And in what sense does a body resemble a handwriting? or how could it be hostile to us? or how has it been taken out of the way?

2. An opinion as ancient as the preceding supposes the handwriting to be the broken covenant which God originally made with Adam. This opinion is found in Chrysostom, Theophylact and Œcumenius, Ambrose and Anselm. Bähr, and others, trace this opinion to Irenæus. Speaking of the handwriting of our debt as affixed to the cross, he says—*quemadmodum per lignum facti sumus debitores Deo, per lignum accipiamus nostri debiti remissionem.*[1] The use of this fanciful analogy can scarce, perhaps, be taken as a formal exegesis, though he regards the handwriting generally as sin. Tertullian is said to hold a similar notion, but his opinion will be seen to be more in unison with our own. Bähr well objects to this view, that errors on this subject are not among those alleged to be held by the false teachers, and that this Adamic covenant, containing principally one prohibition, could in no appropriate sense have such a descriptive plural noun as δόγματα attached to it. The whole paragraph refers to a later transaction altogether than the covenant of Eden.

3. The reformers Melancthon, Luther, and Zuingli thought the reference to be to the accusations of conscience. The guilty conscience resembles a guilt-book, or an indictment.[2] Besides replying, with Bähr, that this exegesis does not tally with the purpose of the paragraph, nor with the idea implied in δόγματα, we may add, that the notion of the Reformers is wholly of a subjective nature, whereas the verse presents an objective view of the work of God in Christ. It tells us what God has done as the means of enabling Him to forgive sins, but their interpretation points to a blessing which follows only from the forgiveness of sin. The act of God is prior to forgiveness—is external in its nature; while pardon, with a quieted conscience, is one of the results of the believing reception of it. An inner conviction, also, cannot be well figured as an outer and written record of many heads against us. These

[1] *Adversus Haeres.* v. 17, 3.

[2] *Unser Gewissen gleich als ein Schuldbuch ist.*—Luther.

critics confound what follows from faith in the cross, with what was done upon the cross that faith might secure such a result. It is one thing to expunge an indictment, and quite another thing to have the blessed consciousness that we actually share in the indemnity.

4. Not a few understand the apostle to refer to the ceremonial law, or the Mosaic law in its ritual part or aspect. Such is the view of Calvin, Beza, Crocius, van Till, Gomar, Vorstius, Grotius, Deyling, Schoettgen, Wolf, Bähr, and others. This is, no doubt, the common view, and it is true so far as it goes. The entire ritual, with its lustrations and sacrifices, had a close and constant connection with sin—"in them was a remembrance of sin every year." It is true that it was abrogated by the death of Christ on the cross, and it is also true that one special error of the false teachers was the inculcation of ceremonial distinctions and observances, and that the apostle has such mischievous teaching specially in view. But it is not the less true that the apostle makes no such distinction between one part of the Mosaic law and another. In the parallel passage in the twin epistle the apostle speaks of the "enmity" produced by the ceremonial law, but that was an enmity of races—between Israel who possessed it, and Non-Israel which wanted it. So that, in order to their union, the cause of separation and mutual dislike must be taken out of the way. But here the apostle speaks not of race and race—nor of Jew and Gentile as separated in blood and creed, but of both as being in the same condition—having a handwriting against them. He does not specify separate parties, he says "us," whether Jew or Gentile. Nay, more, it is to Gentiles, distinguished by the uncircumcision of their flesh, and never placed under the ceremonial law, that the apostle is speaking. That law spoke, indeed, of sin, but it spoke intelligibly only to those who understood its symbols, and obeyed its prescriptions. Still the ceremonial law was against the Gentiles, as it kept them out of the Divine covenant. Moreover, the apostle is writing of a blessing not determined in its distribution by race or blood, but enjoyed by all the members of the church—the forgiveness of sin. But the forgiveness of sin was not secured by the simple abrogation of the Levitical law, for its abrogation is only one, though

an important one, of the many results of the death on Calvary.

5. Therefore we are inclined, with Meyer, De Wette, Davenant, Neander, Böhmer, Huther, and others, to understand the reference of the apostle to the entire Mosaic law. That law presents a condemnation of the whole human race—"that all the world may become guilty before God." Davenant says—"I accordingly explain the handwriting in ordinances to mean, the force of the moral law binding to perfect obedience, and condemning for any defect in it, laden with the ceremonial rites as skirts and appendages." But lest this opinion should imply that the moral law was abolished, he adds—"the law as to the power of binding and condemning is abrogated, and its rites and ceremonies are at the same time abolished." But whatever the handwriting, with its ordinances, is, it undergoes only one process—it is blotted out. The distinction referred to, however true in result, cannot therefore be sustained as an interpretation. So that we take χειρόγραφον, not as denoting the Mosaic law absolutely and in itself, but rather in its indictment. It is against us, at once in direction and operation. It is the *finding* of the law which is against us, as well as its *dogmatic* form. And this, especially, is a bond, a writing which pronounces our sentence of death. This is Chrysostom's view in its result, and also that of Tertullian, who writes—*chirographum mortis*,[1] *symbolum mortis*.[2] Schoettgen, *in loc.*, adduces a similar rabbinical expression; when one sins, God dooms him to die, but when he repents, the handwriting is abolished—הכתב מתבטל.[3] It is not, therefore, so much the law with the authority of legislation, as the law with its power of punishment. It is not the code prescribing duty, but rather as at the same time authorizing the infliction of merited penalty, which becomes the χειρόγραφον. In this view, the δόγματα are a handwriting, or a bond which exhibits and warrants our liability to punishment. But the liability to penalty is expunged, the handwriting is wiped out. The law in itself is not, and cannot be contrary to men, but it has become so because they have failed to obey it. Its precepts are not hostile to them, for obedience to them would secure our welfare. The law has been given, both moral and cere-

[1] *De pudicitia*, xix. [2] *De poenitentia*, vi. [3] *Tançhuma*, fol. 44, 2.

monial; the first has been universally broken, and therefore every man is exposed to its curse; the second presents this melancholy truth in its ritual bloodshedding and expiation; but what the one charged, and the other confessed,[1] *has been obliterated.* The claim of condemnation exhibited by the moral law, and traced in the blood and read by the fires of the Levitical law has now been blotted out; not the moral law itself, as it must be eternal and immutable—having its origin in the Divine nature, and forming an obligation under which every creature is placed by the fact of his existence. "Do we make void the law through faith?" asks the apostle, and his reply is, "Nay, God forbid, we establish the law." If the death of Christ was necessary to cancel the indictment which the law presented, it only strengthens and ratifies its preceptive authority. It follows, however, that if the special purpose of the ceremonial law was to confess the fact of man's exposure to the curse, and portrays the mode of his deliverance from it, then, surely, the curse being borne, and the condemning sentence expunged, the Levitical code has served its purpose, and ceases to exist. What it taught in symbol, is now enforced in reality; what it foreshadowed in type, has now become matter of history. And this it is the special object of the apostle to show as a lesson and caution to the Colossians.[2]

This handwriting had assumed the form of "ordinances." In Eph. ii. 14, the apostle uses the term expressly of the ceremonial law and its positive institutions. But the two places are not entirely analogous. There the apostle describes the ceremonial code as a hedge between Jew and Gentile, and shows how, through its abolition by Christ in His death, the union of the two races was secured, both being, at the same time, and by the same event, reconciled to God. Here, however, as the apostle speaks specially of the spiritual results of Christ's death, and of these as effected by God the Father, he seems, as we have said, to refer to the entire Mosaic Institute, but especially to the ceremonial law, as it was so palpable and

[1] The χειρογ. bore upon it the signature or acknowledgment of the debtor, and so differed from συγγραφή, which contained the signatures of both contracting parties.

[2] Also Lucian, *Prometh.*, Opera, vol. ii. p. 2, ed. Bipont.—τοσοῦτον χρόνον τῷ Καυκάσῳ προσηλωμένος.

prominent a portion of the system, and contained such a number of minute and peremptory enactments.

Καὶ αὐτὸ ἦρκεν ἐκ τοῦ μέσου—"And He has taken it out of the way." The use of the perfect tense adds emphasis to the verb—he took it out of the way, and still it remains out of the way. The apostle says, *καὶ αὐτό*—this very document, terrible as it is; that is to say, He not only blotted out the writing upon it, but He has taken out of the way the parchment itself; or, as Theophylact says—*ἐποίησε μηδὲ φαίνεσθαι.* The idiom *ἐκ τοῦ μέσου* (the contrast being *ἐν τῷ μέσῳ*) is no uncommon one. On the change of construction from participle to verb marking emphasis, see under i. 6. Winer, § 63, I. 2, b. How God has taken it so effectually out of the way is next told us—

Προσηλώσας αὐτὸ τῷ σταυρῷ—"Having nailed it to the cross." The participle occurs only here in the New Testament, but is similarly found in 3 Macc. iv. 9. The allusion is not to the tablet nailed to the cross above the sufferer, as Gieseler assumes, but to the crucifixion of the Redeemer Himself. There seems to be no historical ground for the illustration of Grotius, that it was customary to thrust a nail through papers—declaring them old and obsolete, much in the same way as a Bank of England note is punched through the centre when declared to be no longer of value, and no longer to be put into circulation. The idea of the apostle is, that when Christ was nailed to the cross, the condemning power of the law was nailed along with Him, and died with Him—"Now we are delivered from the law, that being dead in which we were held." Rom. vii. 6. In other words, God exempts sinners from the sentence which they merit, through the sufferings and death of Jesus. The implied doctrine is, that the guilt of men was borne by Christ when he died—was laid on Him by that God who by this method took the handwriting out of the way. Jesus bore the sentence of the handwriting in Himself, and God now remits its penalty; having forgiven you all your trespasses, inasmuch as He has blotted out the hostile handwriting and taken it out of the way, for He nailed it to the cross of His Son. Meyer remarks, that *ἐξαλείφειν* and *αἴρειν ἐκ τοῦ μέσου* are not two really distinct acts, but represent the same thing. We would rather say, that the first term characterizes the act, and the second refers to the completed result; while the third participle—προσηλώσας—defines the external mode of accomplishment.

(Ver. 15.) Ἀπεκδυσάμενος τὰς ἀρχὰς καὶ τὰς ἐξουσίας—"Having spoiled the principalities and powers." We should have expected καί to be placed between the two clauses; but its absence indicates the close connection, nay, the identity of the two acts; or, perhaps, of the process in which the two acts were completed. In blotting out the handwriting, God at the same time vanquished Satan. If ever there was bathos in exegesis, it is in that of Rosenmüller—that when Jesus rose again from the dead, it was seen how vain were the efforts of the Jewish magistrates against Him. Suicer, Junker, and others, take a similar view. The terms have been explained under i. 16, and under Eph. i. 21, vi. 12. We cannot agree with Pierce that good angels are meant; they needed not to be spoiled or triumphed over openly. Hostile spiritual powers are plainly designated. Their reign over man had its origin in his sin; and their usurpation lasted till sin was atoned for, and its power destroyed. Hence Satan is called the "god" and "prince of this world." [Eph. ii. 2;] Luke xi. 22.

The verb ἀπεκδύομαι, which means literally to cast off anything, such as clothing, has been taken by many as referring to Christ's own death, as if he had cast off the flesh in dying—an idea which seems to have originated the reading τὴν σάρκα, in F, G, seen too in the Syriac, and followed by some of the Latin Fathers. Augustine has—*spolians se carne.* So that the figure has been supposed to be that of a naked wrestler. But the diction of the verse is that of avowed and open warfare, and the participle ἀπεκδ. must have the sense of spoiling; conquering, and then making the vanquished a spoil, as is done when a fallen foe is stript of his armour. This last is the idea and image of Meyer, which perhaps is too minute, for the general figure is, that He stript them of all power and authority. The compound form of the verb indicates how completely this was done; ἐκδύειν[1] is used in the sense of *spoliare,* and the Vulgate here renders *exspolians.*

Ἐδειγμάτισεν ἐν παῤῥησίᾳ—"He made a show of them

[1] Joseph. *Bell. Jud.* ii. 24.

openly." The allusion is plainly to the triumph which is celebrated after a battle. His spiritual foes, on being vanquished, were exhibited as a public spectacle. The meaning is not that He exposed their weakness—*τὴν ἀσθένειαν ἔδειξε*, as Theodoret understands it. That is certainly implied, but the idea is, He has shown the fact of their complete subjugation in His triumph over them. There is no ground to give the simple verb the sense of the compound—*παραδειγματίζειν*, and add the idea of shame, as is done by Theophylact, Beza, Röell, Storr, and Conybeare. Such an idea, as well as that of weakness, may be indeed inferred from the humiliating exposure. And it was no private parade, it was done *ἐν παῤῥησίᾳ*—"openly." John vii. 4. Theophylact gives it rightly—*δημοσίᾳ, πάντων ὁρώντων*—"openly, in the eyes of all;"—*kühnlich, frei und frank*, as Meyer paraphrases it.

Θριαμβεύσας ἐν αὐτῷ—"Having triumphed over them in it." The participle is used in 2 Cor. ii. 14, with a hiphil sense, and it here occurs with the accusative, like the Latin—*triumphare aliquem*. Adhering to the hiphil sense—"maketh or causeth to triumph," some would supply *ἡμᾶς*—maketh us to triumph over them. Such an idea only encumbers the sense. The three verbs in the verse do not form a climax. But the spiritual foes are spoiled, and then they are exposed; while the last participle defines the manner and purpose of the exposure—it formed a public triumph. The truth expressed is, that there has been complete and irretrievable subjugation.

But the meaning and reference of the last words *ἐν αὐτῷ* are doubtful. The Syriac and Vulgate, with Theodoret, and the editors Griesbach and Scholz, read *ἐν αὑτῷ*—"in Himself." If the reference be made to Christ, then it is wrong, for God is the nominative; and if to God, then the phrase is not very intelligible. Meyer takes the reference to be to the principal noun of the preceding verse—*χειρόγραφον*. His meaning is, that the expunged and perforated handwriting was a proof of Satan's overthrow. This exegesis, however, gives a fulness of meaning to *ἐν αὐτῷ*, which the words will not bear. They simply mean "in it," that is, in the handwriting. Now it was not in the handwriting simply that God obtained His victory, but in obliterating it, and nailing it to the cross—an idea that could not be expressed by the bare *ἐν αὐτῷ*. "In the cheirograph," and in what he did with the cheirograph, are very different ideas, requiring very different forms of diction.

Opinions are nearly divided as to whether ἐν αὐτῷ refers to Christ or to the cross. Wolf, Musculus, Bengel, Storr, Flatt, Rosenmüller, Bähr, Huther, and De Wette, hold the first view. Our objection to this view is, that in the two verses no mention is made of Christ. The work is wholly ascribed to God—not formally to God in Christ.

And therefore we incline to the other opinion, that ἐν αὐτῷ carries us back to σταυρῷ. Such is the opinion of the Greek Fathers, Theophylact and Œcumenius, of Calvin, Beza, Grotius, Crocius, Steiger, Böhmer, and Olshausen. Origen has no less than eight times for ἐν αὐτῷ the phrase ἐν τῷ ξύλῳ. Epiphanius, Macarius, and Athanasius, read either so, or ἐν σταυρῷ. The reading is a gloss, but it shows the general opinion. In the cross God achieved His victory over the infernal powers—" through death," he " that had the power of death " was destroyed. Through the agency of fallen spirits sin was introduced, and it was the sphere of their dominion ; they could rule in a condemned world, but not in a redeemed one; and when that world was released from death by the death of Christ, the instrument of His death was the weapon of conquest and symbol of victory over them. Most strong is the prevailing opinion of the mediæval Latin church, as seen in Aquinas, Anselm, and others, that this spoiling was in the nether world, and over the dæmons who held the souls of the patriarchs in captivity, and that the triumphal procession was the march of the imprisoned spirits out of the *limbus patrum.* [Eph. iv. 8, 9.] The subject throughout the previous context is God, not Christ; and the whole notion is an idle chimera.

Most glorious is the thought that the church is released from the bond that held it, and delivered from the hellish powers that tyrannized over humanity—a deliverance achieved for it by Him alone " whose right hand and holy arm " could get Him the victory. Redemption is a work at once of price and power, of expiation and conquest. On the cross was the purchase made; on the cross was the victory gained. The blood that wipes out the sentence was there shed, and the death which was the death-blow of Satan's kingdom was there endured. Those nails which killed Christ pierced the sentence of doom—gave egress to the blood which cancelled it, and inflicted at the same time a mortal wound on the hosts of darkness. That power which Satan had exercised was so prostrated, that every one believing on Christ is freed from his vassalage. Christ's death was a battle, and in it God achieved an immortal victory. The conflict was a furious one, mighty and mysterious in its struggle. The combatant died; but in dying He conquered. Hell might be congratulating itself that it had gained the mastery, and might be wondering what should be the most fitting commemoration and trophy, when He who died arose the victor—no enemy again daring to dispute His power or challenge His right, and then God exhibited His foes in open triumph. "The prince of this world is cast out."

All this teaching bore upon the Colossian church and its crisis. Let not the ritual law—which exhibits the condemning power of the whole law—be enacted among you, for it has been fully and formally abrogated. Let not your minds be dazzled or overawed by esoteric teaching about the spirit-world. All those spirits are beneath the Divine Master; if good, they are His servants; if evil, they are conquered vassals.

Now follows the pointed and practical lesson. Already had they been warned against one phasis of error—"philosophy and vain deceit," and a sufficient reason is given. Next is rehearsed their privilege of circumcision and baptism, their death to sin and their life to God. Here their forgiveness is stated along with the means which had been taken to secure it; and this process, so decided and characteristic, lays the foundation for the warning in the verse which we are now to consider.

(Ver. 16.) *Μὴ οὖν τις ὑμᾶς κρινέτω ἐν βρώσει ἢ ἐν πόσει*—"Let no one, therefore, judge you in eating or in drinking,"—test your piety by such a criterion. The participle *οὖν* refers back to the preceding statement, especially to the first clause of the 14th verse. The verb may be followed by the accusative, intimating who are the objects of judgment, while *ἐν* accompanying it sometimes specifies its period, as in John xii. 48, and sometimes its quality, as in Acts xvii. 31, but here it denotes the basis on which judgment is passed, or rather, the sphere in which it is exercised. According to Meyer, βρῶσις, in the writings of the Apostle Paul, is uniformly *actio edendi*, and so distinct from βρῶμα—*cibus*, though in other portions of the New Testament, and among the classics, that distinction is not observed. Some of the lexicographers do not admit the statement, as is manifest by their citations, neither does Fritzsche—but we believe Meyer to be correct. Πόσις is also the act of drinking, in contrast with πόμα, the draught. Though the Mosaic law did not dwell so much on drinks as meats, yet, as we shall see, it included some statutes about drinks and drinking vessels, and therefore we cannot agree with De Wette that πόσις was inserted "for the sake of the alliteration"—*des Gleichklanges wegen.* The eating and drinking are, therefore, a reference to the dietetic injunctions of the Mosaic law. Lev. vii. 20–27, xi. Certain kinds of animal food were prohibited. The Jews were allowed the flesh of ruminant quadrupeds with a cloven hoof, of fishes with scales and fins, and of such insects as the locust, while unclean birds were specified in a separate catalogue. The priests on the eve of ministration were solemnly forbidden the use of wine. Certain kinds of vessels that had contained water, and been defiled, were to be broken, but others were only to be rinsed. The Nazarites did not taste any product of the vine. No doubt the pride of sanctity was strong in the Jewish mind, and the tendency was, both in Essenes and Pharisees, to multiply such prohibitions, and to place around meats and drinks a finical array of minute and complex regulations. The party at Colosse had strong ascetic tendencies, and were apt to sit in judgment upon those who felt that "every creature of God is good, and nothing to be refused." The errorists forgot that the spirituality of Christianity rose far above such physical restraints and distinctions, and that the new kingdom was "not meat and drink, but righteousness, and peace, and joy in the Holy Ghost."

Ἠ ἐν μέρει ἑορτῆς ἢ νουμηνίας ἢ σαββάτων—"Either in the particular of a festival, or of a new moon, or of Sabbath-days." The phrase ἐν μέρει, as in classic use,[1] signifies not simply in

[1] See Wetstein, *in loc.;* Aelian, v. 8, 3. Krebs regards ἐν μέρει as an elegant redundancy, but his examples do not sustain his opinion.

respect of, as Beza, Flatt, Bähr, and Huther give it. It gives a specialty to the theme or sphere of judgment, by individualizing the topic or occasion. Melancthon and Zanchius render—*vicibus festorum.* The Greek Fathers Chrysostom and Theophylact take it as denoting a partial observance, as if the heretics did not retain the whole of the original rule; and Calvin supposes ἐν μέρει to intimate that they made unwarranted distinctions between one day and another. "Feast," or Festival, refers, as is plain from the contrast, to the three great annual feasts of the Passover, Pentecost, and Tabernacles. The "new moon" ushered in certain monthly celebrations, while the sabbaths were weekly in their periods. Some, indeed, such as Neumann, suppose the allusion to be to the grand sabbatic periods of the seventh day, the seventh year, and the fiftieth year. But there is no warrant or necessity for such a reference here, though the apostle says to the Galatians, "ye observe days and months, and times and years." Rom. xiv. 5, 6. The term σάββατον often occurs in a plural form in the New Testament, as if, as Winer supposes, the Syro-Chaldaic form—שַׁבְּתָא—had been transferred into the Greek tongue. Matt. xii. 1; Luke iv. 16; Acts xiii. 14, xvi. 13. Allusions to these feasts, collectively, will be found in 1 Chron. xxiii. 31; 2 Chron. ii. 4, xxxi. 3. The observances of the Jewish rubric, whether in its original form, or with the multiplied and ascetic additions which it presented in those days, laid believers no longer under obligation. They belonged to an obsolete system, which had "decayed and waxed old." Christianity inculcated no such periodical holidays. For it did not bid men meet thrice a year to feast themselves, but each day to "eat their bread with gladness and singleness of heart." It did not summon them to any tumultuous demonstration with "trumpets at new moon," since every division of the month was a testimony of Divine goodness, and the whole kalendar was marked by Divine benefactions—every day alike a season of prayer and joy. Nor were they to hallow the "sabbaths," for these had served their purpose, and the Lord's day was now to be a season of loftier joy, as it commemorates a more august event than either the creation of the universe or the exodus from Egypt. Every period is sanctified—"day unto day uttereth speech, and night unto night teacheth knowledge." Sensations of spiritual joy are not to be restricted to holy days, for they thrill the spirit every moment, and need not wait for expression till there be a solemn gathering, for every instant awakes to the claims and the raptures of religion. The new religion is too free and exuberant to be trained down to "times and seasons" like its tame and rudimental predecessor. Its feast is daily, for every day is holy; its moon never wanes, and its serene tranquillity is an unbroken Sabbath. The Jewish Sabbath was kept, however, by the early Christians along with their own Lord's day for a considerable period; till at length, in 364 A.D., the Council of Laodicea condemned the practice as Judaizing.

(Ver. 17.) *Ἅ ἐστιν σκιὰ τῶν μελλόντων*—"Which are a shadow of things to come." The plural form of the relative has higher authority than the singular, which is adopted by Lachmann, and is found in B, F, G, and in several of the Latin Fathers. The relative is not to be restricted to *σαββάτων*, as Richter argues; nor does it simply connect itself with those festive days, as Flatt takes it. The entire ritual is alluded to—the ritual as God appointed it, and not as overloaded by its self-willed votaries.

The noun *σκιά* may bear two different meanings. It may either signify a shadow projected from a body by its interception of the light; or it may signify, as here, a dim and shadowy sketch of an object, in contrast not only with a full and coloured likeness, but with the object itself. Meyer contends strenuously for the former, viz. that *σκιά* is not *σκιαγραφία*, but simply "shadow," as if the Christian economy threw its shadow back, and this shadow was ritual Mosaism. This idea brings out, indeed, the typical relation which Judaism bore to Christianity. But perhaps the apostle had the figure before his mind which he has elsewhere employed; "the law," he says, "had a shadow of good things to come," and not the "very image of the things." In this expression he distinguishes *σκιά* and *εἰκών*, as being both likenesses, though of a different kind; and in the passage before us, he distinguishes *σκιά* from the reality or substance—*σῶμα*—which it represents. The nouns *σκιά* and *σῶμα* are thus also contrasted by Josephus, when he makes Antipater say of Archelaus—*σκιὰν αἰτησόμενος βασιλείας, ἧς ἥρπασεν ἑαυτῷ τὸ σῶμα.*[1] Photius vaguely renders *σῶμα* by *ἀλήθεια*. The "things to come" are the spiritual blessings of the Christian dispensation, not as Meyer, in accordance with his favourite theory, supposes, blessings to be enjoyed at the Parousia, or second coming. Heb. x. 1. The apostle employs *ἐστί* in the present, not because, as Meyer argues, the blessings are yet future to the present point of time; but either because, as Davenant supposes, he gives a definition, or because the apostle transports himself ideally to a period when ritual Judaism was of Divine obligation, and when it was really the shadow of things yet to come. The connection of *σκιά* with the genitive *τῶν μελ.* forbids the notion of Zanchius and Suicer, that the reference may be to the comparative darkness of the former economy.

Τὸ δὲ σῶμα Χριστοῦ—"But the body is Christ's." A few Codices change the passage by a glaring amendment, and read *ὁ Χριστός*, while A, B, C prefix the article *τοῦ*, a reading which Lachmann prefers. "But the body is Christ's," that is, of Christ's provision and possession. Meyer, taking *σῶμα* in the sense of body, that is, the concrete reality of those things to come, supposes that Christ is here supposed to be its head. But the term body, with its correlative organ—head, invariably refers in Paul's writings to the church—a meaning which cannot in this place be admitted. Chrysostom adopted this sense, and to support it, altered the connection, and clumsily joined this clause to the following verse—"You who are the body of Christ, let no man deceive you of your reward." The same construction is approved by Photius, and also by Augustine, who has *corpus autem Christi, nemo vos convincat*. The meaning is not that Christ is the body, but that He possesses it. The realities so long shadowed out *are* His—all that composes them belongs to Him.

The clause then contains the great truth that the Mosaic economy was no empty congeries of useless and meaningless observances—infantine in character and design; but an organism at once Divine in its origin, and fraught with lessons of striking form. It was a dim outline—*σκιά*—of those substantial blessings which are of Christ, and it served

[1] *De Bell. Jud.* ii. 2, 5. Also Cicero, *de Officiis*, 3, 17.

a gracious purpose during its existence. It was a rudimentary sketch. Its temple with its apartments, vessels, and furniture; its priesthood, in their imposing robes and duties; its altar, with the fire on its hearth, and the cloud of smoke resting over it; its victims, in their age, kind, and qualifications; its rubric, with its holidays, and their special observances; its minute ritual in reference to diet, dress, and disease—all were the faint lines of a sketch which was limned by the Divine pencil for the guidance and government of Hebrew faith and worship. The eye of faith might, as it gazed, be able to fill in the picture, and see in distant perspective the sublime group of a tabernacle filled and inhabited by the Great Spirit; a Priest offering the most costly of victims—the God-man presenting Himself; an altar consecrated by blood precious beyond all parallel; and a sabbatism not only serene and joyous on earth, but stretching away into eternity as a "rest remaining to the people of God." Thus the hieroglyph and substance exactly correspond, though the former be only an adumbration and a miniature.

But not only was there this close and preordained relation between the shadow and the substance, there was also a predictive correspondence. The sketch is taken from the reality, and implies the existence of it. The shadow is the intended likeness of the substance. In other words, Christianity was not fashioned to resemble Judaism, but Judaism was fashioned to resemble Christianity. The antitype is not constructed to bear a likeness to the type, but the type is constructed to bear a likeness to the antitype. It is, in short, because of the antitype that the type exists. The Mosaic economy being a rude draught of Christianity, presupposed its future existence. If it had been an institute without ulterior object, if its rites had contained no prospective delineations, or if its whole design had terminated in present observance, then it could not have received the apostolic designation. But it was a typical system. Now, a type not only pictured out the nature of a future reality, but it foretold its certainty. It showed, and it foreshowed. The sacrifice not only showed that the offerer was under sentence of death, and that only by the substitutionary shedding of blood the awful sentence could be repealed; but it also foreshowed that the great and final oblation of infinite efficacy would assuredly be presented in "the fulness of the time." It not only portrayed the mode, but it gave assurance of the fact—it was at once a symbol and a prophecy. The entire Jewish ritual was so organized, as not only to exhibit a faint and distant likeness to Christianity, but it established the certainty that the new dispensation of which it was an early and elementary copy should be at length organized in perfection and symmetry. The "figure for the time then present" guaranteed the introduction of the figured reality in the time to come. The sign not only preceded, but certified the advent of the thing signified.

Still, the shadow is in itself nothing—it is empty, baseless, and indistinct. The Hebrew ceremonial could not give full instruction by its symbols, and it could only purge "as pertaining to the flesh." It had no power to enter into the conscience, and impart peace and the sense of forgiveness. The blood of an animal could not secure Divine favour. The thief, after restoring fourfold to the man whom he had wronged, and so satisfying him, must also offer a victim on the altar to God, in order that the penalty incurred from Him might be remitted. The man who had been contaminated by any ceremonial impurity, who had touched a corpse, or come into accidental contact with a leper, was by means of an appointed ordeal of ablution and sacrifice restored to his previous status. But the whole apparatus was wanting in spiritual power, and its only virtue was in its connection with the substance to come. That it was a shadow so designed, and not a fortuitous and unmeaning system, is plain from its correspondence with the body which is Christ's, and its consequent fulfilment in Him. The harmony is universal and complete. The great High Priest has come and clothed Himself in humanity—a living vestment far more costly than the robes of Aaron, "made for glory and for beauty;" and all other victims have been superseded by His oblation of Himself. Omniscience is His, and therefore no formal Urim and Thummim glitters on His breast. The Self-sacrifice He presented was pure as the fire from God by which it was consumed, and it has been visibly accepted. He has gone through the starry vail, and into heaven itself, with the names of all His clients inscribed upon His heart; and He pleads the merit of His blood before a mercy-seat not canopied by a cloud, but enveloped in the Majesty of Him who sits upon it. The woven and metallic cherubim disappear in the reality, for the angels having performed their allotted parts in the mystery of redemption, are "ministering spirits to them who shall be heirs of salvation." There is no need now that the law be engraved on stone, for it is written indelibly on "the fleshy tables of the heart." It is no longer required that there be a bath, or a "sea of brass," for believers are washed in the laver of regeneration. The golden lampstand has been extinguished, for the lustre of the Enlightening Spirit fills the House of God. Nay, the entire church on earth is a spiritual priesthood, engaged in appropriate ministrations, serving now, indeed, in the outer court, but soon to be called up into the inner sanctuary.

The argument of the apostle, then, is—why go down to "the weak and beggarly elements"? Who would listen to any sophistry urging him to prefer the shadow to the substance? Such a relapse would be an attempt to roll back the Divine purpose, and impede that religious progress which Christianity had introduced; an effort to restore an intolerable yoke, and rob the new religion of its spirituality and vigour. The result would be to stifle devotion by a periodical mechanism, and degrade obedience into a service of trifles. And therefore the apostle solemnly warns the Colossians not to be imposed upon by such pretences, and not for a moment to submit to teaching which would supplant the real by the ritual, and give them a religion of obsolete externalities for one of vital freedom and spiritual jurisdiction.

(Ver. 18.) *Μηδεὶς ὑμᾶς καταβραβευέτω*—"Let no man rob you of your reward." Theodoret explains the peculiar verb as meaning *τὸ ἀδίκως βραβεύειν*—to confer a reward unjustly. Zonaras, on the 35th canon of the Laodicean Council, has usually been adduced, and he says that the action of the verb is done when this takes place—*τὸ μὴ τὸν νικήσαντα ἀξιοῦν τοῦ βραβείου, ἀλλ' ἑτέρῳ διδόναι αὐτό*, "not to reckon one who has conquered worthy of the prize, but to give it to another." Suidas says more distinctly—*τὸ ἄλλου ἀγωνιζομένου ἄλλον στεφανοῦσθαι λέγει ὁ ἀπόστολος καταβραβεύεσθαι.* The other figure, adopted by Beza, from one of the exceptional meanings of *βραβεύω*, is not sustained by any certain examples. His idea is, let no one usurp the office of a *βραβευτής* against you; while in a similar way a-Lapide, Crocius, and Bengel, generally adopt this meaning—let no one assuming such an office domineer over you, and so prescribe to you how you are to act in order to obtain the prize. Such an interpretation has more in derivation to recommend it than the notion of Luther, Castalio, and Calvin—let no one intercept the prize, or get it before you. The apostle warns them to listen to none of these instructors, for their design was to rob them of that prize, which, as the result of their spiritual victory, Christianity set before them. If they yielded to any of the practices referred to in this verse, then they followed the solicitation of one who would rob them of that "prize of their high calling" for which they had been pressing forward. It is thus a term of far deeper import than the preceding *κρινέτω*, though Photius, Hesychius, Elsner, Storr, Huther, Bähr, and Olshausen virtually identify them. For there is in it not merely the giving of a wrong judgment, but a judgment which involves in it the loss of all that the gospel promises to the winner, a life of glory on high. It is a tame idea of De Wette, to suppose that the prize is the true worship of God, for it is here looked upon not as a prize, but as the means of obtaining the prize. It may be remarked in passing, that Jerome regards the verb as a Cilicism, or a provincialism of the apostle, but others have shown that the word occurs among the classics, as in Demosthenes and Polybius.

The true connection and meaning of the following word, *θέλων*, are not easily ascertained. The agitated question is, whether it should be joined to *καταβραβευέτω*, or to the following words, *ἐν ταπεινοφροσύνῃ*. If it be joined to the former, the meaning will be "willingly"—let no one willingly seduce you; but this would be a counsel to the false teachers as well as to the Colossians. Or it may be, as Grotius gives it—*etiamsi id maxime velit*, "let no one, although he should set his heart upon it, rob you of your reward." Beza finds in the term a support to the sense which he attached to the verb—let no one assume voluntarily the office of a prize-distributor over you, and thus wrong you. Erasmus gives the term an adverbial sense of *cupide, studiose;* and others render it *ultro.* Steiger inclines to a similar opinion, and Tittmann translates—*consulto vel ultro.*[1] But the usage is not well sustained in the New Testament, and the participle is, as Bengel remarks, the first of a series, *θέλων, ἐμβατεύων, φυσιούμενος, κρατῶν*, and each of the participles has its independent construction. It must therefore be joined to *ἐν ταπεινοφρ.*—but how? Olshausen, Wahl, Bähr, Böhmer, Baumgarten-Crusius, and Bretschneider, preceded by Hesychius, Phavorinus, Augustine, Estius, Elsner, Storr, and Flatt, take *θέλων* in the sense of *εὐδοκῶν*, "delighting in"—*affectans humilitatem.* Thus they regard it as a Hebraism formed upon the usage חָפֵץ בְּ—1 Sam. xviii. 22; 2 Sam. xv. 26; 2 Chron. ix. 8; Ps. cxi. 2, cxlvii. 10. Though this usage may be regarded as established in the Septuagint, yet it is not found in the New Testament, nor does it suit here. For the apostle is not wishing to paint the character of the false teacher, but to warn against his wiles. He does not mean to say that the false teacher has a special pride in his own humility, but he means to say, that the Colossians must be on their guard against him, for he will seek to entrap them by means of that humility.

We give *θέλων* its common meaning. Let no man beguile you—wishing to do it by his humility. This is the natural view of the Greek Fathers, of Theodoret, and of Theophylact who says—*ὅτι θέλουσιν ὑμᾶς καταβραβεύειν διὰ ταπεινοφρ. δοκούσης.* So Photius, Calvin, Huther, Meyer, and De Wette. The preposition *ἐν* denotes the means of deception, or the sphere in which the deceiver moves. The humility referred to, as may be seen from the last verse of the chapter, is a spurious humility. Fanatical pride is often associated with this humility, as when, for show, the beggar's feet are washed; and the friar in his coarse rags walks barefooted and begs. And men become proud of their humility—glory in the feeling of self-annihilation. The spirit of the false teacher, with all its professed lowliness, would not bend to the Divine revelation, but nursed its fallacies with a haughty tenacity, and preached them with an impious daring, for he was "vainly puffed up by his fleshly mind."

Καὶ θρησκείᾳ τῶν ἀγγέλων—"And adoration of angels." This is another of the instruments of seduction. The genitive

[1] *De Synon.* p. 130.

τῶν ἀγγέλων cannot be that of subject, as if the meaning were, a worship like that which angels present, or such as man may learn from them—θρησκεία ἀγγελική. Such a view is held by Schoettgen and Wolf, and in its spirit by Noesselt, Rosenmüller, Luther, and Schrader. Tertullian says—*aliquos taxat, qui ex visionibus angelicis dicebant, cibis abstinendum,* etc. *Adver. Marcion,* v. 19.

The genitive is that of object. The attempt of the false teacher was not to get them into an ecstasy such as that felt by the "rapt seraph, who adores and burns," but it was a positive inculcation of angel-worship. Θρησκεία is often followed by the genitive of object.[1] Winer, § 30, 1. The term, whatever its derivation, denotes devotional service. How angels came to be worshipped we may not precisely know, though, certainly, it might not be difficult to account for it, when one sees how saint-worship has spread itself so extensively in one section of Christendom. The angels occupied the highest place which creatures could occupy under the Theocracy. They held lofty station and discharged important functions. The law was "ordained by angels, in the hands of a mediator," nay, the apostle calls it "the word spoken by angels." Jehovah descended with ten thousand of His holy ones, when "from His right hand went a fiery law." The Jews, said Stephen, in his address, "received the law by the disposition of angels." Whatever be the meaning of these declarations, there is no doubt that they indicate some special and important province of angelic operation. Josephus expresses the same opinion—the current one of his nation.[2] No wonder that those beings, so sublimely commissioned by God, and burning in the reflection of His majesty, command human reverence, and are therefore themselves called "gods." Ps. xcvii. 7, compared with Heb. i. 6.

Now, the step from respect to worship is at once short and easy, for it is but an exaggeration. The heart, not content with feeling that a being so near God and so like Him should be held in esteem and admiration, passes into excess,

[1] Herodian, v. 7, 3. Joseph. *Antiq.* iv. 4, 1; iv. 8, 44, etc. etc. Wisdom xiv. 27; Clement, *Strom.* vi. 566. Eusebius, *Hist. Eccles.* vi. 4.

[2] *Antiq.* xv. 5. Eisenmenger, *Entdecktes Jud.* vol. i. p. 808.

and worships where it had honoured. And to fortify itself in the practice, it perverted the angelic office. It raised those creatures from attendants to mediators—from messengers to interested protectors. It would seem that in the days of the patriarch Job[1] such a feeling existed in the early world. "Call now," is the challenge of Eliphaz, "if there be any that will answer thee; and to which of the saints wilt thou turn?" and in another chapter mention is made of an angel interpreter. In the book of Tobit,[2] the Jewish belief is incidentally brought out—that angels formally present prayers to God. In the imagery of the Apocalypse, we find an angel at the altar, having in his hand a golden censer and much incense, that he should offer it with "the prayers of all saints." In the Testimony of the Twelve Patriarchs, and in the book of Enoch, the same notion is prominently exhibited. And thus the prayer offered through the angel, was by and by presented to him. It was first offered to him that he might carry it to God, and then it was offered to him without such ulterior reference or prospect. Again, that angels were entrusted with the presidency of various countries and nations, was another Jewish opinion; and it was with a superstitious people a matter of extreme facility to pass from that obeisance, which might be yielded to a representative of Divinity, to that veneration which is due to Jehovah alone. If a man bent one knee in loyalty, he soon bent both knees in worship; and asked from the substitute what should be solicited from the principal.

That the worship of created spirits was widespread, thus admits of no doubt. The Fathers abundantly testify to it. Origen affirms it of the Jews, and Clement makes the same assertion; both of them, as well as the treatise called the "Preaching of Peter," describing the Jews as λατρεύοντες ἀγγέλοις. An old Jewish liturgy distinctly contains angel-worship, and exhibits one form of it. Celsus also avers it. The Platonic idea of demons—itself, in all probability, a relic of Eastern Theosophy—spread itself, in Asia Minor, and combined with the Jewish superstition. That such practices should

[1] v. 1; xxxiii. 23. Hirzel and Prof. Lee on Job, *in loc.*

[2] xii. 12. Böhmer, *Isagoge in Epist. ad Coloss.* p. 281. Neander, *Geschichte der Pflanzung*, etc., p. 508. Suicer, *sub voce* ἄγγελος.

take root in Phrygia is no marvel, for there they found a congenial soil. Theodoret testifies to their existence, and that they remained in Phrygia and Pisidia for a long time. The thirty-fifth canon of the Council of Laodicea, a city in the vicinity, solemnly interdicted the practice, but did not wholly eradicate it. In the days of Theodoret, the archangel Michael was worshipped at Colosse; and a ναὸς ἀρχαγγελικός was built in his honour, and for a miracle alleged to be wrought by him. Though those historical quotations refer to post-apostolic periods, still they appear to describe the remnants of earlier practices, and they afford at least some analogies that help us to judge of the superstitions which the apostle mentions and reprobates. The Catholic interpreters, Estius and a-Lapide, make a strong effort to exclude this passage, from such as might be brought against the worship of saints.

The two nouns, "humility and worship of angels," are closely connected, and mean a species of humility connected with angel-worship. It was out of a fanatical humility that service was offered to angels. It was thought that the great God was too majestic and distant to be addressed, and they therefore invented these *internuncii*. That the heretical party thought the glory of the Only-Begotten too dazzling for approach, and therefore took refuge in angel-worship, is an opinion of Chrysostom and Theophylact, but in opposition to the whole tenor of the rebuke generally, and of the following clause particularly, for it contains the accusation of "not holding the Head." The true reason and connection are given, as we have given them, by Theodoret.

Ἃ μὴ ἑώρακεν ἐμβατεύων. This clause presents a very strange difference of reading, for the negative is omitted in some MSS. of high authority, such as A, B, D[1], and by several of the Latin Fathers. It is therefore rejected by Lachmann, and his reading is approved of by Olshausen, Steiger, Huther, and Meyer. Olshausen says that μή was added because critics thought that they were obliged to insert a negative. His assertion may be turned against himself; for we might reply that the copyists could not discover the propriety of μή according to their finical notions of grammar; since some, as in F, G, changed it into οὐκ, and others omitted it altogether. The meaning of the clause is not materially different whichever reading be adopted. If the negative be omitted, the clause must be an ironical description. The words "which he has seen" will mean, visions which he professes or imagines to have seen—visions which are the result of a morbid imagination or a distempered brain. We prefer the common reading found in C, D^{111}, E, J, K, in the Vulgate, Gothic, and Syriac Versions, and in so many of the Greek Fathers. The negative μή, and not οὐκ, is rightly employed. Winer, § 55, 3.[1] The participle ἐμβατεύων, found only here in the New Testament, but occurring several times in the Apocrypha, and allied in origin to the similar term ἐμβαίνω, is wrongly supposed by some, such as Erasmus, to signify, to walk in state—as if the expression were taken *a tragicis cothurnis.* It sometimes denotes, to go into the possession of, as in Josh. xix. 49. And then it is usually followed by εἰς. Buddaeus, Zanchius, and Huther assign it such a meaning here. It also has the sense of—to go into, to penetrate into, or to intrude. It is so used of God,[2] and often of man, both in a literal and tropical sense, and is followed sometimes by the dative and sometimes, as here, by the accusative.[3] Phavorinus defines it—τὸ ἔνδον ἐξερευνῆσαι ἢ σκοπῆσαι, and Hesychius explains it by the less intense term ζητήσας. The compound κενεμβατεύειν is employed, in Plato, to denote senseless speculation. From the verb ἑώρακεν, there is no need to deduce the idea of mental perception or knowledge, as Heinrichs and Flatt incline to do —*quae intellectu percipere nemo potest.* The word is often used of visions and visionary representations—Acts xi. 17, ix. 10–12, x. 3; Rev. ix. 17; and of a supersensuous view of God—John i. 18, vi. 46, xiv. 7; 1 John iv. 12.

The reference in the clause—"intruding into what he has not seen"—appears to be the worship of angels. The current theosophy spent no little of its ingenuity upon the spirit-world. It wandered not only beyond the regions of sense, but even that of Scripture. It mustered into troops the heavenly orders. [Eph. i. 21.] This oriental propensity was a prevalent one. The inquisitive spirit pryed into the invisible world around it and above it. It loved such phantasms, and lost itself in

[1] Moulton, p. 603, note 4.

[2] Chrysos. 2 *Hom. in Philip.*

[3] Philo, *de Plant. Noe*, vol. iii. p. 120, ed Pfeiffer. Æschylus, *Persae*, 449. Eurip. *Electra*, 595. Josephus, *Antiq.* xii. 1.

transcendental reveries. The creed of the Zendavesta had its Ormuzd, its six Amshaspands, its eight-and-twenty Izeds, and hosts of Feruers—all of them objects of worship and prayer. Augustine says, with justice, that many had tried the intercession of angels, but had failed; and not only so, but—*inciderunt in desiderium curiosarum visionum.*[1] How the Jewish fancy strove to penetrate the curtain that conceals the unseen, may be learned from the following quotation from a rabbinical treatise.[2] "As there are ten Sephiroth, so there are ten troops of angels, as follows:—the Erellim, Ishim, Benei-haelohim, Malachim, Hashmalim, Tarshishim, Shinanim, Cherubim, Ophanim, and the Seraphim. Captains are set over each of them—Michael over the Erellim, Zephaniah over the Ishim, Hophniel over the Benei-haelohim, Uzziel over the Malachim, Hashmal over the Hashmalim, Tarshish over the Tarshishim, Zadkiel over the Shinanim, Cherub over the Cherubim, Raphael over the Ophanim, and Jehuel over the Seraphim." Tertullian mentions some who professed to divine their asceticism from angelic revelation,[3] a remark which serves at least for illustration.

Some, such as Steiger, have proposed to join the following adverb *εἰκῇ* to *ἐμβατεύων*, and give it the sense of "rashly" or "uselessly." This notion, however, is already contained in the reproof. But the idea with our exegesis is, that the mental inflation of the errorists, which co-exists with his humility and his angel-worship, and prompts him to pry into what is concealed from him, is *εἰκῇ*—it is without ground. It has no warrant. Matt. v. 22; Rom. xiii. 4.

The following clause discovers one prime ground of the heresy, and shows the principal reason why the gospel was not cordially received. It was not intricate enough, it did not deal in any vain speculations, but it claimed and commanded attention to the real and practical, and it showed not the way into the abstruse and recondite. It did not harmonize with current notions of angelology and asceticism, and it was outdone in those respects by Essene Gnosticism. It did not forbid the humble spirit to raise

[1] *Confess.* x. 42.
[2] *Berith menucha* in Eisenmenger, *Entd. Jud.* vii. p. 374.
[3] *Adversus Marc.* v.

itself to the Divine throne; for it taught that the intervening distance was spanned by the mediatorial nature of Christ. It exhibited the angels as "ministering spirits," or fellow-servants; but it held up no eccentric array of visions and phantasms, which might beguile men into fanatical worship and conceited contrition. In the fulness of its revelation it left to no man the claim of discovery, or the merit of invention. He, then, who did not receive it as presented to him, but wished to change its nature and supplement its oracles, so that it might have the air and the aspect of a transcendental theosophy, was "puffed up by his fleshly mind,"—thought himself possessed of a higher knowledge, and favoured with profounder instruction than our Lord and His apostles.

The participle *φυσιούμενος*,—not from *φύσις*, which, in the classical writers, makes *φυσιάω*, but from *φύω*,—signifies inflated. 1 Cor. iv. 6, 18, 19, v. 2, viii. 1. The heretic was blown up with his delusion, verifying the remark—*ἡ γνῶσις φυσιοῖ*—"knowledge puffeth up." He was too proud to learn—too wise to acknowledge any instruction beyond himself. The source of inflation was a "fleshly mind," "he was puffed up."

Ὑπὸ τοῦ νοὸς τῆς σαρκὸς αὐτοῦ—"By the mind of his flesh." The expression is peculiar, but darkly emphatic. *Νοῦς* is mind—not simply intellect, but mind as the region of thought and susceptibility; while *σάρξ* is, as in so many other places, the name of unregenerate humanity. The expression denotes something more than *mens imbecilla.* Nor is it enough to resolve the two genitives into the phrase—*σαρκικῆς διανοίας*, or with Usteri, into *νοήματα σαρκικά*. The genitive is not a mere predicate, but is the genitive of possession. The "flesh" possesses and governs the "mind." The mind did not struggle with the carnal principle, but succumbed to it. It was wholly under the sway of a nature unchanged by the grace of God, and which therefore exercised its predominance to serve and please itself. In all these mental efforts and sentiments concerning Christianity, the false teacher was guided not by any pure regard to the Divine revelation, or by a simple desire to bow to the Divine will; but his "mind" was influenced by motives, and determined by reasonings, which sprung from a nature wholly under the empire of sense and fancy; a nature which was satisfied with an array of external puerilities—which preferred ascetic distinctions to spiritual self-denial—revelled in imaginations that at once sprung from it and lorded over it—and, in short, acting like itself and for itself, coveted and set up a religion of man, but spurned and thrust away that religion which is of God. And thus, in a later century, and in the same country, it was believed that the Holy Spirit communicated to Montanus more and nobler revelations than Christ had delivered in the gospel. The "flesh" could not but have a sensuous system—one resembling itself; and the "mind," acting under its sway, could not but devise a scheme in keeping with such governing and prompting influence. 1 Cor. ii. 14. And, by this means, the abettor of error was "vainly puffed up"[1] that he possessed a deeper enlightenment than the apostles, and a purer sanctity than the churches; and, in his vanity, he dreamed of being able, by his unhallowed reveries, to supply the defects and multiply the attractions of the gospel. The three participles of this verse, and that of the first clause of the following verse, have a close connection—*θέλων* expressing the desire of the heresiarch to make converts by a specious snare—*ἐμβατεύων* portraying one special source and feature of his system—*φυσιούμενος* indicating his moral temperament—and, lastly, *κρατῶν* pointing to the lamentable accompaniment and necessary result—"not holding the Head"—

(Ver. 19.) *Καὶ οὐ κρατῶν τὴν κεφαλήν.* The participle describes a firm grasp—a tenacious hold. Song of Sol. iii. 4; Acts iii. 11; Matt. xiv. 3; Mark ix. 27. The term *κεφαλή*, applied to Christ as Head of His church, has been explained under Eph. i. 22, and alluded to Col. i. 18. Those errorists did not hold the Head, and, indeed, the greater portion of their errors tended to this result. If they worshipped angels, they could not adore His person. If they insisted on circumcision and ascetic penances, they depreciated the merit of His work. If they preached the permanence of Mosaic ceremonies, they mistook the spirit and lost the benefit of the system which He had founded. They did not hold the truth as to His person or His work, His government or His dispensation.

[1] Müller renders—*der von seinem ungöttlichen Weltsinne aufgeblasene.—Lehre von der Sünde*, p. 452.

Those errors on vital points were fatal. So long as cardinal truths are held, many minor misconceptions may be tolerated; but when the former are lost, Christianity becomes a worthless and nominal profession. Bengel says truly, *qui non unice Christum tenet, plane non tenet.*

Ἐξ οὗ πᾶν τὸ σῶμα, διὰ τῶν ἁφῶν καὶ συνδέσμων, ἐπιχορηγούμενον καὶ συμβιβαζόμενον, αὔξει τὴν αὔξησιν τοῦ Θεοῦ— "From whom the whole body, through joints and bands, supplied and compacted, groweth the growth of God." The similar passage is Eph. iv. 16. The first words—ἐξ οὗ, mean, from which Head as the source of life and growth. We should expect the relative in such a case to agree in gender with its antecedent—ἐξ ἧς, and for this reason some copies add Χριστόν. The words are taken by some as masculine, the pronoun being supposed to refer to Him who is the Head —Christ. But though this be the common interpretation, as of Bähr, Huther, and De Wette, we cannot agree with it. It would destroy the harmony of the figure, which has its basis not in Christ as person, but in Christ as Head. Some take the relative as neuter, and in a special sense. Thus Bengel —*ex quo, ex tenendo caput.* We agree, however, with Meyer, that the neuter form refers to the Head—not personally as Jesus, but really or objectively—*nicht persönlich sondern sächlich.* Kühner, ii. § 785; Jelf, § 820.

Πᾶν τὸ σῶμα . . . αὔξει τὴν αὔξησιν τοῦ Θεοῦ. Such is the construction and ending of the sentence—"groweth the growth of God." The form αὔξει occurs only elsewhere in Eph. ii. 21. There is no ellipse here needing the supply of κατά, as Piscator and others suppose; but the verb governs its correlate noun—no uncommon form of syntax. Eph. i. 3, 20, ii. 4, iv. 1; John xvii. 26; Jelf, § 552; Buttmann, § 131, 4, 5; Kühner, § 547, *a*. There is in such an idiom an extension of the meaning of the verb. Often, in such a case, when a relative does not intervene, the accusative has a distinctive or intensive epithet connected with it. John vii. 24; 1 Tim. i. 18; Bernhardy, p. 106; Winer, § 32, 2. Here we have a genitive for a similar purpose. Luke ii. 8. Now this genitive is not to be explained away as a mere Hebrew superlative, as in Storr's paraphrase—*mirifice crescit.* Nor is the exegesis of Calvin, Bähr, and Winer in the third edition of his grammar, up to the full sense—*incrementum quod Deus vult et probat;* nor yet is *κατὰ θεόν* correct, as Chrysostom renders it. It means, as Winer gives it, in his fifth edition —"an increase wrought by God." Winer, § 36, 3 (*b*). The growth of that spiritual body corresponds with its nature—is the result of Divine influence and power. And the means of growth are stated in the intermediate clause. For the body is not only connected with the head, but is also—

Διὰ τῶν ἁφῶν καὶ συνδέσμων ἐπιχορηγούμενον καὶ συμβιβαζόμενον. The first participle *ἐπιχορηγ.* is in the middle voice, and, in an absolute sense, means, "furnished with reciprocal aid." 2 Cor. ix. 10; Gal. iii. 5. *Συναρμολογούμενον* is the word used in the parallel verse of the Epistle to the Ephesians, but the substantive *ἐπιχορηγία* occurs in the same verse. The next participle *συμβιβ.* signifies "brought and held together in mutual adaptation." (See under the second verse.) And this is done *διὰ τῶν ἁφῶν καὶ συνδέσμων*—"by joints and ligatures." The noun *ἁφή* signifies a joint, and so it is generally understood. Meyer supposes it to mean nervous energy or sensibility—*Lebensthätigkeit* —what the Greek Fathers understand by *αἴσθησις*. We may, perhaps, understand it not merely of joints in the strict anatomical sense, but generally of all these means, by which none of the parts or organs of the body are found in isolation. The other anarthrous noun, *σύνδεσμος*, has a meaning not dissimilar, and perhaps refers to those visible and palpable ligatures of flesh and sinew which give to the body unity of organization.[1] Dan. v. 6. Some would assign a noun to each participle—"furnished by the joints and compacted by the ligatures." There appears, however, to be no necessity for this refinement. The apostle describes that unity of the body which is dependent upon its head, and is essential to its growth. The expression *ἐξ οὗ* is neither to be confined to the participles nor restricted to the verb; for the apostle has said, emphatically, "the whole body." It is not this or that organ that grows from its vital connection with the head, while others unconnected perish and die; but the living energy of the head pervades the entire body—pervades

[1] Ἐξ ὀστοῦ εἰς ὀστοῦν ἐμφυόμενα σύνδεσμος ἀμφοῖν γίγνεται κοινός. Galen, quoted by Bähr, *in loc.* Theodoret says—*διὰ τῶν νεύρων ἔχει τὰς αἰσθήσεις τὸ σῶμα.*

it because it is an organic unity, supplied with conductors, and bound together by joints. Means are provided for distributing through it this vitality; there is no barrier to impede it—no point at which it stops. The body, so connected with the head, and so supplied and knit by internal structure and external bands, grows, and all grows, by Divine influence and blessing. The whole church of Christ depends on Him as its head—"out of Him" are derived organization, life, and growth. The idea is well expanded by Theophylact.

The "joints and bands" have been differently understood, and so have the supply and the symmetry. Bengel understands the first noun and participle of faith, and the second noun and participle of love and peace; this last view being held also by Zanchius, who gives it as—*charitas inter membra.* This is also Davenant's notion—"the first substantive represents what unites us to Christ, and the second what binds us to one another." It is a strange idea of Theodoret, that the "joints and bands" are prophets, apostles, and teachers. Böhmer adds, in modification, "but yet as little do we exclude the laity"—"*aber eben so wenig excludiren wir die Laien.*" Such an idea destroys the harmony of the figure. For teachers and taught compose the church, or the body and its organs, and they are held together by what the apostle calls joints and bands. To characterize minutely the spiritual elements of unity represented by these terms, would be pressing too much on the figure. The question is, what power gives vitality and union to the mystical body of Christ? The reply must be, Divine influence communicated by the Spirit, and using as its instruments faith and love. The last grace is specially mentioned in the correspondent passage of the twin epistle. The whole body, so pervaded and united, grows—all grows in perfect symmetry, and in connection with its Head. Without the head it dies—without "joints and bands" it falls into pieces, and each dissevered organ wastes away. The application is obvious. The church can enjoy neither life nor growth, if, misunderstanding Christ's person or undervaluing His work, it have no vital union with Him. If the creed of any community supplant His mediatorship, and find no atoning merit in His blood; if its worship look up to angels, and not to Him to whom "all power is given in heaven and in earth;" if it place its trust in ritual observances and bodily service, it cannot be one either with Him or with other portions of His church. Severed alike from head and trunk—from the vitality of the one and the support and sympathies of the other—it dies in isolation. So it was or would be with him or with them who threatened to disturb the Colossian Church. The entire figure and description are more fully presented in Eph. iv. 15, 16, where we have given a lengthened exegesis.

The apostle still presses home his doctrine. It was no abstract truth which he had enunciated, and he winds up the paragraph by a reference to its pervading lesson—exhibiting the care and caution which should prevent any ordinances of an ascetic nature—such as those which belonged to the Jewish ritual—from being superinduced on Christianity.

(Ver. 20.) *Εἰ ἀπεθάνετε σὺν Χριστῷ ἀπὸ τῶν στοιχείων τοῦ κόσμου.* The *οὖν* of the Received Text has no authority, neither has the article *τῷ* before the proper name. "Since ye died off with Christ from the rudiments of the world," or, have been separated by such a death from the rudiments of the world. The phrase "rudiments of the world" has been already explained under the eighth verse. To be dead to them is to be done with them, or, to be in such a state that they have no longer any authority over us. Thus in Rom. vii. 3, 4, the wife by the death of her husband is said to be so free from conjugal law, that she may marry another man. In Gal. ii. 19, the apostle speaks of being "dead to the law." The dative is used in those two cases, as if there was a consciousness of complete deliverance. The preposition *ἀπό* is here employed to intensify the idea, as if death were followed by distance or removal. Winer, § 47, b. They had nothing more to do with the rudiments of the world—and the rudiments of the world had nothing more to do with them. The apostle again introduces his favourite idea of union with Christ. The death of Christ abrogated the ritual law; and being one with Him in that death, they had died to that law—the *ἀπό* denoting consequent separation. We cannot agree with Huther, in inferring from this passage, that the phrase "rudiments of the world" expresses something more than the Mosaic law, and denotes the ethical life of the heathen world.

He says—"the language implies that the Colossians had served the elements of the world; and if so, then, if you mean the ritual institute by these elements, you must hold what you can never prove, that the majority in this church were of Jewish extraction."[1] But the argument is not conclusive. In Gal. iv. 9, the apostle may refer to heathen elements, so far as they had a ceremonial and sensuous aspect; but the rites of the heathen world—its *στοιχεῖα*, never had any Divine claim or obligation, so that the death of Christ did not formally annul them; whereas the Mosaic law was an ordinance of God's appointment, and only by yielding to it could religious privilege and blessing be enjoyed prior to the death on Calvary. It was by initiation into this rudimentary and worldly system, that the worship of the one God could be engaged in. Heathenism never had any authority over them, whatever might be its actual power. If its ordinances be meant, then the apostle warns against a return to them. This is not the case, for the ordinances against which he cautions were remnants of a system not wholly unlawful like Gentilism, but of one which had enjoyed Divine sanction. In short, the whole paragraph has special reference to Jewish customs. After speaking, in the eighth verse, of the rudiments of the world, he describes the glory of Christ, and affirms that the Colossian believers are circumcised in Him—a reference to the Jewish ritual. Then, having said that the handwriting of ordinances had been blotted out, he adds, as a warranted inference from, and application of the doctrine—let no man judge you in eating and drinking, or in respect of new moons and Sabbath days—another direct allusion to Mosaic institutions. And in fine, as a sample of those rudiments of the world, he quotes—"touch not, taste not, handle not." There were among them, it is true, other practices than such as had been originally Jewish; —an asceticism which was foreign to the Mosaic system, and an angel-worship which was, perhaps, based upon a misrepresentation of traditions connected with it; but still the central error of the false teachers was an attempt to impose the ceremonial yoke, in some of its aspects, on the members of the Christian church, as something which would ensure them a transcendental purity, and bring them into a magical connec-

[1] On the other hand, see Baur, *Paulus*, p. 594.

tion with the powers of the spirit-world. The apostle then asks—

Τί ὡς ζῶντες ἐν κόσμῳ δογματίζεσθε, μὴ ἅψῃ, μηδὲ γεύσῃ, μηδὲ θίγῃς:—"Why, as living in the world, do ye suffer such ordinances to be published among you as 'touch not, taste not, handle not'?" Bähr is wrong in saying that *τί* stands for *διὰ τί*, though the one phrase may explain the other. The word *κόσμος* cannot here mean the physical world, as Schneckenburger maintains,[1] for it must have the ethical meaning which it bears in the previous clause and in verse eighth. It is the sphere of the "weak and beggarly elements." But the Colossians had been translated into the kingdom of God's dear Son, therefore the code of the realm which they had left had no more force upon them. A Russian naturalized in Britain need not trouble himself about any imperial ukase, as if he yet lived under the Autocrat.

The verb *δογματίζειν*, which occurs only here in the New Testament, but sometimes in the Septuagint and Apocrypha, signifies in the classics to pronounce an opinion, as well as to enforce or publish a decree. The latter meaning prevails in the Septuagint, Esth. iii. 9, etc.; 2 Macc. x. 8, xv. 36. Some look on the verb as active. Thus Melancthon has *decreta facitis;* Ambrosiaster, *decernitis;* and Olshausen, "why do ye again set up worldly ordinances?" The majority of commentators take the word in a middle sense, though Beza, Wolf, and Meyer give it a passive significance. Buttmann, § 135, 8. But we cannot see how the use of the middle would imply a censure, any more than the employment of the passive. The middle brings out rather a pointed caution—"why should ye permit the preaching of dogmas? or why should ye allow such dogmas to be imposed on you?" They could not suppress the teaching of the errorists, but they needed not to listen to it, and far less to yield to it. The strong form of the verb almost says, that the apostle suspected a latent tendency in their temperament to listen and be charmed. The apostle, in Eph. ii. 15, calls the Mosaic law, in one aspect of it, by the name *δόγματα*, and he here uses the cognate verb referring to the same institute. The argument is a cogent one. They were dead to such ordinances—

[1] *Theolog. Jahrb.* 1848.

why then should they act as if they lived under them? They did not belong to that κόσμος, of the character of which such ordinances partook. They belied their entire position, and reversed all their relations, if, after being freed by Christ, they again sunk themselves into bondage—if they allowed the handwriting to be reinscribed, and taking the nail out of it, laid it up among their solemn archives as an instrument of revived and extended authority. To submit to the ritual which they had believed to be obsolete, was in direct antagonism to all that Jesus had done for them, and to all which they had willingly acknowledged as His achievement on their behalf. Some of the δόγματα to which the apostle alludes are now given, and they are ascetic in nature. But ere we advance to them, we shall take up the clause which we believe to be joined closely with δογματίζεσθε, viz., the last clause of verse 22.

Κατὰ τὰ ἐντάλματα καὶ διδασκαλίας τῶν ἀνθρώπων. Matt. xv. 9; Mark vii. 7; Isa. xxix. 13. Our reasons for adopting this view will be afterwards stated. This clause describes the source of such δόγματα, and virtually contains another reason why they should not be submitted to. The prime reason is, that believers are dead with Christ to them; but the subordinate reason is, that the edicts are wholly human in their origin. "Why should ye for a moment suffer them to be imposed upon you according to—κατά—or having no higher authority than, the commandments and doctrines of men?" The two nouns differ not, as Grotius supposes, that the former is enacted by law, and the latter enjoined by philosophers; but rather, as Olshausen says, the first is enactment—the second, the principles on which it is based. The first—ἐνταλ., is the dogma in its preceptive and practical form, of which there is a specimen in the preceding part of the verse—"touch not, taste not, handle not;" and the second —διδασκαλία, is the doctrine out of which it arises—the convictions and theories by which it is illustrated and defended. The same general idea has been stated under the eighth verse. Christ is Head, and to Him alone do we owe subjection. Whatever authority ordinances had when the Mosaic economy stood, they have none now—the institute being abolished in the death of Him who is the one Legislator.

And all extra-biblical additions to it were human in their very origin.

(Ver. 21.) *Μὴ ἅψῃ μηδὲ γεύσῃ μηδὲ θίγῃς*—"Touch not, taste not, handle not." These curt dogmas are not the apostle's own teaching, but the mottoes, or prominent lessons, or watchwords of the false teachers.[1] In all probability, the three terms refer to the same general object—abstinence from certain meats and drinks. It is therefore excessive refinement to distribute them according to certain distinctions, either with Flatt, Böhmer, Hammond, and Homberg, referring the first verb—or, with Grotius, the last verb—to marriage; or, with Estius, Zanchius, and Erasmus, giving the first verb an allusion to Levitical uncleanness, special or general. The two critics last named refer the last term to Levitical sacred things, but Michaelis and Storr refer it to impurities. Böhmer, with a strange caprice, finds a reference in *θίγῃς* to the holy oil which the Essenes specially regarded as *labes.* But though the words refer generally to diet, and are so used by the classics,[2] there may be a distinction among them, as they seem to be repeated, along with the negative, for the sake of emphasis. The first and last verbs are somewhat similar, and both represent in the Septuagint the Hebrew—נָגַע. But the first term may here denote that handling which is necessary to eating—the touch which precedes taste; while the last, a sister-term, with *tango* and *touch,* may signify the slightest contact. In Heb. xii. 20, the contrast seems to be this—a beast was not only not to graze on Sinai, but not even for a moment to set a hoof upon it. Thus in Eurip. *Bacchae,* 617, where a similar contrast obtains—"he did not come in contact, far less handle me[3]—there was neither touch nor grasp." The last verb is the most dogmatic—you are not to take certain meats into your hand, nor are you to taste them; nay, you are not even to touch them, though in the slightest degree—you are to keep from them hand, tongue, and even finger-tip. The apostle does not specify the objects to be abstained from, for they were so well known to his readers.

[1] The words would, in modern usage, have the marks of quotation assigned to them.

[2] Xenophon, *Cyrop.* i. 3, 5; i. 11.

[3] Οὐτ' ἔθιγεν οὐθ' ἥψαθ' ἡμῶν.

The connection and meaning of the next clause are matter of various opinion.

(Ver. 22.) Ἅ ἐστιν πάντα εἰς φθορὰν τῇ ἀποχρήσει. The idea of Macknight is altogether unsupported. He supposes the reference of the apostle to be to Pythagorean abstinence from animal food, and he connects this and the previous verse in the following way. Touch not, taste not, handle not whatever things tend to the destruction of life in the using. He takes the maxim of the false teachers condemned by the apostle to be this—abstain from everything the eating of which involves the taking away of life. The idea itself is foreign to the argument, nor can it be supported by the apostle's diction.

The question turns upon the meaning assigned to φθορά, and the supposed antecedent to the relative.

I. A large party take φθορά in a spiritual sense, and suppose the relative to refer to the precepts contained in the preceding verse, as if the warning were—all which maxims tend by their observance to spiritual ruin—lead to the eternal destruction of such as are influenced by them. Some of those who hold this view, give ἀπόχρησις the sense of abuse, as if the apostle wished to say—the law did make distinctions of meats and drinks, but the unwarranted abuse of such a distinction is a fatal course. Others, again, connect the last clause of the verse with the first—all which precepts tend to your own ruin, by your observance of them, for they are an observance based upon the doctrines and commandments of men. Such, generally, are the views of Ambrosiaster and Augustine, a-Lapide, Heumann, Suicer, and Junker.

II. Others suppose the antecedent to be not the maxims, but the things forbidden in them, and among such critics there are two classes.

1. Some suppose the apostle to be still further showing the opinion of the false teachers. According to them, the meaning is, either, all which meats and drinks lead to ruin in the use of them, according to the commandments and teachings of those men; or, all these meats and drinks to be abstained from, tend to destruction by the use of them, if you are to be judged by their opinions and doctrines. The verse, then, would contain this idea—the false teachers forbade the touch-

ing and tasting of certain things, because, in their opinion, the use of them brought certain pernicious results. This opinion is concurred in by Kypke, Storr, De Wette, Böhmer, and Baumgarten-Crusius. There is nothing in the words themselves to contradict it; it may be grammatically defended, and the noun *φθορά* may bear the meaning of spiritual hurt, as in Gal. vi. 8. But it does not appear to us to be in so complete harmony with the context as is the following exegesis.

2. The opinion which we prefer is that which gives the same antecedent to the relative, but understands the clause to be an exposure of the absurdity of such asceticism—"all which things are meant for destruction through the use of them." The meats and drinks about which the errorist exclaimed—"touch not, taste not, handle not," are meant to be consumed by use. They perish or cease to exist, because they are eaten and drunk for the support of life. They are intended for this destiny—*ἐστίν εἰς*—exist for it; God created them to be consumed, and they meet this destiny by being used to the full—*ἀπο*—used to the complete satisfaction of appetite. The verb *ἐστίν* is more than a copula. It means—exists—which things exist. The noun *φθορά* is often used in a physical sense—in the Seventy, Ex. xviii. 18; Isa. xxiv. 3; Jonah ii. 7; and in the New Testament, 1 Cor. xv. 42, 50; 2 Pet. ii. 12; Josephus, *Antiq.* vii. 13, 3. The term *ἀπόχρησις* is not abuse in the English sense of the word—but, "full use." The Latin *abutor* has this meaning also—to use up; as often in Cicero, and also in Terence and Suetonius. It is this using up or consuming of a thing by use contained in the *ἀπο* and *ab*, that gave the term in Latin, Greek, and English, the secondary signification of misuse.

The apostle thus states two objections to the Colossian asceticism. First. It contradicts the design of Providence, which created such meats and drinks for man's use and satisfaction. The apostle, as we have said, uses *ἀπόχρησις*, which does not signify abuse, but full use. The maxims of the false teachers are—"touch not, taste not, handle not;" but the things from which he sternly enjoins this abstinence are, in their own nature, utterly harmless, and not only is the use of them unaccompanied with spiritual damage, but that use is enjoined by Him whose providence has so liberally furnished them for the stay and support of life. The meats and drinks so frowned upon have been created for the very purpose of being consumed, and having served their purpose in this consumption they perish. A religion of asceticism is therefore a libel upon Providence—a surly and superstitious refusal of the Divine benignity. It believes that the eating and drinking of some gifts of Divine goodness is fraught with unspeakable danger, and therefore it makes its selections among them in its "show of wisdom." Strange conviction, that what is physically nutritious may be spiritually poisonous; and that what gives strength to the body may send "leanness to the soul"! No wonder that such a self-righteous and ungrateful practice led by a swift path to a dark and Manichæan theology.

And, secondly, things which are meant to perish in being used up, can have little connection with genuine piety; it does not, and cannot depend on abstinence from them. Our Lord Himself said—"not that which goeth into the mouth defileth a man;" and the apostle declares—"every creature of God is good, and nothing to be refused;" and he speaks of meats "which God hath created to be received with thanksgiving." 1 Cor. vi. 13. It degrades Christianity to make it a system of physical or ascetic distinctions. Spirituality is not based on such external and ceremonial forms. The error, as Olshausen says, "was in looking for holiness in the outward rather than the inward." Such an error has been, alas! too common in the church, and is the result of superstitious indolence and vanity. Men seek to be acted on from without, and to be sanctified as if by the secret and unconscious charm of an amulet; misunderstanding, forgetting, or shunning the mighty work or change which should be going on within. That change is from the centre to the outer life, not from the outer life to the seat of motive and thought. What the lips receive or refuse from "cup and platter," has neither propitiatory merit nor demerit, nor can it exercise a hidden power over heart and mind. The palate may be ungratified and yet the conscience be defiled; the anchorite, while he starves himself, may roll many a vice, as a sweet morsel, under his tongue; for self-denial in corporeal appetite usually takes ample revenge or compensation in spiritual indulgence and pride. And thus it has been often found, that men attach a higher sanctity to abstinence from certain kinds of food and physical refreshment, than to abstinence from sin; and would rather violate a Divine statute, than break a self-inflicted fast.

> What mean they? Canst thou dream there is a power
> In lighter diet at a later hour
> To charm to sleep the threatenings of the skies,
> And hide past folly from all-seeing eyes?[1]

Several things concur in justifying the view we have taken, which is that of the Greek Fathers, of Luther, Calvin, and Beza, of Grotius, Meyer, Steiger, and Bähr. The apostle is speaking of physical things, as eating and drinking, and it is natural to understand φθορά and ἀπόχρησις in their physical sense, and in connection with those elements of forbidden sustenance. Again, the writer places no substantive after the three verbs, and the ellipse imparts a certain emphasis. The objects to be abstained from were yet present to his mind, and it was natural for him to allude to them, and to show that they were designed for use, nay, were of so little permanence and value that they perished in this use. The mimetic clause—"touch not," etc., is inserted, or rather rapidly interjected, as the apostle passes on. It will therefore be best read in a parenthesis. The swiftness of the apostle's thoughts interferes so far with the order of them. He first shows the inconsistency of yielding to ordinances after they had become dead to them; and he meant to point out the source of such ordinances, but the mention of them suggests the pointed quotation of some of them, and then he cannot refrain, in a brief underthought, from exposing their absurdity, ere he formally carries out his purpose of showing their origin and inutility. Lastly, the Greek Fathers understand the phrase in this way. They do not mince the matter, but give φθορά its coarsest meaning. Chrysostom, followed by Theodoret, says—εἰς κόπρον γὰρ ἅπαντα μεταβάλλεται. Œcumenius uses this language—ὑπόκειται ἐν τῷ ἀφεδρῶνι; while Theophylact is yet more explicit—φθειρόμενα γὰρ ἐν τῇ γαστρὶ διὰ τοῦ ἀφεδρῶνος ὑποῤῥεῖ.

(Ver. 23.) Ἅτινά ἐστιν λόγον μὲν ἔχοντα σοφίας—"Which

[1] Cowper.

things indeed having a show of wisdom." The antecedent to *ἅτινα* is the preceding clause—"doctrines and commandments of men." Kühner, § 431, 2. The peculiar form *ἅτινα* represents this idea—all which things, that is, the entire class of them. Kühner, § 781, 4, 5. We do not connect *ἐστίν* with the participle *ἔχοντα*, as some do; but specially with the concluding clause of the verse. *Λόγος* signifies sometimes report or rumour—then mere rumour—then mere talk or pretext—words and only words—*λόγον οὐ πράγματα.* It is thus opposed to *ἀλήθεια.* Diodorus Siculus, 13, 4; Polybius, 17 (18), 14, 5. The word thus means a certain kind of semblance, which in Scotch is called a *sough*—sound without reality. These precepts and commandments had the air, aspect, nomenclature, and pretensions of wisdom. The particle *μέν* might imply the contrast, the apodosis not being formally expressed. Kühner, § 734, 2; Winer, § 63, I. 2, e. This last critic says—the parallel member of the sentence is included in the one with *μέν.* Thus, Heb. vi. 16,—men, indeed—*μέν* —swear by the greater, and the implied contrast is, but God can only swear by Himself. These teachings have a show of wisdom, *μέν*—but none in reality. Or, Rom. iii. 2, "What advantage, then, hath the Jew?—much every way"—*πρῶτον μέν*—"chiefly indeed," but not wholly, "because that unto them were committed the oracles of God." Thus Acts xix. 4. *Ἰωάννης μὲν ἐβάπτισεν*—"John indeed baptized" the baptism of repentance; the implied contrast being—but not so Jesus. So, in the clause before us, the same construction has been found by some,—there is the semblance, indeed, of wisdom, but not the reality. We are inclined, however, to regard the apodosis as existing in *οὐκ ἐν τιμῇ τινι*; but *δέ* is not expressed, because the construction is changed into the dative, following up the case of the preceding nouns, and because the word *οὐκ*, to which *δέ* would be attached, has in it a palpable adversative power. It was worse than hypercriticism on the part of Jerome to say, that the particle was omitted—*propter imperitiam artis grammaticae.* The apostle particularizes and adds, this verbiage of wisdom consists "in will-worship"—

Ἐν ἐθελοθρησκείᾳ. This is worship not enjoyed by God, but springing out of man's own ingenuity—unauthorized devotion, *θρησκεία* being religious service—the outer manifestation of inner feeling. Thus, ἐθελόδουλος is one who is wilfully a slave; ἐθελοκίνδυνος is one who is wilfully in danger. The worship referred to is unsolicited and unaccepted. It is superstition, and probably is the homage paid to angels. Such worship had the feint of wisdom, as it professed to base itself on invisible arcana; and to ask and receive blessings and protection from creatures, whose agency comes not within the range of observation, but who were supposed to be the patrons and defenders of those who could name them in erring and extravagant devotion.

Καὶ ταπεινοφροσύνῃ—"And humility." This has been already explained under the 18th verse. The humility referred to is plainly of that spurious kind, that, in its excess and affectation, could not look up to God, but deemed it wondrous wisdom to invoke angels on its behalf.

Καὶ ἀφειδίᾳ σώματος. The term ἀφειδία is unsparingness, and here unsparingness in the form of severity, or that austere asceticism which the apostle has already reprimanded. In this sense it often occurs among the classical writers.[1] The body is not only kept under, that is, kept in its proper and subordinate position, but it is hated, lacerated, and tormented into debility. The appetites are looked upon as sinful, and are checked—not supplied in healthful moderation. Every species of support is grudged—"to back and belly too." The physical constitution is thus enervated and sickened. Yet its sinful tendencies are only beaten down, not eradicated. Job made a covenant with his eyes, but those fanatics would dim theirs by fasting. The whole process was a cardinal mistake, for it was a system of externals, both in ceremonial and ethics. The body might be reduced, but the evil bias might remain unchecked. A man might whip and fast himself into a walking skeleton, and yet the spirit within him might have all its lusts unconquered, for all it had lost was only the ability to gratify them. To place a fetter on a robber's hand will not cure him of covetousness, though it may disqualify him from actual theft. To seal up a swearer's mouth will not pluck profanity out of his heart, though it may for the time prevent him from taking God's name in vain. To lacerate the flesh almost to suicide, merely incapacitates it for indul-

[1] Diodorus Sic. 13, 60. Thucyd. ii. 51.

gence, but does not extirpate sinful desire. Its air of superior sanctity[1] is only pride in disguise—it has but "a show of wisdom," and is not—

Οὐκ ἐν τιμῇ τινὶ, πρὸς πλησμονὴν τῆς σαρκός. There is difficulty in arriving at a correct interpretation of these clauses, and one reason is, that we have first to solve whether they should be joined or disconnected. It is quite plain that the apostle intends a contrast, and the preposition *ἐν* is repeated.

1. Very many interpreters supply *σώματος* to *τιμῇ*. The Greek interpreters held this view, followed by Pelagius, Calvin, Luther, and other reformers; by Estius, and a-Lapide in the Popish Church; by Daillé, Davenant, and Macknight; and in later times by the lately deceased critics, De Wette and Baumgarten-Crusius. The meaning, then, is—"which things have a show of wisdom in will-worship, humility, and neglecting of the body, not in any honour shown to the body in reference to such things as satisfy corporeal appetite." This is a favourite interpretation, but we cannot receive it. For, as Meyer remarks, it gives *σάρξ* the meaning of *σῶμα*, which had just been previously used—a meaning which it cannot bear. Then, too, this exegesis supplies *σώματος* without any reason, and it restricts the contrast introduced by *οὐκ* to only one member of the sentence. That contrast seems to refer to all the manifestations of this specious wisdom, and not simply to one of them. Besides, this interpretation gives a very feeble ending to the verse; austerity towards the body, is weakly characterized as not giving honour to the body in

[1] Car je vous prie quelle ombre de sagesse y a-t-il en ce caresme par exemple, qu'ils commencerent l'autre jour, après la préface ordinaire de leur carneval? Ou est la raison? ou le sens commun, qui puisse avoüer, s'il est libre, que ce soit sagesse, après s'estre licentié à toute sorte de débauches, et de folies, de penser effacer tout cela avec une poignée de cendres? Que ce soit sagesse de croire, que c'est jeusner, de manger du poisson? Que ce soit sagesse d'estimer, que c'est se sanctifier, de manger des herbes, ou du saumon, ou de la moluë? et que c'est soüiller son âme d'un peché mortel, et digne du feu éternel, de goûter d'un morceau de beuf, ou de mouton, ces quarante jours durant? comme si toute la nature des choses s'étoit changée en un moment, et que les animaux de la terre fussent tous devenus contagieux, et mortels, de bons et salutaires, qu'ils étoyent, il n'y a que quatre jours? Est-ce sagesse d'attacher le Christianisme à une observation si peu raisonnable, et de dire, comme ils font, que ceux, qui mangent de la chair en ce temps, ne sont pas Chrétiens? Il n'y a point d'esprit si mediocre, qui ne juge aisément, qu'il n'y a nulle apparence de sagesse en tout cela; pour ne rien dire de pis.—Daillé, pp. 548-550.

things which satisfy its physical appetites, as if the Colossians needed such a definition. And lastly, this πλησμονή is something more than the gratification of corporeal desire, for in the Pauline vocabulary, σῶμα is only a portion of σάρξ.

2. Another view, which holds the same connection, is that which gives τιμή the sense of value, and brings out this exegesis—which are not of any value, inasmuch as they are concerned with things which serve only to the gratification of the flesh. These are useless prohibitions, and have but a show of wisdom, for they are concerned with matters which minister only to appetite—*quum ad ea spectent quibus farcitur caro.* The participle ὄντα is thus supposed to stand before πρός. This is the idea of Beza and Crocius, and that of Heinrichs is only a worse modification of it. It restricts the meaning of σάρξ, and needs considerable eking out in its construction.

3. Others take the word σάρξ in its full sense, and suppose the apostle to mean that all prohibitions which bear especially against the body are of little worth, for they minister all the while to the pride of corrupted humanity. The last clause is thus nearly equivalent to an earlier one—"vainly puffed up by his fleshly mind." With some varieties, this is the exegesis of Hilary, Bengel, Storr, Flatt, Böhmer, Steiger, Bähr, and Huther. Meyer, in taking the same view, places σαρκός in contrast with σώματος, and πλησμονή with ἀφειδία. He also lays the principal stress of the contrast on the words οὐκ ἐν τιμῇ τινί, as if they stood in antagonism to the λόγον σοφίας. That wisdom is all a pretence—it has no honour in reality or basis. Still, with this otherwise good interpretation, the connection of the last clause appears to be hard, for πρός must signify *um dadurch*, or "all of them tend to." A modification of this view is adopted by Conybeare, who gives the clause a pregnant sense—"not of any value to check the indulgence of the flesh." His reviewer in the *North British Review* applauds the exegesis.[1] We do not accept the sense of fleshly passion for σάρξ, and we cannot believe πρός to be so utterly indifferent in its meaning. In the proposed

[1] Vol. xx. p. 336. "There is really no difficulty in the πρός. As a jocose philologer of our acquaintance observed—'Poor πρός is morally indifferent, and flexible either to checking or promoting.'"

exegesis, πρός must signify "against." It sometimes is so translated, still the idea of hostility is found, not in the particle, but in its adjuncts, as μάχεσθαι, βάλλειν, or as in the New Testament, Acts vi. 1, where the idea of antagonism is found in γογγυσμός, Acts xxiv. 19, where the clause is preceded by κατηγορεῖν, and in Eph. vi. 11, where there is the idea of combat. In all such cases the idea of hostility is implied in the clause, and the preposition only expresses the reference—but there is no such idea implied in the verse before us. The same principle explains the array of classical instances adduced by Peile

4. While we take this general view, we are inclined to regard the verse, from λόγον to τινί, as participial; and with Bähr, closely to connect ἐστίν with πρός. "Which things having, indeed, a show of wisdom in superstition, humility, and corporeal austerity, not in any thing of value, are for, or minister to the gratification of the flesh." Πρός after εἰμί denotes result. John xi. 4. There needs, with this view, the insertion of no explanatory terms, or connecting ideas taken for granted. The verb stands at a distance from the preposition, but is not on that account the less emphatic. The apostle means to condemn those precepts and teachings, and he is about to pronounce the sentence; but to make it the more emphatic he briefly enumerates what they chiefly consist of, and then his censure is, that they produce an effect directly the opposite to their professed design. Their avowed purpose is to lower and abase humanity, and he gives them epithets all showing this object; while he adds with sternness and force, that their only result is to rouse up and inflate unregenerate humanity. That πλησμονή can bear this tropical meaning there is no doubt, as in Hab. ii. 16, where the word occurs with ἀτιμίας; Sirach i. 16, where it is used with σοφίας; and Isa. lxv. 15, where it stands absolutely, but with a spiritual sense. The phrase οὐκ ἐν τιμῇ τινί, then brings out this contrast—those doctrines have in sooth a show of wisdom, in their will-worship, humility, and corporeal austerity, but they have really nothing of value.

The paragraph therefore reprobates superstitious asceticism. The religious history of the world shows what fascination there is to many minds in voluntary suffering. Such asceticism threw its eclipse over the bright and lovely spirit of Pascal. The oriental temperament feels powerfully the fatal charm. As if the Divine Being might fail to subject them to a sufficient amount of discipline, men assume the labour of disciplining themselves, but choose a mode very unlike that which God usually employs.

> The Brahmin kindles on his own bare head
> The sacred fires, self-torturing his trade.
> Which is the saintlier worthy of the two?
> Past all dispute yon anchorite, say you.
> Your sentence and mine differ. What's a name?
> I say the Brahmin has the fairer claim,
> If sufferings Scripture nowhere recommends,
> Devised by self to answer selfish ends,
> Give saintship, then, all Europe must agree
> Ten starveling hermits suffer less than he.

Such delusions are not confined to religious follies, for their origin lies deep in human nature. Men glory in being what their fellows dare not aspire to, and there is no little self-aggrandizement in this self-annihilation. When Diogenes lifted his foot on Plato's velvet cushion and shouted, "Thus I trample on Plato's pride," the Athenian sage justly replied, "But with still greater pride." The apostle utters a similar sentiment; the carnal nature is all the while gratified, even though the body, wan and wasted, is reduced to the point of bare existence. There is more pride in cells and cloisters than in courts and palaces, and oftentimes as gross sensuality. The devotee deifies himself, is more to himself than the object of his homage. The whole of these fanatical processes, so far from accomplishing their ostensible object, really produce the reverse; such will-worship is an impious invention; such humility is pride in its most sullen and offensive form; and these corporeal macerations, so far from subduing and sanctifying, only gratify to satiety the coarse and selfish passions; nay, as history has shown, tend to nurse licentiousness in one age, and a ferocious fanaticism in another. The entire phenomenon, whatever its special aspect, is a huge self-deception, and a reversal of that moral order which God has established.

In the course of expounding this chapter, we have found several illustrations in post-apostolic times. We now present another, which shows how the practices described in this section were viewed in themselves, and condemned at a very early period. The unknown author of that very precious document, the letter to Diognetus, and now rightly included by Hefele among the remains of the apostolical Fathers, speaks in a style worthy of an apostle. He says of the Jews, "But indeed I think that you have no need to learn from me their ridiculous and senseless alarms about their food, their superstition about the Sabbath, their boasting of circumcision, and their pretexts of fasting, and the observance of new moons. How is it right to receive some of the things which God has created for the use of man as fitly[1] created, and to reject others of them as useless and superfluous? How can it be else than impious to libel God, as if He had forbidden any good action to be done on the Sabbath day? How worthy of ridicule their exultation about the curtailment of the flesh as a witness of their election, as though on this account they were the peculiar objects of God's complacency! Who will regard as a sign of piety, and will not much more regard as a mark of folly, their scrupulous study of the[2] stars, and their watching of the moon, in order to procure the observance of months and days, and to arrange the Divine dispensations and changes of the seasons—some into feasts and others into fasts, according to their inclination? I imagine that you are sufficiently informed, that the Christians rightly abstain from the prevailing emptiness of worship and delusion, and from the fussiness[3] and vainglory of the Jews."

Our readers will pardon us for inserting in a note a modern instance of this pride of sanctity covered with a robe of revolting humility. Last year (1854), a new saint was added to the Popish calendar, by name Benedetto Giuseppe Labre, who had made his residence in the Coliseo for many years, and was noted by travellers for his craziness and filth. At the usual mock trial which takes place at a canonization, the pleading of the so-called Devil's advocate against him was rebutted by the so-called God's advocate in the following terms, literally translated from the paper:—"He was a model of humility, abstinence, and mortification, taking only for food remains of cabbage, lemon peel, or lettuce leaves, which he picked up in the streets. He even ate, once, some spoiled

---

1 Καλῶς.

2 Παρεδρεύοντας.

3 Πολυπραγμοσύνης. Opera, *Justini Mart.* vol. ii. pp. 474-476, ed. Otto.

soup which he found on a dunghill, where it had been thrown. All these facts are fully proved by the juridical documents laid before the tribunal." . . . . Having spoken at length of the wooden cup, all broken and rotten, in which he received his soup at the door of the houses, "eternal monument of his voluntary privations," the advocate proceeds: "What more shall I say? A glance cast upon him was sufficient to discover in him a perfect model of poverty. His hair and beard were neglected, his face pale, his garments ragged, his body livid; a rosary hung from his neck; he wore no stockings; his shirt was dirty and disgusting; and to give of him a full idea, let us add, that he was so completely covered with vermin (*pidocchi*), that in the churches many persons kept away from him for fear of catching them!"

CHAPTER III

The apostle leaves his scornful flagellation of the false teachers, and comes to a more congenial occupation. For though it is needful to refute error, it is more pleasant to inculcate truth. If the Colossian believers should act in accordance with their privileges—if they understood how the charge preferred against them by the law had been met with a discharge on the cross of Calvary—if the process of sanctification beginning in their hearts should work outward, and hallow and adorn their lives—if they felt that whatever blessings they enjoyed in part, or anticipated in fulness, sprang from union with Christ, then should they be fortified against every effort to induce them to sever themselves from the Head, and against every attempt to substitute reveries for truth, or human inventions for Divine enactments. Then, too, should they learn that worship does not consist of superstitious invocations, and that sanctification is not identical with fanatical austerities. Let them move in a spiritual region lifted far above those earthly vanities, and let them look down on them as the offspring of a morbid and self-deceived imagination, or the craving and the nutriment of a self-satisfied pride.

(Ver. 1.) *Εἰ οὖν συνηγέρθητε τῷ Χριστῷ*—"If, then, ye have been raised together with Christ," or are in a risen state. The particle *οὖν* is illative, and *εἰ* does not mean "if," as if it betokened uncertainty, but it introduces a premiss on which a conclusion is to be based. It is somewhat of a syllogistic form, as Fritzsche, Kühner, and Meyer suppose, but the notion appears to be a needless refinement. There are few forms of reasoning or inference based upon fact or hypothesis, which cannot be moulded into a syllogism. There is no doubtfulness in the statement, it asserts an actual condition, as in many parts of the New Testament too numerous to quote. Hartung, ii. p. 202. The same meaning must be given to it as in ii. 20. They had been dead in sins, but they had been quickened together with Christ. There may be a reference, as many suppose, to the phrase, "buried in baptism," though there the allusion is to death to sin, not death in it. Now, the restoration of life implies resurrection, for the dead on being quickened do not lie in their sepulchres. The power that reanimated Lazarus immediately cried to him, "Come forth." The nature and results of this spiritual resurrection are detailed under Eph. ii. 6. Union with Christ enjoys a peculiar and merited prominence—"risen with Christ." Their new position laid them under a special obligation, and they are thus enjoined—"seek those things which are above"—

Τὰ ἄνω ζητεῖτε. The reference in *ἄνω* is here, as is proved by the concluding clause, to heaven—"seek things in heaven." There is no occasion to supply *ἀγαθά*, for it is implied. The expression is used in contrast with *κάτω*, and with *τὰ ἐπὶ τῆς γῆς* in the following verse. The same idea is often expressed, as in Phil. iii. 14, 20; Matt. vi. 20, 33; Gal. iv. 26. The region of spiritual death is a nether-world, that of life is an elevated realm—the living not only rise, but they sit with Christ "in the heavenly places." The precise locality is now indicated—

Οὗ ὁ Χριστός ἐστιν ἐν δεξιᾷ τοῦ Θεοῦ καθήμενος—"Where Christ is, sitting at the right hand of God." The ideas of honour, power, and felicity, implied in the declaration will be found under Eph. i. 20. Illustrations or allusions occur in 1 Kings ii. 19; 1 Sam. xx. 25; Ps. cx. 1; Rev. iii. 21; Rom. viii. 34; Heb. vii. 25; Phil. ii. 9.

The clause presents inducements to obey the injunction, "Seek those things which are above." And these inducements lie in the statement of two facts. *First*, they have been raised up with Christ, and therefore they ought to seek things above. Any other search or desire would be very inconsistent. The image seems to be—the region of the dead is beneath; they are let down to their final resting-place. Should, then, a man rise from this dark and deep receptacle, and ascend to the living world, would he set his desires on the gloom, and chill, and rottenness, he had left behind him? Would he place the objects of his search among the coffins, and the mean and creeping things that live on putrefaction? Would he still seek for things below? At the very idea and memory of that locality would not his spirit shudder? And if the Christians at Colosse had been raised from a yet lower condition, and by a still nobler resurrection, should not similar feelings and associations rule their minds? Why should they be gazing downwards from their position, and groping amidst things so far beneath them? Their past state, with its sin and guilt, its degradation and misery, could surely have no attractions for them. Having been brought up, they must still look up; and what they seek must be in harmony with their own pure and elevated position—*Sursum corda.* And, *secondly,* Christ is above in a station of glory. Their union with Him will lead their thoughts to Him. Whatever the character of the things to be sought may be, they are to be found with Christ. Truth and blessing are from Him—promise and hope centre in Him. Whether the "things above" be a fuller glimpse of heaven, a higher preparation for it, or a sweeter foretaste of it; whether it be to learn its songs, reach a deeper sympathy with its enjoyments, or realize a living unity with its population; still, Christ at God's right hand enjoys a special pre-eminence, as those attainments are from Him, and the song, the service, and the inhabitants of heaven have Him as object, or as Lord. As the salvation which they experience comes from that blood by the shedding of which He rose to His glorious position—as there He intercedes so effectually, and governs so graciously, by word, providence, and Spirit—as there He holds heaven in their name, and prepares them for it—as their present life and peace originate in union with Him—a union to be realized yet more vividly when He shall bid them "come up hither;" therefore should their desire stretch away upward and onward towards Him and the scene he occupies "on the right hand of the glorious majesty." "An high look," though it be sin in ordinary things, and be the index of a proud heart, is yet the true aspect of a humble believer.

The form of expression, "things above," while it has a distinctive meaning in Christianity, and is not a mere image, is one that is also based on our moral nature. Local elevation is the instinctive symbol of spiritual aspiration and refinement. Hence the origin of the phrases collected by some commentators from the classics.

(Ver. 2.) *Τὰ ἄνω φρονεῖτε, μὴ τὰ ἐπὶ τῆς γῆς*—"Set your

mind on things above, not on things on the earth." The verb in this verse differs so far from that employed in the preceding, that it refers more to inner disposition, while the former is rather practical pursuit. The sure safeguard against seeking things below, is not to set the mind upon them. The "things above" have been already glanced at. The things "on the earth" are not, as Huther and Schrader suppose, the meat and drinks and other elements of the ascetic system which the apostle condemns, but such things as are the objects of usual and intense search among men. Phil. iii. 19. The apostle does not urge any transcendental contempt of things below, but simply asks that the heart be not set upon them in the same way, and to the same extent, in which it is set upon things above. The pilgrim is not to despise the comforts which he may meet with by the way, but he is not to tarry among them, or leave them with regret. "Things on earth" are only subordinate and instrumental—"things above" are supreme and final. Attachment to things on the earth is unworthy of one who has risen with Christ, for they are beneath him, and the love of them is not at all in harmony with his position and prospects. What can wealth achieve for him who has treasure laid up in heaven? Or honour for him who is already enthroned in the heavenly places? Or pleasure for him who revels in "newness of life"? Or power for him who is endowed with a moral omnipotence? Or fame for him who enjoys the approval of God? Nay, too often, when the "things on earth" are possessed, they concentrate the heart upon them, and the "look and thoughts are downward bent." Bishop Wilson on this place observes—"for things on earth too naturally draw us down, attract us, fix us. Esau's red pottage prevails over the birthright. The guests in the parable turn away to their land, or oxen, or families. The Gadarene mind wishes Christ to depart from its coasts."[1] The things on earth are seen, therefore they are temporal; the things in heaven are unseen, and therefore they are eternal. If the mind be fully occupied with things above, things on earth will be barred out. The apostle adduces another reason, not indeed essentially different, but exhibiting another phasis of the argument—

[1] *Lectures on Colossians*, p. 282, 3rd ed.

(Ver. 3.) Ἀπεθάνετε γάρ—"For ye died." The expression is general, and the apostle does not simply say, ye died to the world—τοῖς κάτω,[1] or *mundo*[2]—and should have no more concern with it, but he says, ye died, that is, with Christ, and all that is out of Christ, or hostile to Him, should cease to excite your attention or engross your industry. The apostle had said in the first verse that they had risen with Christ, here he resorts to a previous point in their spiritual career, and says they had already died. ii. 20. Neither "seek nor savour" the things of earth; for having died, and having been even buried with Christ, your sphere of being, action, and enjoyment, is totally different from your former state. As Luther says—*Wir leben nicht im Fleisch, sondern wir wohnen im Fleisch*—"we live not in the flesh, but we dwell in the flesh." When they did die, their death was but a birth into a new life, for he adds—

Καὶ ἡ ζωὴ ὑμῶν κέκρυπται σὺν τῷ Χριστῷ ἐν τῷ Θεῷ—"And your life has been hidden with Christ in God." The death is past and over, but the life has been hid, and still is in that hidden state—**κέκρυπται**. The peculiar phraseology of the clause has suggested a variety of interpretations. There are many who regard this life as future or eternal life, laid up for Christians with Christ in God. So the Greek Fathers, and many who partly follow them, such as Erasmus, Rosenmüller, Barnes, and Meyer. We apprehend that the apostle speaks not of the resurrection, as Theodoret supposes, but of a spiritual life enjoyed now, though not in the meantime fully developed. That life which we now live in the flesh has a hidden source with Christ in God—its infinite fountain. The idea of Olshausen is somewhat different, for he places the notion of concealment in the nature of the life more than in its source. He says—"the life of believers is called hidden, inasmuch as it is inward, and the outward does not correspond with it." Von Gerlach says—"his life is not in him, but it is in Christ." The exegesis of De Wette is similar. This life, he says, is hidden, being inner as opposed to being visible—*innerlich nicht auf das sichtbare gerichtet ist*—and as being *ideal*, not—*real oder offenbar*. Barnes, again, lays too much stress on the idea of security: eternal life is "safely

[1] Theophylact. [2] Bengel.

deposited"[1] with Christ in God. a-Lapide finds his choicest illustration of the phrase in the seclusion of monastic life. We cannot agree with such as hold that the apostle calls this a hidden life, as being concealed from the world, inasmuch as he counsels them to make the results of it more apparent, and to show their vitality in their modes of action. The mortification of the members which is enjoined in the following verse, is but the fruit and expansion of this life. As it diffuses itself, it carries death with it to all sinful propensities. Now, of this life God is the source, and Christ the channel; and when it is said to be hid "with Christ in God," the meaning is not only that channel and fountain are both supersensuous and invisible, but that our connection with them is also a matter of inner experience—not as yet of full and open manifestation.

This life is hidden *σὺν τῷ Χριστῷ*—"with Christ," for He is its medium, and our union with Him gives us life; and it is hidden with Him *ἐν τῷ Θεῷ*—"in God," not merely as He is now removed from view and exalted to God's right hand, but as He enjoys supreme repose and fellowship in the bosom of His Father. Böhmer's connection of *ζωή* at once with *σὺν τῷ Χριστῷ* is forbidden by the position of the words; and the eccentric and baseless interpretation of Calixtus and Heinrichs needs not be mentioned. The idea of concealment, and not that of security, seems to be principally contained in the verb, for it is placed in contrast with open manifestation at Christ's appearance. If the apostle had meant our future life, then the idea of security might naturally be found in this concealment. But he speaks of present life—life really, though partially enjoyed, life giving a palpable, though feeble, demonstration of its health and vigour. The prepositions *σύν*

[1] "Ac ne molesta sit exspectatio, notemus istas particulas, *in Deo*, et *cum Christo:* quae significant, extra periculum esse vitam nostram, tametsi non appareat. Nam et Deus fidelis est, ideoque non abnegabit depositum, nec fallet in suscepta custodia: et Christi societas maiorem etiamnum securitatem affert. Quid enim magis expetendum, quam vitam nostram manere cum ipso vitae fonte? Quare non est, quod terreamur, si undique circumspicientes vitam nusquam cernamus. Spe enim salvi sumus. Ea vero, quae iam patent oculis, non sperantur. Neque vero tantum mundi opinione vitam absconditam esse docet, sed etiam quoad sensum nostrum: quia hoc verum et necessarium est spei nostrae experimentum, ut tanquam morte circumdati vitam alibi quaeramus quam in mundo."—Calvin *in loc.*

and ἐν express, as Meyer remarks, the first coherence, and the second inherence.

This life is at once divine and mediatorial—God's gift to believers through Christ; and the gift, along with its medium and its destiny, are hidden in the Giver, as the infinite source. But this concealment is no argument against present and partial enjoyment; for one may drink of the stream and be unable either to detect its source, which hides itself far away and high among the mountains, or conjecture at what distant point its deepening current pours itself into the ocean. The life is not said, by the apostle, to be hidden in itself, either from the world or from believers themselves, as so many commentators suppose. True, indeed, it is mysterious. It is not among things of vulgar gaze. It is a strange experience; none can know it save he who has it. For Christians die and yet live; nay, the moment of death is that of life—the instant of expiry is that of birth. Yet this life is now enjoyed—is therefore now a matter of secret consciousness, though much about it is beyond inquiry and analysis. No one can lay bare the principle of physical life; the knife of the anatomist cannot uncover the cord which binds the conscious thinking essence to its material organ and habitation. But the special thought of the apostle is, that the ethereal nature of spiritual life eludes research, alike in its origin and destiny. Its source is too high for us to climb to it, and its destiny is too noble to be written in human language. As to the former, it is hidden with Christ in God; and as to the latter, it shall not be fully revealed till Christ come the second time in glory. But it shall be ultimately disclosed. For Christ, with whom our life is hidden, shall reveal Himself, and we whose life is so hidden with Him shall also appear with Him in glory. When its medium is revealed, its character and destiny shall also be laid bare.

(Ver. 4.) Ὅταν ὁ Χριστὸς φανερωθῇ ἡ ζωὴ ἡμῶν, τότε καὶ ὑμεῖς σὺν αὐτῷ φανερωθήσεσθε ἐν δόξῃ—"When Christ, who is our life, shall appear, then, too, shall ye with Him be revealed in glory." The form ὑμῶν appears, on good authority, to be preferable to the ἡμῶν of the Received Text. The verb φανερωθῇ is opposed to the κέκρυπται of the previous verse. There is concealment now, but there shall be ultimate and glorious disclosure. 1 John i. 2, iii. 2, 5; Rom. viii. 18; 1 Tim. iii. 16; 1 Pet. v. 4. Christ is termed "our life;" and in the former verse our life is said to be hid with Him. He is our life, not simply because he reveals it, and He alone has "the words of eternal life;" nor yet because coming that we "might have life, and that we might have it more abundantly," He "died that we might live," and has given us this blessed pledge—"as I live, ye shall live also;" but specially, because by His Spirit, as His representative, He enters into the heart and gives it life—fans and fosters it by his continuous abode—gratifies all its instincts, and evokes all its susceptibilities by His word and His presence. "If Christ be in you, the body is dead because of sin, but the spirit is life because of righteousness."

When it is said—"Christ our life shall appear," the meaning is, that He shall appear in the character of our life. In this peculiar aspect of His operation shall He make Himself manifest. To appear as our life, implies our relation to Him as His living ones; and the unveiling of the Fountain shall allow the eye to discover the myriads of rivulets which issue out of it; or, as our life is hid with Christ, so, when Christ comes out of His hiding-place, our life shall accompany Him into openness and light. Nay more, as our life, He appears to perfect it, and to give it fulness and finality of development. At present it is checked by a variety of causes. It exists in a body "dead because of sin," and it feels the chill of a mortality that so closely envelops it. The distance, too, implied in the fact—that it is hidden with Christ in God—keeps it from its perfect strength, and induces occasional debility and lassitude; but the revelation of Christ brings it into nearness and vigour. Nay more, at that period, the body is to be brought into harmony with it, and "mortality shall be swallowed up of life." For He who is our life shall diffuse life through us—"change our vile body, and fashion it like unto His own glorious body." The physical frame then to be raised, spiritualized, and imbued with life, shall be a fit receptacle for the living soul within it, which shall then indulge its tastes without hindrance, feeling no barrier to activity in any of its occupations—no stint to capacity in any of its enjoyments. *Hiems nostra*, says Augustine, *Christi occultatio, aestas nostra, Christi revelatio.* Suicer remarks—*gloria capitis est gloria corporis et membrorum.* For the apostle describes, as the consequence of the appearance of Christ our life, that "we, too, shall appear with Him in glory." Rom. viii. 17; 1 John iii. 2. Since He appears as our life, so to appear with Him is, on our part, to appear as partakers of His life. The source, progress, and maturity of our life shall then be fully apparent—how it originated, and how it was sustained—what course it took, and what obstacles it encountered—how it was still supported, and still maintained its hold—how it was felt in our own consciousness, and yet had its hidden spring "with Christ in God"—and what shall be now its high crown and its magnificent destiny—all shall be seen in the living and life-filling brightness of "Christ our life." The followers of Christ shall surround Him in triumph, a dense and glorious retinue—"ye, too, shall appear with Him," and that—ἐν δόξῃ.

It would be wrong to restrict this "glory" to any special aspect of final perfection. It consists, as Davenant, after the schoolmen, says, of the "robe of the soul and the robe of the body." It is here the result of life—*vita gloriosa*,[1] of life in its highest form and fullest manifestation — life diffused through "spirit, soul, and body." Nor is our appearance in glory with Christ a momentary gleam; it is rather the first burst of unending splendour. And it has, or shall have, for its elements—final freedom from the sins and sorrows of earth; perfect holiness beyond the possibility of loss, with unmingled felicity beyond the reach of forfeit; an endless abode in heaven, and in the brightest province of it; the rapturous adoration of God, and unbroken fellowship with Christ; the exalted companionship of angels and genial spirits of human kindred; and the successful pursuit of Divine knowledge in a realm where no shadow ever falls, but where is chanted the high halleluiah, welling out of the consciousness that all this ecstasy is of sovereign grace, ay, all of it sealed to us for eternity, in connection with "Christ our life."

The apostle now descends to particularize certain forms of sins which were very prevalent in heathendom—in which they themselves had revelled during their prior state of

[1] Beza.

gloom and degradation, but which they must now and for ever abandon.

(Ver. 5.) *Νεκρώσατε οὖν τὰ μέλη ὑμῶν τὰ ἐπὶ τῆς γῆς*— "Mortify, therefore, your members which are upon the earth." "Therefore," since such are the peculiarities and prospects of your spiritual state, act in harmony with them; and since you have died, diffuse the process of death through all your members. If the heart is dead, let all the organs which it once vivified and moved die too—nay, put them to death. Let them be killed from want of nutriment and exercise. Similar language is found in Rom. viii. 13, where *θανατοῦτε* is employed; and in Gal. v. 24, where occurs the modal verb *σταυρώσατε*. In *τὰ μέλη*, the allusion is to members of the body, taken not in a physical, but in a spiritual sense. Hilary, Grotius, Bengel, and others, destroy the point of the allusion in regarding sin itself as a body, and its special parts as members. The apostle had strongly condemned asceticism, and declared it in the conclusion of the preceding chapter to be an absolute failure, and he now shows how the end it contemplated is to be secured. There is no reason for Meyer to deny that the apostle regards "the old man" as the body to which such members belong. It is not, indeed, the eye, foot, and hand, as these are in themselves, or as they belong to the physical frame, but as they belong to, and are in subjection to the "old man." The phrase is to be understood in the same spirit as our Lord's emphatic declaration about the plucking out of the right eye, and the cutting off of the right arm. Matt. v. 29. The lust that uses and debases these organs or members as its instruments, is to be extirpated.

And the "members" are characterized as being *τὰ ἐπὶ τῆς γῆς*—"upon the earth." The allusion is to the previous phraseology—"set your affections not on things on the earth." That is to say, earth is the sphere of their existence and operation; and as they belong to it, they are to be killed, for they are in utter antagonism with that higher life which is hid with Christ in God. They are "of the earth, earthy"—their essence is earthy, and so are their temptations, sources, and forms of enjoyment. The man who possesses a life that has its spring in heaven, and seeks and relishes things above, will not stoop to gratifications which are so far beneath him in nature, so utterly opposed to that new and spiritual existence which he cherishes within him, and which grows in power and health in proportion to the thoroughness and universality of the death which is executed on the "members which are on the earth." The apostle then enumerates some of these forms of sensuality.

Πορνείαν, ἀκαθαρσίαν, πάθος, ἐπιθυμίαν κακήν—"Fornication, impurity, lust, and evil concupiscence." These accusatives are in apposition to τὰ μέλη. The first two terms are found in Eph. v. 3, and denote fornication and lewdness. 2 Cor. xii. 21; Gal. v. 19. See especially under Eph. iv. 19, where the second occurs, and is described. But, in fact, the shapes and kinds of lewdness, to be found not only in the pagan worship, and in the symbols carried in religious processions, but also in common life, as depicted on tables and furniture, are beyond description.[1] The term πάθος is too lightly understood by Grotius and Chrysostom, as signifying —*motus vitiosi*, such as anger and hatred; and perhaps too darkly by such as refer it wholly to unnatural lust. The noun does not seem of itself to have this last sense, but it occurs with a special adjunct in Rom. i. 26; and the adjective, παθικός, has an indescribable baseness. It seems here to denote the state of mind that urges and excites to impurity—τὸ ἐρωτικὸν πάθος,[2] that condition in which man is mastered by unchastity, and the imagination being defiled, is wholly at the mercy of obscene associations. It is *morbus libidinis*, as Bengel says. The next term, ἐπιθυμία κακή, refers to the same circle of vices, and is more general in its nature. The four words may be regarded as in two pairs. The prior pair refers to act, the first term more particular, and the second more comprehensive; the second pair to impulse, the first again more special, and the second more sweeping in its nature. They were no longer to be guilty of fornication, or any similar deed of lewdness; they were no longer to be filled with libidinous thoughts, or any other prurient feelings, having their issue in lecherous indulgences.

Καὶ τὴν πλεονεξίαν ἥτις ἐστὶν εἰδωλολατρεία—"And that covetousness which is idolatry." The form ἥτις may cor-

[1] Juvenal, *Sat.* ii. [2] Plato, *Phaedrus*, vol. i. p. 153, Op. ed. Bekker.

respond to the Latin *quippe quae*—since indeed. The reader may turn for the meaning of πλεονεξία, and its occurrence in this connection, to our comment on Eph. iv. 19, v. 3–5. The noun πλεον. has the article, which none of the preceding substantives have, and it alone is the antecedent to ἥτις. Winer, § 24, 3. We believe that it does not characterize any form of sensuality, or *quaestum meretricium*, as the Greek expositors, and others after them, suppose, though it denotes a vice that has its origin in the same selfish or self-seeking depravity. Trench, in his *New Testament Synonyms*, § 24, has some excellent observations on this word, remarking that the πλεονέκτης is as free in scattering and squandering as he was eager and unscrupulous in getting; that monsters of covetousness have been also monsters of lust; and that πλεονεξία is a far deeper passion than mere miserliness or avarice, as being "the fierce and ever fiercer longing of the creature which has turned from God to fill itself with the inferior objects of sense." This desire of having more, and yet more, is idolatry. What it craves it worships, what it worships it makes its portion. To such a god there is given the first thought of the morning, the last wish of the evening, and the action of every waking hour.

(Ver. 6.) *Δι' ἃ ἔρχεται ἡ ὀργὴ τοῦ Θεοῦ*—"On account of which sins cometh the wrath of God." The reading δι' ὅ has also several authorities in its favour. On the meaning of the clause see our exposition of Eph. v. 5. This special wrath is often suffered on earth, and it is not wholly reserved for the other world. Meyer, as in the correspondent place in the Epistle to the Ephesians, denies that the ὀργή is manifested here, and justifies his opinion by pointing to Paul's certain conviction of the near approach of the day of judgment. The sins mentioned in the previous verse are, as we have shown on Eph. v. 6, often visited by penalty on earth. The next clause of the Textus Receptus—ἐπὶ τοὺς υἱοὺς τῆς ἀπειθείας—is excluded by Tischendorf, but without sufficient authority. It is wanting in B, certainly, but this is a solitary MS. witness. The clause occurs in Eph. v. 6, and is there explained, as also under Eph. ii. 2, 3. They who indulge in such vices, not only disobey the Divine statute, but also violate the laws of their own constitution. This ὀργή is more than chastisement, or *κόλασις*, it is direct and punitive indignation frequently inflicted here in the form of physical debility and disease, remorse and stupefaction.

(Ver. 7.) *Ἐν οἷς καὶ ὑμεῖς περιεπατήσατέ ποτε ὅτε ἐζῆτε ἐν τούτοις.* The relative *οἷς* may be either masculine or neuter, as it is referred to *υἱούς*, or to the *ἅ* of the previous verse. Each construction has been vindicated. With Olshausen and Bähr, we prefer the neuter, not only because *περιπατεῖν* is usually employed in connection with things, and not persons, but because the believers in Colosse are said, in the next clause, to have lived in them, and in the 8th verse, to have thrown them all off. Calvin says—*male Erasmus vertit, inter quos.* Meyer prefers the masculine in this first clause, but is obliged to change the gender in reference to *τούτοις* in the second clause. "In which lusts ye too once walked;" "walked" having, of course, its common tropical meaning. But that period was now over—a new era had dawned; and their walk was in a widely different sphere, one in which, by the assistance of the Spirit, they copied the example of Jesus, and sought, and were acquiring a growing preparation for the purity and bliss of heaven.

Ὅτε ἐζῆτε ἐν τούτοις. *Τούτοις*, and not *αὐτοῖς*, on the evidence of A, B, C, D[1], E[1], though *αὐτοῖς* has in its favour D, E[2], F, G, J, K. Flatt, Böhmer, Huther, and others, take *τούτοις* to be masculine; an exegesis which does not give any tolerable meaning. In *ἐζῆτε* there is an allusion by contrast to the *ἀπεθάνετε.* They once lived in such sins. Life is here used in a spiritual, and not in its physical sense, as in 1 Thess. iii. 8. Other instances may be found in the classics—*possemne vivere,* says Cicero, *nisi in litteris viverem?*[1] Libanius describes Alexander as *ἐν Ὀδυσσείᾳ ζῶν*; Aelian (*Hist. Var.* iii. 13) speaks of a people so fond of wine—*ὥστε ζῆν αὐτοὺς ἐν οἴνῳ*; and we have the phrase *οἱ ζῶντες*—they who enjoy life. They had felt supreme enjoyment in such indulgences. So much had they been engrossed with them, and such fancied gratification did they find in them, that they might be said to "live in them." The difference of meaning between the two verbs has been variously understood, but there needs no special definition. They once walked in such

[1] Ep. 9, 26.

lusts, when they lived in them; that is, they were utterly addicted to them, for they believed that life or happiness was to be found in them. Calvin says the verbs differ, as do *potentia et actus.*

(Ver. 8.) *Νυνὶ δὲ ἀπόθεσθε καὶ ὑμεῖς τὰ πάντα*—"But now do ye also put off the whole." The words *καὶ ὑμεῖς* here correspond to *καὶ ὑμεῖς* in the preceding verse, and *νυνί* stands out in contrast with *ποτέ*. The verb is found in Eph. iv. 25. Wolf is wrong in referring *πάντα* to *μέλη*, which is so far distant from it. The phrase *τὰ πάντα* is the entire circle of vices; not, as Winer says, this or that all (intensive), but "the all which is immediately adduced," § 18, 1. A radical and extensive change had taken place; but (*δέ* adversative) they were to "cast off" that slough in which were lodged all degrading sins. The catalogue or class of sins is subjoined.

Ὀργὴν, θυμὸν, κακίαν, βλασφημίαν, αἰσχρολογίαν ἐκ τοῦ στόματος ὑμῶν—"Anger, indignation, malice, calumny, abusive discourse out of your mouth." The apostle observes a different order, and uses some other terms in Eph. iv. 31. Under that place the first four terms repeated here have been explained. Bähr and Trench take *ὀργή* in distinction from *θυμός*, as denoting settled indignation bordering on revenge. This is the Stoical definition—*ἐπιθυμία τιμωρίας*; and it is also the opinion of Origen, as brought out in his exposition of the second Psalm. Still, we think that though *ὀργή* characterizes a habit or state, the idea of visible display is usually associated with it, as indeed the phrase *ὀργὴ θυμοῦ* often found in the Septuagint plainly implies; and, as is manifest from the diction of the previous verse, "the wrath of God *cometh.*" *Ὀργή* is the outburst, or the vice in a palpable form; *θυμός* is the violent emotion that boils within; while *κακία* points to the state of heart in which malice originates, and *βλασφημία* is that calumnious denunciation to which anger so often prompts. As regards *αἰσχρολογία*, which occurs only here, we agree with De Wette and Trench, that its meaning is not to be confined to obscene speech. That it has this express meaning is beyond any doubt, but it also often denotes generally foul or abusive language,[1] and as it is so closely connected with the passion of anger, such may

[1] Polybius, viii. 13, 8; Plut. *de lib. Educ.* 14.

be its meaning here. It is therefore a more comprehensive term than βλασφημία, as the first refers to what especially injures character, and the second to what offends in any sense, not only to what hurts the ear of modesty, but to whatever in any form is scurrilous and indecent—that mixture of ribaldry and profanity which too often escapes from the burning lips of passion. The addition, ἐκ τοῦ στόματος ὑμῶν, may belong to both βλασφ. and αἰσχρ. with the verb ἀπόθεσθε mentally repeated. Nor can we give the words the emphasis which Theophylact attaches to them. "See," says he, "how he recounts the members of the old man," that is, shows how each sins, as "the mind by falsehood, the heart by anger, the mouth by blasphemy, eyes and hidden members by fornication, the liver by evil concupiscence, the hands by covetousness."

From sins of malignity, the apostle passes to sins of falsehood.

(Ver. 9.) Μὴ ψεύδεσθε εἰς ἀλλήλους—"Do not lie to one another." As one of the Greek Fathers says, falsehood ill became them who avowed themselves disciples of Him who said, "I am the truth." The apostle, in writing to the Ephesians, adds as a reason why they should adhere to the truth —"we are members one of another." He does not here say, as some suppose, lie not against or about one another, that is, to the damage of one another; but his meaning is, in all your communications among yourselves, never depart from the truth.

The connection of the following clause is best ascertained by adherence to the literal meaning of the participle, ἀπεκδυσάμενοι—"having put off the old man with his deeds." The Vulgate gives *exuentes* in the present time, and is followed by Luther, Bengel, Storr, De Wette, and Huther.[1] The

[1] We had forgotten to mention an extraordinary interpretation of this verb, ἀπεκδύομαι, as it occurs in ii. 15. Dr. Donaldson, in his book of capricious and destructive criticism, called "Jashar" (London, 1855), in vindication of certain views which he entertains of the character of humanity in general, and of Christ in particular, to wit, His liability to temptation, justifies his theology by quoting the verse referred to, pp. 70, 71. After affirming, with no little vaunt, that all interpreters up to himself have misunderstood it, he says that it must have the same meaning as in iii. 9. He gives the following exegesis—"the principalities and powers" are the potent lords of lust—*duces libidinum*—which rule in our members, and stuck to Christ like the poisoned shirt of Nessus, and these

putting off of the old man, as described by the aorist, cannot be contemporary with the foregoing imperatives, but it precedes them. It is a process consummated, and so Calvin, Bähr, Böhmer, and Meyer rightly understand it. Beza says correctly, that the participles are used *αἰτιολογικῶς*. These participles are not to be taken in the sense of imperatives, as the first class of expositors virtually regards them, but they unfold a reason why the sins condemned should be uniformly abstained from. Lie not one to another, as being persons who have put off the old man; or, as the participle has often a causal sense—since ye have put off the old man with his deeds. De Wette says that such an argument is superfluous, but surely the paragraph may conclude as it began, with an argument. The first argument is, ye are dead; and the second contains one of the results of that spiritual death with Christ.

Ἀπεκδυσάμενοι τὸν παλαιὸν ἄνθρωπον σὺν ταῖς πράξεσιν αὐτοῦ—"Since ye have put off the old man with his deeds." The expressive personality—"old man"—has been explained under Eph. iv. 22. It is a bold personification of our first nature as derived from Adam, the source and seat of original and actual transgression, and called "old," as existing prior to our converted state. This ethical person is to be put off from us as one puts off clothes, and with all his deeds—all the practices which characterized him, and the sins to which he excited. This was a change deeper by far than asceticism could ever reach. For it was a total revolution. Self-denial in meats and drinks, while it prunes the excrescence, really helps the growth of the plant, but this uproots it.

(Ver. 10.) *Καὶ ἐνδυσάμενοι τὸν νέον, τὸν ἀνακαινούμενον.*

He conquered and led in triumph. Not to say, with Mr. Perowne, that the exegesis is "sheer nonsense," and contrary to the entire meaning of the terms, the strain and spirit of the context, and to Paul's theology, we simply reply, that the acute and learned author of the New Cratylus may see that God, and not Christ, is the subject, and that if *ἀπεκδύομαι* must there denote "the putting off from himself" something which clings to the agent, the affirmation of the verse is at utter variance with the purity and spirituality of the Divine Being, Nay, more, Dr. Donaldson says, that "the principalities and powers," those lords of lust which so clung to Christ that they were only flung off by Him when He died, were and must have been in Christ, for they were "created in Him," according to Col. i. 16. Is there any wonder that previous commentators never came to such conclusion?

As the old man is thrown off the new man is assumed. In the Epistle to the Ephesians, the apostle inserts between the off-putting and the on-putting a clause in reference to renewal "in the spirit of the mind," and there using a different adjective he calls the new man *τὸν καινὸν ἄνθρωπον*, but he had previously used the verb *ἀνανεοῦσθαι*. Here, he says *τὸν νέον* [*ἄνθρωπον*], but he adds *τὸν ἀνακαινούμενον*. So that though it be in different forms, both terms are employed in both places. If the verbal term from *νέος* be followed by the epithet *καινός* in Ephesians, and if in Colossians the epithet *νέος* be followed by the verbal term from *καινός*, it is plain that the same general meaning is intended by the apostle. Though *νέος* and *καινός* may be distingu shed, their meaning is thus blended. If *νέος* be "recent," and in this sense be opposed to *παλαιός*, then this recency springs from renewal. The one man is old, for he belonged to a past and former state ; and the other is new, for his assumption was to them but a novelty, a matter of yesterday in their spiritual experience.

This man is new not only in point of time, but of quality or character, for he is renewed—*εἰς ἐπίγνωσιν*. It is not the idea of Paul in this expression, that the new man, still renewing, never grows old, *ἥτις οὐ παλαιοῦται*—as the Greek expositors imagine. Rather would we say, with Calovius, that he is called "*re-novatus*, because he was once *novus* at his first creation," and as the preposition *ἀνα* would fairly seem to imply. Man must be brought back to his original purity, but the process of renovation is continuous, as the use of the present participle indicates. Bähr quotes Augustine as saying—*in ipso animo renati* non est *perfecta novitas.* We cannot take the participle to be simply a predicate of *ἄνθρωπον*, for the construction points out its connection with *νέον*. The new man (the present participle being used) is renewing, as the apostle affirms—*ἡμέρᾳ καὶ ἡμέρᾳ*—in 2 Cor. iv. 6 ; or, as Theophylact says, *ἀεὶ καὶ ἀεί.*

In the phrase *εἰς ἐπίγνωσιν*, the preposition cannot signify the instrumental cause of the renewal, but it denotes the final purpose. The new man is renewed "unto knowledge." The meaning of *ἐπίγνωσις* may be seen under Eph. i. 17 ; and in this epistle, i. 9 ; ii. 2. And that perfect knowledge has a close connection with God, for it is characterized as being—

Κατ' εἰκόνα τοῦ κτίσαντος αὐτόν—"After the image of Him who created him." A large number of expositors connect the clause directly with the participle *ἀνακαινούμενον*, the image of God being the pattern after which the believer is renewed. Meyer joins it more closely to *εἰς ἐπίγνωσιν*, but the meaning is not materially different. The likeness is renewed after the image of God, and the special feature of that image selected by the apostle is knowledge. The knowledge of the renewed man corresponds in certain elements to that of God. Other features of resemblance of a moral nature are referred to in the parallel passage, Eph. iv. 24. That image is said to belong to God the creator, not Christ, as was supposed in the early church, and as is understood by Müller. A peculiar exegesis is adopted by a-Lapide and Schleiermacher, the former making *τοῦ κτίσαντος* the object of the knowledge; and the latter thus explaining the image—*so erneuet, dass man an ihm das Ebenbild Gottes erkennen kann.*

But what creation is referred to? Is it the first or the second creation? Many incline to the first view, as if the apostle meant that man is brought back to that likeness which God gave him on the day of creation. So Calovius, Heinsius, Estius, Schoettgen, and De Wette. But though this be a truth, it is not that precise form of truth conveyed by the apostle's language. It is not of man generally, but of the new man that he speaks—the new man renewed unto knowledge after the image of Him who created him, to wit, the new man. The apostle does not say—who created you. The new man is the converted spiritual nature, not the man himself in proper person. It is this creation of the new man, not that of the man himself, which is ascribed to God. Thus, the parallel passage in Eph. iv. 24 says expressly—"the new man which after God is created in righteousness and true holiness." This new nature is of God, and not of self-development. All creation is indeed from God, and this new creation is no exception. The new man is not the ethical symbol of a mere reformation which a strong will may achieve; nor is it any change of creed, party, or opinions, which is the result of personal examination and conviction. These are but as statuary, compared with living humanity; for however close the resemblance, there is always, in spite of highest art, the still eye and the motionless lip. Yes, God's work is a living power, something so compact and richly endowed, so fitted to our nature, and so much a part of us as to be called a *man*, but at the same time so foreign to all previous powers and enjoyments as to be called the *new man*.

As the first man was made by God, and in His image, so is this new man. The special point of resemblance stated is knowledge. This may have been selected, as an allusion to the boasted knowledge and proud philosophy of the false teachers in Colosse. ii. 2. There are, it is true, many points in which our relative knowledge shall never, and can never, resemble the absolute Divine omniscience. But as the Spirit is the source of our knowledge, no one can predict what amount of it, or what forms of it, He may communicate when the mind is freed from every shadow and bias, and is surrounded with an atmosphere of universal truth. Human language is necessarily an imperfect vehicle of thought, and it may then be dispensed with. "Now we see through a glass darkly, but then face to face,"—our conceptions shall resemble God's in fulness and truth; for no dim medium of intellectual vision shall shade or disturb our views. Immediate cognition shall also be our privilege—"now we know in part, but then shall we know, even as we are known."

In accordance with that strange theory by which Müller would account for the origin of sin—a theory at once above the domain of consciousness and beyond the limits of Scripture, he denies that there is any biblical warrant for the idea that man, having lost the image of God by the fall, has it restored to him under the gospel by the renovating influence of the Spirit of God. His notion of a pre-temporal state, in which man fell, when, how, or where, he does not say, necessitates him to the conclusion, that when Adam fell, man lost nothing, but that there was only awakened in him the consciousness of a previous want and deficiency, so that sinful principles already within him acquired universal dominion over the human race. A transition, on the part of Adam, from an absolutely pure state into one of sin, is not, he holds, necessarily contained in the inspired record. "The narrative of the first sin, as well as the description of that condition which preceded it, does not of necessity lead us to any further idea than that of an initial state in which sin has not yet made its appearance," and does not imply, "that Adam through his fall implanted in human nature a principle previously foreign to it."[1] Müller's inference, of course, is, that it cannot be properly said that the Divine image is restored to man, seeing that on earth, at least, he never possessed it. The passage before us, and the parallel passage in Eph. iv. 24, certainly affirm that the new man is the reflection of the Divine image in some of its features. They do not indeed affirm, in as many words, that he becomes possessed of the same Divine image which he once enjoyed. But the statement is virtually implied. Had man never this Divine image, and does he enjoy it for the first time through faith in Christ? "The new man," Müller says, "is the holy form of human life which results from redemption." Now, not to say that the very idea of redemption, reconciliation, or renewal, implies a restoration to some previous state in which none of them was needed, there being in that state no penalty to be ransomed from, no enmity to be subdued, and no impurity to be cleansed away —let us see what revelation teaches as to man's primeval condition and his possession of the Divine image.

The idea of "non-temporal sinfulness" we must discard as a speculation about which Scripture is completely silent, and which, putting the lapse of ideal humanity beyond the period of paradise, only shifts back the difficulty in proportion, but does not explain it. In Gen. i. 26, 27, and v. 1, we are told that man was created in the image and likeness of God, but no formal explanation of the phraseology is attached. Opinions have varied as to the meaning of the peculiar phrase; some, like Pott, Rosenmüller, and von Bohlen, placing it almost in physical form, rising scarcely as high as the heathen Ovid;[2] some regarding it as a general expression of

[1] *Lehre von der Sünde*, vol. ii. p. 483, etc., 3rd ed., Breslau, 1849.

[2] *Animal mentisque capacius altae, et quod dominari in caetera posset.* Also Cicero, *De natura Deorum*, i. 32. Pythagoras could say, as reported by Diogenes Laertius, that there is a relationship between men and the gods, because men are partakers of the Divine principle. Dio. L. p. 584, ed. Is. Casaubon. Xenophon, *Mem.* i. 4, 14.

the dignity of the race, like Herder, Schumann, Delitzsch, and Knobel;[1] others finding in it the idea of dominion over the lower creatures—like Ephrem, Grotius, and Tuch; and others, as Calvin, and the majority of the Reformers and Theologians, regarding it too exclusively as the symbol of spiritual capacities and powers.

But what do we gather from Scripture? In the edict against murder, Gen. ix. 6, the atrocity of the crime is taught by the doctrine, that "in the image of God made He man." On this express account the life of animals formally delivered into man's hand for meat, has not the sacredness of human life. Further, the Apostle James (iii. 9) exposes the rashness and inconsistency of sins of the tongue, blessing God in one breath, and in another cursing man "made after the similitude of God." If man did not still retain this image of God, there would be no sin either in killing or cursing him. Therefore this image referred to is something altogether independent of the fact or development of sin in man's nature, for it is still possessed, and ought to shield him from violence and anathema.

This image, so unaffected by the fall, plainly results from man's position as a creature. His physical formation is not only noble and supreme, but as a rational and immortal creature, and as God's representative to the lower creation, he bears the image of God. These endowments yet remain to him. He has not been degraded from the erectness of his mien, nor have reason and immortality been penally wrested from him. And thus through himself he still learns what God is, or rather, is enabled to comprehend lessons on the nature and attributes of God by the analogies of his own mental and spiritual constitution. For, when he is told that God knows or loves, he naturally and necessarily forms his ideas of the Divine knowledge or affection, by feeling what these properties are within himself, and by inferring what they must be when resident in an infinite and unchanging essence. Or if he be informed that God is a person, his own conscious and unmerging individuality leads him at once to attach a correct and definite meaning to the term, and he is in himself a living witness against Pantheistic folly and delusion.

[1] *Als beseelte Einheit.* Knobel, *die Genesis erklärt*, p. 18.

But is this all that is meant by the Divine image? Müller says, that it simply consists in "personal essence,"[1] and that man is thereby distinguished from other classes of existences. But we apprehend that the expression reaches deeper than this. There are certain properties or privileges which man has forfeited by the fall, and which are affirmed to have been originally possessed or enjoyed by him. Ignorance and spiritual death now characterize him. But is not spiritual intelligence a portion of the Divine image—the reflection of God's own light? There is also what the apostle, Eph. iv. 18, calls "the life of God," and from that we are now alienated; but would that mere personal essence on which Müller insists, bear any resemblance to God at all, if such vitality did not fill it? A personal essence with the gloom of ignorance within it, and the eclipse of death upon it, could not be recognized as bearing the Divine image. Therefore a mere personality devoid of such intelligence and life, could scarcely be called the image of God, or regarded as constituting the whole of it. And yet, though they formed a portion of that image, they have been lost by the fall, and are reconferred only in Christ. Besides, can any one bear the moral image of God and not be happy—not be a partaker of His immortal blessedness? But dissatisfaction and misery are the doom of fallen humanity, everywhere, and at all times.

That man was once filled with wisdom, purity, life, and happiness, appears to be the repeated statement of Scripture. The theory of Müller consistently says, man never had these on earth, and therefore could not lose them. But the narrative of Genesis, though it do not treat the subject dogmatically, presents the picture of an innocent creature, tempted by the serpent, and doomed for his apostasy to toil and death. Does Prof. Müller believe that the sin of man in an ideal ante-creational state was followed by no penalty? Or was the penalty of this kind, that the sinner was only subjected to another trial in another sphere, with the sad certainty that the germs of evil would ripen into fatal action? The narrative in Genesis must be interpreted in the light of the other and subsequent Scriptures, and they plainly teach that

[1] *Persönliches Wesen.*

Adam's transgression is the primary source of prodigious spiritual loss.

Our belief therefore is, that the Divine image, in which man was made, consists of more than personal essence, or dominion over the inferior creatures. These, indeed, belong to it, and are still retained by man. The gospel, therefore, has no effect upon them save to hallow them. Man did not forfeit manhood by his fall, and of necessity, what is essential to his manhood and his position still belongs to him. For his creational relationship to the God above him and the existences beneath him, could not be impaired, or his annihilation or metamorphosis would have been the result. But while manhood has not been lost, its nobler characteristics, without which the original image would have been imperfect, have been obliterated. What belongs to constitution, fallen man has retained; what belongs to quality and character has gone from him. The latter is a portion of the image as much as the former; the image, not of a Divine essence, but of an intelligent, holy, and blessed Divine person. And those features of the image which have been lost through the fall, are given back to the disciples of Christ.

We do not base any argument on the statement that the fallen Adam begat a son in his own image, whereas the Creator made man in His image. Nor do we imagine that any such notion of a double image of God, one essential and incapable of loss, and another moral and liable to be erased, can be found at all in the use of the two terms צֶלֶם and דְּמוּת, as they are both separated and interchanged in the sacred record. Nor have we begged the question by arguing back from the verse before us, and assuming from the image of the new man created by God, what the image of the first man created by Him must have been. For the apostle does not say that the new man is renewed in knowledge after Him who originally created humanity, but after the image of Him who creates himself—the new man. Indeed, the image conferred in renovation, though generically the same, cannot be in all points identical with that given in creation. It is fuller and lovelier, a richer intelligence with nobler objects of cognition; a higher form of life, having its type in the normal man—the second Adam; both reaching forward to a development to which neither means nor scope could have been found in Eden, or in simple connection with the first man, who is "of the earth, earthy." In fine, we are not sure if Müller's theory does not contain, by implication, what we have advanced. In illustrating the declaration of Paul, that 'in God we live, move, and have our being," he says—"God has willed man to be like Himself, in order that there might be a being which should be capable of fellowship with Him." But surely mere personality could not of itself constitute such a likeness, or lead inherently to such a communion. It must possess other qualities than simple consciousness to give it this resemblance, and fit it for this enjoyment of Him. Therefore these qualities, as we have contended, did and must belong to this first image, and being lost in the fall, are and must be restored to the second image, which characterizes and beautifies the "new man."

(Ver. **11.**) *Ὅπου οὐκ ἔνι Ἕλλην καὶ Ἰουδαῖος*—"Where there is neither Greek nor Jew." The first adverb refers to the preceding clause, "in which sphere of renewal," or simply, the idea of locality being so far sunk, "in which thing;" as in 2 Pet. ii. 11; Prov. xxvi. 20. The peculiar term *ἔνι* is supposed by many to be the contracted form of *ἔνεστι*. Phavorinus defines it by *ἐστίν, ὑπάρχει*. Others regard it as the simple preposition in the Ionic form; "the notion of the verb," as Kühner says, "being so subordinate that it is dropt." Such is the view of Robinson, Buttmann, and Winer, etc. But in this place the idea of the preposition is already expressed by *ὅπου*. There is also the analogy of other prepositions similarly used, such as *ἔπι* and *πάρα*. Perhaps the supposition of the *Etymologicum Magnum* is correct, that *ἔνι* is elliptical, leaving the reader to supply what part of the verb the syntax requires. In all the places of the New Testament where it is used it is preceded by *οὐκ*, and expresses a strong negation. Gal. iii. 28; Jas. i. 17. There is probably in the phrase the idea also of inner existence—where there does exist any inner distinction of Greek or Jew.

The apostle now specifies various mundane distinctions.

Ἕλλην καὶ Ἰουδαῖος, περιτομὴ καὶ ἀκροβυστία, βάρβαρος, Σκύθης, δοῦλος, ἐλεύθερος. The first pair is the natural distinction of "Greek and Jew." The noun ἕλλην, as opposed to βάρβαρος, means a Greek proper, and as opposed to Ἰουδαῖος, signifies one belonging to the Greek world, and perhaps viewing that world as the representative of that civilized heathenism which was brought into close and extensive correspondence with Palestine. Rom. i. 14, 16, ii. 9; Gal. iii. 28. The noun Ἰουδαῖος means a Jew, originally and merely one of the tribe of Judah; but latterly, as that tribe on its return from Babylon was so ascendant, it came to denote any one of the Hebrew race. There is no ground for the idea of the Greek expositors that ἕλλην means a proselyte, and Ἰουδαῖος a native Jew—ἐκ προγόνων, as Chrysostom has it. The second couple of epithets points out a religious distinction—περιτομὴ καὶ ἀκροβυστία, "circumcision and uncircumcision." The "circumcision" is the Jewish world, as Abraham's progeny, with the seal of the covenant in its flesh, and distinguished by its theocratic privileges, while the "uncircumcision" is non-Israel, or all the world beyond the chosen seed, and destitute of religious blessing. It has been said that the apostle uses four pairs of terms, but he drops the use of the καί, and there is no contrast between βάρβαρος—Σκύθης—"barbarian—Scythian." While the epithet ἀκροβυστία applied to the whole world beyond Israel, there were various distinctions in that world itself. The Hellenic section was elevated by refinement and culture, but other portions were debased and wretched. The two terms now under review appear to differ only in intensity. The Scythian is one at the lowest point of barbarism, as we might say—a negro, or even a Hottentot—a savage, or even a Bushman. The Scythian races, represented by the modern Tartar or Cossack races of Asia and Eastern Europe, were regarded as at the bottom of the scale. Scythians, according to Josephus, were βραχὺ τῶν θηρίων διαφέροντες[1]—while Herodotus calls them cannibals—ἀνθρωποφάγοι. Cicero against Piso uses a similar climax—*quod nullus in Barbaria. Quis hoc facit ulla in Scythia tyrannus?* The next two terms represent a social distinction, δοῦλος, ἐλεύθερος—"bond, free," a distinction very common in those countries and times. Some manuscripts, and those of high authority, insert a καί before ἐλεύ-

[1] *Contra Ap.* 2, 37.

θερος, such as A, D[1], E, F, G. It might be used as in the two first couples, for there is a contrast. There are thus three forms of distinction expressed, and one implied—national distinction, religious distinction, and social distinction; and there is also implied the secular distinction between civilization and savagism. The apostle completes his thoughts by adding—

'Αλλὰ τὰ πάντα καὶ ἐν πᾶσιν Χριστός—"But Christ is all and in all." The phrase is idiomatic. Christ is everything to all of them having the new man. To one and all of them He is everything, so far as the sufficiency, offer, and enjoyment of salvation are concerned, or as the apostle says in the similar passage in Galatians, "ye are all one in Christ Jesus."

Now, the meaning of the apostle is not that a man loses nationality on becoming a Christian; or that social rank is obliterated by admission into the church. The blood of Javan was not changed in a Greek, nor the blood of Abraham in a Jew, when both met in a spiritual kingdom. The rude manners of the Scythian might be refined by his faith, but he did not lose his peculiarity of colour or configuration. The chain of the slave was not broken by his religion, any more than the circumcision of the Jew was erased. But the meaning of the apostle is—

First, That such distinctions do not prevent the on-putting of the new man. In other words, such differences of nation, religion, culture, and social position, do not interfere with the adaptation, the offer, or the reception and the results of the gospel. It is fettered by no geographical limits, by no local or lineal peculiarities. The Greek is not nearer Christ for his philosophy, nor the Scythian more distant for his want of it. The incision of the ceremonial knife gave no preference to the Jew, nor was the absence of it any drawback to the Gentile. The slave was as welcome as the freeman—the wandering nomade as the polished citizen. Whatever a man's descent or race, his creed or rites; whatever his language or pursuits, his colour or climate, his dwelling or usages, his position or character—the gospel comes to him with special offer, and adaptation, and completeness, and having embraced it he will feel its renewing power. It does not insist on the Gentile submitting to the Abrahamic rite, nor require the Jew to be initiated into the wisdom of the Greek; it does not stand aloof from the slave till he burst his chain, nor does it command the barbarian to master an alphabet or win the civic franchise ere it can save and change him. No; it comes alike to the synagogue and to the temple, with equal fitness to freedom and to servitude; with equal fulness, freeness, and tenderness to the citizen in the forum and to the wanderer on the wide and solitary steppe. All adventitious distinctions are levelled at its just and loving glance.

Secondly, It is taught by the apostle, that in the church, the sphere of the new man's activity and enjoyments, prior and external distinctions, do not modify the possession of spiritual privilege and blessing. In the spiritual commonwealth, no partition is erected between Jew and Greek; the barbarian is not degraded to a lower seat, nor is any outer court appropriated for the Scythian. The slave does not obtrude though he mingle his voice in the same song of spiritual freedom with his master, and drink out of the same sacramental cup. The Tartar in his sheepskin may kneel with the citizen in his mantle, and each break with the other that bread which is "the communion of the body of Christ." Nay, the faith of the untutored savage may be more earnest, childlike, and fearless in its reliance; may be a fuller source of gladness and triumph than the faith of him whose philosophy may have prompted him to ask other reasons than Scripture may have given, and to fortify his belief with arguments which the simple disciple did not want, and could not understand.

Oh, it needs not that one enjoy the erudition of the schools in order to be taught of God! The graces of civilization are not the necessary soil for the graces of the Spirit. Secular enfranchisement is not indispensable to fellow-citizenship with the saints. In the sphere of the new man, those distinctions which obtain in the world exercise no disturbing or preventive influence. That new man has broken all the ties of the old man, and is not more akin to one race than to another, has no affinities of blood, is not circumscribed by national boundaries, or forbidden by the inequalities of social rank, and by whomsoever assumed, he may be fully possessed. This is the glory of Christianity, that as it is developed in the church, it has none of the barriers or predilections which the epithets of this verse indicate as obtaining in the world, and dividing it into jealous and exclusive ranks and castes, but is at once and fully enjoyed by all the believing possessors of our common humanity. The idea of Theophylact, that the verse refers to the absence of distinctions in the other world, is wholly opposed to the scope and context.

The apostle now particularizes certain graces which they were to assume. He had specified the sins which marked the old man, and now he signalizes those virtues which are connected with the new man. Ye have put on the new man, and ye enjoy the all-sufficiency of Christ—therefore, *οὖν*, ye must manifest your possession of the following elements of Christian character—

(Ver. 12.) *'Ενδύσασθε οὖν, ὡς ἐκλεκτοὶ τοῦ Θεοῦ, ἅγιοι καὶ ἠγαπημένοι*—"Put on, therefore, as the chosen of God, holy and beloved." While *οὖν* refers back to one argument, *ὡς* carries the mind forward to another. In the epithet *ἐκλεκτοί* we recognize the fact of their separation from the world, or the realization in their present state of God's eternal and gracious choice. We incline, with Meyer and Lachmann, to regard *ἐκλεκτοί* as the substantive, and the other two epithets as its predicates. Others, as Luther, Calvin, Bähr, Huther, and De Wette, reverse this exegesis, and take the two following words as co-ordinate substantives. But it is better to take *ἐκλεκτοί* as describing their present position, and *ἅγιοι* and *ἠγαπημένοι* as specifying its character, for election is not determined by character, but determines it. [Eph. i. 4, 5.] The meaning of *ἅγιοι* is consecrated, set apart to God, this consecration necessarily producing holiness of life. This is an appeal to their character, and not simply to their position in the visible church. [Eph. i. 1.] They were also the objects of God's special complacency—"beloved." His eternal and sovereign love did elect them, and now, that election having taken effect, He has special complacency in them. Their assumption of these graces would certify to themselves their election, would be a happy development of their consecration, as well as a proof of its genuineness, and would also endear them yet more to Him, who in love had predestinated them to the adoption of children. These thoughts formed a convincing appeal to them, and could not but induce them to feel and act as the apostle recommends. And so they are enjoined to put on—

Σπλάγχνα οἰκτιρμοῦ. The singular of the last word is preferred to the plural on the authority of A, C, D[3], E, F, G. The singular is also found in several places of the Septuagint. Dan. ix. 18; Zech. i. 16. The phrase is a Hebraism, corresponding to the Hebrew—רַחֲמִים. *Gesen. Lehrg.* p. 671. The following genitive, *οἰκτιρμοῦ*, gives a specific intensity to the clause; it makes it *ἐμφατικότερον*, as Chrysostom says; since the first word of itself might denote kind or merciful emotion. Luke i. 78. The Colossians were not to cherish a hard and unrelenting disposition, that was slow to remit punishment, but forward ever to inflict it.

Οἰκτιρμός, from *οἴ*—*οἶκτος* has more reference to feeling, or commiseration; while the second term, *χρηστότητα*, kindness, is, as the word really implies, that form of kindness which is serviceable to others. Jerome describes it as—*invitans ad familiaritatem sui, dulcis alloquio, moribus temperata.*[1] "To do good" is the injunction, and disciples are to cherish the habit, and to create opportunities for it. Christians are to be obliging in their general demeanour. The last three terms are found in the same order in Eph. iv. 2. *Ταπεινοφροσύνη* is lowliness of mind, opposed to haughtiness and conceit. The adjective, *ταπεινός*, is used often in the classics to denote "mean-spirited." Trench has the excellent remark, that "Chrysostom is bringing in pride under the disguise of humility, when he characterizes humility as the making of ourselves small when we are great, for it is the esteeming of ourselves small because we are so."[2] As the same writer well remarks, "the idea of such a grace is wholly Christian,[3] for the gospel leads man to a feeling of

[1] *Com. in Ep. ad Gal.* v. 22.

[2] *New Testament Synonyms*, § 42.

[3] The statement may not at first sight appear to be correct to its full extent. Æschylus, *Prometh. Vinct.*, makes Oceanus bring the following charge against Prometheus—σὺ δ' οὐδέπω ταπεινός—not even yet are you humble; that is, thou hast not learned submission by thy punishment. A similar result, viz. that of submissiveness, is said by Plutarch to be, in fact, the end of Divine chastisement—ταπεινὸς καὶ κατάφοβος πρὸς τὸν Θεόν—*De sera numinis vindicatione*, cap. iii. Instances also may be found in Plato—ξυνέπεται ταπεινὸς καὶ κεκοσμημένος—*Leges*,

entire and unalterable dependence upon God." Augustine eulogizes this grace by saying, that if asked *quae via sit ad obtinendam veritatem?* he will reply, *primum est humilitas, quid secundum, humilitas, quid tertium, humilitas,* etc. Calvin remarks on the connection, that the graces previously mentioned cannot be cherished without it.

The next term is *πρᾳότης*, meekness. We cannot fully acquiesce in Mr. Trench's idea, that this word describes "exercises of mind which are first and chiefly toward God, or is that temper of spirit in which we accept His dealings with us without disputing or resisting." Neither he, nor Ellicott,[1] who follows him, has produced any direct scriptural instance of such a sense, though certainly he who is truly meek will always bow to God in serene resignation. He who, under the influence of Divine grace, does not resent a human injury, will not quarrel with any Divine allotment. But *πρᾳότης* is here ranked among graces which have specially human relations, such as mercy and long-suffering. Even in *ταπεινοφροσύνη*, the idea is man-ward fully as much as God-ward. In the place it here occupies in the range of virtues, it denotes that want of arrogance or insolence in reference to our fellow-men, which lowliness before God ever tends to produce and increase. *Μακροθυμία* is literally "long-mindedness," and is opposed to what we often call shortness of temper. All the terms of the text receive further illustration in the subsequent clauses.

Now, these virtues certainly suit—ὡς—"the elect of God, holy and beloved." They are in source and essence an imitation on the part of the saint of what God has felt towards him, and they indicate a consciousness of the relation which he sustains to the Divine benefactor. For he has experienced the Divine mercy in its sweep and fulness—there was no frown on the Divine countenance, when he so

iv. p. 113, vol. viii. ed. Bekker, and in other places; Ast, *Lex. Platon. sub voce.* Still, the idea in these places seems to be that of a sense of lowliness inwrought by some depressing event, and forced upon the mind by some painful contrast. This is not the habitual grace of Christian humility, for a man who may feel himself to be deeply humiliated, will yet only recoil into a fiercer pride, and be far, far indeed, from being humble.

[1] *Grammatical Commentary on Ephesians*, iv. 2. London, 1855. [See Ellicott on the present passage.]

abject, insignificant, and withal so provoking and guilty, drew near. God has crowned him "with loving-kindness and tender mercy;" and though he be daily sinning, daily coming short of duty, nay, ever committing positive faults, he is borne with, and he has been long borne with, as "sentence against an evil work has not been speedily executed." Must he not therefore act toward his fellows on the same level with himself, as God from the heights of His glory has acted towards him? And there is need for the exercise of such virtues, for "offences must come;" or, as the apostle intimates in the next clause—

(Ver. 13.) *'Ανεχόμενοι ἀλλήλων, καὶ χαριζόμενοι ἑαυτοῖς, ἐάν τις πρός τινα ἔχῃ μομφήν*—"Forbearing one another, and forgiving one another, if any one have a complaint against any other." The meaning of the first participle has been illustrated under Eph. iv. 2, and we need not in this place repeat the illustration. The sense is, having patience with one another—waiting with composure under injury or provocation, till those who so offend may come to a better mind. The other participle, *χαριζόμενοι*, carries forward the sense—not only are we to forbear, but we are also to forgive. Not only are we to show humility, meekness, and long-suffering as we forbear, but we are also to manifest bowels of mercy and goodness in forgiving. The second participle, *χαριζόμενοι*, is found in a passage almost parallel, in Eph. iv. 32, and it also occurs in the same sense in ii. 13 of this epistle. The pronoun *ἑαυτοῖς* is simply for *ἀλλήλοις*; and the noun *μομφή* denotes "ground of offence or complaint," explained in some of the Codices by the substitution of *ὀργή*. There may be just ground of offence, but it is not to excite to resentment or retaliation. And the apostle proposes for imitation the highest of examples.

Καθὼς καὶ ὁ Χριστὸς ἐχαρίσατο ὑμῖν, οὕτως καὶ ὑμεῖς. Χαριζόμενοι is to be supplied, and not the imperative, *χαρίζεσθε*, with some, nor yet *ποιεῖτε*, as is found in some MSS., such as D[1], E[1], F, G. The conjunction occurs twice, for the sake of intensity (Klotz, *ad Devar.* 635), and *καθὼς καί* introduces an argumentative illustration. In a corresponding passage in the Epistle to the Ephesians, the apostle makes reference to God—"forgiving one another, even as

God for Christ's sake has forgiven you." iv. 32. This difference of person in the two places seems to have suggested the various readings which occur in the old copies. Not a few of them have κύριος, such as A, B, D^1, F, G, and those appear to be almost equal in authority to C, D^3, E, J, K, which have Χριστός, a reading supported, however, by many of the Versions and Fathers. But here forgiveness is specially ascribed to Christ. If Christ forgive sin, the inference is, that He is Divine. Pardon is a Divine prerogative, yet Christ exercises it. And it is not on His part a venturesome act, nor one which is provisional, and cannot take effect till it receive the sanction of the Father, but it is at once full, decided, and final. The Saviour gave the paralytic patient a complex benefit in a single act, when He said to him as he lay helpless on a couch at His feet, "Thy sins be forgiven thee." And if Christ forgive sin, He is entitled to do so, for He has made provision for it in His sufferings and death. May He not Himself dispense the fruits of His atonement, and pardon those for whom He died? The general idea is the same as that of Eph. iv. 32. Christians are to forgive one another because Christ has forgiven them, for His example has all the force of a formal command. They are also to forgive one another as He has forgiven them—fully and freely, at once and for ever; not pardoning seven times, but demurring to the seventy times seven; not insulting him who has injured them by the rigid exaction of a humiliating apology, or stinging him by a sharp and unexpected allusion to his fault; not harbouring antipathy, but forgetting as well as forgiving; not indulging a secret feeling of offence, and waiting for a moment of quiet retaliation; but expelling every grudge from their hearts by an honest and thorough reconciliation. Meyer expressly condemns the reference, found by Chrysostom and Theophylact, to the medium by which Christ forgives, to wit, His own death, their inference being, that we ought to lay down our lives for others. We should also demur to this full form of expression on the part of these Fathers as being a necessary deduction here. The doctrine is found, however, in other parts of Scripture, as in 1 John iii. 16. But perhaps we may be warranted to say, that as in the case of Christ's pardoning us, there was a self-denial even unto death—so with us, there should be self-denial too. There may be a painful effort, but it should be made—the forgiveness may cost us no little sacrifice, but we must not shrink from it. Such a doctrine seems to be implied, though we cannot say as firmly as Chrysostom, that the proper interpretation of καθώς demands it—τὸ γὰρ, Καθὼς, ταῦτα ἀπαιτεῖ.

(Ver. 14.) Ἐπὶ πᾶσι δὲ τούτοις τὴν ἀγάπην. The construction still depends on ἐνδύσασθε of the 12th verse. Looking at the figure implied in the verb, some, such as Gataker and Meyer, give to ἐπί the sense of "over," as if the meaning were—on those other parts of spiritual raiment throw this, as an over-dress. But such an exegesis appears to press the figure. Nor can the preposition bear the sense which Calvin puts upon it of *propter*, that is, ye cannot exhibit these graces unless ye have love. Ἐπί means "in addition to," with the idea implied, that what follows is chief or best. Luke xvi. 26. In addition to all these, as last and best, "put on love." Ἀγάπη is the grace of love, on the beauty, propriety, and excellence of which the apostle so often insists. [Eph. i. 1, 4.] We take the next clause in its plain sense—

Ὅ ἐστι σύνδεσμος τῆς τελειότητος—"Which is the bond of perfectness," that bond which unites all the graces into completeness and symmetry. Ἥτις is the reading of the Received Text, but ὅ is found in such high authorities as A, B, C, F, G. It weakens the sense to regard the clause as a species of Hebraism, as if it meant "a perfect bond;" or as Erasmus renders it in his paraphrase—*perfectum et indissolubile vinculum*. Such is the view of Melancthon, Vatablus, Balduin, Michaelis, Calovius, Estius, Grotius, Wolf, Rosenmüller, and Flatt. The apostle here calls love, not perfection, but its bond, or that which holds together all the graces which constitute it. Some, indeed, as Bretschneider, Bengel, Usteri, Böhmer, De Wette, and Olshausen, take the term in the sense of *fasciculus*, *Inbegriff*—not that which binds, but that which is bound up. In a similar sense, Calvin and Böhmer take it for *summa*. The two interpretations differ, as do the German words *Band* and *Bund* (*Bündel*), or the English bond and bundle. There is one passage of Herodian appealed to, where the word has such a meaning—πάντα τὸν σύνδεσμον τῶν ἐπιστολῶν, the whole package or bundle of letters. But that is not the common meaning of the term, either in the classics or the New Testament. The noun τελειότης, as an abstract term with the article, describes moral perfection as a whole. Perfection consists of many graces, each in its own place and relations, each in its own circle and sphere—but they are held together by love. Did they exist singly, or in separate clusters, perfection would not be enjoyed; were they fragmentary, and not coalescent, symmetry of character would be lost.

For love is the product of the other graces, the fruit of their ripe development, so that in their perfect state they should throw around them this preserving cincture. Love itself is, at the same time, the highest element of this perfection, and forms the nearest resemblance to Him of whom it is said—"God is love." It creates perfection, but here it is specially represented as a bond which sustains it. No grace is complete without it. Without it, knowledge is but a selfish acquisition, purity an attempted personal gain, and zeal a defective struggle; uninspired by it, faith is but an abortive and monopolizing grasp, and hope an exclusive anticipation. Sin is essentially selfishness in a variety of forms, and not till such selfishness be fully put down, can the semblance of perfection be enjoyed. Love to God and to every one that bears His image, as the fulfilment of the law, imparting fervour and breadth to every grace, giving odour to the blossom, and being itself the fruit, is the bond of perfectness. A heart replete with this love maintains all its spiritual acquirements in health and vigour. Bound up in this zone, every Christian excellence fills its own place, and keeps it, and the whole character is sound, does not distort itself by excess, nor enfeeble itself by defect. [Eph. iv. 15, v. 2.]

Love is thus regarded here, not as a congeries of graces, which make up perfection—as Bengel says—*amor complectitur virtutum universitatem.* It is more its office than itself which the apostle regards. It is not looked upon here as containing perfection within itself, but as so uniting the other graces that it gives them perfection and keeps them in it. Meyer shrewdly says, that if love, as a bundle, contained all the other graces in it already, how could the apostle bid them assume love in addition to them?—ἐπὶ πᾶσι τούτοις. If they were to put on all its parts, how could they assume it as something still distinct? Huther takes the neuter ὅ as referring to the preceding clause,—love, the putting on of which is the bond of perfection. But the apostle's idea is, not that the putting on of the love, but that the love, when put on, is the bond of perfectness. Our view is not unlike that of Chrysostom and Theodoret. Some of the older interpreters labour to reconcile the statement of the apostle with his doctrine of justification by faith, and Romish writers pressed them hard on the subject. Crocius and Schmid refer this perfection simply to the unity or integrity of the church, which love creates and preserves. But though this be not the precise meaning of the apostle, it is certainly included under his statement, and this idea, coupled with the phraseology of Eph. iv. 3, may have led one of the copyists to insert ἑνότητος. What is the bond of perfectness to an individual is also the bond of perfectness to a church.[1] [Eph. iv. 3, 14, 15, v. 2]; 1 Pet. iii. 8.

[1] "Let us consider that charity is a right noble and worthy thing; greatly perfective of our nature; much dignifying and beautifying our soul. It rendereth a man truly great, enlarging his mind unto a vast circumference, and to a capacity near infinite; so that it by a general care doth reach all things, by an universal affection doth embrace and grasp the world. By it our reason obtaineth a field or scope of employment worthy of it, not confined to the slender interests of one person or one place, but extending to the concerns of all men. Charity is the imitation and copy of that immense love, which is the fountain of all being and all good; which made all things, which preserveth the world, which sustaineth every creature; nothing advanceth us so near to a resemblance of Him, who is essential love and goodness; who freely and purely, without any regard to his own advantage or capacity of finding any beneficial return, doth bear and express the highest good-will, with a liberal hand pouring down showers of bounty and mercy on all His creatures; who daily putteth up numberless indignities and injuries, upholding and maintaining those who offend and provoke Him. Charity rendereth us as angels, or peers to those glorious and blessed creatures, who, without receiving or expecting any requital from us, do heartily desire and delight in our good, are ready to promote it, do willingly serve and labour for it. Nothing is more amiable, more admirable, more venerable, even in the common eye and opinion of men; it hath in it a beauty and a majesty apt to ravish every heart; even a spark of it in generosity of dealing breedeth admiration, a glimpse of it in formal courtesy of behaviour procureth much esteem, being deemed to accomplish and adorn a man: how lovely, therefore, and truly gallant, is an entire, sincere, constant, and uniform practice thereof, issuing from pure good-will and affection!"—Barrow's *Works*, vol. i. pp. 250, 251, Edinburgh, 1841.

The apostle still continues his exhortation—

(Ver. 15.) *Καὶ ἡ εἰρήνη τοῦ Χριστοῦ βραβευέτω ἐν ταῖς καρδίαις ὑμῶν*—"And let the peace of Christ rule in your hearts." The reading *Χριστοῦ* is preferred to the common one of *Θεοῦ*, on good authority, such as A, B, C[1], D[1], F, G, and various Versions and Fathers. Some regard this peace as the result of the preceding admonitions—the peace of mutual concord. Such is the view of no less distinguished critics than the Greek expositors, and of Calvin, Grotius, Vatablus, Calovius, and Meyer. Chrysostom's illustration is as follows: —"Suppose a man to have been unjustly insulted, two thoughts are born of the insult, the one urging him to vengeance, and the other to patience, and these wrestle with one another. If the peace of God stand as umpire, it bestows the prize on that which calls to endurance, and puts the other to shame." We cannot embrace this exegesis, for we regard it as narrow and unusual. "Peace" is commonly with the apostle a far higher blessing than mere harmony with others, or the study of Christian union. It is with him synonymous with happiness, that calm of mind which is not ruffled by adversity, overclouded by sin or a remorseful conscience, or disturbed by the fear and the approach of death. Isa. xxvi. 3. This view is, generally, that of Luther, Bengel, De Wette, Bähr, Olshausen, and Huther. Nor is it out of harmony with the context. For nothing is more fatal to such "peace" than the indulgence of those foul and angry passions which the apostle warns them to abandon in the preceding verses (5 to 9), and there is nothing so conducive to its purity and permanence as the cultivation of those serene and genial graces which are enjoined in verses 12, 13, and 14. It is almost as if he had said—those vices being dropt, and those virtues being assumed, the peace of Christ shall therefore reign within you, and its happy sensations you will be led naturally to express "in psalms, hymns, and spiritual songs."

It is called "the peace of Christ," a phrase not essentially different in meaning from the common one, "peace of God." It is given by Christ, or produced and perpetuated by His Spirit. It is the Redeemer's own legacy—John xiv. 27, "My peace I give unto you; let not your hearts be troubled, neither let them be dismayed." Christ has secured this peace in His blood as Mediator, and He has the right to dispense it as the result of the reconciliation or atonement.

And such tranquillity, which in its highest aspect is Christian felicity, was not simply to be in their hearts, but it was to "rule" in them; it was not merely to have existence, but it was to exercise supreme command. For such is the meaning of βραβευέτω, as it naturally comes from its original and literal signification of presiding at the games, and then of distributing the rewards of victory. Both senses have, however, been separately maintained by critics; Chrysostom adhering to the idea of adjudication—κριτὴς καὶ ἀγωνοθέτης; and Œcumenius employing in explanation the verb μεσιτεύειν. Calvin, Erasmus, and Vatablus look upon it as the figure of a wrestler who himself wins the prize—let this peace obtain the prize and keep it; but the view is against sound philology, for the word is never used of the combatant, but only of the umpire. Nor can we accept the view of Huther, Wahl, and Bretschneider, who refer generally to the idea of βραβεῖον implied in ii. 18, and understand the apostle to say, "let the peace of God confer its rewards upon you." Nor is there more foundation for the opposite idea of Kypke, who supposes it to mean specially, "let the peace of God distribute the prize of love in your hearts." The general and very frequent sense we have already assigned to the verb is preferable, and such is the opinion of many commentators, supported by numerous examples. Diodorus Sic. 13, 53, etc.; Wisdom x. 12. Loesner has collected many examples from Philo. This peace was to possess undisputed supremacy—was to be uncontrolled president in their hearts.

'Εν ταῖς καρδίαις ὑμῶν. Let it not be a state of mind admired or envied, but one actually possessed; let it not be hovering as a hoped-for blessing on the outskirts of your spirits, but let it be within you; let it not be an occasional visitant, often scared away by dominant and usurping passion, but a central power, exercising a full and unlimited administration. Let it so govern, and happiness will be the result, every source of disquietude and element of turbulence being destroyed. The apostle thus wished the Colossians highest spiritual welfare, that their souls might enjoy unbroken quiet.

A peace, which is not the peace of Christ, is often rudely disturbed, for it is but a dream and a slumber in the midst of volcanic powers, which are employing the time in gathering up their energies for a more awful conflict. There is no question, if a man possessed and cherished the ripe consciousness of his interest in Christ, if he had full assurance, and felt that God was for him—if the elements of sinful passion, either in its fouler forms of sensuality, or its darker aspects of malignity, were subdued; and if "the gentleness of Christ" were at home within him, and all the graces which possess a kindred character were around him, bound and held together by that "love which is the bond of perfectness," that then he would enjoy a peace or a bliss second only to the elevation and felicity of heaven. Phil. iv. 7. And it was no audacity in them to seek or cultivate that peace, for to it they had been called.

Εἰς ἣν καὶ ἐκλήθητε—"To which ye were also, or indeed were, called." This verb is often used by the apostle. Eph. iv. 1. The possession of this peace was a prime end of their Christianity. The gospel summons a man, not to misery, but to happiness—not to internal discord, but to ultimate peace. And they were called to the possession of it—

Ἐν ἑνὶ σώματι—"In one body;" not *εἰς ἓν σῶμα*—"into one body," that is, so as to form one body. But the meaning is, that they already formed one body, or that unitedly they had been called to the possession of peace. And the apostle adds—

Καὶ εὐχάριστοι γίνεσθε—"And be ye thankful." [Eph. v. 4, 20.] Not a few take the adjective in the sense of friendly, as if the apostle bade them cherish amicable feelings to one another. This is the view of Jerome, of Calvin, Suicer, a-Lapide, Bähr, Steiger, and Olshausen, who give *εὐχάριστοι* the sense of *χρηστοί* in Eph. iv. 32. Calvin renders *amabiles sitis;* and Conybeare "be thankful one to another." With Huther, Olshausen, De Wette, and Meyer, we prefer the meaning "thankful"—that is, towards God. The former sense abounds in the classics, and though the latter is found there too, yet it seems to be wholly contrary to the usage of the kindred terms in the New Testament. For there is every cause of thankfulness to Him who had called them to the possession of such peace. If that peace dwelt within them, and reigned within them—if Christ had at once provided it for them, and summoned them unitedly to its enjoyment, surely profound gratitude was due to such a benefactor.

(Ver. 16.) *Ὁ λόγος τοῦ Χριστοῦ ἐνοικείτω ἐν ὑμῖν πλουσίως*—"Let the word of Christ dwell in you richly." Lachmann and Steiger propose to read this clause parenthetically, and to join the previous *γίνεσθε* to the following participles—*διδάσκοντες*, etc. But nothing is gained by such a distribution. For *Χριστοῦ*, a few authorities and Fathers read *Θεοῦ*; and the Coptic and Clement read *κυρίου*. "The word of Christ" is the gospel, the doctrine of Christ, or the truth which has Christ for its subject. In fact, Christ is both the giver of the oracle and its theme. By *ἐν ὑμῖν* is meant, not simply among you—*unter euch*, as Luther translates, or as De Wette contends. Let the Christian truth have its enduring abode "within you"—let it be no stranger or occasional guest in your hearts. Let it not be without you, as a lesson to be learned, but within you, as the source of cherished and permanent illumination. Let it stay within you—*πλουσίως*, abundantly. That is, let it be completely understood, or let the soul be fully under its influence. Let it dwell not with a scanty foothold, but with a large and liberal occupancy.

Different ideas have been formed of the best mode of dividing the following clauses of the verse. Our translators, following the Peschito, Chrysostom, and Luther, Calvin, and Beza, add the words "in all wisdom" to the clause which we have already considered. But the idea of wisdom is better joined to the following clause, which refers to mutual teaching—"in all wisdom teaching and admonishing one another." Our translators, too, so point the verse as to make psalms and hymns the material of instruction, whereas it seems better, and more appropriate, to keep the clause distinct, thus—"Let the word of Christ dwell in you richly; in all wisdom teaching and admonishing one another: in psalms, hymns, and spiritual songs, singing with grace in your hearts unto the Lord."[1]

[1] Τίς ἐστιν ὁ λόγος τοῦ Χριστοῦ; τὰ λόγιά εἰσι τοῦ ἁγίου εὐαγγελίου καὶ τῶν θεοφόρων ἀποστόλων καὶ τῶν θείων προφητῶν· Πῶς δὲ ἐνοικεῖ ἐν ἡμῖν ὁ λόγος τοῦ θεοῦ ἐν

The words *ἐν πάσῃ σοφίᾳ* are thus connected as they are in i. 28, and such is the view, among others, of Bengel, Storr, Bähr, Steiger, Olshausen, and Baumgarten-Crusius. See under i. 28, where the participles—*διδάσκοντες, καὶ νουθετοῦντες*—occur, though in reverse order, and where they are also explained. The anakoluthon which occurs in the construction is almost necessary, and gives special prominence to the ideas expressed by the participles. The duty enjoined in this clause has a very close connection with that enjoined in the preceding one. Unless the word of Christ dwelt richly within them, they could not fulfil this duty; for they could not teach and admonish unless they knew what lessons to impart, and in what spirit to communicate them; but the lessons and the spirit alike were to be found in the gospel. Mutual exhortation must depend for its fitness and utility on mutual knowledge of the Christian doctrine. Sparing acquaintance with Divine revelation would lead to scanty counsel and ineffective tuition.

Ψαλμοῖς, ὕμνοις, ᾠδαῖς πνευματικαῖς, ἐν τῇ χάριτι ᾄδοντες ἐν ταῖς καρδίαις ὑμῶν τῷ Θεῷ. Both the conjunctions (*καί*) which appear in the Received Text seem, on good authority, to be mere euphonistic insertions. Some take the words down to *χάριτι*, as connected with the preceding participles—"admonishing one another in psalms, hymns, and spiritual songs." Our objection is, that while metrical or musical compositions are not the common vehicle of instruction or admonition, they are specially connected with sacred song. The datives, without the preposition, denote the materials of song. The phrase *ἐν τῇ χάριτι*, according to Huther and De

πάσῃ σοφίᾳ; διὰ τῆς ἀκροάσεως καὶ ἀναγνώσεως καὶ μελέτης τῶν θείων γραφῶν· Ὅταν ταῦτα συχνῶς τε καὶ ἐπιμελῶς μελετῶμεν, τότε καὶ ἡ μνήμη πληροῦται, καὶ ὁ νοῦς πλουτίζεται, καὶ ἡ καρδία ἐξερεύγεται, καὶ τὸ στόμα ἐκχέει πλούσια τῆς θείας διδασκαλίας τὰ νάματα· Ἐπειδὴ δέ τινες μετὰ ὑπερηφανείας καὶ ἰδιογνωμοσύνης μελετῶντες τὰς θείας γραφὰς πίπτουσιν εἰς τῶν αἱρέσεων τὰ βάραθρα, ἄλλοι δὲ ἀμαθῶς καὶ ἀπερισκέπτως αὐτὰς ἀναγινώσκοντες, καὶ μὴ διακρίνοντες τὴν ἐντολὴν ἀπὸ τῆς συμβουλῆς, γίνονται δεισιδαίμονες καὶ κεκαυτηριασμένοι "Τὴν ἰδίαν συνείδησιν·" διὰ τοῦτο εἶπε τὸ, "Ἐν πάσῃ σοφίᾳ," ἤγουν, ἵνα μετὰ παντὸς εἴδους σοφίας, καὶ τῆς πνευματικῆς δηλονότι καὶ τῆς σχολαστικῆς, καὶ τῆς εὐλαβητικῆς διαθέσεως καὶ τῆς ὀρθῆς διακρίσεως καὶ ἀναγινώσκωμεν, καὶ μελετῶμεν τὰς θείας γραφὰς, καὶ διδάσκωμεν δι' αὐτῶν καὶ ἑαυτοὺς καὶ τοὺς ἄλλους· ΝΙΚΗΦΟΡΟΥ ΘΕΟΤΟΚΟΥ ΤΟΥ ΑΣΤΡΑΧΑΝΙΟΥ ΚΑΙ ΣΤΑΥΡΟΥΠΟΛΕΩΣ ΑΡΧΙΕΠΙΣΚΟΠΟΥ ΚΥΡΙΑΚΟΔΡΟΜΙΟΝ, ΤΟΜΟΣ ΠΡΩΤΟΣ, p. 155, ΕΝ ΑΘΗΝΑΙΣ, 1840.

Wette, means "with a grateful spirit." 1 Cor. x. 30. It appears to us wholly out of the question on the part of Calvin, Beza, a-Lapide, Bähr, and many others, to take the words as denoting εὐσχημόνως, "gracefully"—*sine confusione.* We prefer, with Estius, Steiger, and Meyer, to regard the phrase as meaning by the influence of grace, given, as Chrysostom remarks, by the Spirit. Luther joins the phrase erroneously to the preceding term. The following dative, τῷ Θεῷ, indicates Him in honour of whom this sacred minstrelsy is raised, and the formula ἐν ταῖς καρδίαις describes the sincerity of the service, —the silent symphony of the heart. Tischendorf appears to us to have forsaken his own critical principles in retaining the singular form τῇ καρδίᾳ, for he has confessedly against him A, B, C^1, D^1, F, G, the Syriac which reads ܒܠܒܘܬܟܘܢ, and the Vulgate, which has—*in cordibus vestris.* For remarks on the different terms, and their distinction, the reader is referred to what has been said by us under Eph. v. 19. We have there said that probably by Psalms may be understood the Hebrew book of that name, so commonly used in the synagogues; that the hymns might be other compositions divested of Jewish imagery and theocratic allusions, and more adapted to the heathen mind; while the spiritual odes were freer forms of song, the effusion of personal experience and piety, and do not simply point out the genus to which the entire class of such compositions belonged.

Still the sentiment hangs on the first clause—"let the word of Christ dwell within you nobly." These sacred songs, whether in the language of Scripture, or based upon it, could be sung in the right spirit only when the indwelling "word" pressed for grateful utterance. When the gospel so possessed the heart as to fill it with a sense of blessing, then the lips might be tuned to song. Experimental acquaintance with Christianity could only warrant the chanting of the sacred ode.[1]

[1] The following is a portion of Basil's encomium on the Psalms, referred to by us in Ephesians:—"Psalmody is the calm of the soul, the repose of the spirit, the arbiter of peace: it silences the wave, and conciliates the whirlwind of our passions, soothing that which is impetuous, and tempering that which is unchaste. Psalmody is an engenderer of friendship, a healer of dissension, a reconciler of those who were inimical; for who can longer account that man his

(Ver. 17.) *Καὶ πᾶν ὅ τι ἂν ποιῆτε, ἐν λόγῳ ἢ ἐν ἔργῳ, πάντα ἐν ὀνόματι Κυρίου Ἰησοῦ*—"And whatever ye do in word or in deed, do all of it in the name of the Lord Jesus," or "Whatever ye are in the custom of doing," etc. On the use of *ἂν* with the present, see Winer, § 42, 3, *b*, (*β*). This concluding precept is general in its nature. Some take *πᾶν*, with Flatt and Bähr, in an absolute case, others think it better to regard it as repeated in the plural form *πάντα*. Meyer takes the whole clause, as far as *ἔργῳ*, as an absolute nominative. There is an earnest rapidity in the composition which may easily excuse any rhetorical anomaly. The rule laid down by Kühner is, that a word of special importance is placed at the beginning of a sentence in the nominative, to represent it emphatically as the fundamental subject of the whole sentence, § 508. No doubt, special emphasis is laid on *πᾶν*, for the apostle's idea is, that while some things are done formally in the name of the Lord Jesus, *everything* should be done really in it. The imperative *ποιεῖτε* is to be

enemy, with whom to the throne of God he hath raised the strain? Wherefore that first of blessings, Christian love, is diffused by psalmody, which devises the harmonious concert as a bond of union, and connects the people in choral symphonies. Psalmody repels the dæmons; it lures the ministry of angels; a weapon of defence in nightly terrors, a respite from daily toil; to the infant a presiding genius, to manhood a resplendent crown, a balm of comfort to the aged, a congenial ornament to women. It renders the desert populous, and appeases the forum's tumult; to the initiated an elementary instruction, to proficients a mighty increase, a bulwark unto those who are perfected in knowledge. It is the church's voice. This exhilarates the banquet; this awakens that pious sorrow which has reference to God. Psalmody, from a heart of adamant can excite the tear: psalmody is the employment of angels, the delight of Heaven, and spiritual frankincense. Oh! the sapient design of our Instructor, appointing that at once we should be recreated by song, and informed by wisdom. Thus, the precepts of instruction are more deeply engraven on our hearts: for the lessons which we receive unwillingly have a transient continuance; but those which charm and captivate in the hearing, are permanently impressed upon our souls.—From hence may not everything be acquired? Hence mayest thou not be taught whatever is dignified in fortitude, whatever is consummate in justice, whatever is venerable in temperance, whatever is sublime in wisdom? Here the nature of penitence is unfolded; patience is here exemplified. Is there a blessing to be named, which here resides not? The splendours of theology beam effulgent; Jesus is predicted; the resurrection is announced; judgment is proclaimed; the sword of vengeance is unsheathed; crowns of glory glitter; speechless mysteries astonish. All these are treasured up in the book of Psalms, as in a common treasury of the soul."—Boyd's translation, London, 1834.

supplied. The plural *πάντα* individualizes what has been put collectively under the singular *πᾶν*. As for the whole of what you do in word or in act, let every part or separate element of it be done in the name of the Lord Jesus. The apostle has just spoken of formal religious service, and surely it is to be done in the name of the Lord Jesus. But not it alone —all speech and action must be imbued with the same spirit.

But what is meant by the phrase—"in the name of"? [Eph. v. 20.] The Greek Fathers explain it widely—*αὐτὸν καλεῖν βοηθόν*. Jerome is farther in error when he renders it—*ad honorem*, for that would represent *εἰς* with the accusative. Vitringa, *Observat. Sac.* p. 327, says that the phrase corresponds to לְשֵׁם. It rather corresponds to בְּשֵׁם, and strictly means—by his authority, or generally, in recognition of it. To speak in His name, or to act in His name, is to speak and act not to His honour, but under His sanction and with the conviction of His approval. This is the highest Christian morality, a vivid and practical recognition of Christ in everything said or done. Not simply in religious service, but in the business of daily life; not merely in psalms, hymns, and spiritual songs, but in the language of friendship and of bargain, of the forum and the fireside; not simply in deeds which, in their very aspect, are a Christian compliance, such as almsgiving, or sacramental communion, but in every act, in solitude and in society, in daily toil, in the occupations of trade, or negotiations of commerce. This is a high test. It is comparatively easy to engage in religious discourse, but far more difficult to discourse on everything in a religious spirit; comparatively easy to do a professedly Christian act, but far more difficult to do every act in a Christian spirit. In the one case the mind sets a watch upon itself, and speaks and acts under the immediate consciousness of its theme and purpose, but in the other, the heart is so influenced by religious feeling, that without an effort it acknowledges the name of Christ. Men may for the occasion solemnize themselves, and word and act may be in direct homage to Christ, but the season of such necessity passes away, and the sensations it had created lose their hold. Thus the associations of the Sabbath fade during the week, and the emotions of the sanctuary lose themselves in the market-place.

Still, the apostle does not inculcate any familiar or fanatical use of Christ's name, it is not to be mixed up with the phrases of colloquial life. A man is not to say, in Christ's name I salute thee, or in Christ's name I buy this article or sell that one, charter this vessel, or engage in that speculation. But the apostle means, that such ought to be the habitual respect to Christ's authority, such the constant and practical influence of His word within us, that even without reference to Him, or express consultation of Him, all we say and do should be said and done in His spirit, and with the persuasion that He approves. Christianity should ever guard and regulate amidst all secular engagements, and its influence should hallow all the relations and engagements of life. This is the grand desideratum, the universal reign of the Christian spirit. The senator may not discuss Christian dogmas in the midst of national interests, but his whole procedure must be regulated, not by faction or ambition, but by that enlightened patriotism, which, based on justice, is wise enough to know that true policy can never contravene morality, and is benignant enough to admit that other states are interlinked with our progress, and that the world is one vast brotherhood. The merchant is not to digress into a polemical dispute while he is concluding a sale, but love of profit is not to supersede rectitude, nor is the maxim, that there is no friendship in trade, ever to lead him to take undue advantage, or accomplish by dexterity what equity would scarcely permit. The tradesman, as he lifts his tool, is not to say, in Christ's name I strike; but in the spirit of Him who was among His disciples, "as one that serveth" is he faithfully to finish the labour assigned him, ever feeling himself to be under the "great taskmaster's eye." Art, science, literature, politics and business, should be all baptized into the spirit of Christ.

Εὐχαριστοῦντες τῷ Θεῷ καὶ Πατρὶ δι' αὐτοῦ—"Giving thanks to God even the Father by Him." The sentiment is found in Eph. v. 20, more pointedly and fully expressed, and in almost the same connection. As ye give thanks to God by Christ, so think all and speak all in Christ's name, who is the medium of thanksgiving. Blessings come through Him, and through Him thanks are to be rendered. With this clause, Kypke wrongly connects the previous one, thus—

"always in the name of the Lord Jesus giving thanks to God."

The apostle now comes to the inculcation of some special duties belonging to social and domestic life. Steiger, after Chrysostom and Theophylact, has remarked, that only in Epistles addressed to Asiatic churches do such formal exhortations occur, and he endeavours to account for it by the supposition that the liberty proclaimed by the false teachers had developed a dangerous licentiousness and taught a kind of Antinomian exemption from the rules and obligations of morality. It is true, as Meyer replies, that no direct polemical tendency is discernible in this section: still there must have been some reason why, in his letters to Asiatic communities, Paul dwells so strongly on this important branch of ethics. We may have little more than conjecture, yet we know that the apostle penned no paragraph in vain, and that there must have been more than accident in the fact that conjugal duty is not mentioned in the Epistles to Rome, Philippi, and Thessalonica, but is specially dwelt upon in those to Ephesus and Colosse, as also in the Apostle Peter's epistles to churches in the same region. The exhortations tendered by Paul to Titus as a Cretan pastor, when he touches on the same subject, have more of a general character, and those found in the epistle to the church in Corinth were called forth by peculiar queries. But here, and in the twin epistle, the apostle places special stress on the conjugal relationship, and its reciprocal obligations; as also on the relative duties of parents and children, of masters and slaves. Chrysostom gives, as the reason, that in such respects these churches were deficient, though he does not specify the source of such deficiency. His own homilies supply one form of illustration, for they abound in severest reproofs against the indecencies, luxuries, and immoralities of wedded life, and the picture is evidently taken from the state of manners that prevailed in the Byzantine capital, in which the discourses seem to have been delivered. It would thus appear that in the Asiatic cities there was great need to enforce the duties originated by the marriage tie, and it may be, that forms of false doctrine had a tendency to excite spurious notions of so-called Christian liberty. It is easy to conceive how a creed of boastful freedom would speedily work its way among slaves. The reader will not forget how, at the period of the Reformation, the principles of a licentious liberty were not only received, but to a great extent acted out by the Anabaptists of Munster.

(Ver. 18.) *Αἱ γυναῖκες, ὑποτάσσεσθε τοῖς ἀνδράσιν*—"Wives, submit yourselves to your husbands." The *ἰδίοις* of the Received Text has no good authority, and some manuscripts, such as D[1], E[1], F, G, add *ὑμῶν*, an evident gloss. The injunction has been fully considered under Eph. v. 25–33, where it is enforced by a special argument, and a tender analogy derived from the conjugal relation of Christ and His church. The submission which is inculcated on the part of the wife is wholly different in source and form from that slavery which is found in heathen lands, for it is the willing acquiescence which springs out of social position and wedded love, and is dictated at once by a wife's affection, and by her instinctive tendency to lean on her husband for support. The very satire which is heaped upon a wife who governs, or who attempts it, is a proof that society expects that fitting harmony of the hearth which the gospel recommends. The early and biblical idea of a wife as that of a "help meet," implies that she was to be auxiliary—second, and not principal in the household. Thus unity of domestic administration was to be secured by oneness of headship.

The apostle subjoins as a reason—*ὡς ἀνῆκεν ἐν Κυρίῳ.* Adopting a different punctuation, many, from Chrysostom to Winer and Schrader, join *ἐν κυρίῳ* to the verb *ὑποτάσσεσθε,* as if the meaning were—"be submissive in the Lord." The order of the words seems to forbid such an exegesis, and *ἐν κυρίῳ* is united by its position to *ἀνῆκεν*—"as is fitting in the Lord." In the imperfect form or time of the verb is implied, according to Winer, an appropriate hint that it had not been so with them at all times. § 40, 3; Bernhardy, 373. The translation then is—"as it should be in the Lord." This obligation of submission commenced with their union to the Lord, sprang out of it, and had not yet been fully discharged. It is therefore not a duty which had only newly devolved upon them, but its propriety reached back to the point of their conversion. Their union with the Lord not only expounded the obligation, but also enforced it.

Though the general strain of these exhortations be the same as in the Epistle to the Ephesians, there is usually some specific difference. In the other epistle he says, "wives, be obedient to your own husbands *as to the Lord*," where ὡς points out the nature, and not simply, as Ellicott thinks, the aspect of the obedience enjoined. The spirit of the obedience is referred to in Ephesians, and the becomingness of that spirit in the clause before us. How different from heathen principles, either that of Aristotle—*mores viri lex vitae*; or that of Cato, as repeated by Livy, that wives are simply *in manu virorum*.

(Ver. 19.) *Οἱ ἄνδρες, ἀγαπᾶτε τὰς γυναῖκας, καὶ μὴ πικραίνεσθε πρὸς αὐτάς*—"Ye husbands, love your wives." The duty is touchingly illustrated in Eph. v. 25, 26. The implication is, that the submission of the wife is gained by the love of the husband. Though the husband is to govern, he must govern in kindness. This duty is so plain that it needs no enforcement. The apostle then specifies one form in which the want of this love must have often shown itself—"and be not bitter against them." The tropical use of the verb is as obvious as is that of the noun in Eph. iv. 31. The verb, which is sometimes followed by ἐπί in the Septuagint, is here followed by πρός.[1] There is no doubt that the inconsistency here condemned was a common occurrence in heathen life, where a wife was but a legal concubine, and matrimony was not hallowed and ennobled by the Spirit of Him who wrought His first miracle to supply the means of enjoyment at a marriage feast. The apostle forbids that sour and surly objurgation which want of love will necessarily create; all that hard treatment in look and word, that unkind and churlish temper which defective attachment so often leads to. Wives are to submit, not indeed to guard against a frown or a chiding, but to ensure a deeper love. So that if this love is absent, such obedience will not be secured by perpetual irritation and fault-finding, followed by the free use of opprobrious and degrading epithets.

In Ephesians, the apostle proposes as the example Christ's love to the church in its fervour, self-sacrifice, and holy purpose, and also enjoins the husband to love his wife as himself,

[1] The verb occurs in the same sense in Philo, and is to some extent explained by Plutarch. See Kypke, *in loc.*

as being in truth a portion of himself (ὡς containing in it a species of argumentative comparison), but here the injunction is curt and unillustrated, followed only by the prohibition of a sin which a husband's indifference will most certainly induce. It would almost seem, however, as if the phrase, "as is fitting in the Lord," enforced both the duty recorded before it, and that which stands after it. Tertullian, in his address to his wife, written before he became a Montanist, describes the happiness of a marriage in the Lord in the following glowing terms:—"How can we find words to express the happiness of that marriage which the church effects, and the oblation confirms, and the blessing seals, and angels report, and the Father ratifies? What a union of two believers, with one hope, one discipline, one service, one spirit, and one flesh! Together they pray, together they prostrate themselves, and together keep their fasts, teaching and exhorting one another, and sustaining one another. They are together at the church and at the Lord's supper; they are together in straits, in persecutions, and refreshments. Neither conceals anything from the other; neither avoids the other; neither is a burden to the other; freely the sick are visited, and the needy relieved; alms without torture; sacrifices without scruple; daily diligence without hindrance; no using of the sign by stealth; no hurried salutation; no silent benediction; psalms and hymns resound between the two, and they vie with each other which shall sing best to their God. Christ rejoices on hearing and beholding such things; to such persons He sends His peace. Where the two are, He is Himself; and where He is, there the Evil One is not."[1]

[1] "Quale jugum fidelium duorum unius spei, unius disciplinæ, ejusdem servitutis! Ambo fratres, ambo conservi, nulla spiritus carnisve discretio. Atquin vere duo in carne una; ubi caro una, unus et spiritus. Simul orant, simul volutantur, et simul jejunia transigunt, alterutro docentes, alterutro hortantes, alterutro sustinentes. In ecclesia Dei pariter utrique, pariter in convivio Dei, pariter in angustiis, in persecutionibus, in refrigeriis; neuter alterum celat, neuter alterum vitat, neuter alteri gravis est; libere æger visitatur, indigens sustentatur; eleemosynæ sine tormento, sacrificia sine scrupulo, quotidiana diligentia sine impedimento; non furtiva signatio, non trepida gratulatio, non muta benedictio; sonant inter duos psalmi et hymni, et mutuo provocant, quis melius Deo suo cantet. Talia Christus videns et audiens gaudet, his pacem suam mittit; ubi duo, ibi et ipse; ubi et ipse, ibi et malus non est."—Tertull. *ad Uxorem*, ii. 9.

From conjugal the apostle naturally passes to parental duty.

(Ver. 20.) *Τὰ τέκνα, ὑπακούετε τοῖς γονεῦσι κατὰ πάντα*—"Children, obey your parents in all things." The wife is generally to be submissive, but children are to be obedient, to listen and execute parental commands, and to exemplify a special form of submission for which the filial relation affords so many opportunities. [Eph. vi. 1–3.] The love of the child's heart naturally leads it to obedience. Only an unnatural child can be a domestic rebel. Where the parents are Christians, and govern their children in a Christian spirit, obedience should be without exception, or—*κατὰ πάντα.* The apostle, speaking in reference to Christian parents, for his epistle could reach none but children of that class, takes no heed of any exception. The principle involved in his admonition is, that children are not the judges of what they should or should not obey in parental precepts.

The best reading of the following clause is *τοῦτο γὰρ εὐάρεστόν ἐστιν ἐν Κυρίῳ*—"For this is well-pleasing in the Lord," not as the older form had it, "well-pleasing to the Lord." The construction is similar to that of the 19th verse, the specific difference of thought being, that in the former case submission is an appropriate thing in the Lord; while in this case filial obedience is marked with special approbation, as being well-pleasing in the Lord. Resting on Christian principle and motive, it meets Divine approbation. In Eph. vi. 1, the apostle calls it—*δίκαιον*, a thing right in itself, and then he quotes the fifth commandment to show that such a duty is also inculcated in Scripture, but here he regards it simply in a religious aspect, and awards to it Christ's approval.

(Ver. 21.) *Οἱ πατέρες μὴ ἐρεθίζετε τὰ τέκνα ὑμῶν*—"Ye fathers, do not provoke your children." [Eph. vi. 4.] Authorities of no mean note give us *παροργίζετε*, a reading adopted by Griesbach, Scholz, and Lachmann, but which might slip into the text from Eph. vi. 4, though, certainly, it is found in A, C, D[1], E[1], F, G. The verb, as in 1 Macc. xv. 40, Deut. xxi. 20, is to irritate, to fret, to rouse to anger, and not, as in 2 Cor. ix. 2, to stir up to emulation. Fathers are spoken to since training is their duty, and because this peculiar sin which the apostle condemns is one to which they, and not mothers, are peculiarly liable. The paternal government must be one of kindness, without caprice; and of equity, without favouritism. The term includes greatly more than what Burton understands by it—"do not carry their punishment too far." The child, when chastised, should feel that the punishment is not the result of fretful anger; and when it obeys, its obedience should not be prompted, or rather forced, by menaced infliction. If children, let them do what they can, never please their father, if they are teazed and irritated by perpetual censure, if they are kept apart by uniform sternness, if other children around them are continually held up as immeasurably their superiors, if their best efforts can only moderate the parental frown, but never are greeted with the parental smile, then their spirit is broken, and they are discouraged.

Against this sad result the apostle warns—

Ἵνα μὴ ἀθυμῶσιν—"Lest they be disheartened." The composition of the verb shows its strong signification. Children teazed and irritated lose heart, renounce every endeavour to please, or render at best but a soulless obedience. The verb occurs only here in the New Testament, but is found in the Septuagint, 1 Kings i. 16, etc., and in several of the classical authors. What the apostle guards against has been often witnessed, with its deplorable consequences. In the Epistle to the Ephesians, he speaks more fully, and enjoins the positive mode of tuition—"but bring them up in the nurture and admonition of the Lord." The young spirit is to be carefully and tenderly developed, and not crushed by harsh and ungenerous treatment. Too much is neither to be demanded nor expected. The twig is to be bent with caution, not broken in the efforts of a rude and hasty zeal. Approbation is as necessary to the child as counsel, and promise as indispensable as warning and reproof. Gisborne on this place well says—"To train up children as servants of God, as soldiers of Jesus Christ, for a future existence in preference to the present life; to instruct and habituate them, in conformity with their baptismal vow, to renounce the world, the flesh, and the devil, and to live not unto themselves but to that Redeemer who died for them; this is universally the grand duty of a parent. This well-known duty the apostle, though he does not name it, presupposes as acknowledged and felt by the Colossians. In the discharge of this duty, and in every step of their proceedings, he directs them to beware, as parents, of provoking their children to anger; that is to say, as the original term evidently implies, of exercising their own authority with irritating unkindness, with needless and vexatious severity; of harassing their children by capricious commands and restrictions; of showing groundless dissatisfaction, and scattering unmerited reproof. To act thus, the apostle declares, would be so far from advancing the religious improvement of children, that it would discourage them. It would not only deaden their affections towards their parents, but would dispirit their exertions, and check their desires after holiness."[1]

Following the same order of thought as in the Epistle to the Ephesians, the apostle next turns him to the other members of the household, the slaves. It is probable that the false philosophy inculcated, with regard to them, certain notions of freedom which were not merely unattainable, but the belief of which might only aggravate the essential hardness of their lot. Steiger has referred to the fact that the Pharisees gave a special prominence to political freedom (John viii. 33), and he says, drawing his authority from Philo, that the Essenes held a doctrine which would, if carried out to practice, lead to a philanthropic revolution. At all events, they condemned slave-masters as not only unjust, but impious, and destroyers of a law of nature—*θεσμὸν φύσεως ἀναιρούντων*. The false teachers, if they held similar views, might inculcate this abstract doctrine, which, whatever its inherent truth, could not in those days lead to anything but discord and bloodshed. The apostle, on the other hand, applied himself to things as they were, and while he attempted to moderate an evil which he could not subvert, he laid down those principles, by the spread of which social bondage first was shorn of its grievances, and then lost its very existence. We have already stated, under Eph. vi. 5–8, the relation in which the gospel stood to the slaves, how it raised them to spiritual brotherhood, and gave them a conscious freedom which chains and oppression could not subvert. It so trained them, and so tutored their Christian masters, that slavery in a Christian

[1] *Familiar Exposition of the Epistle of Paul to the Colossians*, London, 1816.

household must have existed only in name, and the name itself was ready to disappear as soon as society was leavened with the spirit of Christianity.

The injunctions here delivered are much the same as those in the Epistle to the Ephesians. The reader is invited to turn to the prefatory remarks to our comment on Eph. vi. 5. The apostle does not speak vaguely, but hits upon those vices which slavery is so apt to engender—indolence, eye-service, and reluctance in labour.

(Ver. 22.) *Οἱ δοῦλοι ὑπακούετε κατὰ πάντα τοῖς κατὰ σάρκα κυρίοις.* [Eph. vi. 5.] The master of the slave is only so—*κατὰ σάρκα*, the relationship is but corporeal and external, the contrast being—the real master is the Lord Christ. No distinction can be established between *κύριος* and *δεσπότης* in the New Testament, either in their Divine or human application. The principle of the obedience is *κατὰ πάντα*, as in verse 20. Refractoriness on the part of the slave would at once have embittered his life, and brought discredit on the new religion which he professed, but active and cheerful discharge of all duty would both benefit himself, promote his comfort, and recommend Christianity.

Μὴ ἐν ὀφθαλμοδουλείᾳ ὡς ἀνθρωπάρεσκοι—"Not with eye-service, as men-pleasers." [Eph. vi. 6.] The plural form of the first noun is preferred by some, as being the more difficult reading, but the singular has A, B, D, E, F, G, in its favour. Yet Tischendorf has rejected it in spite of all this testimony. The Codices D, E, F, G, have another, and perhaps more correct spelling—*ὀφθαλμοδουλίᾳ*. In Eph. vi. 6, the apostle uses *κατά*, but here *ἐν*. In the former place they are enjoined to obey in singleness of heart, as unto Christ—" not according to eye-service "—that is, not in the style of eye-service; here they are asked not to serve in eye-service, that is, in the spirit of it. Slaves have usually but the one motive, and that is, to avoid punishment, and therefore they only labour to please the master when his eye is on them. They are disposed to trifle when he is absent, in the hope that their indolence may not be detected. But Christian slaves were to work on principle, were to do their duty at all times, and from a higher motive, conscious that another eye was upon them, and that their service was really rendered to another master. Such a conviction would prevent them being *ἀνθρωπάρεσκοι*. See under Eph. vi. 6, where we have noticed the necessary connection of this vice with slavery.

'Αλλ' ἐν ἁπλότητι καρδίας φοβούμενοι τὸν κύριον—"But in singleness of heart fearing the Lord" (Christ). ***Κύριον*** is preferred to ***Θέον*** on undoubted authority. [Eph. vi. 5.] Singleness of heart (1 Chron. xxix. 17) is that sincerity which the heathen slave could scarcely possess, for he would often seem to work, and yet contrive to enjoy his ease under the semblance of activity. Duplicity is the vice which the slave uses as his shield. He professes anxiety when he feels none, and he exhibits a show of industry without the reality. For this singleness of heart could only be secured by such a motive as the gospel presents—"fearing the Lord"—standing in awe of His authority over them. They would not be men-pleasers if they bowed to Christ's authority, for then their aim would be to please Him; nor would there be eye-service, if they wrought in singleness of heart, for such a feeling would lead them to conclude the task in hand, irrespectively of every minor and personal consideration.

(Ver. 23.) In this verse the common reading is *καὶ πᾶν ὅ, τι ἐὰν ποιῆτε*, but the better reading is *ὃ ἐὰν ποιῆτε, ἐκ ψυχῆς ἐργάζεσθε, ὡς τῷ Κυρίῳ καὶ οὐκ ἀνθρώποις*—"Whatever ye are in the way of doing, work it heartily as to the Lord, and not to men." They were, in any task that might be assigned them, to labour at it, to work it out, and that without grumbling or reluctance, not only doing it honestly but cheerfully, as Chrysostom says—*μὴ μετὰ δουλικῆς ἀνάγκης*. [Eph. vi. 6.] The heathen slave might do everything with a grudge, for he had no interest in his labour, but the believing slave was to act with cordiality, plying his toil with alacrity, for he was serving in all this industry no human master, but the Lord, who had bought him with His precious blood. Let this be the feeling, and there would be no temptation to fall into eye-service, men-pleasing, and duplicity of heart or conduct. The apostle says without reservation—"as to the Lord, and not to men." There is no necessity to take *οὐκ* as meaning *οὐ μόνον*. The immediate object of the service must be man, but the ultimate object is the Lord; the negative, though absolute in form, being relative in sense. Winer, § 55, 1.[1] The service, whatever its nature, or its relation to man, was ever to be felt and viewed as an act of obedience done to Christ. See under verse 17. In doing it to others, they did it to Him; and to Him, with such claims upon their love and fealty, they could not but give suit and service heartily. As usual, in the parallel place in Ephesians, the thought is given more fully, and the relationship of the slave's labour to Christ is twice noted. Besides, not only was the servant to work as here—ἐκ ψυχῆς—"from the heart," pointing out his relation to his work, but he is enjoined also to labour—μετ' εὐνοίας—that is, "with good will" to his master. The apostle adds yet further—

(Ver. 24.) *Εἰδότες ὅτι ἀπὸ Κυρίου ἀπολήψεσθε τὴν ἀνταπόδοσιν τῆς κληρονομίας*—"Knowing that from the Lord ye shall receive the reward of the inheritance." With this persuasion within them, they should be able to follow out the inspired admonition, and such knowledge would form a motive of sufficient energy and life. Serving the Lord in serving man, they would receive their reward from Him. Winer, § 47,[2] represents ἀπό as denoting that the recompense comes immediately from Christ, its possessor. Their masters are in no sense to be the dispensers of that reward. Christ Himself shall bestow it. The compound noun, ἀνταπόδοσις, is found only here in the New Testament.[3] That remuneration is the "inheritance." [Eph. i. 11–14.] Also Col. i. 12. The genitive is that of apposition, such as is found in Eph. iv. 9; 2 Cor. v. 25. See our Commentary on Ephesians, iv. 9. The inheritance is heavenly glory, 1 Pet. i. 4, and that is their prospective blessing. They had no inheritance on earth, nothing which they could call their own; they could not even realize property in themselves—but an inheritance rich and glorious awaited them. In the hope of it—and the enjoyment of it could not be very distant—they were to work, and suffer and wait, and in the possession of it they would find immediate and ample compensation. [Eph. vi. 8.] There is no room here for

[1] Moulton, p. 594. [2] *Ibid.* p. 463, note.
[3] But sometimes in the classics. Elsner, *in loc.*

the Popish doctrine of merit. *Nota hoc,* says a-Lapide, *pro meritis bonorum operum, contra Novantes;* but Bähr adduces the terse reply of Calovius—*filiis haereditas non confertur ex obedientiae merito, sed jure filiationis.*

The *γάρ* of the next clause, as found in the Textus Receptus, cannot be received, as it is only an interpolated gloss—*τῷ Κυρίῳ Χριστῷ δουλεύετε*—which the Vulgate renders, *Domino Christo servite,* "serve ye the Lord Christ." Perhaps, as Meyer says, the imperative is preferable, *γάρ* being spurious. It is thus a summation of the whole—"the master, Christ, serve ye." The use of the indicative is foreign to the passage, which is injunctive. Since the Lord gives such a reward so rich and blessed, serve ye Him. Look above and beyond human service, and with such a bright prospect in view, serve the Lord Christ. Your masters on earth have no absolute right over you: the shekels they may have paid for you can only give them power over your bodies, your time and your labour; but the Lord has bought you with His blood, and has therefore an indefeasible claim to your homage and service.

(Ver. 25.) *Ὁ γὰρ ἀδικῶν κομίσεται ὃ ἠδίκησεν.* The *δέ* of the Stephanic is rightly replaced by *γάρ*, on the evidence of A, B, C, D[1], F, G, and many of the Versions. The construction of the clause is idiomatic—"the wrong-doer shall receive what he has wronged." Winer, § 66, b, says it can scarcely be called a brachylogy, for it is somewhat, as is said in German,—*er wird das Unrecht erndten*—that is, he does not receive the wrong itself, but the fruit of it, or the wrong, in the form of punishment. He shall be paid, as we say, in his own coin. The wrong-doer shall bear the penalty of the wrong.

The question is, to whom does the apostle refer? 1. Some suppose him to mean the slave, as if to warn him, that if he failed in his duty he must expect to be punished. This is the notion of Theophylact, Bengel, Storr, Flatt, Heinrichs, and De Wette. This exegesis may have the support of the mere words, but it does not tally with the concluding clause—"there is no respect of persons with Him." Is the fact that the Judge has no respect of persons an argument that an unjust slave shall not escape punishment? The phrase, "respect of persons," usually implies that an offender, simply for his rank and station, escapes the penalty—a mode of partiality not at all applicable to slaves. The argument of Bengel is only ingenious—*tenues saepe putant, sibi propter tenuitatem ipsorum esse parcendum.*

2. Others regard the verse as indicating a great general principle, applicable alike to the master and his slave. Such is the view of Jerome and Pelagius, Bähr, Huther, Baumgarten-Crusius, and Trollope. Jerome says, *quicumque injuriam intulerit, sive dominus sive servus, uterque.* . . . But the same objection applies to this view as to the former. So that we incline to the third opinion, which is, that the words refer to the master, the view of Theodoret, Anselm, Aquinas, Erasmus, Beza, Calvin, Estius, and Meyer, while De Wette allows its possibility. The connection of the thought seems to be—"you are Christ's servants, and you shall receive the reward from Him. Injustice you may in the meantime receive from your earthly masters, but they shall be judged for it, not at a human tribunal, where their rank may protect them, but before Him who in His decisions has no respect of persons. Therefore, ye masters, give your slaves what is just and equal." There is, besides, a strong tendency in any one who owns slaves, and exercises irresponsible power over them, to treat them with capricious and heedless tyranny. The statement of the apostle, then, contains a general truth, with a special application to the proprietors of slaves, and is therefore the basis of the following admonition. Meyer rests another argument on the current meaning of the participle ἀδικῶν in the New Testament, which, he says, with the exception of Rev. xxii. 11, denotes *Unrecht zufügen,* not *Unrecht thun.* In fact, our translators have given the word at least eight different renderings. Ten times have they rendered it "hurt," eight times have they rendered by "do wrong," as in the case before us, twice simply by "wrong," twice by "suffer wrong," once by "injure," once by "take wrong," once by "offender," and once by "unjust." The predominant idea is not, to act unjustly, but to injure, and refers therefore more probably not to the slave forgetting his duty, but to his master, tempted by his station and power to do an act of injury towards his servile and helpless dependants.

Καὶ οὐκ ἔστι προσωποληψία—"And there is no respect of persons." [Eph. vi. 9.] Rom. ii. 11; Acts x. 34; Jas. ii. 1, 9.

(Chap. IV. Ver. 1.) The division of chapters is here very unfortunate. The apostle, while he stooped to counsel the slave, was not afraid to speak to his master.

Οἱ κύριοι, τὸ δίκαιον καὶ τὴν ἰσότητα τοῖς δούλοις παρέχεσθε—"Ye masters, afford for your part to your servants what is just and equal," or rather "reciprocal." [Eph. vi. 9.] The verb in the middle voice, has in it the idea, "as far as you are concerned." Acts xix. 24. The principal term, and the one about which there is any dispute, is *ἰσότητα*. What does the apostle mean precisely by it? Not a few understand by it equity in general. Such is the view of Robinson, Wahl, Bretschneider, and Wilke, in their respective lexicons, and also of Steiger, Huther, and De Wette, in their respective commentaries. Others, again, like Erasmus, a-Lapide, and Böhmer, look on the words as denoting impartiality—do not in your treatment of your slaves prefer one to another, give them the like usage. In the only other passage of the New Testament where the word occurs, it denotes not equity, but equality. 2 Cor. viii. 14: "But by an equality, that now at this time your abundance may be a supply for their want, that their abundance also may be a supply for your want; that there may be equality." In this verse equality is the idea—your abundance and their want, their abundance and your want, being in reciprocal adjustment. In the passage before us, we incline to follow the older expositors, Calvin, Zanchius, Crocius, as also Meyer, who give it such a sense.

The meaning is not very different from that of the corresponding passage in Eph. vi. 9—"ye masters, do the same things unto them," which we have explained as meaning what Calvin has called the *jus analogum*. While we agree with the general view of Meyer, we think him wrong in his special application of it. He regards the *ἰσότητα* as involving that spiritual parity which Christian brotherhood creates. Slaves are your equals, and they should be treated with such equality. This exegesis is based on the supposition that Christian slaves only are meant, a supposition which, we think, cannot be admitted. The slaves are told how to behave toward their masters, whether these masters are Christians or not; and the master is admonished how to conduct himself toward his slaves, whether these slaves be Christians or not. The apostle speaks to Christian slaves and Christian masters; but such slaves might have heathen masters, and such masters might have unconverted slaves. There is no warrant, then, for saying, that the apostle only teaches the duty of masters towards Christian servants. Whatever the religious creeds of their serfs, they were to give them what is just and equal. The equality lay in reciprocal duty; if the slave is bound to serve the master, the master is bound equally to certain duties to the slave. The elements of service have a claim on equal elements of mastership. Equality demands this, that he shall give the slave all to which he is entitled, not with a view to please men, but to please God—"doing it heartily as unto the Lord." Such property had its duties as well as its rights, and the equality lay between the exercise of such duties and the enforcement of such rights. The phrase *τὸ δίκαιον* means what is right, irrespective of all considerations, that is, what the position of the slave as a man and a servant plainly involves. Right and duty should be of equal measurement. The apostle did not bid the masters demit their mastership, for he does not mean by *ἰσότης*, equality of rank with themselves, for such an elevation would imply greatly more than the bestowal of personal freedom. Masters are still called so, as they still stood in that relationship, but Christianity was to regulate all their transactions with those placed under them and owned by them. And with regard to their Christian slaves—the equality which Meyer contends for was certainly to guide them—the equality so well explained in the Epistle to Philemon.

One powerful reason the apostle adds—

Εἰδότες, ὅτι καὶ ὑμεῖς ἔχετε Κύριον ἐν οὐρανοῖς—"Knowing that ye too have a master in heaven." The participle has its common causal sense. It is not material to our purpose whether the reading be *οὐρανῷ* or *οὐρανοῖς*. The sense is—ye are under law yourselves to the highest of masters—you are in the position of servants to the heavenly Lord. As ye would that your Master should treat you, so do you as masters treat them. Let the great Master's treatment of you be the model of your treatment of them. If the masters realized this fact, that in this higher service their slaves, if Christians, and themselves were colleagues, ransomed by the same price, the same service appointed to them, and the same prospect set before them, a tribunal before which they should stand on the same level, and an inheritance in which they should equally share, irrespective of difference in social rank upon earth, then would they be kept from all temptations to harshness and injury towards their dependants. Who does not recollect the touching language of Job? "If I did despise the cause of my man-servant, or of my maid-servant, when they contended with me; what then shall I do when God riseth up? and when He visiteth, what shall I answer Him? Did not He that made me in the womb make him? and did not one fashion us in the womb?" xxxi. 13–15.

That the apostle in such admonitions pursued the wisest course, the Servile wars of Rome are abundant evidence. The principles inculcated by him lightened the burden, and their practical development in course of time removed it. So numerous were the slaves, that in very many cases they far outnumbered the freemen—as in Attica, where the proportion was at least four to one. Probably very many of them were to be found in all the early churches.

The apostle lays down three positions fatal to slavery. *First,* he denies a common theory of the times, which seems to have regarded slaves as an inferior caste, either born so, as Aristotle affirms, or brought into servitude, as Homer sings, from mental imbecility.[1] For he pleads for reciprocity, and thereby admits no distinction but the one of accidental rank. And, *secondly,* he declares that certain duties to slaves spring from natural right, an idea the admission of which would not only at once have put an end to the incredible cruelties of Spartan and Roman slave-owners, but which did also, by and by, as it leavened society, prompt Christian men to give liberty to their servants, made like themselves in God's image, and as entitled as themselves to a free personality. *Thirdly,* he avows that in the Christian church there is neither "bond nor free," and thus provides and opens a spiritual asylum, within which

[1] Euripides, too, says of the slave race—οὐχ ὁρᾷς ὅσον κακόν.

equality of the highest kind was enjoyed, and master and slave were not in such a relationship recognized. For master and slave were alike the free servants of a common Lord in heaven. In the meantime, as Chrysostom says, Christianity gave freedom in slavery, and this was its special distinction.[1] The same Father tells what spiritual benefit Christian servants had often imparted to their masters' households, and Neander states that a Christian female slave was the means of bringing the province of ancient Georgia to the knowledge of Christ.[2]

[1] Τοιοῦτον ὁ χριστιανισμός. *In loc.* 1 Cor. xix.

[2] *Memorials*, p. 306. Bohn, London.

CHAPTER IV

THE apostle now passes to more general admonitions. But he places prayer in front, and he delights to contemplate it as the "ladder" which connects earth with heaven, by which the soul rises to highest communion, and spiritual blessings, like descending angels, come down to our world.

(Ver. 2.) *Τῇ προσευχῇ προσκαρτερεῖτε*—"Continue in prayer." The apostle knew the benefit of prayer from his own experience, and he is therefore anxious that they should pray with persevering energy, and give himself a prominent place in their intercessions. [Eph. vi. 18.] Rom. xiii. 12; 1 Thess. v. 17. They prayed, and the apostle was well aware of it, but he exhorts them to "continue in prayer." They were never to suppose that prayer was needless, either because their desires had been gratified, or God had bestowed upon them all His gifts. But as they were still needing, and God was still promising, they were still to persist in asking. This perseverance was a prime element of successful prayer, as it proved their sincerity, and evinced the power of their faith. They were to pray and wait, not to be discouraged, but still to hold on—wrestling in the spirit of him who said, "I will not let thee go except thou bless me."

Γρηγοροῦντες ἐν αὐτῇ ἐν εὐχαριστίᾳ. The phrase *ἐν εὐχαριστίᾳ* is not connected with the preceding *τῇ προσευχῇ προσκαρτερεῖτε*, but with the words last quoted—"watching in it with thanksgiving." The present form belongs only to the later Greek. *Phrynichus*, ed. Lobeck, pp. 118, 119—*ἐγρήγορα* perfect of *ἐγείρω* being employed. Eustathius, *ad Odyss.* 1880; Sturz, p. 157; Buttmann, § 343. It would be an unworthy view to refer this language to the practice of ancient Christianity, which was compelled by persecution to spend so many hours of the night in devotional exercises. Such tame formality is not involved, but it still clings to humanity, and is found not only "in the confusion of Paternoster and Ave

Marias among the Catholics," but also "in the no less pious babbling of many a pietist *keeper of the hours*."[1] The apostle enjoins, not physical, but spiritual wakefulness, as in Eph. vi. 18, where he employs ἀγρυπνοῦντες. They were to be ever on their guard against remissness. If a man refuses to sleep that his attention may not be interrupted, his watching argues the value he places on the end desired. To prayer, Christians are to give themselves with sleepless anxiety, and are ever to watch against all slackness or supineness in it, and against all formality and unbelief. 1 Thess. v. 6; 1 Pet. v. 8. They were not to become torpid or careless, but were to beware of spiritual sleepiness in their devotions. And along with prayer, they were to be wakeful "in thanksgiving." Olshausen lays too great stress upon the phrase when he says that by ἐν εὐχαριστίᾳ the more general προσευχή is more accurately defined. He adds, "that the prayer of a Christian, in the consciousness of his experienced grace, can never be anything else than a thanksgiving." But the apostle in no sense nor form identifies prayer with thanksgiving, he only classes thanksgiving along with prayer. See under ii. 7. Still there are so many grounds for thanksgiving that it cannot be omitted in any approach to the throne of grace. While we ask for so much, there is also much for which we ought to give thanks. We must give Him credit for what He has done already, while we ask Him to do more. There are many reasons of thanksgiving, and not the least of them is the privilege of prayer itself. Prayer and thanksgiving co-exist only on earth. They shall be separated in the other world, for in the region of woe there is only wailing, and in that of glory there is only melody.

(Ver. 3.) The apostle wished himself to be specially included in their supplications.

Προσευχόμενοι ἅμα καὶ περὶ ἡμῶν—"Praying at the same time also for us." We cannot suppose, with some critics, that Paul means only himself when he uses ἡμῶν. True, indeed, he immediately uses the singular, still he seems first to include others with himself. But we cannot say that Timothy is the only person meant besides himself. These others may have been persons circumstanced like the apostle, and probably

[1] Stier, *Reden Jesu*, Matt. vi. 7.

comprised at least those whose names are mentioned in the concluding salutations. The Greek expositors dwell on the apostle's humility in asking the prayers of the Colossian church, Theophylact adding that the circumstance also shows —τὴν δύναμιν τῆς φιλαδέλφου εὐχῆς. Yes, and it also shows that the apostle was no Stoic, that he felt the need of those prayers, and set a high value on them. For the circumstances in which he was placed had a depressing tendency, and he seems, not indeed to have lost confidence in himself, but to have had some apprehension that from age and infirmity he might yield, or appear to yield before them. But he knew the power of prayer. "Human entreaty has shut up heaven, and has again opened it. At the voice of a man the sun stood still. Prayer has sweetened the bitter fountain, divided the sea, and stilled its waves. It has disbanded armies, and prevented conflict; it has shortened battle, and given victory to right. It has conferred temporal abundance, as in the case of Jabez; and given effect to medical appliances, as in the case of Hezekiah. It has quenched the mouths of lions, and opened the gates of the prison-house. As Jesus prayed by the river, the dove alighted on Him; and as He prayed on the hill, He was transfigured. The glory of God was manifested to Moses when he asked it, and the grace of Christ to Paul when he besought it. Not a moment elapsed between the petition of the crucified thief and its glorious answer. Ere Daniel concluded his devotion, the celestial messenger stood at his side. The praying church brought down upon itself the Pentecostal effusion."[1] The prayer which he wished to be offered for them was this—

Ἵνα ὁ Θεὸς ἀνοίξῃ ἡμῖν θύραν τοῦ λόγου—"That God would open to us a door of discourse"—that is, an opportunity of preaching. Mr. Ellicott, on Eph. i. 17, assigns to *ἵνα* three meanings in the New Testament—a telic, hypotelic, and ecbatic meaning, and he adds, that "our criticism, admitting the third and denying the second after verbs of entreaty, is somewhat illogical." He prefers the second, or covert telic sense. But surely our admission of an ecbatic sense of *ἵνα* in the New Testament, does not compel us to admit in such a construction as the one before us, a hypotelic sense. Nor do

[1] Eadie, *The Divine Love*, etc., p. 184, 1855.

we feel the harshness which Winer alleges to be in the telic sense of *ἵνα* after verbs of entreating. In short, the hypotelic sense is more ingenious than sound. The result, as future, and as the effect of conscious instrumentality, is subjectively regarded under the aspect of design. The subject of a prayer is rarely so blended with its design as to obscure it when it is prefaced by *ἵνα*, for that subject still assumes to the writer's mind the idea of purpose, and therefore there is no need to drop or modify the proper telic sense of the conjunction. Here the opening of the door of utterance was to be the subject of prayer, and they were to pray *in order that* it might be granted. While the theme was on their tongue, the prompting of a final purpose was felt in their hearts. The suppliants naturally looked at the end, while they repeated the theme, and thus the apostle proposes this theme to them under the aspect of an end which they were to keep steadily before them at a throne of grace.

We cannot agree with those who think that by *θύραν τοῦ λόγου* is meant simply " the mouth," as the medium of speech. Yet a great number hold this view, such as Thomas Aquinas and Anselm, Calvin and Beza, Cajetan and Estius, a-Lapide, Zanchius, and Bengel. In the New Testament we find *θύρα* used in the secondary sense of occasion, or opportunity. Acts xiv. 27; 1 Cor. xvi. 9; 2 Cor. ii. 12; Rev. iii. 8. The figure is so natural and apparent, that it occurs frequently among classical writers, both Greek and Latin. While the exegesis referred to does not come up to the meaning of the words, that of Chrysostom and his followers goes beyond it, when they thus explain *θύραν* as—*εἴσοδον καὶ παῤῥησίαν*, an idea borrowed from Eph. vi. 19. The apostle longed for liberty, not for itself, but for the opportunity which it gave him of preaching the gospel. He might, indeed, in his captivity, find some opportunity of preaching, but he longed for uninterrupted licence. Nay, his own personal liberty was nothing to him but in so far as it gave him an unhampered sphere of evangelical labour. The opening of the door of his prison would be the opening of a door of discourse to them, and specially to him, for his design was—

Λαλῆσαι τὸ μυστήριον τοῦ Χριστοῦ—" To speak the mystery of Christ." The infinitive is that of result. Winer,

§ 44. On the meaning of *μυστήριον*, see under Eph. i. 9, iii. 4, and especially vi. 19. Christ is the subject of that mystery, it has Him for its theme. See also under i. 26. It was the apostle's special function to act as a hierophant, or to make it known. It was by the proclamation of it that its blessings were to be enjoyed, and the apostle longed to speak it. His attachment to the mystery was in no way weakened by the persecution which for his disclosure of it had come upon him.

Δι' ὃ καὶ δέδεμαι—"For which yea I am bound." Winer, § 58, 4, 2. The form *ὅ* is preferred to *ὅν*, as being the reading of A, C, D, E, J, K, etc. See under i. 24. These chains lay upon him because he unveiled the mystery in its full extent. He had been imprisoned for preaching it, but still, if liberated, would he preach it again. Thus, at length, the apostle converges those prayers upon himself. In praying for the others, as he requested them, particular reference was to be made to himself, and his inability, through his bonds, to proclaim the mystery of Christ. These bonds had not deadened his love to it, and he longed to proclaim it in this aspect of it as a mystery, viz. its adaptation to the Gentile races. Eph. iii. 8. The special cause of his imprisonment was his proclamation of the gospel to the Gentiles, and his admission of converted heathens into the church without respect to the Mosaic law. They had, therefore, special reason to remember him in their prayers. Hallet[1] says well, "that we Gentiles are indebted inconceivably more to the Apostle Paul than we are to any man that ever lived in the world. He was the apostle of the Gentiles, and gloried in that character. While Peter went too far toward betraying our privileges, our Apostle Paul stood up with a courage and zeal becoming himself. For us in particular, as for the Gentiles in general, our invaluable friend laboured more abundantly than all the apostles. For *us* he suffered. He was persecuted for this very reason, because he laboured to turn *us* from darkness to light, and to give to *us* the knowledge of salvation upon our repentance towards God, and faith in our Lord Jesus Christ. How dear, then, should his memory ever be to us!"

[1] *Notes*, etc., vol. i. p. 382.

(Ver. 4.) Ἵνα φανερώσω αὐτὸ, ὡς δεῖ με λαλῆσαι—"That I may make it manifest as I ought to speak." Quite peculiar is the connection invented by Bengel—"δέδεμαι, ἵνα φανερώσω, *vinctus sum ut patefaciam. Paradoxon.*" We do not agree with Beza, Bähr, and De Wette, that the two conjunctions (ἵνα) are parallel, and both depending on προσευχόμενοι, for the last one appears simply to develop the order of thought. They were to pray in order that God would open a door of utterance for him, and this in order that he might preach the gospel with all his original boldness and freedom. The one ἵνα, therefore, depends upon the other—"praying in order that God would open a door of utterance for me to speak the mystery of Christ, in order that this being granted I may make it manifest as I ought to speak." Some understand by the phrase, "as I ought to speak," the moral qualities of preaching—but Meyer thinks that the apostle refers simply to freedom of speech, to absence of physical restraint, or to unlimited power of travel from land to land. But the comprehensive phrase, "as I ought to speak," may comprehend both sets of ideas, and certainly the context does not limit it to the latter. It is true that imprisonment deprived the apostle of the power of preaching at all, but when he says, "as I ought," the pregnant phrase refers not simply to his commission, as the world's apostle, and to the licence of travel which it involved, but also to the spirit in which such duty should be discharged. For it might be surmised that what Paul had suffered for the gospel had lessened his love for it, or modified his views of the office which he held. And may we not suppose that the apostle wished the world to understand, that if he were liberated, there would be no abatement of his zeal, no subduedness of tone in his speech, no mutilation of his message, and no accommodation of it so as to avoid a recurrence of the penalty, but all his old fervour and power, all his former breadth of view, and all his uncompromising hostility to Jewish narrowness and bigotry—"that I may make it manifest as I ought to speak." The form of request presented to the Ephesians is more pointed. He twice asks them to pray for him, that he may speak with boldness, and he graphically depicts himself as an ambassador in chains.

The exhortations of the two following verses refer to the outer aspects of Christian conduct, or such aspects of it as present themselves to the world. While they were to set their affections on things above, and mortify their "members which are upon the earth;" while they were to put off certain vices, and assume certain virtues, culminating in love; while they were to be exemplary in every social relation—as husbands and wives, parents and children, masters and servants; and while they were to be instant in prayer for themselves and for the apostle, all this ethical code referred to personal and mutual spiritual duties within the church. They must, however, in ordinary circumstances, come in contact with unbelieving heathenism around them. If they shrank entirely from such company, the inference of the apostle would be realized—"for then must ye needs go out of the world." But they were not to go out of the world because it was bad, they were to remain in it for the purpose of making it better. And that their conduct might exercise such a beneficial influence they were thus enjoined—

(Ver. 5.) *'Εν σοφίᾳ περιπατεῖτε πρὸς τοὺς ἔξω*—"Walk in wisdom towards them which are without." The verb *περιπατεῖν*, when, as here, it has an ethical sense, is sometimes followed by *κατά*, as in Rom. viii. 4, xiv. 15, 1 Cor. iii. 3, but more usually by *ἐν*; the shade of difference being, that in the former case, the ideas of source and similarity are implied, and in the latter the character or sphere of walk is principally indicated. The phrase *οἱ ἔξω*—"those who are without," is found in 1 Cor. v. 12, and in 1 Thess. iv. 12, and points to persons beyond the pale of the church, and not simply or prominently the false teachers, as Junker supposes. Those without should be surrounded with every inducement to come in. No barrier should be thrown in their way, but the attractive nature of Christianity should be wisely exhibited to them. And as the life and practice of those within the church is what they especially look at and learn from, so the apostle says, "walk in wisdom—*πρός*," in reference to them. The admonition, as contained in Eph. v. 15, is more general, and wants the pointed application which it bears here.

The "wisdom" here enforced is more than mere prudence.

[Eph. v. 15.] It means that while Christians are to abstain from such sins as disgrace their profession, and are to preserve a holy consistency, adorning the doctrine of God their Saviour; they are also to exhibit, at the same time, not only the purity of the gospel, but its amiability, its strictness of principle in union with its loveliness of temper, its generosity as well as its rectitude, and its charity no less than its devoutness and zeal. Let "those without" not be told of Christian self-possession in a tone of irritation, or of Christian happiness while uneasiness sits on the brow of the speaker. Let no one wrangle about the duty of peacemaking, or bow his face to the earth as he tries to expatiate on the hope of the gospel. The world's Bible is the daily life of the church, every page of which its quick eye minutely scans, and every blot on which it detects with gleeful and malicious exactness. The same wisdom will assume the form of discretion in reference to time and place. Unwise efforts at proselytism defeat their own purpose; zeal without knowledge is as the thunder shower that drenches and injures, not the rain that with noiseless and gentle descent softens and fertilizes. The great Teacher Himself has said, "Give not that which is holy unto the dogs, neither cast ye your pearls before swine, lest they trample them under their feet, and turn again and rend you." Matt. vii. 6.

Τὸν καιρὸν ἐξαγοραζόμενοι—"Redeeming the time." Conybeare renders—"and forestall opportunity." The clause has been explained under Eph. v. 16. The general meaning is "purchasing, or seizing on the opportunity." The preposition *ἐκ*, in composition, according to Ellicott, directs the thought to the undefined times or circumstances out of which, in each particular case, the *καιρός* was to be bought; a notion different only in aspect from our view given under Eph. v. 16, which takes *ἐκ* to represent "out of another's possession," a view which appears to us to be more in harmony with the spirit of the figure. The immediate reference is to the injunction of the preceding clause. Every season for exercising such wisdom is to be eagerly improved, or no opportunity for its display is to be trifled with or lost. The idea of the Greek expositors is foreign to the purpose—"the time is not yours, but belongs to those who are without, for whose good you must employ it." So Theodoret—*οὐκ ἔστιν ὑμέτερος ὁ παρὼν αἰὼν, χρήσασθε αὐτῷ εἰς τὸ δέον.* Not less away from the point is the definition of Augustine—*Quid est redimere tempus, nisi cum opus est, etiam detrimento temporalium commodorum, ad aeterna quaerenda et capessenda spatia temporis comparare.* The reason annexed in the Epistle to the Ephesians, "because the days are evil," is not found in the passage before us.

The next verse, though it contains a sentiment which is of great moment by itself, is yet closely connected with this which goes before it.

(Ver. 6.) *Ὁ λόγος ὑμῶν πάντοτε ἐν χάριτι, ἅλατι ἠρτυμένος*—"Let your conversation be always with grace, seasoned with salt." The phrase *λόγος ἐν χάριτι* is, according to Robinson, equivalent to *λόγος χαρίεις*. But the noun *χάρις* signifies, perhaps, that gracious spirit which rules the tongue, and prompts it both to select the fittest themes, and to clothe them in the most agreeable and impressive form. Sirach xxi. 16; Luke iv. 22; Sept. Ps. xlv. 3. It is not that *χάρις τοῦ λόγου* which Plutarch ascribes to the courtly Alcibiades, or that graciousness or blandness of tongue which is but mere politeness. It is vastly higher than what Bloomfield understands by it—"terseness of thought and smartness of expression." Chrysostom says well, "it is possible to be simply agreeable—*χαριεντίζεσθαι*—but we are to beware that this agreeableness fall not into indifference." In Eph. iv. 29, the apostle gives a different and negative form of advice, but adds as the needed characteristic of Christian conversation—"that which is good to the use of edifying."

To show his meaning yet more fully, the apostle employs a strong metaphor—"seasoned with salt." The participle employed is the ordinary culinary term. The figure represents speech as liable to become insipid, or to lose spiritual piquancy unless it be seasoned with salt. The form *ἅλατι*, from *ἅλας*, seems to have belonged to the popular speech.[1] Salt has various applications in Scripture, such as the salt of the covenant and the salt of the sacrifice, and appears to be the symbol of what is quickening and conservative in its nature.

[1] Suidas affirms that it is used only in the phrase *ἅλασιν ὕει*. Buttmann, however, says that the word is only a euphonious form for *ἅλσιν*, § 58. See also Suicer, *sub voce*, where there is much curious information.

We therefore demur to the notion of many commentators, that the term here refers principally, if not wholly, to wisdom. The Attic salt, indeed, was that wit which gave zest and sparkle to Athenian conversation. But it was not wisdom in any special sense. Nor can we agree with Meyer and Böhmer, that salt is, in Matt. v. 13, Mark ix. 49, 50, or Luke xiv. 34, the symbol of wisdom. It is rather the symbol of that spiritual conservative power which Christianity exerts on society and the world. Here it stands in explanation of *χάρις*, not specifically of *σοφία*. True, indeed, *χάρις* involves *σοφία*, gracious words must be always wise words, but wisdom is here employed to characterize the walk, and grace to describe the "fruit of the lips." The conversation which *λόγος* denotes is to be seasoned with this condiment, that it may be in itself free from every pernicious taint and quality, that it may be relished by those who hear it, and that on them it may exercise a beneficial influence.[1] In Eph. iv. 29 the apostle says, "let no corrupt speech proceed out of your mouth." Christian speech is not to be insipid, far less to be corrupt, but it is to possess that hallowed pungency which shall excite interest in the inquirer, and that preservative flavour which may influence for good the mind and heart of those who, being without, are disposed to put questions to the members of the church. For the apostle subjoins as a reason—

Εἰδέναι πῶς δεῖ ὑμᾶς ἑνὶ ἑκάστῳ ἀποκρίνεσθαι—"That ye may know how it becomes you to answer each one." Though in certain cases the infinitive may stand for the imperative among the classical writers, there is no reason to adopt such a supposition here. Winer, § 43, 5, *d*. Tremellius and Storr,

[1] Baldwin (Professor Witebergensis, 1624) has a most extraordinary comment on this place. He understands the apostle to refer to wit—"De salibus, et jocis in sermone hic est quaestio." And he subjoins the following permissions and regulations:—"Modus tamen in jocis homine gravi ac prudenti, multò magis Christiano dignus est, qui et si præcisè et secundùm omnes circumstantias præscribi non potest, ex his tamen regulis dignosci potest. 1. Joci sint docti qui moralia quædam sua urbanitate tacitè instillant. 2. Ad jocandum non abutamur sacris scripturis. 3. Jocantes omnes non seipsos tantùm sed et aliorum sales libenter audiant. 4. Obscura si qua fortè excidunt, ambitu verborum tegenda sunt. 5. Non jocemur semper in aliorum gratiam, ne nos ipsos prostituamus. 6. Jocemur in tempore: nam apud tristes jocari intempestivum est, ut et in re seria. 7. Joci non sint affectati."—P. 240.

however, translate by *scitote*, while Grotius, Bengel, and Huther regard the verb as a kind of ablative gerund, *sciendo*. But the infinitive, as in other places, denotes the object, Matthiae, § 532. The Greek expositors commit a blunder, we think, in giving the phrase "every one" too extensive a meaning, and including in it the members of the church. Thus Theodoret, ἄλλως γὰρ τῷ ἀπίστῳ καὶ ἄλλως τῷ πιστῷ, etc. Chrysostom lays too much stress on external condition, for he says "a prince must be answered in one way, and a subject in another, a rich man in one way, and a poor man in another," and he adds a sarcastic reason, that the minds of rich and powerful men are feebler, more inflammable, and undecided—ἀσθενέστεραι, μᾶλλον φλεγμαίνουσαι, μᾶλλον διαῤῥέουσαι. Ambrosiaster has a similar train of illustration. That of Primasius is better—*aliter paganis, aliter Judaeis, aliter haereticis, aliter astrologis, et caeteris est respondendum.*

For it is of those without that the apostle speaks, and each, as he puts his question, is to have a gracious and effective answer. "Death and life are in the power of the tongue."[1] Prov. xviii. 21. One kind of answer will not suffice for all, but each one is to be answered as he should be. Therefore the necessity of the "grace" and of the "salt." The question might refer to various things. It might refer to evidence or to doctrine, to ritual or to ethics. It might embody an objection, suggest a difficulty, or contain a peculiar solution. It might be a query, in which lurked a satire, or one that argued a humble and inquiring mind. It might be as aimless as Pilate's interrogation, "what is truth?" or it might be the

[1] "And we may generally observe, that men of the weakest minds are oftentimes the most garrulous; they unconsciously try to make up in number of words what is obviously wanting in weight and wisdom: whereas men of much grace and sound intellect try to say much in few words: they bring massive thoughts within small compass: there is hardly anything they dread more than to seem to be talking much, and yet to be really saying nothing. And it is well worthy of remark also, that he never speaks much to edification who knows not when to cease to speak. It is one thing to speak much, and another to speak with effect. Much talkativeness and much grace seldom go together. Speaking and thinking aright are widely different operations of the mind; and the one is often possessed in an eminent degree, while the other is almost entirely wanting. We may generally lay it down as a rule, *that there is far the most depth where there is the least noise.*"—Watson's *Discourses on the Colossians*, pp. 370, 371.

result of such an idle curiosity as that which moved the Athenian gossips on Mars' hill to say, "we would know therefore what those things mean." Or it might indicate a state of mind in which mingled feelings were in operation, as when the Jews at Rome came to the apostle's lodging to hear of him what he thought. The tone of one querist might be that of scorn, of another that of earnest inquiry. One, as he asked information, might show that conviction had made some progress; another, that his previous thoughts had been gross misconceptions. But each was to be answered as was becoming—according to the contents, the spirit, and the object of his question—answered so that he might at once receive enlightenment and impression, be charmed out of his hostility, reasoned out of his misunderstanding, guided out of his difficulty, awakened out of his indifference, and won over to the new religion under the solemn persuasion that it was foolish to trifle any longer with Christianity, and dangerous any more to oppose the claims of a Divine revelation, enriched with such materials, fortified with such proofs, and commended by such results to universal reason and reception. 1 Pet. iii. 1, 15; 2 Tim. ii. 25, 26. According to those passages, meekness is one special element of the Christian answer.

In fine, wholly out of place is the notion of Pierce, that the answer here referred to is that which Christians were often obliged to make to heathen rulers when summoned to appear before them. Elton, in his exposition of this epistle (1620, London), makes the following pithy application:—"Wouldest thou then be able to speak fitly, and to good purpose on euery occasion, as in one particular case, in time of distresse, in time of trouble, and vexation of body or minde, wouldest thou be able to speake a word of comfort, and as the Prophet saith, Isa. i. 4, know to minister a word in time to him that is weary? Oh then let thy tong be euer poudred with the salt of grace, haue in thy mouth at all other times gracious speeches, and certainly then thou shalt not be to seeke of sweete and comfortable words in time of neede. Many come to their friends whom they loue well, and wish well vnto, in time of their trouble, haply lying on their sicke beds, and are not able to affoord them one word of spirituall comfort, onely they can vse a common forme of speech, aske them how they doe, and say, they are sorry to see them so, and then they haue done: here is one speciall cause of it, their mouthes are not seasoned with gracious speaches at other times; they vse not to season their speech with grace at other times, and so it comes to passe that when they should, and (it may bee) would vse gracious and comfortable words, they cannot frame themselues to them, but euen then also, they are out of season with them; learne thou therefore to acquaint thy selfe with holy and religious speeches, let thy mouth at other times be exercised in speaking graciously, and then (doubtlesse) though thou canst not speake so eloquently, as some that foame out nothing but goodly speaches, yet thou shalt be able to speake to better purpose, because (indeede) it is not mans wit, but Gods grace, that seasons speach, and makes it profitable and comfortable."

The apostle did not wish to burden the epistle with any lengthened or minute account of his private affairs. There was much which all interested in him would naturally wish to know—his health, his means, his prospects and plans. But the bearer of the epistle would make all necessary communications, and one so recommended as Tychicus was, would be eagerly listened to as he spoke to them of the aged prisoner at Rome.

(Ver. 7.) *Τὰ κατ' ἐμὲ πάντα γνωρίσει ὑμῖν Τυχικὸς ὁ ἀγαπητὸς ἀδελφὸς, καὶ πιστὸς διάκονος, καὶ σύνδουλος ἐν Κυρίῳ*—"Of all that concerns me Tychicus shall inform you—the beloved brother and faithful minister and fellow-servant in the Lord." The phrase *τὰ κατ' ἐμέ* is a common one in Greek, as Elsner and Wetstein have abundantly shown. Tychicus is honoured with three appellations. *First*, he is called "the beloved brother," one of the sacred brotherhood, bound together by the tie of a common fatherhood in God. His apostolic dignity did not fill Paul with reserve toward any fellow-believer, but he owned and loved as a brother every one who was with himself in Christ. Besides this common spiritual relationship, Tychicus must have endeared himself to the apostle, and therefore possessed his entire confidence. See under Eph. vi. 21. He was, *secondly*, "a trusty servant," and as such carried this epistle, and was charged with these oral messages to Colosse and to Ephesus. The term *διάκονος* may mean, generally, one who has spent his time and energies in connection with the church and that apostle who was one of its ornaments and bulwarks. In Eph. vi. 21 he is called, as here, "the beloved brother and trusty servant," but the apostle adds in this place a third epithet—*καὶ σύνδουλος*—"and fellow-servant." Official service of a general nature is implied in *διάκονος*, but under this term the apostle speaks of him as a colleague. See under i. 7. The words *ἐν κυρίῳ* are referred by De Wette to all the three epithets, and by Meyer to the last two of them. The meaning is not different whichever view be adopted. But as the first two names have distinct and characteristic epithets attached to them, and the last has none, perhaps *ἐν κυρίῳ* is to be specially joined to it, for the fellowship in service is marked by the common object and sphere of it—"the Lord."

(Ver. 8.) There are in this verse two marked differences of reading. The Textus Receptus, followed by Tischendorf, reads *ἵνα γνῷ τὰ περὶ ὑμῶν*—"That he might know your affairs;" but the other reading is *ἵνα γνῶτε τὰ περὶ ἡμῶν*—"That ye might know our affairs." The last appears to be the most natural. The apostle had just said, "All about me shall Tychicus tell you, whom I have sent for this purpose, that ye might know how it fares with us," and then he adds of him and Onesimus, "they will inform you of all things here." Whereas, if the reading of the Received Text be adopted, a new idea is introduced—"that he might know your affairs"—and one out of harmony with the twice expressed design of the mission. The common reading has the support of C, D[3], E, J, K, the Syriac and Vulgate Versions, and many of the Fathers. The other reading has, however, A, B, D[1], F, G, the text of Theodoret and Jerome. The phrase, *εἰς αὐτὸ τοῦτο*, refers to what has been said, viz. "all my state shall Tychicus declare unto you;" and he adds, "I have sent him *for this very purpose.*" Is it conceivable that now the apostle should introduce another and very different purpose after this strong assertion? It is objected to this reading that it is copied from Eph. vi. 22. But surely, in two epistles written at the same time, and carried by the same bearer, might not the same commission be given to him for both churches, and in the same words? If the other clauses of the commission are the same, why should this clause vary? The declared result is the same in both places, and for both churches—"that he might comfort your hearts"—and there is no reason to suppose any difference in the process, for their hearts were to be comforted by a direct and full knowledge of the apostle's condition. The various lections may have arisen from omitting the syllable τε before τά, from their resemblance. One ancient Father has γνῷ τε τά. Bengel takes γνῶ for the first person. The new reading is adopted by Scholz and Lachmann as editors, recommended by Griesbach, vindicated by Rinck, and followed by Meyer, Baumgarten-Crusius, Olshausen, and Huther. The reading then is—

Ὃν ἔπεμψα πρὸς ὑμᾶς εἰς αὐτὸ τοῦτο ἵνα γνῶτε τὰ περὶ ἡμῶν—"Whom I have sent unto you for this very purpose, that ye might know our affairs." In the verb ἔπεμψα is a common idiom. Tychicus could not be sent off till the letter was finished, and yet he says, forestalling the act, "I have sent him." The Colossians were in distress at the apostle's condition, and in sorrow for his imprisonment; but when Tychicus should tell them how he was circumstanced, and what his views and feelings were, how his mind was unruffled and his courage unsubdued, he would comfort their hearts—καὶ παρακαλέσῃ τὰς καρδίας ὑμῶν.

Tychicus was not to be despatched on this errand by himself. He had a companion whose history and change had been striking and peculiar in their nature.

(Ver. 9.) Σὺν Ὀνησίμῳ τῷ πιστῷ καὶ ἀγαπητῷ ἀδελφῷ—"Along with Onesimus, the faithful and beloved brother." Onesimus carried with him another and more special testimonial and introduction to his master, Philemon. Onesimus had been a slave—had fled from his owner, and had, during his exile, been converted by the apostle. He was sent back in his new character, "not now as a servant, but above a servant—a brother beloved, especially to me, but how much more to thee, both in the flesh and in the Lord." On being converted he had become, and is now eulogized as, "a brother;" and whatever may have been his delinquencies as a slave of Philemon, he is now commended as a faithful brother—one the genuineness of whose Christianity might be safely trusted. He was also "one of themselves"—Ἐξ ὑμῶν,

Colosse being either the place of his birth or his ordinary abode.

Πάντα ὑμῖν γνωριοῦσι τὰ ὧδε—"They shall inform you of all matters here." The phrase is of much the same meaning as *τὰ κατ' ἐμὲ πάντα* in verse 7, only the last is more personal, and the one before us more general in its nature. The apostle knew well the anxiety of the Colossians about him, and he wished them to be amply gratified.

The epistle is now brought to a conclusion by the introduction of a few salutations. Those who send their greetings to Colosse, were either personally, or at least by name, known to the church. The Syriac translator, in rendering the Greek term "salute," reverts to the old Hebrew form, and makes it —"ask for the peace of."

(Ver. 10.) *'Ασπάζεται ὑμᾶς 'Αρίσταρχος ὁ συναιχμάλωτός μου*—"Aristarchus my fellow-prisoner saluteth you." Aristarchus was a Macedonian, and a native of Thessalonica. Acts xix. 29, xx. 4, xxvii. 2; Philem. 24. He had been much in Paul's society—was with him during the riot at Ephesus, and several of his journeys in Syria and Greece—was with him too when he sailed for Italy, in order to follow out his appeal to Cæsar, and seems to have remained with him in Rome. He is here termed a "fellow-prisoner," but in Philemon only a fellow-labourer; whereas in this epistle Epaphras is named a fellow-servant, but in Philemon a fellow-prisoner. From such an exchange of those epithets, it has been inferred that the imprisonment of Aristarchus was not compelled but voluntary. There was no charge against him, and no prosecution. He seems to have attached himself to Paul, and he willingly shared his imprisonment, that the apostle might enjoy his service and sympathy. Probably, as Meyer suggests, his friends shared in his confinement by turns. It was Aristarchus who was with him when he wrote to the Colossians; but Epaphras had taken his place when, about the same period, he wrote to Philemon.

Καὶ Μάρκος ὁ ἀνεψιὸς Βαρνάβα. By *ἀνεψιός*, allied to *nepos*—nephew—is to be understood not nephew but cousin —*geschwisterkind*—"sister's son," by which term our translators themselves probably meant cousin. Num. xxxvi. 11.

Hesychius defines it thus—ἀνεψιοί, ἀδελφῶν υἱοί.[1] There seems no good reason to doubt that Mark is the John Mark referred to in Acts xii. 12, 25, xiii. 5, 13, xv. 37–39. He was the occasion of the well-known dispute and separation between Paul and Barnabas. On a former missionary tour, he had left them, and "went not with them to the work." Paul, therefore, thought it not good to take him,—"and the contention was so sharp between them, that they parted asunder the one from the other." Whether Paul or Barnabas was right in his opinion about Mark we know not. His desertion of a former enterprise seemed to justify Paul's opinion, and perhaps Barnabas thought too kindly of a near relation. Yet his subsequent conduct seems to warrant the substantial soundness of the judgment of Barnabas. Mark was apparently reconciled to Paul afterwards, and may have given the apostle ample reason to retract his censure. It may be, too, that the very dispute about him awakened within him renewed energy and perseverance. Again does Paul mention him with high commendation, 2 Tim. iv. 11,—"Only Luke is with me. Take Mark, and bring him with thee: for he is profitable to me for the ministry."

The name of Barnabas seems to be presented by Paul as a kind of passport to Mark. Barnabas must have been a name familiar to the Colossian church. His character must have endeared him to all who knew him, or had heard of his hearty evangelical labours. By birth a Levite, of the island of Cyprus, he was at a very early stage of its history converted to Christianity. At once he disencumbered himself of his worldly possessions, and devoted himself to the spread of the gospel. It was he who introduced Paul to the church in Jerusalem, and such was the confidence reposed in him, that he was sent as the deputy of the mother-church to Antioch, to bring back a faithful report of the progress of the gospel in that city. On his visit to the Syrian capital, the sacred historian says of him, Acts xi. 23, 24, "Who, when he came, and had seen the grace of God, was glad, and exhorted them

[1] Lobeck, *ad Phrynich.*, says—"*Pollux dicit filios filiasque fratrum et sororum dici* ἀνεψιούς, *ex his prognatos* ἀνεψιαδοῦς, ἀνεψιαδᾶς." It is thus the same with ἐξαδελφός—"first-cousin." The word rendered "nephews," 1 Tim. v. 4, as the translation of ἔκγονα, signifies, as it often does in Old English, not brothers' and sisters' children, but *nepotes*—descendants generally, and especially τέκνα τέκνων.

all, that with purpose of heart they would cleave unto the Lord. For he was a good man, and full of the Holy Ghost and of faith: and much people was added unto the Lord." Barnabas, finding the field so ample and so inviting, went at once to Tarsus, and brought Saul with him to Antioch, and such was the great success of their joint labours in preaching Christ, that "the disciples were called Christians first in Antioch." Barnabas next went up to Jerusalem with funds to relieve the poor saints, and then Paul and he visited many places in company. He is found soon again at Antioch, and he was delegated to go up to Jerusalem to secure a settlement of the angry controversy as to the observance by Christians of the Mosaic law. Returning to Antioch with the apostolic finding, he continued some time there "teaching and preaching the word of the Lord." It was after this period that Paul and he had the sharp contention about the fitness of Mark for the missionary tour which they had sketched for themselves. The last account of him is in these words—"and so Barnabas took Mark and sailed unto Cyprus." There seems every reason to believe that the society of Barnabas had a salutary effect on the mind of Paul, and at a period, too, when he might not be fully conscious of his powers and qualifications, nor be able to realize the high destiny which lay before him. Barnabas thus stood on the confines of the apostolic college, though he was not within it, and next to its members, he occupies a distinguished place in the early church. Such, in fine, was the zeal and success of this "Son of Consolation," such his prominence among the brethren, and so identified was he with the apostles, that he seems to be classed among them. Acts xiv. 4. So that we are disposed to infer that the mention of him here was not simply to point out Mark from others bearing the same name, but also to secure for him, through his relationship to Barnabas, a cordial welcome and reception at Colosse.

Περὶ οὗ ἐλάβετε ἐντολάς—"Concerning whom ye received instructions." The antecedent is not Barnabas, as Theophylact supposes, but Mark. What these commands were, or by whom enjoined, what they contained, or when they were delivered, we know not. Some suppose that they were sent at this period by Tychicus—a supposition which the tense of the verb will not warrant. Vain is all conjecture, such as that of Anselm and Schrader, who think that the apostle alludes to previous advices of an opposite nature, which are here recalled; or that of Grotius, who refers the missive to Barnabas; or Huther, who ascribes it to some Christian community—*von irgend einer Gemeinde;* or Estius, who so naturally assigns its origin to the Church of Rome.[1] Not a few imagine that the following clause contains the instructions—

'Εὰν ἔλθῃ πρὸς ὑμᾶς, δέξασθε αὐτόν—"If he come to you, receive him." But against this view is to be noticed the plural form *ἐντολάς*, implying that there was a variety of commands; and the omission of the article shows that it has no reference to what follows. This view, adopted by Calvin and Baumgarten-Crusius, seems, however, to have originated a various reading—*δέξασθαι*, found in D[1], F, G, and in the Syriac Version and Ambrosiaster—"concerning whom ye have received commandment *to receive him*, should he come to you." Such a reading at once betrays its exegetical origin. The present reading cannot be disturbed. We are therefore ignorant of these *ἐντολαί*, in their origin and purpose. But the apostle adds, parenthetically, for himself, concerning Mark, "if he come to you, receive him." Mark evidently purposed a journey which might lead him to Colosse, and the Colossians were to give him, should he come among them, a kind reception. The verb *δέχομαι* is used, both in the classics and New Testament, to denote the welcome which one gives to an honoured guest—a *guest-friend*, as the Germans translate the Greek *ξένος*. Matt. x. 14, 40, 41; Luke ix. 5, 48. The apostle continues the list of salutations—

(Ver. 11.) *Καὶ 'Ιησοῦς ὁ λεγόμενος 'Ιοῦστος*—"And Jesus, who is named Justus." Of this Jesus Justus we know nothing. Chrysostom and others would identify him with the Justus mentioned in Acts xviii. 7. That appears to have been a proselyte—this was a born Jew.

The proper punctuation of the remaining clause is matter of doubt. It has been commonly read—*οἱ ὄντες ἐκ περιτομῆς*, with a stop, "who were of the circumcision," namely,

[1] The view of Reuss, in his *Geschichte der Neutest. Schriften*, is both unnecessary and extreme, for he supposes by this language that there had been sent a previous epistle to the Colossians, which has been lost.

Aristarchus, Mark, and Jesus Justus. And then the apostle adds—"these only are my fellow-workers to the kingdom of God." But it is plain that the apostle had many other fellow-workers, and that he means, that among the believing Jews these only had co-operated with him. Such a necessary limitation of meaning has suggested another form of punctuation, which puts a stop after Ἰοῦστος, and commences with οἱ ὄντες ἐκ περιτομῆς a new sentence—"these being of the circumcision, they alone were my fellow-workers;" or, "of them of the circumcision, these alone were my fellow-workers." This construction is adopted by Lachmann, Steiger, Huther, and Meyer. In such a case the phrase οἱ ὄντες ἐκ περιτομῆς, is a species of anacoluthon. Such a construction, however, seems awkward. Indeed, by the first form of construction, the same result is obtained; for it is plain that in οὗτοι μόνοι, the writer limits himself to the circumcision. By "the kingdom of God," the apostle means the church—as a divine institute; and they were his colleagues not in the kingdom, but "unto the kingdom," that is, unto its furtherance and consolidation. The preposition εἰς has often such a signification. To consolidate and extend this kingdom was the end of his apostolical mission. These three Jews were the only parties of their race who lent him any assistance for this purpose at Rome, and of whom therefore he adds—

Οἵτινες ἐγενήθησαν μοι παρηγορία—"Who indeed have been an encouragement to me." The Syriac renders—"and these only," ܘܗܢܘܢ ܒܠܚܘܕܝܗܘܢ. The noun occurs only here. It signifies originally an address or exhortation, then it came to denote the result of such exhortation—comfort.[1] Still we apprehend it is comfort in the form of encouragement. The other believing Jews plagued the apostle, and he complains of them in the epistle to the Philippians, that they preached Christ "even of envy and strife—of contention, not sincerely, supposing to add affliction to my bonds." Phil. i. 15, 16. As the apostle of the Gentiles, and the zealous maintainer of the free and unconditioned admission of men to the church, without any reference to the law, Paul was an object of bitter prejudice to many Christian Hebrews. The names which follow are, therefore, those of persons of heathen birth.

[1] Kypke, *in loc.*

(Ver. 12.) Ἀσπάζεται ὑμᾶς Ἐπαφρᾶς ὁ ἐξ ὑμῶν—"There salutes you Epaphras, one of you." i. 7. As a Colossian himself, Epaphras had a deep interest in them, and sends them his affectionate greeting. The apostle further characterizes Epaphras as a servant of Christ—δοῦλος Χριστοῦ. Some insist on putting no comma between ὑμῶν and δοῦλος. The reading of highest authority seems to be Χριστοῦ Ἰησοῦ—"a servant of Christ Jesus." This good man, probably the founder of the Colossian church, could not forget them—for he was one of them by birth; and, as a servant of Christ Jesus, and one of their pastors, he had also a deep spiritual affinity with them. And not only so, but the apostle describes him further—as

Πάντοτε ἀγωνιζόμενος ὑπὲρ ὑμῶν ἐν ταῖς προσευχαῖς—"Always striving for you in his prayers." Though he was absent, he did not forget them. The best scene of memory is at the throne of grace. In proportion to the fervour of one's affection will be the importunity of his petition. Love so pure and spiritual as that of Epaphras will produce an agony of earnestness. There will be no listless or fitful asking —but a mighty and continual wrestling of heart. And the apostle witnesses that for this end Epaphras supplicated—

Ἵνα στῆτε τέλειοι καὶ πεπληροφορημένοι ἐν παντὶ θελήματι τοῦ Θεοῦ—"That ye may stand perfect and full-assured in all the will of God."[1] The Stephanic reading πεπληρωμένοι is not based on sufficient authority. The language of the clause is very expressive. Epaphras prayed that they might stand, and neither wander nor fall—stand perfect and full assured—every grace of the Spirit within them, and their minds possessing an undoubting and imperturbable persuasion on every point of Divine instruction, or of "the whole will of God." It is a needless refinement on the part of Meyer to connect ἐν παντὶ θελήματι so closely with στῆτε, as the *Local-bestimmung;* and to take τελ. καὶ πεπλ. as the *Modal-bestimmung.* For the words ἐν θελήματι are, in our view, closely allied to τέλειοι καὶ πεπλη.—that they might be perfect and fully assured *in* the whole will of God. And we are the more confirmed in our view when we turn to ii. 2, where the noun πληροφορία

[1] Ulphilas has here the expressive term *allavaurstvans*—all-doing—*omnoperantes.*

occurs in the phrase—"full assurance of understanding." And the allusion is plainly to the dangers which beset the Colossian church, and against which they are warned in the second chapter,—dangers in the form of seductive spiritualism and false philosophy, and against which the grand preservative was a perfect and full assured knowledge of the whole will of God. An imperfect or dubious acquaintanceship with that will would at once lay them open to the stratagems of the false teachers, who headed their errors with the title and varnished them with the semblance, of the "Divine will," and claimed for their theosophic dreams and ascetic statutes Divine authority. See under ii. 2. The preposition ἐν is not to be taken as εἰς, with Grotius; nor *secundum*, with Storr; nor yet *durch—through*, with Bähr. The apostle subjoins a further testimony to Epaphras in the following verse. But there is no little variety of reading as to the quality or virtue ascribed to him. The Received Text reads—

(Ver. 13.) *Μαρτυρῶ γὰρ αὐτῷ ὅτι ἔχει ζῆλον πολὺν ὑπὲρ ὑμῶν*—"For I certify, in his favour, that he has great zeal for you." This verse is confirmatory (*γάρ*) of the preceding. Instead of *ζῆλον πολύν*, A, B, C, etc., have *πολὺν πόνον*; while D^1, F, G have *πολὺν κόπον*. Some, again, read *πόθον*, and some *ἀγῶνα*. The best reading appears to be *πόνον*—the Vulgate rendering it *multum laborem*. The other readings —*ζῆλον, πόθον*, and *ἀγῶνα*—may have been so many glosses on the more difficult term *πόνον*, which occurs only elsewhere in the Apocalypse. *Πόνος* is toil or travail—such as that which attends a combat.[1] Hesychius defines it by *σπουδή, ἐπίτασις*. It occurs several times in the Septuagint. This *πόνος* led to the previous prayerful *ἀγών*. This stress of spirit begat the anxious solicitude in prayer which the apostle has described in the former verse. But the pains and prayers of Epaphras were not confined to Colosse, for the apostle adds—

[1] An old commentator on Colossians thus defines right zeal:—"1. Let it not be a pretended zeale as in *Ioash*. 2. Nor a superstitious zeale as in *Paule*. 3. Nor a passionate zeale, only for a fit, as in *Iohn* at his first entrance. 4. Nor a malitious zeale as in persecutors, that thinke they doe God good seruice in vexing men wrongfully. 5. Nor a wrong intended zeale, such as is the zeale of merit-mongers. 6. Nor a contentious zeale, such as theirs that make needlesse rents in the church. 7. Nor a secure zeale that is a zeale not raised by godly sorrow, or that is carried without care or feare of falling away. 8. Nor an idle

Καὶ τῶν ἐν Λαοδικείᾳ καὶ τῶν ἐν Ἱεραπόλει—"And for them in Laodicea, and for them in Hierapolis." Laodicea and Hierapolis were cities of the same region as Colosse. See Introduction, chap. i. All the three towns were in Phrygia, and Epaphras was well known to the churches in them. He bore their names on his heart before the Lord in fervent and uninterrupted intercession.

(Ver. 14.) *Ἀσπάζεται ὑμᾶς Λουκᾶς ὁ ἰατρὸς ὁ ἀγαπητὸς, καὶ Δημᾶς*—"There salutes you Luke, the beloved physician, and Demas." That this Luke was Paul's companion does not appear to admit of any doubt; nor is there any reason for denying the old opinion, that he was the author of the third Gospel. He is styled "the beloved physician," either to distinguish him from others of the same name, or to specify the peculiar office in which he had endeared himself to the apostle. The health of the apostle, as they might know, had been signally benefited by his medical skill, and that this might be at all times available to his patient, Luke attached himself to his person, accompanied him in several of his missionary tours, was with him in his voyage to Rome, and remained with him in the Italian metropolis. Luke is mentioned in Philem. 24; 2 Tim. iv. 11. It is said in Ecclus. xxxviii. 1, 2, "Honour a physician with the honour due unto him for the uses which ye may have of him, for the Lord hath created him, for of the Most High cometh healing." Sir Thomas Browne, however, in the first chapter of his *Religio Medici*, says, that "several circumstances might persuade the world he had no religion," and among them he mentions—"the general scandal of my profession." It was, indeed, a common saying,—*ubi tres medici, duo athei.* Luke might have been an example to the profession. His physico-spiritual character is happily delineated in the following epigram:

zeale that is all words without workes: the word is rendred labour sometimes, and it is certaine true zeale is spent about good workes. 9. Nor an ouercurious zeale, shewed either by sticking too much to the letter of scripture, or by prying into or harsh censureing of the lesser faults of others. 10. Or a bitter zeale, that spends it selfe in rayling and fiery reproches, railers seldome stand long. 11. Or an ignorant bold zeale such as was in the Iewes. Or lastly a selfe conceited zeale, when men trust too much to themselues, and their owne iudgements."—Byfield. London, 1615.

"Pandit evangelii et medicinæ munera Lucas
Artibus hinc, illinc religione valens.
Utilis ille labor, per quem vixere tot aegri
Utilior per quem tot didicere mori." [1]

Who Demas was, we know not. He seems to have been the person who afterwards left the apostle on account of his love of the world; and the name has no distinctive or eulogistic epithet added to it, as if the apostle had suspected this future estrangement—an estrangement which we are perhaps not warranted to identify with absolute apostasy. 2 Tim. iv. 10. The word itself, as has been remarked, is Greek, and not Hebrew, as Schoettgen thought; for he supposes it to be a Greek form of דימי, ending in *ας*, and not *ιος*—as *δήμιος* would mean *carnifex.* It is probably a contraction of *Δημήτριος*.

(Ver. 15.) *Ἀσπάσασθε τοὺς ἐν Λαοδικείᾳ ἀδελφοὺς, καὶ Νυμφᾶν, καὶ τὴν κατ' οἶκον αὐτοῦ ἐκκλησίαν.* The various readings in the verse are not very important. Some read *Νύμφαν* as a female name, and write *αὐτῆς*, like B, in agreement of gender. Others, for the opposite reason, support the form *αὐτοῦ*; while A, C, and others, read *αὐτῶν*, but *αὐτοῦ* seems to have highest authority. "Salute the brethren in Laodicea, and Nymphas, and the church in his house." The Colossian church was, in the apostle's name, to salute the sister church in Laodicea, especially not forgetting in such a greeting Nymphas, and the church in his house. The first *καί* points out Nymphas as worthy of distinction, and probably the last *καί* introduces the explanation. The church in his house could not, as Bähr supposes, be the whole Laodicean church; nor can the words, as some of the Greek Fathers opine, mean simply the family of Nymphas, all of whom were Christians. Some portion of the Laodicean believers, for what reason we know not, statedly met for worship in the house of Nymphas; and Meyer has shown that if *αὐτῶν* were the right reading, as he thinks it is, such a use of the plural is not against Greek usage.

(Ver. 16.) *Καὶ ὅταν ἀναγνωσθῇ παρ' ὑμῖν ἡ ἐπιστολὴ, ποιήσατε ἵνα καὶ ἐν τῇ Λαοδικέων ἐκκλησίᾳ ἀναγνωσθῇ, καὶ τὴν ἐκ Λαοδικείας ἵνα καὶ ὑμεῖς ἀναγνῶτε*—"And when this

[1] Webster and Wilkinson's *New Testament*, p. 206.

epistle has been read among you, cause that it be read also in the church of the Laodiceans; and that ye too read that from Laodicea." The construction ποιήσατε ἵνα belongs to the later Greek. Matthiae, § 531, 1. Nor should we say that in such a case ἵνα is ecbatic, for though result be described in the clause which follows it, design is clearly expressed by the verb which precedes it. The apostle alludes to the public reading of his letter in the churches, and recommends an exchange of epistles. The epistle sent to Colosse and read there was to be sent to Laodicea, and read there too. The words παρ' ὑμῖν signify "among you," not by you; and ἡ ἐπιστολή is the one which the apostle was at that moment writing. But the difficulty lies in determining what the Colossians were to read in turn, or what document is meant by the phrase τὴν ἐκ Λαοδικείας—"that from Laodicea." The apostle's language is not explicit, inasmuch as the Colossians would understand at once the reference made by him. But the question is, does ἐκ point to the origin or authorship of the epistle, or only to its present locality? Was it an epistle which had come to Paul from Laodicea, or would it need only to be brought out of Laodicea in order to be read at Colosse?

The expression is pregnant and idiomatic.

1. Many have taken it to mean a letter which Paul himself had received from the church in Laodicea. Theodoret, Photius, Calvin, Estius, Erasmus, Beza, van Til, Baumgarten-Crusius, and others, hold this view, though they can only conjecture as to the nature and contents of such a document. But the principal support of such a view is the assumed meaning of ἐκ, in the phrase ἐκ Λαοδικείας. It is argued that ἐκ denotes origin. True, but the texture of the verse shows that the epistle is supposed to be in Laodicea, when they were to try and get it *out* of that city. It was to be brought from Laodicea to them, and by their own endeavour. Besides, as Dr. Davidson remarks, "It is difficult to conceive of the mode in which the apostle's injunction could have been carried into effect. It is very unlikely that the Laodiceans kept a copy, or that Paul knew of it. Or if it be conjectured that Tychicus and Onesimus, the bearers of the Colossian letter, carried that which the apostle had received from the Laodiceans, the idea is inconsistent with ποιήσατε ἵνα καὶ

ὑμεῖς ἀναγνῶτε τὴν ἐκ Λαοδικείας; implying *endeavour* to get the Laodicean epistle."[1] Nor is there any hint in the epistle to the Colossians, that it is a reply to any queries or communications, the reading of which might cast light on those of its statements which served the purpose of an answer.

2. Others take it for some epistle written at Laodicea, either supposing it, like Theophylact, to be the First Epistle to Timothy, according to the common subscription; or like Lightfoot, the First Epistle of John; or as Jablonsky opined, an epistle written to the Colossian pastors generally; or as Storr and Flatt would think, one specially addressed to Epaphras. Such suppositions are as easily refuted as they are made. Philastrius of Brescia, Schultess, Stein, in his appendix to his commentary on Luke, and Schneckenburger, suppose the Epistle to the Hebrews to be intended. It cannot be the early uncanonical production now known by the title of the Epistle of Laodicea, a document which Hutter translated out of Latin into Greek, and of which Jerome said—*ab omnibus exploditur.* Marcion, in his canon, according to Tertullian, gave the Epistle to the Ephesians the title of the Epistle to the Laodiceans. [Commentary on Ephesians, Introduction, p. xxv.]

3. The more probable opinion is, that it is an epistle sent by Paul to Laodicea at this very period. The epistles were to be interchanged. And the interchange is naturally this—that the Laodiceans read the epistle which had been sent to Colosse, and the Colossians the epistle which had been sent to Laodicea.[2] Wieseler argues that the epistle meant is that to Philemon. But it is hard to prove that either Archippus or Philemon was a Laodicean. It would certainly be strange for the Colossian church to send Paul's charge to the minister of another church, when, according to Wieseler, there was an epistle destined for individuals in the same community. Then, again, as has been observed, what is there in the private letter to Philemon to make it of general use at Colosse? Again, many, as Bähr, Steiger, Böhmer, and Anger, who hold that the Epistle to the Ephesians is a circular letter, believe it to be here meant, while some maintain that its original destina-

[1] *Introduction*, vol. ii. p. 134.
[2] *Chronologie des Apost. Zeitalters*, p. 452.

tion was Laodicea. But how, it might be asked, how did the apostle know that the encyclical epistle should have reached Laodicea just at the time when his letter should arrive at Colosse? The spirit of the injunction in verse 16, seems plainly to imply that both letters were despatched at once, and the same might be inferred from the apostle's desire expressed in ii. 1, that the Laodiceans as well as the Colossians should be aware of his intense solicitude for them. Tychicus, as Meyer suggests, would travel through Laodicea to Colosse, and he would there impart the oral confirmation that the letter referred to by the apostle was lying at Laodicea. This arrangement being known to the apostle gave precision to his language. One difficulty in our way is the fact that Paul bids the Colossian church salute the brethren in Laodicea. Why do so, it is asked, if he himself despatched a letter at the same time to Laodicea? But the salutation sent through the Colossians would manifest the apostle's desire that both churches should cherish a sisterly attachment, and the transmission of the apostle's salutation to Laodicea would be a fitting occasion for the interchange of epistles.

But will the phrase *τὴν ἐκ Λαοδικείας* bear such a meaning? There is no doubt that it may, the preposition showing that the letter was there, and to be brought out of that city. The idiom means that the letter was there, or would be found there, and was to be carried thence. Thus, Bähr refers to Luke xi. 13—*ὁ πατὴρ ὁ ἐξ οὐρανοῦ δώσει πνεῦμα ἅγιον*—where the particle *ἐξ* characterizes the descent of a gift out of heaven, and from One who is in heaven. Matt. xxiv. 17 has also been referred to—*ἆραι τὰ ἐκ τῆς οἰκίας αὐτοῦ*—but the similarity of construction is not so close. The case of *ἀπό*, in Heb. xiii. 24, and the reverse one of *εἰς* in Luke ix. 61, come under a similar law. Compare 2 Cor. ix. 2; Phil. iv. 22. The law is based on what is called the attraction of prepositions, when, for example, instead of a preposition denoting rest being used, the idea of motion is attracted from the verb, which either expresses it or implies it, and a preposition signifying such motion is employed. Kühner, § 623; Winer, § 66, 6. The idea of fetching the epistle out of the city of Colosse was present to the writer's mind, and so he says *ἐκ*—the epistle to be gotten *out*, and not *ἐν*—the epistle now lying *in* Laodicea. This ascertained usage puts an end to the objections of the Greek expositors, who affirm that this view would necessitate such a phrase as *τὴν πρὸς Λαοδικέας*.

The inference, of course, is that this epistle is lost, like many others of the apostle's writings. Probably it was wholly of a temporary and local nature, and therefore has not been preserved.[1] An inspired writing is not necessarily a canonical one.

[1] We subjoin a copy of the spurious epistle referred to on p. 292 :—

1. Paulus apostolus, non ab hominibus, neque per hominem, sed per Jesum Christum, fratribus qui estis Laodiceæ.	1. Paul an apostle, not of men, neither by man, but by Jesus Christ, to the brethren which are at Laodicea.
2. Gratia vobis, et pax a Deo Patre et Domino nostro Jesu Christo.	2. Grace be to you, and peace from God the Father, and our Lord Jesus Christ.
3. Gratias ago Christo per omnem orationem meam, quod permanentes estis et perseverantes in operibus bonis, promissionem expectantes in die judicii.	3. I thank Christ in every prayer of mine, because ye continue and persevere in good works, looking for that which is promised in the day of judgment.
4. Neque disturbent vos quorundam vaniloquia insimulantium veritatem, ut vos avertant a veritate Evangelii, quod a me prædicatur.	4. Let not the vain speeches of any trouble you, who pervert the truth, that they seduce you from the truth of the gospel which is preached by me.
5 Et nunc faciet Deus, ut qui sunt ex me, perveniant ad perfectum veritatis Evangelii, sint deservientes, et benignitatem operum facientes, quæ sunt salutis vitæ æternæ.	5. And now may God effect it, that my converts may attain to a perfect knowledge of the truth of the gospel, be beneficent, and doing good works which are connected with the salvation of eternal life.
6. Et nunc palam sunt vincula mea, quæ patior in Christo, in quibus lætor et gaudeo.	6. And now my bonds which I suffer in Christ, are manifest, in which I rejoice and am glad.
7. Scio enim quod hoc mihi est ad salutem perpetuam, quod factum est orationibus vestris, administrante Spiritu Sancto.	7. For I know that this shall turn to my salvation for ever, which is secured through your prayer, and the supply of the Holy Spirit.
8. Sive per vitam, sive per mortem, est mihi vivere vita in Christo, et mori gaudium.	8. Whether by life or by death; [for] to me shall be a life in Christ, to die will be joy.
9. Et ipse Dominus noster in nobis faciet misericordiam suam, ut eandem dilectionem habeatis et sitis unanimes.	9. And our Lord Himself will grant us His mercy, that ye may have the same love and be like-minded.
10. Ergo, dilectissimi, ut audistis præsentiam Domini, ita sentite, et facite in timore; et erit vobis vita in æternum.	10. Wherefore, my beloved, as ye have heard of the coming of the Lord, so think and act in fear, and it shall be to you life eternal;
11. Est enim Deus, qui operatur in vobis;	11. For it is God, who worketh in you;

This interchange of epistles was a salutary custom; it made an epistle sent to one church to become, in reality, the common property of all the churches, and it led in no very long period to the formation of the canon of the New Testament.

(Ver. 17.) *Καὶ εἴπατε Ἀρχίππῳ. Βλέπε τὴν διακονίαν ἣν παρέλαβες ἐν Κυρίῳ, ἵνα αὐτὴν πληροῖς*—"And say to Archippus, Take heed to the ministry which thou hast received in the Lord, that thou fulfil it." Archippus is mentioned also in Philemon. There is no ground for the opinion of Michaelis, Storr, Wieseler, and Theodoret, based on the Apostolic Constitutions, vii. 46,[1] that Archippus was a Laodicean. Philem. 2. What the motive of the apostle in sending him this exhortation was, we do not know. It would be an unwarranted suspicion, on the one hand, to suppose that Archippus was in danger of proving unfaithful; and it is no less a baseless notion of Bengel, on the other hand, that he was either in sickness or old age, and not far from the end of his career. The form *εἴπατε* is peculiar. Winer, § 15. In construing the exhortation, it serves no purpose to take back *ἵνα* from its place, and read *βλέπε ἵνα*, for what then should come of *αὐτήν*? 2 John 8. The phrase "in the Lord" has not the same meaning as "from the Lord," with which some

12. Et facite sine peccato quæcunque facitis.

13. Et quod optimum est, dilectissimi, gaudete in Domino Jesu Christo, et cavete omnes sordes in omni lucro.

14. Omnes petitiones vestræ sint palam apud Deum; estote firmi in sensu Christi.

15. Et quæ integra, et vera, et pudica, et casta, et justa, et amabilia sunt, facite.

16. Et quæ audiistis et accepistis, in corde retinete, et erit vobis pax.

17. Salutant vos omnes sancti.

18. Gratia Domini nostri Jesu Christi cum spiritu vestro. Amen.

19. Hanc facite legi Colossensibus, et eam, quæ est Colossensium, vobis.

12. And do without sin whatever things ye do.

13. And what is best, my beloved, rejoice in the Lord Jesus Christ, and avoid all filthy lucre.

14. Let all your requests be made known before God, and be firm in the doctrine of Christ.

15. And whatsoever things are sound, and true, and of good report, and chaste, and just, and lovely, these things do.

16. And those things which ye have heard, and received, keep in your hearts, and peace shall be with you.

17. All the saints salute you.

18. The grace of our Lord Jesus Christ be with your spirit. Amen.

19. Cause that this Epistle be read among the Colossians, and the Epistle of the Colossians to be read among you.

[1] Τῆς δὲ ἐν Φρυγίᾳ Λαοδικείας Ἄρχιππος, p. 187, ed. Ueltzen, 1852.

would identify it. It points out the source of the ministry, not simply, but by describing the sphere in which it was given and received. It was "in the Lord"—the recipient was in union with the Lord himself, and the ministerial function was conferred upon him, and accepted by him under no foreign influence, obligation, or motive. Whatever this ministry was, and we cannot determine its nature, whether it be the diaconate specially or the pastorate generally, it was therefore a divine office which Archippus held. He had "received it in the Lord," and the charge was, that he was to see to it "that he fulfilled it." Acts xii. 25. This was to be his solicitude, to discharge all the duties which such an office laid upon him, and to fill up with holy activity that sphere which the Lord had marked out for him. There is no occasion to adopt the idea of Grotius, that the verb πληροῖς is any imitation of the Hebrew מלא, as applied to the consecration of a priest, for the word is found with a similar sense in the classics and in Philo. Some suppose that Archippus was holding office in the absence of Epaphras, others that he was a son of Philemon, and deacon under his father as pastor. It has been said, that it marks the free intercourse of the early churches, when such an address should be made by a church to one of its ministers. Only it should be borne in mind, that the church was simply the vehicle of communication. It was an admonition of Paul to Archippus through the church. The idea of Theophylact is, that Paul sends him the admonition so openly, for this purpose, that when he had occasion to rebuke any members of the church, they might not deem him bitter or censorious, for they would recall the apostle's charge to him, and esteem him for so faithfully obeying it.

(Ver. 18.) *Ὁ ἀσπασμὸς τῇ ἐμῇ χειρὶ Παύλου*—"**The salutation of Paul with mine own hand.**" Having employed an amanuensis in writing the previous portion of the epistle, the apostle authenticates it by adding his salutation in his own hand. 1 Cor. xvi. 21; 2 Thess. iii. 17. What associations and feelings that handwriting would excite! Many an eye would be moistened as it gazed upon it. Not only does he write the salutation himself, but he adds, with his own hand too, the remaining clauses.

Μνημονεύετέ μου τῶν δεσμῶν—"**Remember my bonds**," a brief but pathetic request. The alternative view of Heinrichs is a very miserable one—*stipendio mihi mittendo.* Nor can we, with Olshausen and others, confine the mode of remembrance craved by the apostle simply to supplication for him. As Meyer says—*jede Beschränkung ist unbefugt*—"every limitation is unwarranted." Every possible form of remembrance they were besought to cherish. With every mention of his name, or allusion to his work, his chain was to be associated. Every picture which their mind's eye formed of him was to be that of a prisoner. When they felt their obligations to him as an apostle, they were to think of his captivity. Their freedom of religious observance was to suggest to them, by the contrast, his incarceration. When they asked a blessing on their spiritual benefactors, they were not to forget the fetters of him—the apostle of the Gentiles. "Remember my bonds." When his right hand penned the salutation of the previous clause, no wonder he felt his bonds so keenly, and spoke of them, for at the same moment his left hand was chained to the right arm of the Roman soldier who kept him.[1] And now he bids them farewell—

Ἡ χάρις μεθ' ὑμῶν—"**Grace be with you.**" The adieu is brief, but expressive. The apostle concludes as he began, with an earnest benediction, a prayer for fulness of blessing, alike for their present and eternal welfare. The *Ἀμήν* of the Received Text is not well authenticated, and the subscription, though correct, is necessarily spurious.

[1] ["The remark of Eadie is just, that as the apostle used his hand to write, he felt his bonds yet more keenly; but, in all probability, it was not the *left*, but the *right* hand that was bound to the soldier that guarded him. Smith, *Dict. Antiq.*, *s.v.* 'Catena,' p. 207."—Ellicott.]

INDEX

INDEX OF GREEK TERMS MORE PARTICULARLY REFERRED TO